A History of Everyday Things
The birth of consumption in France, 1600–1800

Things which we regard as the everyday objects of consumption (and hence re-purchase), and essential to any decent, civilised lifestyle, have not always been so: in former times, everyday objects would have passed from one generation to another, without anyone dreaming of acquiring new ones. How, therefore, have people in the modern world become 'prisoners of objects', as Rousseau put it? The celebrated French cultural historian Daniel Roche answers this fundamental question using insights from economics, politics, demography and geography, as well as his own extensive historical knowledge. Professor Roche places familiar objects and commodities – houses, clothes, water – in their wider historical and anthropological contexts, and explores the origins of some of the daily furnishings of modern life. *A History of Everyday Things* is a pioneering work that sheds light on the origins of the consumer society and its social and political repercussions, and thereby the birth of the modern world.

DANIEL ROCHE is a Professor at the University of Paris and author of several works on the Enlightenment and on the history of society, including *The Culture of Clothing* (Cambridge, 1994).

This book is published as part of the joint publishing agreement established in 1977 between the Fondation de la Maison des Sciences de l'Homme and the Press Syndicate of the University of Cambridge. Titles published under this arrangement may appear in any European language or, in the case of volumes of collected essays, in several languages.

New books will appear either as individual titles or in one of the series which the Maison des Sciences de l'Homme and the Cambridge University Press have jointly agreed to publish. All books published jointly by the Maison des Sciences de l'Homme and the Cambridge University Press will be distributed by the Press throughout the world.

Cet ouvrage est publié dans le cadre de l'accord de co-édition passé en 1977 entre la Fondation de la Maison des Sciences de l'Homme et le Press Syndicate of the University of Cambridge. Toutes les langues européennes sont admises pour les titres couverts par cet accord, et les ouvrages collectifs peuvent paraître en plusieurs langues.

Les ouvrages paraissent soit isolément, soit dans l'une des séries que la Maison des Sciences de l'Homme et Cambridge University Press ont convenu de publier ensemble. La distribution dans le monde entier des titres ainsi publiés conjointement par les deux établissements est assurée par Cambridge University Press.

A History of Everyday Things

The birth of consumption in France, 1600–1800

Daniel Roche

University of Paris

translated by Brian Pearce

CAMBRIDGE
UNIVERSITY PRESS

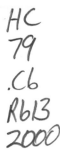
#4118502

PUBLISHED BY THE PRESS SYNDICATE OF THE UNIVERSITY OF CAMBRIDGE
The Pitt Building, Trumpington Street, Cambridge, United Kingdom

CAMBRIDGE UNIVERSITY PRESS
The Edinburgh Building, Cambridge, CB2 2RU, UK http://www.cup.cam.ac.uk
40 West 20th Street, New York, NY 10011–4211, USA http://www.cup.org
10 Stamford Road, Oakleigh, Melbourne 3166, Australia
and Editions de la Maison des Sciences de l'Homme
54 Boulevard Raspail, 75270 Paris Cedex 06, France

Originally published in French as 'Histoire des choses banales' by Librairie
Arthème FAYARD, 1997 and © Librairie Arthème FAYARD 1997.

First published in English by Editions de la Maison des Sciences de l'Homme
and Cambridge University Press 2000 as 'A History of Everyday Things'.
English translation © Maison des Sciences de l'Homme and Cambridge
University Press 2000

First published 2000

Printed in the United Kingdom at the University Press, Cambridge

Typeset in Plantin 10/12pt [VN]

A catalogue record for this book is available from the British Library

Library of Congress cataloguing in publication data

Roche, Daniel.
  [Histoire des choses banales.   English]
  A history of everyday things: the birth of consumption in France,
1600–1800/Daniel Roche; translated by Brian Pearce.
    p.   cm.
  Includes bibliographical references.
  ISBN 0 521 63329 X (hb). – ISBN 0 521 63359 1 (pb)
    1. Consumption (Economics) History.   2. Consumer behaviour –
History.   3. Social history.   I. Title.
HC79.C6R613   2000
399.4'7'0944–dc21   99-23258   CIP

ISBN 0 521 63329 X hardback
ISBN 0 521 63359 1 paperback
ISBN 2 7351 0840 6 hardback (France only)
ISBN 2 7351 0841 4 paperback (France only)

To Fanette

Contents

Acknowledgements

This book belongs to a train of thought which began with *Le peuple de Paris* in 1981 (English translation *The People of Paris*, 1987). It could not have been completed without the friendly exchanges and discussions that took place in the seminar which for over fifteen years I conducted along with J.-C. Perrot. I should like to express here once more all my gratitude as a friend for my debt to him and for the borrowing I have made from his work and his research. I should like also to thank, for their help and encouragement, Fernand Arnaud, Nicole de Blomac, Jacques Bottin, Jean Boutier, Isabelle Brian, Alain Cabantous, Roger and Anne-Marie Chartier, Natacha Coquery, Alain Croix, Robert Descimon, Maurice and Marie-Claude Garden, Claude Grignon, Dominique Julia, Steven Kaplan, Bernard Lepetit (a friend too soon lost), Dominique Margairaz, Vincent Milliot, Philippe Minard, Robert Muchembled, Patrick and Odile Nerhot, Nicole Pellegrin, Gilles Postel-Vinay, Daniel Reytier, Jean-Michel Roy and Denis Woronoff. I should like to repeat very warmly my thanks to Aline Fernandez and all my friends at the *Institut d'histoire moderne*, as well as to those at the *Ecole normale supérieure*, Pierre Dockes of the University of Lyons, John Brewer, Gérard Delille and Laurence Fontaine at the European University of Florence and to those at the Universities of Pisa and Venice, at the *Scuola normale superiore* and at the Max Planck Institute at Göttingen who listened to and discussed some of the propositions contained in this work – particularly to Franco Angiolini, Vincenzo Ferrone, Giovani Levi, Mario Mirri and Mario Rosa, Hans Erich Bödeker and Jürgen Schlumbohm and Patrice Veit.

Introduction: culture and material civilisation

'Philosophy still too often confines itself to the realm of speculation. Rare are the thinkers who risk taking hold of the objects of real life. How many speculative thinkers there are for one man who thinks like Montaigne, Franklin, Hume!' Historians can apply to themselves this reflection by Karl Gottlob Schelle, placed at the beginnings of his *Art of Taking A Walk*, which is also an 'art of living'. The ambition which he proposed to everyone, at the end of the eighteenth century, was to reconcile philosophy with everyday life, 'to set in harmony the necessities of life with the concerns of studious reason'.[1]

At the end of the twentieth century, my history of everyday things aims to respond to this intellectual injunction. Thinking about the historicity of what constitutes the texture of our ordinary life does not imply a vulgar materialism, even if it does indeed, in a way, mean re-materialising the principles of our knowledge and so achieving a better grasp of our relation to things, our mediation with objects and the world around us.[2]

Nowadays two reasons combine to make us interested in the history of material civilisation, material culture, everyday life. In the first place, it is a way of contributing to a more general re-reading of economic and social history, of being faithful to our personal intellectual origins, but also a way of re-discovering the questions that impel European and American historians to seek understanding of the dominant economics of consumption and commercialisation, their birth and development, and the nature of the frontiers that separate these from the societies they have emerged from and to which it is easy to contrast them.[3] Secondly, this intellectual and cultural history aims to explain those phenomena of life which, individually and collectively, derive from appropriation. That is why we do not counterpose production to consumption, economic dimension to social distribution; for 'production . . . is directly consumption, consumption is directly production', and a commodity . . . is, in reality, a very queer thing, abounding in metaphysical subtleties and theological niceties'.[4]

Our culture treats as commonplace the object and its role in society. It forgets the place and function of the object, or else wishes to see in it only the expression and means of our utter alienation.[5]

It is of this material culture that I aim to attempt a history. The early modern epoch, between the seventeenth century and the beginning of the nineteenth lends itself fairly well to this task.[6] Not because there is a clear transition from the traditional sphere of exchange and gift to that of the invention of the market and the consuming of commodities, but because the descriptions that have been given of it show how, in a world wherein objects are scarce, we can perceive dawning a primary multiplication of consumptions and the beginnings of a circulation which did not operate solely upon the separation of persons from objects, the symbolic from the economic. To understand differently the relation established between what is produced and what is consumed presumes, where France is concerned at least, a primary change of attitude from that governing historical analyses which have put production and supply in the forefront.

The actual concept of material culture has not often been defined. However, in 1978 J.-M. Perez provided a sufficient and firm basis for thinking about it, in *Nouvelle Histoire*.[7] A useful and utilitarian notion in the sphere of archaeology and anthropology,[8] it also enables historians of all periods and all areas of culture to link together a mass of facts which are marginal to what is essential – politics, religion, sociology, economics – or, in other words, to study 'men's responses to the constraints imposed by the settings in which they live'. These 'constraints' lead to a variety of reactions and adaptations through which the 'natural' is revealed as being fundamentally cultural, with needs and desires embodying themselves in objects and values.

In order, therefore, to understand the relation between objects and the consumption of objects one has to reconsider the classical counterposing of infrastructures to superstructures, of realities to representations, of the facts that are subject to symbolic or intellectual explanations to those which involve material and economic significances. Objects and the relations, physical and human, which they lead to cannot be reduced to mere materiality any more than to mere instruments of communication or social distinguishing marks. They belong not only to the cellar or the attic, or to both at once, and, consequently, they have to be set in the networks of abstraction and sensibility which are essential to the understanding of social facts. No doubt material life establishes in history 'the border which . . . separates the possible from the impossible',[9] as Braudel put it, but it does this by imbricating social contexts of information and communication which organise the significance of things and goods, and not through the succession and clear separation of temporalities favourable to types of behaviour.

This we have learnt from recent histories of the book, of clothing and of the sciences. The contribution made by material bibliography and the history of reading shows that the materiality of a book conditions the meaning that it can convey.[10] The book thus has to be set among all the texts and products that are subject to interpretation: the generality of the systems of signs. The forms assumed by the text, the way the paper is cut and the make-up of the pages all have their effects on the voice, on ways of reading, by shaping the possibilities of understanding and taking-in.

The same applies to clothing, a social fact of communication which also expresses the evolution of the culture, sensibility and intelligence of the producers and the tolerance of the consumers. Fashion, between freedom and constraint, lends itself to all the influences of distinction and power. Clothing can be seen as being in the forefront of the agents of the 'civilisation of manners' and of 'court civilisation', while never becoming detached from the profound link that binds the world to the person.[11] This is what Denis Diderot tells us when he relates the adventure of his dressing-gown: one's clothes express one's being, and every change of clothing results in transformations of the person and of the things that surround him.[12]

The history of chemistry teaches us that, throughout centuries, men sought by analysing bodies to reach the sublimation and quintessence of the essential metals and materials, the fundamental substances. The chemical revolution of the eighteenth century mastered those primary bodies, which were soon analysed and re-made. 'Water, earth, air and even fire then changed their register. They ceased to belong to the world of things and joined the world of objects which we manipulate freely.' Furthermore, scientists soon took an interest in the residues of their analyses and in products that had previously been considered inferior.[13] The obsession with 'spirits' which had held up progress gave place to productive operations. Metaphysics, which had hindered physics, lost ground. The chemistry of colours and that of organic substances emerged from this break with the ideal and the spiritual which had dominated the economy of the elements. Becoming aware of the importance of the materiality of men's productions, in their connections with the creative intelligence at work in all human activities, presupposes an examination of the actual notion of material culture. The first stage proceeds through this break, or this transcendence, with its interpretation, which is regularly and ably illustrated in the *History of Everyday Life*.[14]

As a publishing phenomenon, and an impressive example of the popularisation of history, the history of everyday life coincides initially with

that of a collection begun in 1938, the first book in the series, written by
Jerome Carcopino being *La Vie quotidienne à l'apogée de l'Empire romain*
[*Daily Life in Ancient Rome*, London, 1946], which has been continually
reprinted and translated. Outside this collection, the same interest in-
spires chapters, which it is fair to put in this category, that appear in
numerous works devoted to the history of regions, towns, social groups
and famous places. 'Daily life' can be seen as a convenient event-ordered
way of grouping facts which do not fit into more easily defined categories
such as economy or society. It is particularly and most often a not very
analytical way of grasping the history of civilisation and culture. Dia-
chronic linking brings together a great variety of facts through the logic
alone that is dictated by their repetition, their universality and, so to say,
their triviality.

Thus, J. de Saint-Germain's *La Vie quotidienne à la fin du Grand Siècle*[15]
follows a winding track through eighteen chapters, beginning with one on
casual labourers, lackeys and soldiers, followed by one devoted to 'day-to-
day life' and others on traffic, sport, hunting, fishing, the growth of Paris,
the primary social concerns, the emancipation of women, vagrants,
prisons, firemen, writers, lampoonists, speculation, the winter of 1709,
the reaction of the authorities to famine, policing, tax-farmers, the degrees
of religious feeling, the Police State, entertainments and games. This a
description of reality which has its charm but in which we perceive, behind
all the learning and real knowledge of the facts concerned, the survival of a
wholly positive conception, that of a history that asks no questions. It
corresponds well to a horizon of reference in which the event, specifically
the act of discovery – Palissy and ceramics, Newton and his apple, Pasteur
and his little dog – in short, the appearance of providential objects, is what
is essential. This attitude was for long the sphere of interest of antiquaries
and learned Academicians. In the period since the Second World War it
has remained that of a vast public of writers and readers who share an
interest in social settings, the constraints of geography, the imperatives of
tradition, and folklore. Since 1960 the collection has included popularisa-
tions (in the best sense of that word) of university research on religions,
regions and social groups. It constitutes a mirror of the last past and, often,
an expression of our nostalgias. The governing idea is that of rejection of
the measurable, of a totality without hierarchy, of a triviality which is
interesting because it responds to our need for historical exoticism.

With Lucien Febvre, Robert Mandrou, Fernand Braudel and Guy
Thuillier,[16] in the *Annales* and elsewhere, thought has taken another
turning with a view to giving rigour to an impressionistic form of history.
The principal idea is that civilisation has a subsoil, a domain in which
routine, inertia, minimal consciousness have the greatest influence, a

space where silence reigns over experiences which are common but, for the most part, lived through in private, a lengthy temporality marked by weak breaks, barely visible changes, and wherein habits, customs and traditions prevail which elude easy datings and familiar social divisions. For Braudel, more exactly, it is one of the means by which 'to define the context in which pre-industrial economics operated and to grasp it in all its richness',[17] both by the limits that characterise it (the limit set by resources and needs, the limit set by the possibilities offered through mastery of nature, the evolution of techniques and mentalities) and by the interplay established between the strata that are comprised in it. From material life to the market-economy, from that to the development of capitalism, reality is made up of superimposed strata which, though interlinked, are yet in part dissociated from each other. The stratum of material life is sheltered from control by the civilisation of the market. Times and spaces have their own dynamic.

The lesson taught by the *Annales* has been learnt. Historians have tried to grasp the real weight of everyday life and sought to provide a history of what seemed to have no history: material life and biological behaviour, history of food, history of the consumption of food and clothing, history of diseases. All these studies have called into question certainties regarding the efficacy of the model of *homo oeconomicus* as a way of understanding ancient societies. Taking account of the contribution made by anthropological work[18] they have emphasised observation of practices and actions both individual and collective, the questions posed by memory, transmission, change in the attitudes and habits that structure the universe in which mankind evolves, and whatever bring together or set against through *habitus* (P. Bourdieu) or the logics of situation (K. Popper).

The main question that arises from this transition from 'everyday life' to the idea of 'material life' is ultimately : 'Why and how can human beings live as they do, and why do they put up with it ?'[19] Can one find a meaning for the totality that everyday life presupposes which takes account both of social relations (and the way that these intervene in the relation between production and consumption) and of the intellectual and feeling-governed conditions which sanction them? In other words, we wish to keep Braudel and Labrousse's contribution to economic and social history while integrating in it the project of a cultural history 'sensitive to the way in which ideas and practices are articulated with the social world, sensitive also to the splits that divide a society, the diversity of ways of using shared materials and codes'.[20]

The history of attitudes to the object and the commodity in our society is of capital importance here. It assumes that a history of consumption is a way of reconciling subject and object, inferiority and exteriority. The main argument of the history of material civilisation is the relation of people to things and objects.[21] It has to take account of the process of contestation which begins with the passage from a civilisation of scarcity and a stationary economy to one of development and plenty. At the birth of the new millennium we are constantly discovering the dilemma of progress. A huge responsibility arises from the confrontation of the Western world with traditional civilisation: object and consumption, development itself, have been at once the white man's good luck and his burden.

Behind this fact lies a two-fold snare: that of nostalgia, which sees in all ancient societies the world we have lost because their values can no longer be ours, because happiness is behind us when our future is no longer meaningful on this earth, or is within our reach only in the beyond: and that of commodity, fetishism, of productivism and the eulogising of a development without limits or problems, the other side of which, we need to realise, is profound loss of reality, reification in relation to things and the triumph of signs, which means the triumph of money which is its symbol. The history of everyday things and of their consumption and that of the understanding of those usages and forms of behaviour which create material and intellectual markets reduce to their proper place, as an ideological and philosophical construction, both in authenticity and alienation.

Doubt lies indeed at the heart of growth. From the appearance of the first indications that an extraordinary increase in the production of objects was possible a debate began about the moral value of things, about the gap widening between the development of trade and industry, proofs of civilisation, and the decline of solidarities. Is not man surrounded by objects a prisoner, as we were reminded by Jean-Jacques Rousseau and by Adam Smith himself?[22] Undoubtedly it is the very interpretation of materiality that is being challenged.

In the relation of man to objects the whole West seems to adhere to an ancient dualism which conditions our intellectual choices and our moral and political justifications. The construction of the subject in a process of creative appropriation of objects and of the world, which for Hegel depended on a simultaneity situated at the centre of the theory of knowledge, has become the cause of an alienation of the subject, which Karl Marx placed at the heart of a theory of *praxis*. Man's labour, the source of value, loses its meaning when the individual is deprived of control over what he has created, when objectification produces alienated subjects because the producer and his product are separated, because the juridical and social formation registers a severance between man and the world.

This view, which conditions, more or less, our choices, presupposes the existence of an earlier world more authentic and richer than ours. It puts in the forefront the negative effects of the Industrial Revolution and assumes the possibility of a future in which conflicts will be resolved by new social relations. Recent history has put an end to the political dimension of the Marxist dream, conceived as a decisive break, but it has not done away with the accusation levelled at objects and material culture. The consumption which is submerging Western societies is still the domain of false images and alienation, the 'system of objects',[23] the sphere in which man is the dupe of signs. The object is a gadget, a fetish, a relic of the past, the expression of a bourgeois ideology, the mark of what is ephemeral and useless.

Following the example given by research which, in Great Britain and the United States, has sought to break away from this traditional explanation, the present history of everyday things aims to appreciate differently our ordinary practices and the place of objects in everyday experience, the relations of usage and exchange that they dictate when they are scarce and their term of life has a value different from ours, when society is less complex and when social relations depend not only on economic forms but, equally, on symbolic values – in short, when men's productions are at the heart of the individual's identity and his relations with the family and the group.

'Any object, even the most ordinary, embodies ingenuity, choices, a culture.'[24] A body of knowledge and a surplus of meanings are attached to all objects. We grasp this in the way they are acquired, in which morality, distinctive principles and personal choices play their parts in deciding how much of one's budget is to be devoted to them; in the way they are used, in which there are manifested a doctrine and a morality of use within the norms and rules of propriety; and in the way they are possessed, in which the magnificence and squandering of the great contrast with the ostentatious underconsumption of the bourgeois or the compulsive consumption of the *nouveaux riches*.[25]

If we accept that the external world of objects is not the sphere of our total alienation but the medium of a creative process, and that the relation of individuals to social reality proceeds through objectification, the history of consumptions enables us to understand better the continuity of the material and the symbols, the effort of intelligence and crystallised labour which is conserved in the least of objects, the unity of representations and realities. It is not possible to isolate the world in its fortuitousness, nor ideas in their purity without risk.[26] We have to understand the limits of the possible, that is to say, how possibilities of change occur, how different temporalities coexist at the same moment, how negative and positive effects overlap when breaks happen. Growth can claim its share in liberation, just as it can set in place its production of alienation. George

Simmel sees in this the principal theme of 'the tragedy of culture',[27] since development promotes consciousness and equality at the same time as it programmes disappointment amid plenty and inequality.

The present book seeks to contribute to an understanding of the transformations undergone by what, for want of anything better, we call traditional society, which passes gradually from an economy of salvation, scarcity and morality to an economy aiming at happiness on earth, relative plenty and utility. We know that the changes began before the Industrial Revolution, since they were already at work in urbanisation and the cultural movements resulting therefrom.[28] A more complex society and increased opportunities for distinction and means of information were operational with commercialisation and its networks. The process of abstraction of things and practices was started off by schooling, by calculation, by objects themselves. The technical system presiding over responses to demand was at a turning-point, and we can see that it was not independent of the social order, that it allowed of a rationality achieved through co-ordination, as with energies; that the norms which established the regularity of products had values which were symbolic as well as practical.[29] A material and intellectual relation to space, to setting and to resources was being modified, along with standards of living and ways of life. The system of social exchange was transformed when the inhabited space, the relation to cold and warmth, to night and day, to the body and its disciplines, to conventions of dress, to furnishing and decoration were gradually modified by productive capacities and by the simultaneous evolution of codes of usage and sensibilities – when, through different consumptions or different ways of using things, the subjects could construct themselves differently and re-adjust their relation to the collective.

This history does not aim to break with that which has made it possible to identify the social topography of objects, to verify their multiplication, to show the increase in specialised spaces and in the rise of partitions between the private and the public, the occupational and the intimate, work and leisure. It seems to me to be too easy to criticise with hindsight works which have helped advance our understanding of olden times, whatever can be said about their inadequacies or intellectual limitations. It is also necessary that these works be read and understood.[30] However, as I began in 1989 with *The Culture of Clothing*, I should like to broaden their subject-matter and re-examine the history of the relation between a society and its goods from the standpoint of our analysis of the mediations involved. Consumption does not exhaust the history of objects: it calls for an anthropological interrogation of an epoch and enables us to respect the link between history and the social sciences.

Part I

Production and consumption

I   The natural framework and the human framework

In the society of the Ancien Régime, as in other societies, the relation between production and consumption was based upon an asymmetrical relation. One can consume only what has been produced, but the transformation of goods precedes the demand for them. For economists this relation applies universally. For historians of material culture it depends on capacity to consume and on numerous constraints, and reveals forms of behaviour the changes in which indicate more than economic fluctuations. The dependence or independence of societies in relation to objects, the responses made to the pressures of natural settings and the choices men make are undoubtedly concretised in this association wherein production corresponds, broadly, to supply and consumption to demand.[1] The economy does not totally exhaust the relation of man to things and objects, but it remains the most general framework when the market is established, even if several phenomena of exchange and circulation, such as gift or theft, do not depend upon it directly. In order to understand this imbrication of the market and what does not belong to the market – the non-commercial sphere of the private and symbolic economy – we can either analyse the transformation of goods and their commercialisation or investigate, in the context of scarcity and stability, the various factors – moral, intellectual, religious – which affect consumption and its social inequalities.

Goods in history

It is men's activity as producers and consumers that creates goods, through their labour and the value with which they endow objects, both utility and symbolic value being possible contributors to this. This transformation of objects into goods and wealth has a long history and is oriented towards two poles: that of access to natural goods and that of the hierarchy of values, which raises the problem of luxury goods and, therefore, of differences in consumers' behaviour.

As we observe every day, natural goods may all possess a history in which one could read how they were appropriated by men, who then transformed them into wealth. Our civilisation is now becoming aware that if these goods should be lacking, all of its foundations would collapse. Air, water, forests, the products of the soil are the basis of food, clothing and housing, and the relation which is then established determines a major link between men and material civilisation. But how are we to recognise what is necessary and indispensable for survival which will subject the consumer's relation to nature to strong constraints without eradicating it all together, when historically technology has not been able to change or solve the problem of needs?[2]

Natural goods, use and exchange

'A commodity is . . . a thing that by its properties satisfies human wants of some sort or another', Marx reminds us. There can be no exchange value without use value: in particular, goods can satisfy needs without founding immediate value. For centuries peasants did not pay for water, but that is no longer the case today.

The hierarchy of and the frontiers between use values and exchange values can change. The concrete and everyday dimensions which appear when we analyse the inventories made after someone's death reveal this plainly to the historian of patrimonies. Among the possessions assembled, some objects are easily classifiable, but where are we to place silverware and jewellery, which figure in both the circuit of exchange and that of use? Goods can have a high symbolic value in social relations, yet, when necessity compels, their owners or the family that inherits them do not hesitate to mobilise them as a financial reserve.

Thus, in the seventeenth and eighteenth centuries, as a general rule, water was not sold. It was a natural good, accessible to most people by means of inexpensive procedures. However, the growth of towns resulted in an increase of consumption and the towns then entered into a system of production and commercialisation of water which engaged the municipal authorities in far more than supervision and regulation, since it implied the building of aqueducts and pipes and the installation of machinery and pumps. Water became a form of wealth but, in most cases, it was paid for out of the inhabitants' taxes and indirect taxation. Direct access continued to be inexpensive.

Indirect access and distribution, however, hardly reached Parisian households before the end of the eighteenth century, and then only in a very small part of the town. Elsewhere they came still later, but already through a system of commercialisation or even of subscription or privilege. The water-carriers' market, free but regulated and supervised, supplied everyone's needs. The carriers fetched water from the river, where it cost nothing, or from the fountain, where it had been paid for through taxation, and then sold the contents of their pails to housewives or their homes. This natural good had entered into the circuit of exchange, and that happened already in the Middle Ages. An entire section of the population still lived outside the trade in water, but this trade gained ground progressively. Water, which was at the heart of the technical system of pre-industrial societies, also created forms of social behaviour which varied in space as in time and which could reflect hierarchies of income as well as various choices. This is a sphere of mass consumption which enables us to understand how complex in former times was the relation to production and resources.

The same demonstration could be made regarding air. What good is more available and more accessible without cost? It was at the end of the eighteenth century that people began to think about its consumption. In the main, this thinking resulted from the great debate about the importance of fresh air for health and neo-Hippocratism. It involved administrative and medical authorities who, in the course of a large-scale investigation in which values both material and sentimental figured, raised the question of civilisation's relation to this natural good, which seemingly lacked both cost and weight.[3] Particular places where it was consumed attracted their attention: prisons, where the density of population was already creating an unbalanced climate; cesspools, where the stench was proving fatal to the men who had to empty them; cemeteries, where the accumulation of graves was contributing to urban pollution (their transfer beyond the walls was to alter profoundly, and not without difficulty, a fundamental relation to death and the sacred); mines, where the requirements of exploitation and increased output came up against established techniques which included ventilation. An entire society pondered on the meaning and the cost of the new equipment needed to cope with the evolution of a form of behaviour in relation to everyday needs and a familiar natural good.

Ice offers another illustration.[4] In the old society ice was something very scarce and reserved for the rich, because it was hard to transport and conserve. However, before the sixteenth century, human ingenuity, responding to the consumer-demands of court elites, especially in Italy, managed to find sites for the production of ice and to invent methods of transport and techniques of immediate preservation which did not require much knowledge of physics or chemistry. In the seventeenth and eighteenth centuries natural ice became a form of wealth and entered into the general circuit of consumption, and thereafter it was traded in. The Paris corporation of lemonade-sellers owed part of its prosperity in summer to the sale of iced and cooled drinks which were no longer the exclusive of Versailles and the rich.

Many other examples could be given. Take wood, which enters into all of life's uses, from the most necessary to the most luxurious. We observe a comparable evolution and mobilisation, at both ends of the chain (the relation between production and consumption), on the part of the peasants, defenders of usages and customs, the big wood-merchants and the large-scale landowners, with the monarchical state at their head, who were concerned with profitability. The value of this natural good cannot be reduced to an economic definition, since other values, symbolic and sentimental, complicate usages regarding both heating and domestic and urban lighting.

The identification of production and consumption with supply and demand emerged from the thinking of the political arithmeticians of the late seventeenth and the early eighteenth centuries, William Petty and Boisguilbert. This idea is, of course, more verifiable in the long than in the short term: economists learnt to take account of time-differences. It was connected with an historical tradition directed mainly towards the study of production, therefore of supply, based on the history of prices and their relation to the market.[5] In turn consumption itself enters into this relationship between goods and prices between demand and the market. It is at the heart of transactions, because the nature of objects and appearances is at the centre of their construction, leading to an organisation of distinct and hierarchised commodities. One has also to take into account the behaviour of consumers and not only the tendency to imitate, even if this remains essential in the hierarchy of consumptions.[6] The history of consumption must include analysis of demand, and therefore of the structuring of needs, the classification of consumers, the circuits of distribution and the spatial organisation of supply. Small-scale trade, especially, has a place here which has been insufficiently emphasised.

The nature of goods, the relationship to objects

In natural goods and their transformation through use we soon see the phenomenon of luxury and superfluity appearing. Ice provides the best example, but the history of the bath is equally eloquent. 'Ten centuries with no bath!' said Michelet, already in the middle of the nineteenth century. The relationship of men to objects here takes on a different meaning. 'The economists of the eighteenth century sensed vaguely that there is an order in needs which causes a distinction to be made in the nature of goods.'[7]

The contrast between natural or real needs and needs that are subject to opinion, between 'comfort and luxury', needs due to necessity, on the one hand, and luxury, even ostentation on the other, dominates the shifting frontier between degrees of use and of social visibility that are highly diverse. It distinguishes different spheres of consumption, but also of production and distribution: the sphere of personal and useful consumption; that of the superfluous 'the second order of needs', what is pleasant; and that of the useless, 'the third order of needs', which is also that of the greatest symbolic and social identification. In the realm of commodities, and still more in that of luxury, we are remote from the elementary necessities (consider clothing) and have now entered the world of transformation through labour, the triumph of added value, although dependence on natural resources has not ceased. Old-time industry, the clothing economy and the luxury sector of earlier ages depend upon those resources entirely for their raw materials and for the transformation and transport of these products. At the same time, however, those goods, which are less and less primary and are oriented towards luxury, represent quantities of investment and of labour that are connected.

Labour and money alike go into resources and necessities, but even more into the superfluous. Circulating capital is larger than fixed capital, emphasising the role of the merchant, who leads the dance of profit and accumulation until at least the middle of the nineteenth century.

Several questions thus arise for the historian of consumptions who seeks to understand the relation between supply and demand and consumers' choice. In the first place, whoever controls the circuits enjoys an exceptionally favourable situation. The case of the entrepreneur presents, however, a problem which is both economic and social. The old society does not yet appreciate his true place, even though he is already a decisive agent of transformation, since, by his capacity for innovation and invention he was to be the decisive actor in the change observable between the first and second halves of the eighteenth century.[8] Secondly, what is it that impels men to go into business and invest their money, and what enables these entrepreneurs to see ahead and imagine a result of their activity? Everyone's consumption in the sphere of goods of the second and third orders, as in that of objects of necessity, is based upon this ability and upon the way in which the entrepreneur acquires the intellectual tools required for it.[9] Finally, how are we to understand the dynamic of consumption which is at work behind these motivations of production and trade? How to understand demand, and the market which results from it, which goes beyond necessity, and the way in which it incites to transformation? We have to look for the answers on the side of capacity to consume, and that, yesterday just as today, is measured by the income of households.[10]

Consumption was a reality well before the industrial and commercial revolution that began in the eighteenth century. It was inseparable from the family dimension, in which expenditure was organised not round the individual, the isolated economic agent but round the parents-and-children group, that dynamic collectivity within which individual identities were formed, especially in the days before expanded and large-scale school attendance. In expenditure, and therefore in the choices which are a feature of everyday economy, there mingle in a complex way the factors of socialisation, cultural and anthropological but also social and economic, the level of income and the gaps between levels, and also the perceptions of the persons concerned. Family consumption is not only the product of these conditions, it is also a way of defining oneself and behaving, in accordance with a set of norms of identity and knowledge, of rules which are, primarily, the concern of mothers of families. In the old society the models of consumption were bound up not with economic capacities alone, and the principle established in the nineteenth century by Engel can be applied to them only partially.[11] Actually, variation in consumer behaviour is inseparable from a relation with incomes and family usages the dynamic of which is based on differentialisation and imitation.

This point is essential for understanding how the consumption of clothing has evolved in the modern period. Two principles are simultaneously operating: that of the stationary economy, the appearances and rules of which are determined by social situation (the habit makes the monk, everyone should consume according to his rank – the central argument in conceptions of good manners since Erasmus), and that of the economy of luxury, in which the practitioners and interpreters of fashion talk up the desire to mark oneself off from inferior groups, from which ensues the commercialisation of needs and the construction of new social identities for the individual. This example lets us see what the historian must expect from a re-reading of the rules of material civilisation. He has to combine two approaches – that of the economy and its interpretation, in order to understand how societies function and the relation between consumption and production, and that of social and cultural analysis, which takes account of the imperatives of private and public life, the norms which manifest themselves in the choices of material culture.

The end of the seventeenth century and the beginning of the eighteenth were a special moment for thinking about these matters. We find there the roots of what would emerge in definitive form thanks to Adam Smith, but

also and especially the foundations for an economics, analytical, thought-
ful and rational, exemplified by the work of Boisguilbert, who formulated
the theory of an economy driven by demand.[12] In the context of crisis,
wars, currency disturbances and jerky price-increases, awareness that 'a
large population does not by itself produce wealth' dictated the idea that
the population's consumption is alone decisive. This is merely an indicator of the relation between production and consumption on which
depend capacities for growth and expansion. Three precepts are thus to
be found at the heart of the debates in the France of the Enlightenment: a
break with the mercantilist tradition and its two supreme indices of
prosperity, money and population (money was now seen as a means, and
population as a test); fascination with private interest, since the individual, as actor in the economy, decides for himself his capacity for choice;
and social differentiation in consumption, which has a different weight
for different economic actors and social categories and induces effects
that are not uniform.

Consumption by the poor has an excellent economic result because,
with little money available to the individuals and households concerned,
taken severally, it makes possible rapid resumption of activity by the
production circuits and guarantees their survival. Large-scale consumptions of bread and clothing have immediate consequences. Consumption
by the rich, however, is slower and heavier and gives rise to the question of
how goods are used. Here we come upon the 'dispute about luxury',
which refers back to concern with the moral aspect of economics: the
prosperity of a few millionaire financiers does not make up for the
impoverishment of the poor people upon which it is based. This debate
was set going as a result of the growth of towns and the social fragmentation of the consumptions for which this growth provided the shop-
window. Luxury thus remained a major problem for Ancien Régime
society, because needs were not defined by pure economic relations (do
such exist nowadays?) and because the consumptions it motivated cast
light on the functioning of demand, which, moreover, was not the same
for all sectors and periods.

The primacy of the agricultural sector bore down with a weight that
was clearly revealed in the crises analysed by C.-E. Labrousse, even if his
study of demand can do with further refinement.[13] Production and consumption by unearned income, taxes and purchases depended upon
eighty per cent of the population. Quesnay was not mistaken in his
Tableau économique: the social product of the peasants' labour more than
covered the non-economic expenditure of society – luxury, the administration, the army, the church and religious activities, prestige and the
arts.

Relationship to objects, the nature of standards

On the social and cultural side, consumption presents the questions of how people are apprentices to its rules and how one can understand the ways in which these rules are internalised. In other words, why are certain forms of behaviour approved of and encouraged, and why do people agree (or fail to agree) to conform to them? This problem is linked with a great problem in philosophy because freedom and constraint are involved.

The historian can offer no simple answer, especially because he has to take account of a historiography which stresses too strongly the dependence and the constraints of necessity which are characteristic of the lives of society's lower orders. The old society was obviously a society of scarcity. Another society, with more fluid consumptions, emerged very soon in the aristocratic world and in the towns, but this spread only very slowly to the rural areas and the lower orders in general. My own generation is doubtless the last to have observed this world, which is rapidly disappearing into the past, in proportion as objects become more numerous, more accessible, because less expensive, and more mobile. At the same time, however, the social frameworks of ordinary life are changing, in step with that development.

The family was at the heart of this transformation, because, in town and country alike,[14] it was the unit of production and consumption. The influence of family life was felt in two ways. In some sectors, particularly in manufacture, a tendency appeared here and there to separate labour from the family unit of consumption. This often happened also among urban craftsmen: the movement, once begun, would quicken in the eighteenth century and still more later on. The modern age sees a modifying of family feeling, with the development of a family sensibility, a conception of private life and new expressions of feeling for children. The withdrawal into the 'family nucleus', the importance ascribed to the values of intimacy, the different relations established between generations, the new ways in which the different ages of life find expression, the differentiated effects of age – everything that goes to make up the distinctive features of the parental and family relations in the West has its consequences for consumption, whether this be measured at the macro-economic level or micro-economically, at the household level. The birth of the intimate thus provided the subject of an enquiry into the material environment in Paris, based on a confrontation of family values with objects possessed,[15] such as the bed and the bedroom, the fireplace and the kitchen range.

What, then, were the norms that constituted the 'domestic science' of the family economy, the rules which organised the time, space and

manners appropriate to consumption? On the production side, great
works dealing with the rural economy and rustic dwellings, from Charles
Estienne to Liger, offer lessons in old-time agronomy and a family economy inherited from Antiquity, presented in all its aspects.[16] On the
consumption side, family record books, private accounts and guardians'
accounts show how the strategies and styles peculiar to domestic life were
a field in which rules, knowledge and usages confronted each other. The
schooling of boys and girls[17] also played an important role, as it aligned
the girls' culture with that of the boys, in their apprenticeship to elementary knowledge (reading, writing, counting), even if this happened with a
time-lag and a gap in content, while, at the same time, the school refined
and accentuated the definition of women's work and role. By forming
good housewives and pious mothers, this education had a considerable
influence on consumer behaviour within families.

The economy of everyday life was bound up with the autonomisation
of private life and the way in which this was organised in relation to
places of labour and of leisure. The urban craftsman would have specific modes of consumption depending on whether he was an apprentice
and dependent on his family or on the club of his craft, an independent
journeyman, or a master-craftsman involved in representative functions. Jacques-Louis Ménétra offers in his diary examples of this for the
three phases of his life. Study of consumption is linked with these different social situations which are neither wholly separate nor uniformly
homogeneous.

Persons appear who offer definitions of 'educative consumption', such
as the teacher Verdier who, in 1777, asked in his *Cours d'éducation*: how
are those pupils to be educated who are destined for the highest professions and employments? Verdier is aware that he is responding to a new
need. His concerns are similar to those of the doctors and apothecaries
who at the time, on the initiative of Dr Tissot, were propounding diets,
'health regimes' adapted to different social categories. In each case the
family played a role, for it had become less than an economic and
emotional relationship which aimed to nourish and bring up children in
accordance with a new division of tasks.[18] The issue is how to achieve a
better understanding of the way that growth starts up in a stationary
economy, the way in which it is connected with a consumers' revolution
and levels out, while not abolishing the differences within society.

Stability and change

Two major phenomena govern the relation between production, population and consumption: dependence on the natural setting, and the

demographic regime which tends to self-regulation so as to maintain the balance between numbers of population and resources available. The constraint imposed by the natural framework must be conceived as operating within a certain model of technical environment, through the totality of living conditions, and not as a deterministic relation. The ecological dimension of our epoch has contributed to this tendency in which what matters is to show the variability of man's power to control nature. The old regime of consumption was set within a model of relations with the worlds of vegetation and animal life, the ecosystem as a whole, the sun, crops, woods and water. It laid the foundation for adapting demography to resources.

From the geographical picture to rural history

Any consideration of the relationship between the natural setting, development or agriculture and the history of material culture must start from the French tradition of the geographical picture[19] established by Vidal de la Blache. We know that France is many sided, with its five hundred cheeses, its regions defined by permanent features, the little districts which are all different, its peasants and their works. This historical and physical vision provides the basis for regional geography. Yet Vidal de la Blache's *Tableau* includes, in spite of all that, only general and constant features. It congeals the movement of nature and history alike, from the standpoint of a situation achieved, and to some extent leaves in the dark the dynamism of the relations established between rural societies and natural settings.[20] The regional framework adopted blurs the influence of other levels of spatial reality, the dimensions and functions of which have altered with the passage of time. It fails to take account of the different scales that apply where individuals and groups are situated in many relations. Life organises itself and the ecological dimension, which can be perceived at different levels, becomes established through the plot of land, the field, ownership, exploitation, the soil, boundaries. What we see first of all is the heritage of old landscapes and of their transformation, which can still be observed after many centuries. Then we learn of fluctuations, such as the history of the climate, which has its own movements, connected with those of forms of vegetation and of their utilisation. We need also to take account of the phases of human intervention – ground-clearing, hydraulic development, abandonment of soils, large-scale re-afforestation, meaning the way that landscapes have evolved in response to demand and changes in needs. Finally, we have to look into the question of how contemporaries analysed the relation between the natural setting and rural society.

From this analytical division, which is that of the *Histoire de la France rurale*,[21] I shall take certain features which are needed if we are to understand the historical foundations of material civilisation. From this comes the concept of rural space associated with the elements of the natural setting developed for agricultural production, both of crops and of animals. If rural space is commonly contrasted with urban space, it is not so much because this lays down a rigid frontier between them but because of urban space's greater density of population, and, above all, because different functions appear in it. As early as the eighteenth century Richard Cantillon, in his *Essai sur la nature du commerce en général*, put forward a model of the way the economy functions and real wealth is produced, even perhaps a model of the market. He developed an economic sociology based on relation to the earth as source of value, distinguishing between landowners, farmers and wage-labourers, to whom he added traders and craftsmen. This was the hierarchy which defined the distribution of incomes and the structure of demand, the actual organisation of consumption and expenditure. The town dominated the country because it held the mastery, in respect of landownership and of politics, imposing models of consumption. It was the town, ultimately, that altered the natural space and caused the balance to vary as between areas that were intensively exploited and those what were only more or less developed, where the relation was more discontinuous, the forests and mountain pastures, or else the spaces kept in reserve, intermediate, depending on phases of occupation, but never wholly left to themselves.

The relation to the rural space, aiming at large-scale satisfaction of many needs through agricultural production can no longer be seen in a deterministic way. The weight of the natural factors varies from one period to another and in accordance with agro-technical attitudes, as is apparent from the geographical history of the vine, which has been thoroughly studied from R. Dion to M. Lachiver and G. Garrier.[22] Two major factors of localisation operate in different ways and account for the overall process of evolution. There is the role played by the towns and the roads which organise demand and possibilities of access to the production-sites. Roads and rivers, together with coastwise traffic, favoured expansion beyond the original bounds which had been fixed long after the invasions by church demands, the work of vine-growing bishops and abbots, the glory of princes and the profit of merchants. The rise of the vineyards steadily accompanied the rise of the towns, taking place at their very gates, and, according to Garrier, demand always had to reckon with inadequate supply.[23] It may seem artificial to separate here towns from countryside, in that the town-dwelling landlord is often a vine-grower who sells his produce everywhere, and also in that vines are often

found around towns. Nevertheless, certain localisations are highly dependent on the natural conditions of the place. Improvement of complex
soils in areas exposed to the sun and away from fogs led to vineyards being
established on stony hillsides with cleared soil, preferably facing south.
After choosing favourable locations, large-scale vineyards were developed, to meet the first consumer demands. Some plantations disappeared
because changes in taste, helped by transport conditions, altered their
capacity to meet demand. From the seventeenth until the nineteenth
century, Parisians found the little wine of Suresnes drinkable – perhaps
even delicious. A charming local product, this was eventually abandoned,
like many other minor wines of Northern France which the citizens' thirst
had kept at the limit of production-capacity.

These desertions, and sometimes some revivals, call in question the
idea that growing-areas and supply were stable. To be sure, one can agree
that, until the nineteenth century, the peasant community was stable and
had adapted to the natural conditions and to the technological environment which underwent little change. From this resulted a permanence of
agrarian practices not much open to alteration. The problem therefore is
to discover how change could come about, both on the general plane and
at a local and family level. The opening-up process, doubtless facilitated
by schooling and by the circulation of recipes, was connected with external demand, the imperatives of new consumptions, road-building policy
and administrative measures which had the effect of ending the isolation
of certain areas.[24] New crops established themselves – maize in the
seventeenth century, the potato in the eighteenth, and the chestnut.
Agronomists and peasants saw all of these contributing in various ways to
changes in the landscape, but they also, through changing dietary habits,
altered the style of material culture and social relations. When we understand change and turn away from a static notion of history, we try to
ascertain the possibilities for adaptation possessed by the agro-system on
which everything depended.

Natural and developed space

The living cover of vegetation, heath and forest played a major role in this
change. After the great land-clearances of the twelfth and thirteenth
centuries, this cover was determined by the mastery of fire and re-
establishment of 'the full world' after the Black Death. It was no longer
attacked except on a limited and localised scale, though such onslaughts
increased from the eighteenth century onward. For rural France this
space, both free and yet under control, mastered and yet often magical
and marginal, has defined long since the main lines of the landscape. It

was there that species both vegetable and animal were selected, and sometimes transformed by the introduction of new varieties (the pine and the sweet-chestnut tree, in the forests) and specific kinds of fauna (deer for the nobles to hunt).

Similarly, in this living eco-system ponds and rivers became important. It was in connection with a fundamental element in old-time diets in which a great deal of fresh-water fish were eaten, that sheets of water were developed and protected, as an important source of income for land-owners, contributing to the wealth of great estates both secular and ecclesiastical. In some parts of France, such as Dombes, the monasteries and the rural communities controlled the entire system of ponds and supplied the neighbouring towns with fish.

In the seventeenth and eighteenth centuries the general principles for domesticating the natural setting were established, but the relation of man to nature was not passive. It consisted of the transference of old elements, both vegetable and animal and the introduction of new components, with a variety of changes in the balance. This could sometimes bring about considerable alteration in the ordinary life of the peasants: for example, the great royal and aristocratic hunting preserves were developed around Paris partly at the expense of grain-growing fields. A change in the balance in a set of practices can have many consequences. As regards consumption it is through the variations in available resources that attitudes and appropriations are to be understood.

These attitudes and appropriations are most easily visible in the developed space, the sphere of labour and the basis of peasant life. The land, meaning the soils in all their variety and with their productive capacity reconstituted by men, determines the entire organisation of country life, as ownership of land, through its fundamental prestige, defines the divisions in society. It is in a daily relationship with the land that is experienced the capacity to maintain and renew a world in which everything has its own importance, with actions and implements, practices and ideas, all dominated by the cyclical return of the seasons, of works and days.

The exploitation of the earth's riches was always restricted by shortage of fertiliser. There were no chemical fertilisers and not much of the natural sort. The shortages and deficiencies of organic matter conducive to increased yields could be made up for only by the system of fallows, which kept out of production a third or a half of the productive land. Agronomists applied their efforts to solving this problem, by extending universally the principles of a 'green revolution' which had been tried out in Northern Italy, Holland and England, based on more extensive planting of fodder crops. The fallow system stood firm because without it there would be no cattle, without cattle there would be even less fertiliser in the form of manure, and without that it would be impossible to maintain yields that were already poor. Like wheat, it was a 'necessary evil' that restricted the surfaces from which a return could be got. But the fallow system was also at the heart of the question of animal husbandry: in the relation between production and consumption it was an element which was indispensable but calling for care. Agricultural France of the seventeenth and eighteenth centuries was not merely the great grain-growing plains and open fields of the country's North, which resulted from a long evolution and an adaptation to natural conditions under the pressure of increased urban demand. This was only one of the ways of adaptation presented by the peasant realm. In other regions, the mountains, the bocages, the Mediterranean South, different systems operated, with ecological rates which the agronomists of the time did not always understand immediately, because they did not find there the landscape they were used to and the dominant model of the great grain-growing plains that provided the criterion by which they estimated all farming practices.

Here we see how important were variations in mastery of the developed space and how necessary it is to appreciate the criteria, intellectual and practical, that contemporaries applied in relations with the setting in which they found themselves. We have to measure the nearness and the distance between the agronomist's field and that of the peasant, to distinguish between the concrete meaning of ideas and their ideological usefulness, and to compare the rational choices with the technical possibilities of the localities and the social structure. In this way we can discover the meaning of a history of agronomy in the modern epoch, in its context and its missions.[25]

The natural foundations of material culture are associated with a constant interaction between production and cultivated space. This relation depends on a balance, variable according to regions, between three components in the landscape: the *ager*, the *sylva* and the *saltus*, to employ the classical terminology which was familiar to agronomists in the period between Humanism and the Enlightenment. These three elements are complementary and form a set which was not to be much altered until the major transformation of the nineteenth century.

Cultivated land can be regarded as a single ecological unit without any anachronism. It was the sphere of existence of the peasantry, both vine-growers and cereal-growers. G. Durand has shown very well how, thanks to the daily comings and goings across the country roads, through conflicts and agreements on boundaries, profound relationships were woven, relationships that are essential for an understanding of peasant culture and of attitudes to nature and the possibility of change.[26]

In the 'old forest' that bounds the landscape other practices are at work. Here and there, peasants encountered juridical limits (remember the Code Colbert and the reformation of the forests) or else imaginary ones: the stranger and the strange was always to be found in the depths of the woods, a place without rules, but these very woods supplied the rural economy with all its customary building materials. The growing demand for timber from towns and ironworks gave rise to scientific and academic inquiries as well as giving rise to riots.[27] Forestry could be in conflict with customs, and a change in use could rouse rural communities faced with new constraints to resist them. Fierce competition developed around necessary but scarce and coveted produce, competition in which peasants were set against landowners, country-folk against townsfolk, the administration against merchants, foresters against ironmasters – the country, the town, the factory all in mutual conflict. It was then that a specific criminality appeared at times to break the tension caused by these new practices brought in from outside, because a disturbance of the balance calls for a search for new ways of thinking.

Between the fields and the forests, the *saltus* is the space occupied by grazing-land, wet pastures taken from grasslands or marshes, meadows and heaths of the hills and mountains. For the peasants it is a transitional zone the cultivation of which can upset the general situation of the local economy, like re-colonising of the forests. It is undoubtedly the least stable of the three elements, but nevertheless it has a role to play, because it makes possible large-scale cattle-raising and provides additional resources.

The balance between the three elements obviously differs in accordance with ecological settings. It varies, too, depending on the type of control exercised by the rural communities and lordships, collective usages and common pasture. Moreover, the pasture-space is not entirely coincident with the *saltus*. In the Mediterranean regions, bush and moors provide wood and also grass for goats and sheep. In Brittany the heaths beside the sea and their furze enter into the agricultural system by offering conditions for animal husbandry, particularly horse-breeding, which the cultivation and the development of artificial meadows would sweep away. In the pastures of moderately mountainous areas animal husbandry is often predominant. In the summer pastures higher up an original setting survives, the key to the economy of the mountains and of the seasonal movements of men and beasts. Shepherds play a special role. They are good intermediaries between the forces of nature and those of society. They pass through all the circles of agricultural space. For their neighbours there is always something of the sorcerer about them. Their image also shows the overlapping of these three different landscapes, and points up how plain and mountain may even complement each other.

These elements are indeed complementary. Except in the grain-growing areas they are adapted to a polycultural economy which roots the peasantry in stability and tradition, one of the bases of which continues to be the defence of community usages. In the eighteenth century men become aware both of the natural and historical constraints upon them and of the rigidity which these constraints imply. This was an agricultural system in which productivity was low and technique clumsy, and which was acutely sensitive to all departures from normality, both meteorological and economic, a system that would be subjected gradually to a powerful pressure of demand.

The Revolution, with its agrarian disturbances, was to mark a decisive break, because it supported property ownership in the exclusive and domanial sense recognised by the bourgeois class of victorious property-owning townsfolk.[28] The Revolution thus meant a setback for collective and extensive utilisations of the land and of the intermediate and forest zones. For political and social reasons the ecological balance entered a phase of change, because the relation to institutions, to rights and customs, already questioned, was now challenged. The stability due to the controls exercised by the lords and the communities and by the parish, had survived till then. It was within these entities, variously represented on the map of the kingdom and more or less active, that the constraints of technique and the possibilities of transformation were expressed, by means of leases, discussions and regulations governing the harvesting of crops. The whole technical system depended on the relation to natural conditions and adapted itself thereto, regardless. It made possible the ideal of subsistence farming along with, in normal times, a marketing of surpluses for the provisioning of the towns which brought about a decisive transformation of certain regions, as J. M. Moriceau has shown in the case of the farms of the Ile-de-France.[29] It was not immediately adaptable to the increase in population which occurred in the eighteenth century.

If we are to understand how, in this context, change was possible and how the principal features of the consumption–production relation were modified, we have to take account of two concrete dimensions; that of the population's self-regulation and that of the possibility of an agricultural revolution.[30] Demographic studies have shown that, after a long period of steady-state and with numerous local variations, the eighteenth century saw a period of growth. The population as a whole grew, and also the number of town-dwellers, most of whom had come from the country. All these people had to be fed. Before this time a homeostatic regulation of the population's size seems to have functioned, governed by the amount of food available. Crises, the effects of which were variously interpreted, restored a balance. These crises were severe when the system of cultivation was altered, with increased dependence owing to specialisation, particularly in grain growing, and with economic and epidemiological effects into the bargain, having consequences that differed according to people's social position. Labrousse showed that in 1947. We now know the capacity of agriculture as a whole to reproduce itself, with each crisis giving younger people the opportunity to establish themselves on properties made available by deaths. The ecological balance was maintained, along with the entire agrarian structure. The self-subsistence of a mass of small peasants, small-scale landowners, semi-independent and semi-wage-earning, was safeguarded. The big landowners – noble, ecclesiastical, bourgeois – who marketed the greater part of their harvests, farmers and share-croppers, large-scale or small-scale entrepreneurs à la Cantillon served as intermediaries between variable demand and dispersed production which was heterogeneous in every way.

An increase in economic and political analyses, starting from the first half of the eighteenth century reflected awareness of the demographic problem. It was due to a false perception which Montesquieu reproduces in his *Lettres persanes* and *Esprit des lois* and the positive intellectual effects of which we can understand nowadays.[31] France's intellectuals believed that the population was declining. Administrators and thinkers on social problems sought ways to understand the working of the productive mechanisms: e.g., Quesnay, in the article 'Man' in the *Encyclopédie*. A science of observation of population changes arose, with statistical apparatus, investigations and debates,[32] and this gradually established that, in reality, the population was growing. Present-day historians take note of this, even if they diverge as to the causes and effects of this growth – mortality, age at marriage, family planning. The accepted figure gives 22,000,000 French in the kingdom in the 1720s and at least 28,000,000 in the 1790s.

This growth, which depended mainly on adaptation of employment, set in motion in the rural areas various processes of fragmentation of holdings or of transfer to wage-earning. The formation of large farms could create a centre of attraction for transformed labour-power. The zones of proto-industrialisation, where agricultural and manufacturing work were associated, could record high densities of population, as we see in Valentinois, Perche, Flanders and Normandy, dominated by Rouen. Migration relieved some of the pressure, finding an outlet in the towns, but mobility failed to check the growth, on the contrary its effect was to keep it up. It removed only surplus population from the countryside, and sent back part of the income earned, which served to pay taxes and finance dowries and even the purchase of land. Finally, it endowed the rural world with a more optimistic outlook, regarding possibilities of expansion, an outlook which was also readier to contemplate change. To judge by the results of the concatenation of economic and demographic mechanisms, the thrust of population growth set going responses that were indispensable if it was to be maintained, in terms of production and distribution. This forms part of investigations, still today not entirely resolved, regarding consumption.

The debate on the agricultural revolution seems to be reviving. Even if, as must be agreed, the expression is hardly appropriate, it does indicate an issue. Demand was certainly increasing in quantity, and probably in quality as well. How did supply follow it, at all levels of society? The answer is not to be found merely in terms of arable yields, though those did show significant increases in some areas, but in the overall evolution of the agrarian system and the accumulation of results achieved in the regions. The increased demand for labour doubtless operated in its own way. Then there was the bringing under the plough of newly cleared land, despite marginal costs and the reduction in fallows, together with the diffusion of new crops – buckwheat, maize, potatoes – the 'little outposts' dear to Marc Bloch, meaning all the products used for self-subsistence, but the introduction of which altered the old dialectical balances, while changes were taking place in economic and social relations. Investment of labour in gardening could also bring returns. In the zones of proto-industrialisation the fragmenting of holdings and part-time work for factories made possible an increase in population. Finally, some of the increase was connected with improvements in the road network which favoured the marketing of such products as wine: this was noticeable in Alsace, in Beaujolais, and in the corn-growing areas of northern France, which were encouraged by the take-off of prices after 1740. Without any major technical transformation having occurred, an overall evolution was undoubtedly beginning.

These changes were accompanied by agronomists' study of the rural scene, which, as in Lavoisier's case, measured effects without completely changing their technical data, which were not to undergo a thorough upheaval until the nineteenth century. These writers were organised in 'societies of agriculture and economy' and they expressed themselves in periodicals and memoirs. Naturalists and chemists took part in a debate which ranged over all the problems of the power of nature and that of mankind: the grain famine, the diseases of crops, the balance of the *saltus*, of animal husbandry and the forest, the shortage of woods, the models of cultivation available, the art of managing one's property and the social economy, English agronomy and its results, which showed that animal husbandry could free agriculture from the tyranny of corn (this model functioned throughout France without any alternative, except in some regions).

Two conceptions of the change soon came into conflict.[33] For some, it happened through the introduction into the old system of a new element, a machine, a procedure, a product hitherto unknown – in short, through things. For others, it was the consequence of the transformation of structures and the actions of men who changed their practices. The question interested thinkers of all sorts, because the answer to it changed one's view of the relation of men to things and the acceptance of scarcity or abundance. The growth which led to agricultural production involved the consumption of non-agricultural goods as well.

In order to understand the pressures upon the supply of labour and the increase in the active population through women and children being drawn into work, we need to place the phenomena of consumption in the framework of the family and take account of the plurality of incomes from wages. A family's expenditure might increase even when wages failed to follow prices and so cause an increase in global demand. Intensive development of exchange and use of money introduced countryfolk to *exchange value* and broadened their taste for new things. New consumptions could spread in a society in which there was an ever-increasing contrast between rich and poor, but in which existed a wide hierarchy of unequal incomes. The constraint of subsistence must, therefore, be seen as relative and the specific character of consumer behaviour better appreciated.

Relations between generations, life-style ethnic and cultural allegiances are at the origin of forms of solidarity which are not superimposed on those which have their basis in production-relations. It is from this standpoint that the study of models of consumption is decisive: it can enable us to know which were the social scenes in which envy, imitation and conflict are at work.[34]

The frontiers of production were beginning to move, and this aroused a will to know, an attentiveness which shifted from the exterior, where mercantilism reigned, to the interior, a realm where the role of more numerous and more diverse consumers challenged a system of old-established balances. Consumption itself questioned the moral and intellectual frameworks of old practices based on scarcity and stability. In the more fluid and mobile France of the towns, this experience began much earlier.

For the peasant world we can adopt the conclusions formulated for Alsace by J.-M. Boehler:[35] neither a revolutionary take-off nor a static history but an agriculture placed between tradition and innovation. It is no longer appropriate to contrast an archaic sphere of production, anathematised by the reformers, with an enlightened agriculture worthy of praise but not understood by the peasant masses. Modernity was able to slip in everywhere, including small-scale cultivation. It was able to supply a majority of peasants who were short of resources with substitute products and, failing that, to improve global productivity by getting everyone to work. The material foundations, the technical aspects inseparable from the social context explain a struggle for survival and the coexistence, to varying degrees of new and traditional methods. The principal elements of the eco-system – wood, water, soil – were then utilised as much for the peasants' own consumption as for sale, divided in varying proportion between self-subsistence and the market. The Auvergne peasant aimed at self-sufficiency through polyculture and the communal right to cut wood, while the vine-grower of the Beaujolais or the Bordelais had entered the world of the market, like the Ile-de-France farmer.

The economic geography of France revealed by study of the records of the *Maximum* during the Revolution shows an extreme diversity of articles habitually consumed and an extension in the spheres of sale of products in 1793.[36] We find a greater amount of trade than could have been supposed, even in very isolated rural areas, and production that is very heterogeneous in quality and definition – in short, a picture of 'what is commonly sold'. The isolation of regions has been reduced: if the areas from which they show their supplies differ greatly in extent and intensity, there are now few that are completely independent.[37] Paris is very dominant, but everywhere else the diversity of the products consumed passes through urban filters, by virtue of a rationality of provisioning which is partly national and strongly regional. The diffusion of products marketed and taxed during the Revolution enables us to perceive the encounter on the ground between the logics of supply in a marketing sphere and those of demand as observed in the geography of tastes and choices, which are not entirely superimposable. Local and national goods divide the market of exchange in accordance with variable lines of influence and force. While textiles, hardware, groceries and colonial drysalteries circulate all over France, the basic foodstuffs – wine, oil, salt – are less widely represented in the markets.

At the end of the eighteenth century the cartography of the *Maximum* reveals the country's productive forces, the unevennesses of development and of trade, but also a regional and national geography of consumptions. In both cases we see that Paris and the North of France are winners, with the difference between town and country clearly expressed in the number of places where food can be obtained and in the variety of products on sale.

2   Towns, trade and inventions

Until the middle of the nineteenth century it was the land and landowner-ship, the land and work on the land that provided the foundation for the practices of the population and their ideas about everyday life and the future: that population was mostly rural. What mattered was to adminis-ter a patrimony well and to pass it on. What organised people's time was the principle of an eternal return. What allotted roles and established authority between men and women was relation to a continuity of works and days. True wealth lay not in the movement of goods but in the meadows, the ploughlands, the domain which it was one's duty to en-large. This alienation was no less important than that defined by Marx, because it immobilised the village.[1]

The problem of possessions and their value, and of how to multiply them, the question of resources and means of subsistence, and that of productive transformation were all bound up with this condition, which the Physiocrats endowed with theoretical significance and of which they analysed the political consequences. Innovation, they said, presupposed two changes: one concerning a hierarchy that was the basis of privilege and esteem, the other concerning attitude to a culture of conformism and stability. The opening-up of country life was included in the economic and social prospect which the Physiocrats' doctrine set at the heart of 'the order of the fields', so as both to justify it and to speed up its development.

For the Physiocratic 'sect', the expenditure of the upper strata of society, the landlords, the Court, the army, the church and, of course, the towns is of supreme importance. The peasants' labour, the sole producer of real wealth, pays for all needs, both of subsistence and reproduction, together with the expenditure of the 'unproductive class'. The latter's expenditure is fundamental in regulating the movements of the economy. Dr Chesnay's *Tableau* reveals the process which unites production, circu-lation and consumption, depending upon the land and the mobilisation of its net product. The country is the centre, with the village marginal, but it is there that take place the to-ings and fro-ings of a general transform-ation.

The economic debate thus emphasised the positive character of the increase in expenditure and consumption. It also showed the importance of cultural factors in the transformation of rural societies. The progress of literacy was vital. To be sure, geographical difference persisted. The North retained a lead established long since over the South and the West, and there were differences as between the sexes, with women catching up more or less, but with difficulty, with the men's rate of progress. But the eighteenth century saw an overall adjustment, beginning in the towns, with their evolution moving in the same direction as the regions around them. The increase in information was not a negligible factor. What mattered was the diffusion, direct and indirect of, for example, much news and knowledge regarding agricultural activities, and the bringing of the peasant world into contact with urban circles. The diffusion by pedlars of almanacs, which underwent a partial change in tone and content, the multiplication of exchanges by post made possible by the improvements in roads and postal services after 1750, and the expanded distribution of the press through subscription, both individual and collective, all contributed to an initial opening-up which had unifying effects in respect of everyone's consumption.[2]

Furthermore, an entire economy of circulation of information from town to country affected important social segments of rural society – the lords of manors, the priests, the townsmen who owned land, the well-to-do peasants, the postmasters, in other words all those whose way of life, habits and cultural means had an indirect fall-out on the peasants' ways. The absenteeism of lords has to be looked at from this standpoint: by their mere presence the rural notables incited improvements, because they demonstrated other ways to live. Those who owned estates around towns, in the rural areas dominated by those towns, were not indifferent to the way their property was managed, since they derived a considerable proportion of their resources from it. They resided on their estates for part of their time, thereby displaying ways of life that came from elsewhere and were no less exotic to the country-folk than the country-folk's ways were to the incomers. In this connection the servants who accompanied the latter played an important part. Links could thus be formed which had effects that, though certainly slow, proved decisive in that they suggested comparisons and prospects that were different. The principal actors in this process were, let it not be forgotten, those who held the keys of both 'unproductive expenditure' and development.

It was, indeed, among those notables who were able to accept the risks involved in change that, gradually, the economic relations took shape which led to the improvement of the countryside. Their role was all the more preponderant in that it was coupled with their function in the apportionment and distribution of income from land. Here once more Cantillon offers a convincing analysis: one-third of the resources produced went to the notables, as their expenditure not only on subsistence but, above all, on the goods and luxuries that they bought in the towns.[3] By the choices they made the landowners determined how economic activity and employment was allotted. As independent individuals they propelled the imitative consumption which moralists denounced, along with urban corruption. This consumption we must seek out in the urban framework, so as to show how a different economic system functioned, and in the features of a cultural exchange that was the basis of the 'town' spirit.

The weight of the town

Since long before, the ancient relationship uniting town with country had been experienced in men's minds as the expression of a state of dependence. The caricatures produced during the Revolution which show the privileged orders bearing down with all their weight on the peasant crushed beneath them were exacerbated echoes of that time-honoured notion of rural exploitation. At the same time, however, the relationship was being modified in so far as urbanisation began to dictate exchange and trade, wherein new powers of attraction appeared within the urban fabric. While the hierarchy of the towns was still largely determined by the factors that were responsible for the success of the old cities and had created the urban geography of France, especially after administrative unification, the power of economic and utilitarian phenomena is to be felt more strongly when it comes to defining or picturing the town.

Monuments, privileges, numbers

Scholars define the town by three criteria which already emphasise its originality as a special centre of consumption.

The first of these criteria relates to architecture. The urban scene is characterised by both enclosure and monumentality. Behind walls, and in buildings and dwellings different from those observed by travellers in the country, a different form of life is adumbrated. In the seventeenth and eighteenth centuries fortified walls became less significant in proportion as the Kingdom's defensive strategy came to be organised on the frontiers, and as internal disturbances ceased. Municipalities knocked down their ancient walls, those symbols of an urban patriotism that was on the way out. But the relationship between country and town did not change all at once, and entry to towns continued to be controlled – because the second criterion defining the town is privilege, particularly exemptions and fiscal freedoms. While the townsman is, to begin with, a protected consumer, less subject than the countryman to the hazards of military incursions, he is also a favoured consumer. The customs barrier defined by the toll houses emphasises the advantages on both sides: there are those who pay the *tailles* and those who are exempt from them through collective redemption, and there are those who pay the tolls and those who do not have to.

This change in status encouraged, one presumes, production as well as consumption. The town has a lower tax burden and some of its resources are derived from consumption itself. Furthermore, it possesses a right to control its expenditure which is much greater than that allowed to the peasant communities, and this despite increased supervision by the King's agents.

The Paris toll,[4] the results of which enabled Lavoisier to undertake one of the first attempts made to analyse urban consumption, supplies an example of this. It was an indirect tax which benefited first the royal treasury and then the town: in 1789 four-fifths of the 35 million *livres* came from entry duties. Necker noted in his *Traité de l'administration des finances* in 1787,[5] that the toll constituted one-eighth of all the Kingdom's tax revenue and corresponded to a consumption of 250 million *livres*. 'There are no two provinces of France all of whose taxes put together equal the total duties levied on Parisians' consumptions' commented in 1789 the forgotten author of *Les Etrennes financières*.[6] The taxes fall upon all objects, starting with drinks (20 million out of 35 million in Paris) – burgesses, owners of land in Paris, religious communities, the *maréchaussée* and various officials being exempt from paying this tax. Then it was the turn of all foodstuffs (meat, cereals, fodder, all 'merchandise of weight') drysalteries, groceries, hardware, iron goods, ices and fuel. The more rigorous supervision of the collection of the toll and the building of the 'wall of the Farmers-General' gave inspiration to song-writers:

Pour augmenter son numéraire et raccourcir notre horizon,
La Ferme a jugé nécessaire de nous mettre tous en prison.[7]
[To increase their takings and restrict our outlook, the tax-farmers have resolved to put us all in prison.]

A debate started which is mainly of interest because it shows how a town defended its consumption privileges. The rate of duty charged was bearable, as compared with the amounts furnished by *agrément du domicile* in so far as it was paid in part by the producers, provided that the vices of the tax-system (inequality of exemption, cheating on both sides, pomp and arrogance of the administration and its agents) were not taken to excess.

A lampoon described, on this occasion, the necessary balance in household consumption: 'the four objects of prime necessity for existence, namely, corn, meat, wood and drink'. Another, *Observation sur l'injustice et l'immoralité des droits d'entrée dans les villes*, describes the budget of the Parisian craftsmen[8] in order to justify familiar practices.

Eventually, Lavoisier found in the toll a means of evaluating the national wealth and so of better relating taxation to income, by establishing an equivalence between production and consumption, the former of these being accessible to statistics only in irregular fashion. To calculate average expenditure in relation to the number of inhabitants he introduced the idea of difference in consumer habits between rural areas, small towns and large towns, which he supported by an analysis of expenditures – those of families, of hospitals and of the Army. For the upper fringe of consumers Lavoisier calculated expenditure on the basis of indirect fiscal resources.[9] We see here how the privileges and obligations of towns gave rise to a spirit that was different from that which prevailed in the village communities, and we see also to what extent their establishment conflicted with social reality and gave rise to much questioning, in which the original character of urban consumption becomes clearly apparent.

That consumption was related to the number of inhabitants[10] is the third criterion defining town-life. Discussions about the acceptable threshold of population – 1,500 or 2,000 or more – show the interest taken in learned circles in new ways of classifying that were needed in order to measure and understand the differences (as also for the requirements of policing, administration and technology), so as better to solve the problems of provisioning the towns. The map showing the towns of France was practically stable after the seventeenth century. However, though the century of the Enlightenment did not see the birth of new towns, it did witness the development and transformation of more or less ancient sites that were being drawn, to one degree or another, into the genesis of the modern town.

What scale can we adopt for this phenomenon, and what were its repercussions on changes in material culture? For fiscal reasons the towns usually rejected censuses or failed to acknowledge them. Evaluations, even those made later, by administrators who considered, with Moheau, that 'there can be no well-run political machine or enlightened administration in a country where the number of the population is not known' enables us to outline the dimensions of the urban movement. If we put them together with the calculations made by historians[11] we arrive at the hypothesis that, in 1700–25, the town population amounted to about four million, and that by 1790 it had reached five to six million, an increase of the order of 15–20 per cent. From that time one Frenchman in five was a town-dweller. This growth took place between 1740 and 1775 and thereafter slowed down.

We must nevertheless take note of important variations. The North and the East of France were urbanised mainly along the axes of circulation and the major river-valleys, together with all the coastal areas. The South had towns from ancient times and possessed a somewhat different urban tradition, with its big market-towns in which the ways of life and sociability were rooted in citizenship. The differentiation was not equally shared in all parts of the territory: some towns which were pioneers in the seventeenth century saw their growth slow down (Rouen, Angers, Chartres), while others advanced until the 1770s and then stabilised (e.g., Caen). The great Channel and Atlantic ports, from Dunkirk to Le Havre and from Nantes to Bordeaux, progressed, as also did Marseilles, all being carried along by the impetus of trade and colonial development. Inside the country industrial and manufacturing towns experienced similar rates of growth and a comparable rise in population: St Etienne, Nîmes, Lyons and Strasbourg. Heading the list, Paris increased its population by over a third, going from 400-500,000 inhabitants around 1700 to 600,000, even perhaps 700,000 around 1789. Lavoisier gave the capital about 600,000 souls, and it is obvious that this evaluation directly affected his estimate of consumption.

The size of the population in each town is important, but we must not neglect the status of the urban network or the hierarchy created in this network by the capacity of the urban driving force to attract people and hasten exchanges, and so to change behaviour.

Stability and growth of towns

The form of life of the towns was thus, on the whole, static. This corresponded to an old-established functional stability, in which what mattered most was administrative, judicial, fiscal and religious tasks. What distinguished a small town from a market-centre was that it had offices, courts, religious communities, buildings which went with these various functions, and an entire population which lived by the activities involved – collection of duties, dispensing of justice. The whole life of the old cities, with its processions and hierarchies was subordinated to the institutions established there.

The economy modified this form of life through a different acceleration, by promoting both employment and the circulation of commodities. Small-scale trade, fairs and markets, local proto-industrial manufactories outside the walls but under the town's control – as in the case of textile production, when demand grew and tasks evolved – and a variety of industries carried out within the walls came increasingly to characterise town life, driven by trade, various services and the redistribution of things.

Economists and observers of morals acknowledged the usefulness of the town. It was at once the point of maximum concentration of expenditure by the landowners, the centre of a financial redistribution which also affected the peasants who sold their produce, and the heart of an intensive creation of value by the labour of its craftsmen and of an acceleration of all movements of exchange and control. At the end of the seventeenth century Alexandre Lemaitre noted in his study of the phenomenon of capital cities, chapter 45, 'On the origin of towns', that the peopling of cities was connected with mutual aid, defensive support and the good faith that ensured the foundations of their administrative and political development,[12] which changed its economy through the growth of population, of consumptions and of secondary activities. In the first quarter of the eighteenth century, as we have seen, Cantillon made the town the principal location of expenditure by landowners, a place in which, while the link with politics was maintained, the separate character of expenditure was increasing. At the end of the eighteenth century Condillac, in *Le Commerce et le Gouvernement considérés relativement l'un à l'autre*, Adam Smith in *The Wealth of Nations* (1776, and soon translated into French) and Nicolas Desmeunier in *L'Economie politique*, written for Panckoucke's *Encylopédie méthodique* after 1780, all said the same: the town was now the centre for the social division of labour, the principal gearing of growth and of the problems facing society. They all stressed the interaction between economic, social and cultural phenomena.

The town's attractiveness to the landowners was due to 'enjoyment [there] of agreeable company'. Condillac, following Cantillon, introduced here an explanation of the link existing between the various forms of cultural activity and the economy. The typology and hierarchy of the towns was based upon exchange, the concentration of wealth and the circulation of money. Demand established a geography and a society. For Condillac, 'wealth is shared between the towns in proportion to the consumption that takes place there' and consumption was the basis for growth, in consequence of 'a way of living'. The inhabitants, old and new, were faced with new forms of behaviour and acquired new habits. Everyone's needs developed, bringing about urban growth and affecting the rural economy, the participants in which also reacted, though more slowly, to the attractions of the urban Enlightenment.

This multiplication of needs resulted from movements of population. An influx of labour-power was needed by the active towns, and, whether temporary or lasting, it caused an activation of demand which manifested itself in consumption not in a uniform way but through activities of appropriation that were associated with economic capacity (incomes) and cultural capacity (tastes). The diversity of demand was determined by the mobility of the population, the increase in demand swelled total income.

That consumption created growth can be clearly seen in the economy of reception. Every year, at the end of the Ancien Régime, a floating population moved through Paris: between 100,000 and 150,000, according to police estimates.[13] A few travellers but mostly seasonal workers, temporary migrants who became integrated and anchored through marriage to a Parisian: a majority of men, but a considerable number also of women (between 10 and 20 per cent, according to different calculations) – all discovered the ways of life typical of Paris. The hierarchy of furnished rooms and hotels enabled them to find lodging when hospitality and the charitable networks proved inadequate. In every case the problems presented were proportionate to each person's capacities, either in establishments that were different for rich and poor or in one and the same hotel where each person found what suited him.

The Parisian hotel responded to very varied needs and incomes. It was the first shop-window of new things that the town offered. The difference between Paris and the rest of the kingdom was, certainly, not absolute partly because migration implied stages and successive periods and partly because it also comprised a lot of trial and error, with many departures and returns. Every year, some of the newcomers went back to their original locality, barely altered by their brief experience, whereas others, after a life spent saving up in hope of return were quite transformed, as in the case of the Auvergnat elite of the nineteenth century.[14] On their return they gave their villages the benefit of viewing what they had acquired, displaying new objects and new needs.

The town presided over three great upheavals. It opened the way to other attitudes to new objects, and also to new habits. It created a setting favourable to different forms of demographic and sexual behaviour, through birth control. It prepared other economic attitudes for the family and established a different way of looking at the social hierarchy. While this is easy to see happening in the village, where economic, spiritual and cultural authority were clearly perceptible, it is harder to grasp in the town, where, owing to all sorts of confusions, relations between persons were transformed in a way that favoured sundry freedoms. All these changes were based also on the creation of different time-scales: the Church, the Army, the police and trade provided the town with temporal reference-points centred round measurement and division. The progress of urbanisation affected even the relation between work and leisure, because work and what was not work could be kept separate more easily in the town than in the country A new phase of consumption was being prepared.

The towns and consumption

The towns maintained a movement that was begun by the demographic change in the rural areas and the increase in population. They created jobs and activated the circulation of incomes. This movement, which was not accompanied by complete changes in technique or definitive structural changes, was speeded up by circulation in the sphere of exchange. The towns were the centres of an economic organisation based on the accumulation and redistribution of rent from land, taxes and profits from trade and manufacture.

Land rent, taxes, trade

The role of land rent was accentuated in the eighteenth century by several factors, revealed earlier by C.-E. Labrousse and made clearer recently by J.-Y. Grenier.[15] The amplification of demand, carried forward by the movement of population, led on to a striving for land and so to increases in farm rents and prices. The table of 'good prices' favoured sellers rather than buyers, especially the wage-earners among the latter, as wages did not rise with prices.

In times of crisis consumers' choices focused massively on necessities, basic goods, poor-quality corn instead of wheat. People did without comforts, which had a bad effect on manufacturing and trade. Crises emphasised very strongly social differences and the contrast between town and country. In normal times the surplus from rent was spent in town, where it helped to develop a new type of society, so that landowners, whether noble or bourgeois, were induced to reside in towns. The nobility, who had entered to a considerable extent into the towns' representative organs, had to persist in this role in order to continue to participate in power. Similar mechanisms brought back to the cities part of the Church's income, which served to maintain the life-style of its members and the displays associated with worship, as well as being redistributed in charitable and hospital work: this constituted a large share of what was spent to help the most deprived elements and the unemployed. All of which gives an idea of the diversity of the incomes that were mobilisable and of the movement their consumption could set going.

Taxes furnished the towns with a second source of capital, which disadvantaged the rural areas as it was largely invested in urban equipment:[16] the buildings and monuments of the government, large-scale town planning schemes (royal or municipal), the great hospitals built in the seventeenth century (financed also, one supposes, out of the Church's land rents and even by private charity), and the erection of barracks. The Farmers-General Wall and Ledoux's toll-houses can be seen as excessive symbols of this redistribution, since in their case indirect taxation supplied the architectural magnificence 'necessary' for its own levying. Such investment fed much expenditure, set business and building work going and supported a wide range of crafts.

It is understandable that the Court was increasingly made one of the targets of criticism inspired by defence of the public weal and by hostility to increased taxation and royal expenditure. By its monumental extent and the numerousness of its personnel, by the futility, whether real or imaginary, of the expenditure it entailed (for example, a dress to be worn when one was presented to the King could cost the equivalent of 1,500 to 3,000 days of wage-labour in 1780), the Court seemed to embody the waste and indebtedness of the Ancien Régime's latter end.[17] This was, however, only one aspect of the redistribution of the net product, being in the forefront of the luxury economy. When it no longer supported the crafts of Paris, they suffered crisis. Eighteenth-century criticism of the Court reveals how the levying of taxes was thought of in relation to phenomena of consumption, but also shows that this was a major moment of transformation of the relation between the state and its subjects.

As Alain Guéry has shown, the conception of taxation under the traditional monarchy was based on the idea of gift and reciprocal exchange.[18] The King's right to levy part of his subjects' incomes was justified only if this contributed to the general good. The processes of redistribution might be immediate, without giving rise to criticism, in the form of gifts, appointments or lands conferred on loyal supporters, but most of the revenue had to be devoted to the public service. To this conception of a fiscal system based on the idea of giving there corresponded a general notion of royal and Court consumption, justified by the magnificence indispensable to the representation of sovereignty. The monarch's expenditure manifested in outward forms the visibility of power and the fundamental principle that everyone should consume in accordance with the requirements of the rank and status. This is one of the keys to the economy of scarcity and the contrast there could be between the upper reaches of society and the masses who were often reduced to bare necessities.

The sumptuary laws, the actual application of which remains unknown, entered in two ways into the consumption system. On the social plane, they reserved certain consumptions to certain ranks. *Bourgeois* and their wives had no right to wear garments woven with gold or silver, nor to own pearls, nor to purchase expensive crockery. The Court and the aristocratic families in the towns lived in a separate sphere of consumption. On the economic plane, however, the sumptuary laws were aimed at restricting waste and controlling luxury consumption by the aristocracy.[19] At the end of the seventeenth century these laws lost some of their protective power in the social sphere. From the standpoint of mercantilism they aimed at restricting export of currency, thereby transforming into an economic purpose something that arose from a certain conception of society.

At the same time we observe the result of a century-long growth in the tax burden, which was nevermore to be checked. To this must be added the increasing importance of indirect taxation and duties on consumption, whether these affected indispensable goods or utilities, since they fell upon salt and beverages, groceries, fashionable garments and tobacco.[20] These levies, which affected different classes differently, were at the heart of the system of consumption and the constraints which organised it. The economists Mirabeau, Quesnay and Roussel de la Tour interested themselves in taxation, and, long before this time, Vauban and Boisguilbert had shown that it was necessary to know 'the capacity of peoples to pay taxes'.[21] Raising the question of the fiscal arrangements in the eighteenth century meant tackling the problems of consumption.[22] Few economic thinkers had any good to say of indirect taxation. Most denounced it for its injustice and because it restricted circulation and exchange. *Aides*, *gabelles*, *traites*, with their different forms as between regions and flagrant geographical inequalities, together provided the state with over half of its resources (49 per cent in 1726, 57 per cent in 1788). If the population and the theoreticians denounced this form of tax it was less on account of the reality, which they did not measure (historians relativise it, since the increase has to be set in relation to the increases in population and production), than for the arbitrary assessment, the unfair collection methods, and the opportunities for enrichment open to those who operated the system, the *traitants* and farmers-general.

Turgot, inspired by his administrative experience as an *intendant* and instructed by his relations with Physiocrats like Quesnay and Dupont de Nemours, as well as with liberals like Gournay, put forward an original critique of the fiscal system. The burden of taxation, he said, fell not only on consumers but also on property-owners. If it affected wage-earners, that was due to its unfairness and the obligation to raise the amount.[23] 'Two things alone enter into trade: the produce of the land, and labour.' Here we encounter again the idea of redistribution of land rent, as imagined by Cantillon: the consumption of some always forms the income of others.

Indirect taxes, which ultimately affect the cultivators and landowners, can check growth, because they hinder redistribution. Hence the lesson which Turgot reads to the state: 'When a government imposes a tax on a community, it does not know what it is levying from the people. The always vague knowledge that it obtains concerning current consumption cannot inform it about the variations to which this consumption is susceptible, about the reduction in consumption that will result from the tax itself, or about the increase in fraud due to the larger amounts involved. It does not know whether the disturbance in the balance established between the values of different goods will influence trade in commodities that it has not desired to tax.' Two problems come together here: lack of knowledge about differences in consumption, which Lavoisier tried to remedy, and the curbing effect of taxes on consumption. Both are hindrances to growth and to the freedom of all consumers, townsfolk included – the latter being, perhaps, more immediately sensitive to the injustice of the form of tax than to its general consequences or the movement of the economy.

A third group of incomes accumulated in the towns and was very largely invested and spent there, namely, the profits of trade. Large-scale speculative trade – '*à la grande aventure*', as people still said – is well known to us: its expansion, favourable to the balance of exchanges, was very rapid, perhaps growing by 4 per cent per year between 1716 and 1748 and by 1.5 to 2 per cent after 1778, following a phase of stability, dominated by colonial relations. This was the origin of the enrichment of the great trading cities and the ports, with their population of shipowners, merchants and sailors. It was inseparable from the internal redistribution and continent-wide relations that drove the activity of places like Lyons, Strasbourg and Lille. It was the force behind that small-scale retail trade in which it is hard to draw a line between transformation, making, sale and re-sale. All these forms of trade flourished thanks to organic relations, credit links, social connections and even political associations, where municipal institutions were concerned. Moreover, the towns all benefited from equipment and from the improvement in roads and means of transport.

Central to what was being transformed and circulated was the merchant. He was one of the principal urban factors in the speeding up of consumption. He was neither wholly converted to the '*laisser-faire, laisser-passer*' doctrine of the liberals nor frankly opposed to monopolies and regulations, which he knew how to turn to his own profit. Specialised in re-sale and transactions on commission, his outlook was international and maritime, so that he could engage in several kinds of activity, banking and the fitting-out of ships. The merchant was the Proteus of the growing towns, haunted by a dream of ennoblement. The economy as a whole would be unable to function without him. To him was due a big share in the diversification of consumptions.[24]

Business and industry, trade and services

Three sectors of the urban economy were to benefit specially from the circulation of incomes and supply of jobs, factors which at the same time contributed to the development of this economy.

The first of these was manufacturing and industrial activity. In the textile sphere particularly the increased and diversified demand of the markets helped to take productive work out of the towns, though still under their authority. Unlike the concentrated forms of manufacture created by urban capital, the workshops of proto-industrialisation were dispersed, in the cases of nail-making, hardware and textiles. This arrangement benefited from cheap peasant labour-power, less regulation and, above all, the mobilisation of whole families for the work. The process often involved a return of the population in zones that were poor and densely populated, where they depended on the towns and trade as suppliers of raw materials, purchaser and supervisor of the products and seller of them in the world outside.

Urban consumption and trade were thus again advantaged, whereas the circulation induced by expenditure of income was hardly begun among the rural population, even though they started to respond to external influences tending to change their behaviour. Of this we can judge from the complaints raised by textile merchants concerning the peasant workers who argued and scrounged, keeping for themselves a small quantity of the cloth they made in their homes. A section of the peasantry who were engaged in industrial work enjoyed favourable conditions. This was the case where high-quality products were concerned such as the linen cloth woven by the peasants of the Valentinois. The peasant workers offered better resistance to demographic pressure and to control by the merchants. Some of them became well-off while others escaped from poverty: most of them improved their lot and came to adopt, to some extent, the consumption-pattern of townsfolk.[25] The many exchanges that passed through the towns had a direct effect on urban consumption. In the building that went on we see the outcome of investment both public and private. It expressed the enrichment of the ruling classes and also their aspiration towards betterment: the construction and furnishing of the town-houses of the aristocracy in Paris provides the best example of this,[26] and the long-term rise in rents illustrated the profits that ensued. Everywhere, building work drew in seasonal workers – and increased employment. We can still see the results in the scene presented by our major ports, at Rouen, Bordeaux, Nantes, and by Lyons. Speculative development and reconstruction of dwellings to house an increasing population accompanied the shaping of a habitat the interior of which was transformed by urbanisation both private and public. This, while in accordance with concerns that had been entertained since the Renaissance, was now renewed and strengthened through the utilitarian efforts of the architects and administrators of the Enlightenment.[27] These investments, whether costly or modest, resulted in the appearance of new districts – in Paris, around the Odéon and to the west of the *faubourg* St Honoré – and especially facilitated experiments in the new economy of interior decoration. The emergence of blocks of flats contributed further to the diversifying of the activities of developers and of the ways of life of town populations. In the most active cities segregation began to appear.

Just as all this building work led to changes in ways of life, so also all sorts of objects, both semi-industrial and craft-produced, satisfied current needs and fresh aspirations. Creators and producers mobilised their practical intelligence and their sensibility to construct the *décor* of life and promote changes in tastes. What were most produced were objects needed in huge quantities to meet the needs of everyday life. Here we encounter a general phenomenon apparent long before the Industrial Revolution. The production of clothing supplies numerous examples,[28] but other sectors, crockery and furniture, were no less dynamic. The response to increased demand came from the guild workshops but also from the work done by home-workers and by innumerable workers who evaded the regulations.

In this phase of the demand–supply circuit the making of luxury goods also occupied a special place, where the great deal of value added by labour justified the high price of products that were out of reach for most people and reserved for clients who were rich and often eager to buy. Expressions of this fact were to be seen in the big towns and especially Paris, where fashionable dressmakers or the most famous mercers, such as Lazare Duvaux and Mademoiselle Bertin, no longer actually made things but had these made for them. Both groups were outwardly engaged only in business, but this did not rule out artistic invention and creation.[29] In Paris they marked themselves off from the '*mécaniques*', who often had to work with their own hands, and from the general run of mercers, who made and sold all sorts of things – from textiles, skins, metal-wares and the numberless accessories of everyday living. Those at the top of the profession sold pictures, prints, candelabra, centre-pieces of gilded copper and bronze, cut-glass chandeliers, statues in bronze, marble, wood and other materials, pendulums, clocks and watches, cabinets, chests, cupboards, tables, shelves, pedestal-tables made of expensive wood and gilded, marble tables and other commodities and curiosities suitable for the ornamenting of apartments.[30] 'They were go-betweens, inciters and coaches who stirred up interest, hastening the evolution of styles, cleverly holding their clients breathless.'[31] Their actual work was carried on between purchase and manufacture, between supply and sale. Their transforming activity and their role as intermediaries between the guilds – cabinet-makers and joiners, painters and gilders, sculptors and carriage-builders, metal-founders and engravers, metal-founders and gilders, workers in bronze, glaziers, mirror-makers, dealers in inlaid ware – was of capital importance. As the merchant Jacques Savary puts it, they sustained and animated consumption and trade through an extensive activity of importing and exporting. At the top of the pyramid of guilds, they had understood the power to expand possessed by trade in the service of a clientele that was itself at the top of the world of wealth and prestige.

The third sector of employment connected with the development of towns was that of services, what is now called the tertiary sector. Services gave rise to many forms of activity – the office-workers and agents of the administrations, together with those of the merchants. They were directly connected with exchange and transport, and consequently with urban consumption, while at the same time they influenced the rural world by recruiting labour-power, especially for transport work. Along with the domestic servants, the workers carried out the various tasks which the prevailing level of technology made necessary.

Domestic servants accounted for an increasing proportion of the active population of the towns: 26 per cent in Caen, perhaps 15 per cent in Paris, sometimes more. Carrying water and wood, looking after interiors both modest and rich, cooking, making beds, ironing, cleaning – nobody could do without these helpers. They played a dual role as intermediaries between the town and the village and as links between social groups. Both the men and the women among them were mostly provincials without any special training, whom town life transformed, either by integrating them (the heroes of novels, such as Marivaux's Jacob make much of this positive aspect of the urban theatre of appearances) or by thrusting them into a marginal existence that justified denunciations of a social mobility that was contrary to social order. By leading them to either success or failure the town revealed its power to change people, essentially through accustoming them to new habits. The employment of domestic servants was a form of conspicuous consumption characteristic of the rich: while its immediate purpose was to confirm prestige, it also showed the power of imitation.

Contemporaries reacted in contrasting ways to the development of towns. For advocates of growth the urban phenomenon was a bearer of civilisation and the virtues of 'sweet commerce', whereas the economists and observers of morals, Rousseau-ists like Mercier and Rétif, saw in it an incitement to corruption of the human race. In these two attitudes were confronted the different ways of grasping the social reality of ordinary life, between passivity and activity, the greater or lesser capacity for appropriating things and habits, the hierarchy of needs, how one ought and how one was able to live.

The experience of urban life

Concentration of functions caused the growth of the modern town, and this growth assigned to each town its place in the urban hierarchy.[32] Transformation of material habits was favoured there by the accumulation of cultural capital and the dynamic of inventions.

The links between circulation, exchange and information

The town performs its part when it enjoys the necessary resources and equipment and when it is at the centre of an assemblage of developments which are unevenly located all over the territory concerned. Roads and waterways made it possible for the market to function, for goods and persons to move about, and also for information and orders to be transmitted.[33]

From the cross-lane to the great royal road, from the stream that could be used only for part of the year to the canal developed and exploited on a permanent basis, the transport system operated less as a network than through a series of overlapping levels. Not until the first quarter of the nineteenth century would people conceive of all these ways of communication in terms of a reticular organisation, with ordering and subordination of each component, all inter-related. It was then that roads would produce their decisive effects on rural economy and its relations with the towns.

Road-building policy and the organisation of waterways between the time of Colbert and that of Necker anticipated to some degree the growth of towns by establishing major internal links, with Paris at the centre of the Kingdom's unification by means of transport. This work was accompanied by that of the engineers of the Department of Bridges and Highways and of the construction sites, which encouraged, in Burgundy and Languedoc and, to a smaller extent, in Brittany, the activity of the provincial Estates.[34] In 1789, with 25,000 kilometres of well-laid roads, more in the North than in the Centre or the South, the Kingdom, though still unbalanced and not adequately responsive to all the requirements of economic growth, displayed a picture that was rather exceptional in

Europe, even compared with England.[35] An initial culture of circulation and mobility had been created before the general opening-up of the countryside which took place after 1830 through the general construction of local roads. The villages would then cease more quickly to remain isolated and facilities for access to the towns, limited until then, would be increased. Migration would follow, and mediations, both symbolic and material, would be strengthened.

In the old society the mobility of sellers and buyers was organised through the transport system and the general network of markets and fairs.[36] These sites for exchanges regained their typical features, illustrating well the outlook of the seventeenth-century economists who, led by Cantillon, preached the virtues of circulation and consumption for promoting the hierarchised growth of towns. There was a certain degree of permeability and obvious connections between the two levels of commercial encounter.

In the middle of the eighteenth century Turgot, in his article on 'Fairs and markets' for the *Encyclopédie*, put forward a view which conformed to the desire to improve circulation by doing away with regulations and privileges. Though of the same nature, these two institutions did not serve to ensure periodical trade and connection between the different pieces of the urban chessboard in the same way. The fair, which Turgot saw as covering an entire province, enjoyed liberties and might be a major international gathering. The 'rendezvous of nations' was most often a country gathering: three-quarters of the 4,264 fair sites in 1789 listed by D. Margairaz were parishes of fewer than 2,000 inhabitants, where agricultural produce was bought and sold in large quantities. Many fairs were devoted to the sale of animals and almost all of them diffused through the countryside the products of crafts or manufactures that were controlled by the towns. A fair was a big break in agricultural life, with its monthly and, still more, quarterly rhythm. As for the market, which Turgot defined as the natural commercial sphere 'of a town or a locality', it represented the elementary level of town life and was combined with secondary and tertiary activities. It responded to a local need and was organised in accordance with rhythms that were faster, in most cases weekly. It ensured in every case the polyvalent relations between town and country, with the fluidity and openness of transactions carried out under supervision.

For the consumers, markets, urban and rural, remained the special *locus* of the moral economy, where the police kept an eye on prices and watched over the movements of speculators.[37] Small-scale producers with something to sell were fond of markets, because they saw in them a way to escape the tyranny of the big merchants. Both market and fair were under the ruler's authority, and they were created and supervised with a view to encouraging the monetarisation of the economy and exchanges. Nevertheless, we should not reduce the market to its primordial role in the grain trade, which set the advocates of the moral economy against those of political economy, the public weal against the market of the invisible hand.[38] On the ground a certain freedom of action was, indeed, allowed to the local authorities. This freedom, which lends itself to definition as a 'pragmatic economy', was essential if the producers were to continue to bring their crops to the market. It was through the markets and fairs, too, that most exchanges were effected, other than those in the shops, and the widest variety of commodities passed through them.

In the history of consumption, the history of fairs is, however, an essential element. More than was the case with the market, the fair brought together all the vital factors needed for intensifying demand and even creating it. Because it was frequently associated with the festival of a patron saint, it accompanied exchange with entertainment, enjoyment, a fete. In an economy of scarcity it was the shop-window of plenty and superimposed many other links upon the commercial relationship. The fairs of major commodities – Beaucaire in Provence, La Guibray, near Caen – retained these features of celebration. Like the markets and fairs of the rural areas they broke 'the circle of ordinary exchanges' and the monotonous cycle of works and days.

Fairs displayed the spectacle of urban commodities as well as attracting large-scale trade and contributed to variation in exchanges, which increasingly involved products that were more disparate and of poorer quality, wholesale dealing in small quantities and retail trade, and, consequently, the widest possible public. In his *Mémoires d'un touriste*, Stendhal bears witness, in relation to the fair at Beaucaire, to the eve of decisive changes in large-scale trade.

On every street, in the meadow, on the bank of the Rhone, there are crowds all the time. At every moment somebody uses his elbow on you in order to get ahead. People are hurrying, everybody is in haste to get to his business. This activity is embarrassing and offensive at first, but it is also amusing. Singers gesticulate and bawl in front of the bass-viol and horn that accompany them. Soap-sellers come after you offering first-quality scent which they have brought from Grasse. Street-porters, swaying beneath enormous burdens carried on their heads, shout a warning when they are already upon you. News-vendors make themselves hoarse through crying summaries of telegraphic messages received from Spain. It is a crowd, a throng such as they can have no idea of in Paris . . . The trip to Beaucaire is a fete for everybody.[39]

Hubbub and movement, miscellany of products offered for sale, a variegated public, traders from all countries, nobles of Languedoc and

Provence, bourgeois from the towns, notables and yokels, a wide range of different pleasures displayed which may promote changes in people's ways, 'all the practices that can be accomplished only slowly now vanish, everyone is lively', writes Stendhal, splendidly. Theatricalising of exchanges and commercialising of entertainments, presence of the theft that redistributes, cheating of every kind, prostitution: the fair at Beaucaire, seen by the iron merchant imagined by the novelist, gives concrete form to the share of reality and invention propitious to the promotion of the growth and civilising trade of the towns.

The town's cultural patrimony

In the cultural and economic spectacle provided by fairs and markets the material exchanges that took place were inseparable from the fluidity of communications. In formation, knowledge and consumption were interconnected. What was typical of urban life here was the complexity of the social relationships that it helped to create – on the one hand by diversifying to the uttermost social categories and the ways in which these were grouped (by levels of incomes, by stratification of estates and associations), by multiplication of the opportunities for sociability offered by popular and religious practices, 'society' occasions or meetings between educated people, and on the other by imposing upon the continual heterogeneity of face-to-face encounters freer rules that favoured expression of individualism.[40] Here too the old principles linked with the values of the moral economy and stability coexisted with the new rules brought in by the consumer economy, by the morality of obsolescence, which honoured imitation and change.

By bringing different branches of knowledge together and mingling opportunities for seeing people and things differently, the town widened the intellectual horizon to the utmost limits of civilisation. In the commercial sphere it soon became necessary to connect to the network of stock-exchanges, chambers of commerce, commission-agents and business houses: this happened in Bordeaux, Lyons, Marseilles and Paris.[41] In the cultural domain opinions clashed and doubtless clarified through contradiction and open discussion. The two meanings of the word 'commerce' reinforced each other, illustrating the effects of an accumulation that was both intellectual and material, an accumulation of technology and ways of thinking. Business and exchange fostered a distinct sociability, which also benefited from tendencies long encouraged by urban culture.

The wealth of the urban patrimony was partly due to the educational advantages which had been amassed over a long period and were strengthened by the Catholic Reformation. Schools, colleges, seminaries and universities were found there, and their presence or absence was one of the factors determining the hierarchy of cities.[42] In the capital and the regional metropolises every means was available not only for social reproduction but also for promoting through culture a social mobility which, though limited, certainly happened. School and college spread norms of social life which were also rules for the consumption of things. While conforming to the civilisation of manners they also created new needs. Specialised occupations such as that of the master-scriveners, who were both experts in and teachers of writing, linked directly here the transmission of a body of knowledge with its practical application.

The eighteenth century saw a spread of acculturation and produced new varieties of education: schools of drawing, boarding-schools with up-to-date curricula that were wider than those of the colleges, military schools, schools run by the Christian Brothers that were not alien to the interest of commerce and technology, courses provided by the Academies. A great variety of methods of teaching appeared, reflecting the new needs and expectations of families whose preferences in matters of education were conditioned by a broader strategy of development. More was done for the education of girls. This abundant growth challenged the immobilism and mistrust that could be found among the philosophers regarding more widespread education. The economists themselves were divided on the question, but the liberals and Physiocrats favoured schooling which, if not freed from prejudices, would be at least effective in bringing about a general transformation.[43]

Other urban institutions helped to familiarise the public with opportunities for meeting, through the circulation of written and printed matter of every sort, newspapers and posters included.[44] Though a large proportion of publications of that time served cultural institutions, the church and the economy, the press supported above all 'the works of the town', by spreading information of every kind. Posters informed the public of market prices and goods for sale as well as of entertainments. Among the books published chiefly in Paris and the provincial metropolises, in Lyons, Rouen or Toulouse, the majority were little works of utilitarian purpose, manuals and reference books covering all branches of knowledge and practical activity. Science, art, technique gradually competed victoriously with more traditional subject-matter.

Printed matter contributed to a substantial degree to changing behaviour with regard to economic information, credit, trust and the publishing of technical procedures.[45] Although we know a lot about the role of the journalism of advertising and the services rendered by local announcements, after 1776, in the *Journal de Paris*, we have not so far entirely measured its consequences and impact on France's economic life, which was supported less than was the case in England by special teaching inspired by the requirements of the world of businessmen keen on technical manuals. The diffusion of information was accompanied by efforts in collecting and rationalising it which could guarantee the reliability of news, like that of technical procedures. It led also to thinking about the personal and ostentatious expenditure which was connected with the stimulation of demand, as we perceive from the success of *Poor Richard's Almanack*, issued by Benjamin Franklin,[46] as also to greater familiarity with elementary methods of quantification. Printed matter, which implied a different way of understanding the mechanisms of the market and of distribution, contributed to the commercialising of persons as well as of things. The 'small ads' used for recruiting competent staff, including servants, and those that offered houses and furniture of all sorts for sale, were examples of the effectiveness of a new society, a new conception based upon incitement to buy.

The dynamic of inventions

The enrichment of the towns' cultural patrimony was due also to the appearance of inventions in all spheres. The intellectual aspect of this development was related to historical conditions in which one could conceive of new things, and the question bears the same significance whether we concern ourselves with procedures of intelligence or those of materiality.[47]

No invention, technical or intellectual, can be made in pure abstraction, not one can be separated from the capacity of a setting to communicate and regulate discoveries through norms that are at once technical, scientific or social. The inventor and the invention of the Century of Enlightenment have to be thought of not so much through legends that serve to illustrate genius and finalism as through study of the conditions of production and publicity. Setback and rejection matter no less than success and recognition. What is essential is the way in which the theories and methods manage to establish themselves in the markets of ideas and techniques.[48] The history of technologies shows that they are not applied sciences but possess a degree of independence, expressed in conflicts about functions in the workplace, between the craftsman, the technician and the engineer, or in debates about the rationality of methods or materials.[49]

In the tradition of the crafts, materials and their interdependence were measured in terms of weight or time, more than by calculation of powers of resistance or fracture. Carpenters considered the densest timber more solid than iron, fountain-makers considered lead stronger than copper, masons considered thick lime more adhesive than the thin sort, because it was heavier. One of the things that engineers, inspectors of manufacturies, academicians and military men had to do was to challenge the established practices of craftsmen and impose appropriate criteria and norms. Duhamel du Monceau denounced, in *L'Art du briquetier et du tuilier* the mysteries, prejudices and usages 'dominating all the mechanical arts. To do away with prejudices and restrict the workers' practices to what is necessary, or better, would call for a great deal of work which is not always allowable for those to undertake who would most like to do it.'[50] The eighteenth-century town prepared the conditions for a far-reaching change of attitude on its building-sites, in its workshops, on the roads and canals that transported commodities, and in the experiences of builders or manufacturers. It is this evolution of practices which enables us to understand the evolution of consumptions and their relation to a state of civilisation in which the town demands and receives more or less from nature.

The culture of invention in the seventeenth and eighteenth centuries was related both to the monarchical state and to the town and its social imperatives. In the first place, it was connected with the State and remained a matter of administration and official valuation. All the specialists and services of the monarchy were brought in to appraise inventions which they themselves might have put forward: the Royal Household, the offices of the Army or of the Secretariats of State, the office of trade, the Paris lieutenancy of police, the intendants, consuls and municipalities, the academies (especially the prestigious Academy of Sciences) and the provincial estates. The channels for recognition and validation were numberless and often there was tense exchange of correspondence about them, between different experts and various levels of authority.

Thus, in Lyons, regarding everything that was concerned with silk goods and the technique for making and preparing them, requests and replies circulated between the intendant, the municipality and the controller-general in Paris. Technical inventiveness was conceived as belonging in the framework of a utilitarian notion of public service, in the logic of the functioning of the state, whether administrative or collective, municipal and urban. Expertise, especially that carried out by the academicians, evaluated both capacity and effectiveness of realisation, but also possibilities of acceptance. The *dirigisme* of encouragement and recognition conflicted with routine and the traditional obstacles. It was the natural reforming attitude of the administrative elite who wanted to convince society that progress was possible. In this domain the arbitration exercised by the state did not slacken until the end of the Ancien Régime, including the brief phases of liberalism.

It was then that the urban figure of the inventor enjoyed prestige. This did not relate to a logic of profit but to a consistency of useful service which, in order to obtain a 'privilege' that gave both a legal safeguard of ownership and the possibility of exploiting the invention, placed this and its technique under the protection of scientific experts. Only later did criticism of the inventor's privilege, in the name of liberty, see the state and the urban authorities pamper entrepreneurs and throw into the balance of an invention's success economic outcome and profit, the logics of the market. Under Necker's administration the action of the state and of investors caused the content of the monopoly to change and come close to the English system of patents. Three features showed at that time the vitality of the urban setting, its interest in technical innovation. Of the 1,300 inventors listed, two-thirds were urban craftsmen, the rest being divided between a large nucleus of representatives of cultivated and rich circles and a small group of speculative entrepreneurs and manufacturers. Two-thirds of them came from provincial cities, among which the first place was taken by the capitals of commerce and manufacture, with the remaining third coming from Paris. And the majority of the methods examined concerned the key sectors of the urban economy: textiles, building, and, later, metal-working, chemistry and ordinary consumption.

The shift in technical and economic culture indicated by the multiplication of inventors and inventions showed the modernity of the town, rooted in supervision and quality, generalised by its power of impulsion and command. The position of Lyons, capital of high-quality silk-weaving, its work made regular by encouragement from Paris, was very significant in this connection. The cultural patrimony of the Enlightenment was enriched by the communications established through networks of technical consultation. The upsurge of invention showed once more the common motivation which brought together material change and intelligence, social transformation and growth. Creations and discoveries began at this time to reach the sphere of everyday life, in habitat, in equipment both domestic and collective. From the useful to the indispensable, objects gradually transformed the consumers' world, their way of living along with the symbolic meaning of usages. The modern town enables one to think about the way that an unequal development took place at the moment when economic growth and the first significant expansion of technique began.

3   Ordinary consumption and luxury consumption

In the agricultural and urban economies the transformation brought about by exchange and the circulation of incomes gives rise to the problem of ordinary consumption and luxury consumption. The correlation between means of subsistence and rates of growth of population was, in fact, marked by an increase in the possibilities offered, even though the forms of growth and the differences between regions as regards innovation remain debatable. While the world of agriculture avoided rationalisation, as it was still relatively untouched by systematic quest for profitability and lacked machinery and fertiliser, there was already perceptible a pressing need for intensification and a clash between new and traditional methods.[1] The examples of Flanders and Alsace show the predominant role of labour in the numerous experiments carried out and, despite obstacles, the successes obtained.

This fresh breeze, encouraging both intellectual activity in the agricultural sphere and hopes of profit for entrepreneurs, was able to affect only slowly the domestic economy, urban as well as rural. The epoch of scarcity had doubtless given way to one of relative scarcity, first in the towns and then in the country, following social developments which were not entirely linear and top–down. The demands of a servant born in Ouche but enriched by years of work in Paris were no longer the same as those of his peasant family. The seasonal migrants and the itinerant pedlars also influenced this improvement in consumer habits[2], rooted in practices drawn from a complex culture that was not reducible to the mere logic of subsistence.[3] Ways of spending varied, just like families' strategies in managing their affairs.

What should be produced, what could be shared, what was one to consume? These questions, which might be put to any society, had particular importance in modern France. The answers to them related to the gap between the necessary and the superfluous, in accordance with scale of incomes, social imperatives and symbolic representations, but it would change, because the passage of time transformed the superfluous into the necessary. The dispute about luxury was thus to

54

play an essential part in the transition from the moral to the political economy.[4]

In order to appreciate the consumers' point of view one must also be able to avoid restricting one's sources to the archives of the aristocracy and the rich. However, sources are lacking for the expenditure of the lower classes and the peasants in the seventeenth and eighteenth centuries. Family record books, accounts and guardianship papers still to be studied concern most often the higher income groups. Only in the nineteenth century, when industrialisation threw society into confusion and the consequences of urbanisation seemed intolerable, did philanthropists, thinkers and researchers seek to understand the phenomena that were threatening the social order and to find remedies for them. Following Villermé and Le Play, and mobilised in learned societies, headed by the Institut, Christian and socially minded doctors and economists, whether enlightened or not, made their way to the bedsides of the nascent proletariat and inquired into the relation between resources and cost of living.[5]

The beginnings of the 'social question', which was accompanied by an investigation of ways of life, led to the organisation of social statistics.[6] The result was to throw light on the role of income as an economic factor, something which had until then been either overlooked or treated as secondary by theoreticians of the economy.[7] But, of course, these findings cannot be applied retrospectively to the seventeenth and eighteenth centuries, even if they can provide models for the study of consumption by social categories throughout history.[8] The 'budget' concept, which appeared at the beginning of the eighteenth century, nevertheless makes it possible to grasp the outlook of a social group and an epoch regarding its own habits of consumption, on the basis of observations of the principal elements in ways of life. Economists, philosophers and administrators found here a way of measuring the evolution of a relation between resources and needs. The historian can then compare a series of theoretical budgets, calculated from a wide range of information and the purpose of which went far beyond scientific study, being aimed at political and social targets, through the reconstitution of budgets based on family or group accounts which revealed the science of household management.[9]

Budgets à la Marshal Vauban

The thing came before the word. The word 'budget' did not exist when Vauban revealed, in his *Dîme royale* of 1707, the reality of a peasant family's expenditure. This revelation resulted from numerous observations made by the Marshal. A soldier, the principal creator of the Kingdom's fortifications, a witness to the problems faced by the population owing to continual war, and, as the owner of a lordship in Morvan, someone who knew the value of money, he combined with concrete knowledge, acquired on the ground during protracted rides around the provinces, familiarity with the economic theories of his time and a reformer's conscience. The questions that he put to the ruling circles and Louis XIV himself were those that critics of the King's policy and economists concerned with crisis had compiled.

Vauban's thinking and the secret writings which caused him to be disgraced were not far removed from the concerns of La Bruyère, Fénelon or, on another plane, Boisguilbert.[10] The poverty of the people was related to increased burdens of taxation, to the nature of the taxes and the way they were raised and to problems of the relation between direct and indirect taxation. Given the state of the Kingdom, the weight of taxes caused a blockage in the economic circuits, and everyone, landowners as well as administrators, wondered what new forms of taxation might be conceived that would not reduce the poorest to starvation. By calculating expenditure in relation to incomes, consumption in relation to means, Vauban aimed to supply an answer to this question and, by deduction, to measure the overall capacity of the economy to weather the storm.

It was in this turmoil, as J.-C. Perrot has shown, that an intellectual and financial tradition began which thought about the state's resources in a new way, starting with what was taken from the population, the receipts, and then calculating the expenses, the outgoings. The consequences of this way of looking at the matter were twofold. On the one hand, it led to debates and intellectual exchanges, both pragmatic and theoretical, among the ruler's counsellors and agents. From the Court to the *intendances*, from the police to the *Parlements*, the relation between the monarch and his subjects emerged from this somewhat shaken. On the other hand, it threw a serious shadow over the state's capacity to initiate inquiries to measure the Kingdom's revenue, with a view to linking the investigation of resources with a tax system that grew more and more rapacious, inquiries in which the judges were also parties to the case. Here we glimpse one of the major difficulties in the evolution of ideas and realities, even though the reformist trend can be credited with a movement of discernment which favoured administrative utilitarianism and, eventually, reforms.[11]

The context, the clandestine echo beneath the censorship, which was one of the active forms of publicity given to disturbing works, certainly contributed to the success of Vauban's *Dîme royale*, which the author at first circulated from hand to hand, and amplified the resonance of his proposals. More than a dozen editions of the work appeared, in France and throughout Europe. It provoked controversies in which there participated the best analysts of the society of that time. In *La Facture de la France* (1707) Boisguilbert maintained that it was not possible to levy taxes on all products of the soil. Gueuvin de Rademont in *Le Nouveau Traité sur la Dîme Royale* (1713) introduced figures and commentary thereon into the debate. Pottier de la Hestroye, with his *Réflexions sur la Dîme royale* (1714), refined Vauban's estimates, but the model provided serves as back-cloth, so to speak, for economic investigation right down to the middle years of the century and offers one of the keys for dealing with the problem of consumption's relation to resources.

The Marshal-economist presented his thoughts, at the end of a discussion of the incomes of the taxpaying social groups,[12] to the King and the ruling circles. The category of agricultural labourers and urban craftsmen deserved, he considered, to be given special attention owing to its numerical importance,

through the services that they render to the state, for it is they who do the hard work in town and country without which neither they nor others could live. They it is who provide all the soldiers and sailors, all the servants, male and female. In short, without them the state could not continue to exist. That is why one ought to be gentle with them in matters of taxation, so as not to burden them with more than they can bear.

Vauban quotes two cases which he analyses on the basis of a precise questionnaire – number of days for which pay was received, number of journeymen per master, time lost from work – so as to calculate the men's gains and their expenses, their net income and their basic consumption. The two social types he used for his demonstration were not abstractions. The craftsman was chosen from among the linen-weavers, i.e. from one of the most active and most representative sectors of production. Vauban had probably observed him while in Normandy, in the Rouen area where the first steps in proto-industrialisation were being taken. As for the agricultural labourer, he represented one of the most numerous groups in the active population of the primary sector – the worker who had no income other than wages, the man who was at the service of, and dependent on, the sharecroppers, farmers and landowners.

The weaver's income was related to his ability to make linen. Vauban estimated that he could produce, on the average, six ells per day, or a little over seven metres, which, with an average price of two sols per ell, meant that he received twelve sols for his working day. This exercise assumed that average estimates could be made on the basis of observations and items of information that were easy to obtain in a region where there was already standardised and large-scale production destined for both internal and external markets; but it was not simple, since it called for a capacity for abstraction comparable to that required for calculations in political arithmetic. We know that the exercise did not proceed without some hesitation, since Vauban left traces in his manuscripts of other possible choices of figures. 'Ten ells of certain types of linen, which makes twenty sols. But that would need a very clever workman, for most such men earn no more than fifteen or sixteen sols. Let us assume . . .' The phrase tells us, clearly, that the demonstration is based on a hypothesis. Vauban wished to speak of a case as close as possible to reality, without denying differences that could be due to the quality of the product or the skill of the worker.

Though most of the craftsmen in big towns like Paris, Lyons, Rouen, etc., usually make more than twelve sols – for example, the cloth-workers, shearers, wool-drawers, hatter boys, locksmiths and suchlike, who make from fifteen up to thirty sols, yet there are some who make less than twelve, such as the weaver, and that seems a fair average to take for the other arts and crafts.

For the calculation to be accurate it was necessary to take account also of the actual time spent at work, deducting the days when no work was done – Sundays and holidays, the days when the weaver had to go to the market or the fair to find things he needed for his work, not to mention idleness due to freeze-ups and bad weather (weather conditions being very important for work with thread) or to illness or fatigue. Altogether, the year of 365 days was reduced to 180 working days, and so an income of 108 *livres* on which direct tax (tithe, *gabelle*) had to be paid. For a family of four persons, that left a net income, depending on how heavy their burdens were, of barely 90 *livres*. This burden was too heavy for a craftsman who had only his hands to depend on, but who had to pay rent for his house, to furnish it, to clothe himself and his family, and to feed a wife and children 'who often are incapable of earning much'. For this reason the fiscal burden ought to be moderated, calculated at the rate of one-thirtieth.

Vauban made his demonstration again for the case of the labourer who carried out all the hard work of the countryside – mowing, reaping, threshing, cutting wood, ploughing, clearing land, helping builders – taking into account the seasonal variations in the man's work. At nine sols per day that made 90 *livres* per year, from which taxes had to be deducted, so that what was left to sustain the labourer and his family (four persons) was 75 *livres* and a few sols. Thus a threshold of resources was reached within the bracket of 75–90–100 *livres*! The acuteness of the reasoning and its 'modernity' deserve as much admiration as its outcome. Vauban invented the notion of the average wage, on the basis of actual ability to work, and embodied it in two types that were socially representative, since they were not individual and isolated consumers but responsible agents in a domestic nucleus.

From gains to expenses

Calculating expenditure was a very much more complicted task. Vauban did it in the same way, in both cases, with an extra capacity for abstraction, so as to establish what was needed for a family of four. The principal expense was food – Vauban estimated this at ten *sétiers de Paris*, half of wheat and half of rye – which represented an average annual amount of sixty or seventy *livres*. The labourer would be left with between five and fifteen *livres*, and the weaver with between twenty and thirty. Here, too, there is obvious simplification of the reality: the choice of measure, the calculation of average price, the quality of the corn – each indicator could be open to correction. The mere estimation of the passage from grain to flour, depending on the region or the moment, could give rise to endless speculation. A little more poverty, a little more affluence could still tip the balance. In the main, though, the demonstration had been accomplished, and its pivot was the weight of taxation. To increase that burden any further was impossible if the people were not to be ruined, and with them the state of which they were the sole support. The system of the *dîme royale* would allow the problem to be solved.

For a stratum which was at the very bottom, or almost, of the scale of incomes, the evaluation of expenses showed that they were at the edge of the threshold beyond which a family would be tipped into poverty and want. The strength of the argument was based on the construction of a model of consumption *a minima*, wholly subject to the constraint of subsistence, since it was impossible to fall below what was required for the needs covered, for living and for renting accommodation. Vauban was well aware of the marginal character of the situation he envisioned. The labourer with his fifteen *livres* and the weaver with his thirty had to 'pay rent for his house, or pay for repairing it, to buy some utensils, even if that meant only a few earthenware bowls, clothing and linen, and to meet all his family's needs for a whole year'. Vauban took account of the family's additional resources. The father might find some extra jobs, and the mother might help to meet their expenses by sewing, knitting stockings, lace-making, cultivating a little garden, keeping a cow, a pig, a goat or some chickens, or working a piece of land. The family's diet sometimes improved. Bacon appeared in more substantial meals, a supply of milk was not negligible, a little butter or oil added a note of refinement, slight but inexpensive. All the same, however one looked at it, the labourer or the weaver would have much difficulty in getting to the end of the year.

In putting forward a model for a more equitable fiscal policy Vauban, already, was wagering on the invariability of social facts, which is still today one of the problems facing the social sciences. He emphasised the inertia and feeble capacity for innovation that resulted from a situation in which the burden of feeding one's family crushed everything else. As Halbwachs put it, 'the gleaner's share' would for long amount to little in the wage-earner's purse.[13] Below the level of Vauban's two examples there was nothing to tax; above that level there was flexibility and potential that gave room for discussion. The variability of wages between regions is well-established, along with the difference in the wages paid in town and country respectively, and nothing in the reality revealed by archives contradicts Vauban.[14] Also, the significant place he accords to time in his calculations corresponds to a well-known variety of attitudes towards the relation between work and leisure that gave rise to disputes between the religious and the civil authorities and reflected conflict between economic and moral concerns. Vauban was observing a worker whose activity was not yet fragmented and organised like that of the industrial wage-earner. While time was already money, it was also freedom, and submission to facts of nature and culture that were inescapable. However, the worst case does not cover all possible situations, but merely shows the way in which one section of society asked itself how corporations and estates might be saved from disintegration.

Another question arises when we read the budgets in *La Dîme royale*. Quite plainly, they were compiled by leaving out every necessary article of consumption except corn and bread. This is also a basic text in the history of consumption. We have to admit, with Vauban, that expenditure on food dominated everything else. This was a structural feature of popular expenditure that would continue to apply after the Industrial Revolution. But we know, too, that though the structure of budgets alters in consequence of income changes, this does not happen in linear fashion. In the nineteenth century and at the beginning of the twentieth it is the marginal exceptions that enable us to understand the direction of movement, the dispersion as much as the average.[15] That should make us think about the idea that to identical incomes there may correspond different consumption-profiles, depending on technical and natural constraints.

Why then does Vauban, like so many others, proclaim 'the sovereignty of bread'?[16] Because that statement did conform to everyday reality, in which the bulk of the population got the calories it needed from bread and cereal products. The life of consumers was governed by need for an adequate ration in a world where imponderable forces constantly threatened production and distribution. There was also the question of status and recognition of the parental bond that still existed between the monarch and his subjects. And there was also the fact that, for the people, bread had a symbolic as well as a material meaning.

Bread was one of the most powerful structural features governing life both public and private under the Ancien Régime,[17] because it had religious as well as customary significance, figuring in both the Eucharist and gifts. Steven Kaplan has given due acknowledgement to Simon Linguet, one of the rare thinkers of the eighteenth century who did not associate bread with happiness and showed that it was by no means the universal foodstuff that everybody, from the mercantilists to the Physiocrats and from Voltaire to Rousseau, wanted to see it as. Bread was also an indicator of dependence. 'Bread-making is doubly criminal towards the human race: it increases the poor man's slavery and serves only the sensuality of the rich.'[18] Nobody, or almost nobody, paid attention to this acute thinker when he put his finger on the chain of dependences created by the tyranny of corn, the danger of cereal monoculture, the exaltation by the Physiocrats of the 'viceroys of the Beauce'. Linguet showed that one might at least question this way of seeing the link between production and consumption and consider that capacity to resist crises of food supply was based not merely on control of the corn market but also on variety in sources for subsistence, something that Vauban had already suggested.[19] When need to subsist takes priority over temptation to get rich it can lead to paths other than a cereal monoculture that promotes the sovereignty of bread. Here we are between two economic capacities, which it is almost impossible to know how to balance. On the one hand, self-subsistence covered by production carried out by the family, an ideal difficult for many to realise despite various strategies of production and consumption (clandestine cultivation, kitchen gardening, poultry, gleaning, use of collective commons and pastures, especially in forest areas, small-scale cattle-raising, textiles). On the other, the market and commercialisation, which could not be avoided where some essential products were concerned – salt, iron – as well as superfluities, notably in areas of cereal monoculture and vine-growing.

Vauban's reduction to a single indicator corresponds mainly to his line of argument. He could not, of course, be unaware of the variations in consumption that resulted from price movements during crises and the responses of different regions to these changes, or were due to factors such as social status, capacity for self-subsistence, possible choice of a cheaper cereal, or resort to solutions of economic expediency that were not very inviting (administrators and police in Paris had experience of that).[20] By unifying the terms for comparison Vauban established a description of the population's consumption of food that was massively based upon the country's resources of corn, which were to serve as indicator in subsequent thinking on the subject until the arrival of the transport revolution. The two-and-a-half *sétiers* that the Marshal allowed for families of wage-earners and craftsmen, representing 55 per cent of a weaver's income and 66 per cent of that of an agricultural labourer, and which meant, doubtless, 800 grammes of bread per day per person, constituted thereafter a common reference. Down to 1750–60 the evaluations made were much the same, or else higher – three *sétiers*. At the end of the eighteenth century (in the findings, for example of Moheau and Lavoisier) they began to fall, to 2.4 and 2.2 *sétiers*, a reduction which might reflect two things at once, namely, improvements in observation and calculation and increase in population, which could have led to a decline in the share of cereals and changes in everyone's diets.

Eighteen-century budget investigations

Vauban's model budget was to last out the century but was modified through confrontation with both realities and theories.[21] There were those, such as Le Pelletier, who were to discuss the number of persons in a family, which might be six rather than four. Others already took account of the variations due to the life-cycle of households: two persons to start with, then children, who increased expenditure until they moved out. This was an important consideration in measuring the relation between consumption and expenditure. Another modification resulted from discussions on measurement of the time spent working and on the noteworthy differences in levels of wages and supplementary resources as between town and country. In short, all the parameters of the chain composed by Vauban could be removed and replaced or added to. What harvest? What variety of corn? What unit of measurement? What flour? What bread, or even what porridge? What hunger in relation to age? Behind the principles of the ideal type, concrete situations were found, and greater precision was sought in order to understand these better.

Advances in statistical information and a slowing down in the rhythm of crises made it possible to expand the questionnaire. Between 1715 and 1730 Le Pelletier, Pottier, La Jonchère and Boulainvilliers circulated and debated Marshal Vauban's evaluations. With six persons aboard, the family ship would certainly sink if it received no more than nine sols per day. According to Le Pelletier it would need at least five times that sum if it was to sail serenely. In his *Mémoire sur la taille tarifiée* (c.1720), the Abbé de St Pierre emphasised variations in wages, which could be twice as high in town as they were in the country, and he took up again the matter of the number of working days. Le Pelletier posited for his enlarged household a diet that was less monotonous: to bread he added cider and also herring, which gave plenty of calories and was a symbolic foodstuff in the ports of the West and North.[22] The cost of food still made a big hole in the family income – 80 per cent – but the rest was better guaranteed than in Vauban's margins of dependence. La Jonchère counted more than fifty-four pounds of bread, at three sols per pound per day, and added to this 273 pounds of meat, at eighteen sols per day, 182 pounds of wine at 0.9 *livres* per day, candles thirty-nine *livres*, salt ten *livres*, rent and heating 200 *livres*, and clothes and laundry (wigs included) another 200 *livres*. Altogether, in the townsman's budget, calculated for an income of nearly 960 *livres*, food accounted for 53 per cent, of which barely 10 per cent was spent on bread, and the remaining expenditure went on superfluities.

How authentic the patterns of consumption are that we perceive in these budgets depends on how much their composers knew, but the latter were not independent of the context of their thinking, as both Vauban's supporters and his critics were concerned, like him, about the great problem of taxation. The scope of their investigations was to get broader still and their continuity would benefit from the progress in economic publications which resulted from the administration's increased interest in knowing the factors in the people's budgets – wages, prices, numbers of population – an interest which was no less than that of the writers who contemplated reforms. Four overlapping questions provided the framework for the evaluations made. How were they to understand the evolution that they sensed was taking place? How could the problems of pauperism be solved? How were they to reconcile income from work and income from savings? Finally, how to safeguard the ways of life that had been achieved?

Administrators tried to evaluate changes in the people's resources. Thus, M. de Véran assembled, in the Arles area, the elements of such an investigation between 1750 and 1790. In 1754 the Provençal day-labourer earned 296 *livres* and his wife 56. The expenditure of this childless couple exceeded 350 *livres*. It went to a great extent on food, with consumption of about 100 *livres* of corn, but also of oil, salt, wine and vegetables – 254 *livres* altogether. What was left, ninety-eight *livres*, paid rent and taxes, with little left over for superfluities. The labourer in the Arles area earned more than Vauban's Norman wage-earner, but his standard of living was not much better, even though his food-budget took into account some indispensable extra expenditure. When M. de Véran compared the situation in the country with that in the town he showed also a reduction in dependence on cereals and an increase in expenditure on clothing. Thirty-odd years later he made further calculations. Wages had gone up, income being now 476 *livres* and expenditure on food had also increased (approximately 347 *livres*), so that the Arlesian household had a good hundred *livres* left for paying the rent (which had risen) and acquiring new clothes. This demonstration showed a relative improvement, the results of which were precarious, dependent on how basic choices were made – whether to have children, and, if so, how many – but it left out the element of risk, of illness and accidents such as could happen at any moment. The burden of taxation soon reached its limit.

Similar questions preoccupied the members of the Royal Society of Agriculture in Aunis and Saintonge when they calculated in 1763 the expenditure of a husbandman.[23] 189 *livres* 13 *sols* for one person: 110 *livres* for food, half of this going on bread, a quarter on drink, a quarter on sardines, herrings, garlic, onions and butter '*pour sa soupe*'. The Academicians reckoned that taxes (*taille*, poll-tax), implements and fodder took twelve *livres*, rent fifteen *livres*, heating and lighting nineteen *livres* (nearly ten per cent), together with laundry (a change of shirt every eight days), clogs (four pairs made of sapwood or three of hard wood), clothes (shirt, collar, handkerchiefs, stockings, gaiters, hat, cap, 'secondhand coat or jacket', waistcoat of linsey-wolsey or thick flannel), nineteen *livres* per year if he only half-used his clothes: altogether, for this detailed list, more than twenty-five *livres* with bedclothes, small items of furniture and cost of mending tools. The 'indispensable' expenditure of the wage-labourer in Aunis had thus got bigger than what Vauban allowed him. A mode of consumption was here in process of change: the share given to clothing and appearances was taken into account because in that sphere, supply and demand had changed.[24] We can imagine both the increase in purchases, facilitated by lower prices for second-hand goods or what could be found in the old-clothes market, and the anticipation connected with a branch of consumption the rhythms of which were longer-spaced-out than those of food-supply.

Poor people's budgets, assistance budgets, savings budget

Provincial economists became more numerous. In 1764 those of the municipality of Abbeville set out a budget for a weaver in that town:[25] 388 *livres* income and 312 *livres* necessary expenditure for four persons. In this case food made up two-thirds of consumption, with forty per cent accounted for by bread alone, but other expenses appeared and also, with the seventy-six *livres* remaining, 'the comforts of life'. The food ration was diversified in quantity and in quality: it was no longer uniform, but allowed for difference of needs depending on age and sex. The decline in the 'necessary' element might indicate a noticeable improvement, but for the authorities it also pointed to the precariousness of a domestic economy constantly endangered by crises and which it was impossible to burden any further.

For this reason all those who waged the struggle against pauperism, organising or managing charity or assistance, were also interested in budget evaluations. Poorhouses, workhouses, prisons were subjected to investigations and reports.[26] Experts from the Royal Academy of Sciences, Tenon, Lavoisier and Dupont de Nemours, made it their business to work out the cost of a day in a poorhouse. It seemed to them impossible to reduce it below seventeen *sols* and reasonable to keep it at twenty-two *sols*, or between 500 and 669 *livres* per year, since the poor never stopped eating.[27] This was more than the amount of income and annual expenditure allowed for by the administrators at about the same date. These evaluations gave rise to another discussion, about the time spent at work. Both state and church were trying to cut down the number of holidays, thereby increasing the amount of work done and also reducing opportunities for immorality. In this utilitarian convergence, reduction in supply and production and multiplication of occasions of sin had the same consequence.[28] By thinning-out the number of holidays they hoped to increase production and the incomes of families while reducing incitements to superfluous expenditure and waste. The supervision of *bachelleries* and gatherings of young people and the severe treatment of taverns and pleasure-gardens, dancing and merrymaking, drunkenness and the pleasures of affluence, descriptions of which we can read in the writings of strict ecclesiastics and the publications of administrators, testify very clearly to the existence of expenditure on leisure activities, on Sundays and holidays,[29] which both authorities wished to restrain because it encroached on other ways of spending time and money. Already in his day Vauban had complained of the loss of earning-time. 'There are about thirty holidays in a year, besides the Sundays, and I believe there may be even more.' (He included thirty-eight holidays when he calculated the weaver's income, but his uncertainty was all the greater because of variations between dioceses.)

We could abolish half of them, to the advantage of the craftsmen in the towns and the peasants in the country who, using these fifteen or twenty extra working days, might very well make enough to pay their taxes and have something over. That would be of inconceivable benefit to them if they knew how to profit by it.[30]

Thus, there would be 275 working days. After 1765 calculations became more numerous, and were repeated. M. de Bielefeld gave only 240 days devoted to work, while the Royal Society in Aunis went for 245, and detailed how the other 120 were lost: 52 Sundays, 28 other holidays, ten days of *corvée* (forced labour) on the roads, twenty days lost through bad weather and another ten through illness. Time thus became an essential dimension of the budget. The income earned did not cover all aspects of the expenditure calculated for the 'husbandman', especially if he had a family to support. Between the reduction of expenditure and the increase of earnings the gap was small but not negligible.

'More work, less activity' is a slogan that it is easy to imagine for the advocates of growth who operated according to the idea expounded by the academicians of Châlons between 1775 and 1777 when they launched a competition to find ways of reducing begging.[31] We meet them in the normative analysis of lower-class budgets provided by the Abbé Malvaux, perpetual secretary of the Academy of Champagne, taking as his example the Méreau family, or in that of the Abbé Leclerc de Montlinot, canon of Soissons, or in that of the Pilons. Lavoisier used comparable methods and came to similar conclusions for 'the expenses of a small rural household consisting of a labourer, a woman and three children'. Consumption was becoming diversified, expenditure was increasing, and earnings were menaced by spending on superfluities and by the risk of under-employment. The increase in general productive activity raised, moreover, the question of investment and saving.

In his *Projet pour enrichir l'espèce humaine ou Economie politique* (1763), Joachim Faiguet de Villeneuve resumed the debate on the length of working time, basing himself on study of the role of the guilds, and demonstrated with detailed figures the ability of individuals to economise on their expenditure.[32] To this end he presented a picture showing three economic persons belonging to the same social group, namely, the wage-earning craftsmen: a young journeyman at the start of his career; a worker-artist who was an established and competent employee; and an old wage-worker at the end of his working life. He also allowed for the way the life cycle affected earnings and expenditure, by making the first man twenty years old, the second thirty-five and the third fifty. (The average age of marriage was, for men, around twenty-seven.) In a *Mémoire sur les fêtes* he allotted 285 working days per year to all three, but he did not allow for illness or for weather conditions (which did not matter much in the towns, except for certain trades – building and textiles), and for the urban cases he did not deduct any days for *corvée*. His standpoint was that of the moralists and of the economists who advocated greater profitability to be attained through longer work. This table summarises all these data:

	Journeyman	Artist	Big wage-earner
Ages (years)	25	35	50
Work (days)	285	285	285
Earnings (livres)	356	498	712
Food (livres)	182	219	220
Housing (livres)	24	40	40
Clothes (livres)	40	40	40
Total expenses (livres)	246	299	300
Savings (livres)	110	199	412

It is hard to establish how Faiguet calculated these figures. The figure for rent is that for a Parisian occupying one room, which was the situation of three-quarters of the wage-earning population, who spent in this way between forty and fifty *livres* during the 1760s.[33] The evaluation of payments for food doubtless takes account of a difference in quality, mainly as betweeen the twenty-five-year-old and the thirty-five-year-old. While the weighting relative to income decreases (51 per cent, 43 per cent, 30 per cent), it stays the same (73 per cent) relative to total expenses, which is contrary to Engels' law: 'The lower a family's income, the greater is the proportion of it that has to be spent on food',[34] but this makes us a little doubtful of the calculation. Similarly, while we can accept that expenditure on clothes does not change, it is not out of the question that the amount has been underestimated where the first case is concerned. And, of course, this model refers in every case to a bachelor, not to a household, which would alter all the items that compose it.

Faiguet's purpose is plain: in order to put an end to pauperism and increase production, people must be encouraged to save. His argument advocates individual economic development: the gains that come with age and qualification should be invested so as to produce more income. By neglecting the family dimension Faiguet was advocating a veritable revolution, both economic and cultural. Whereas in the domestic economy, when scarcity prevailed, savings were limited (they were a reserve, not an investment), in the developed economy money ought to be invested in land, be put into circulation or into industry.

This model, which broke with the practices of marginal waste characteristic of festive popular culture, and with unprofitable savings, thus aimed at drawing the consumer into a broader, credit-based movement. It was not out of touch with reality, if we remember the way that Jacques-Louis Ménétra traversed cycles of activity and expenditure. When young, the journeyman increased his earnings, whenever possible, so as to increase expenditure that was largely due to symbolic and festive occasions, when several days' earning sometimes disappeared in a few hours. When settled down and married, the glazier hesitated between the standards of his youth and investment in new enterprises outside the guild framework. His wife urged him to be prudent, keeping control of expenditure which had to meet the needs of four persons, and setting aside part of his earnings.[35]

The last axis of the budget culture of the Enlightenment was situated deliberately beyond calculations on the threshold of survival, far from the cost of the marginalised man, and related in another way to general economic concerns. It was based both on defence of an established standard of consumption and in the context of a crisis which threatened this standard. We can see it being drawn up in Lyons in 1770–90.[36] Recourse to a budget was here connected with the struggle waged by the master silk-weavers against the merchants who controlled the supply of raw materials and the outlets for sale. Threatened with proletarianisation, the Lyons craftsmen demanded guarantees for a scale of prices for their work. Here was no new demand, for it had long figured in conflicts in Lyons and elsewhere, but, this time, the master-craftsmen used as their chief argument the need to protect a certain life-style. The interest of this for us is due also to the fact that it had for its setting an active urban development and involved a large number of persons: at least, in 1786, 7,000 masters and 18,000 wage-earners, to whom must be added their wives and children – altogether, in any case, 40 per cent of the active population. Here we see that economic growth could benefit a substantial proportion of a town's population, while at the same time we are made aware of its precariousness and the human and social cost.

The composing of these Lyons budgets has to be seen as placed at the meeting-point of two politico-intellectual traditions, that of negotiation between the crafts and the authorities and that of the drawing of distinguished Academies into study of the contemporary economy. From the first came the guild idiom[37] and the organicist aspect of a group concerned to prove their claims and liberties, now threatened by the egoism of the big merchants – in Lyons before the municipality, in Paris in the chambers of commerce. From the second we learn that there was not a complete separation between the guild culture and the interests of the local intellectual elite.[38] By setting, in 1777, the subject for a competition as 'means to remedy the difficulties being experienced by manufacture', the elite showed their awareness of a situation which left 'resting' 5,000 out of 10,000 looms, and concerned themselves with the impoverishment that menaced a large number of families in the town. Local patriotism and economic utilitarianism were combined, even if the arguments used to support the remedies proposed were drawn from the domestic economy, including an appeal for austerity in consumption.

The context of the pre-Revolution years accounts for the variations observable in different versions of the craftsman's budget between 1770 and 1790. The final presentation of the demand upheld in Paris by Denis Monnet, representing the master-silkweavers, adjusted the data so as to allow for the evolution of prices (both buying and selling), and of wages. For a working period evaluated at 296 days per year (we note how the desired reduction in holidays had progressed since Vauban's time) he calculated a capacity of production of the order of two-and-three-quarters ells per day, providing an income of 1,800 *livres*. This was what the master could earn together with his wife, who worked, one journeyman and a servant who had to be paid. It was the market rate, without any protective price-list, left to free negotiation. Expenditure was reckoned for six persons (which assumed two or three children, the figure varying from one version to another) and came to 2,049 *livres*. Food took various forms: bread accounted for 45 per cent, and then there was wine, meat, vegetables and 'sweets', making up 38 per cent. Clothes, their upkeep and renewal, for all members of the household, came to 15 per cent. Workshop and tools cost 33 per cent. Rent, heating, wood and candles were estimated at less than 10 per cent. A small margin was left, which corresponded to education expenses and to the miscellaneous costs associated with urban life. From the standpoint of those who compiled this budget, it could not be cut down further, and in that attitude we can perceive the defence of a certain status. The master-silkweaver's independence and the life-style, open to change, diversified and enriched, that was enjoyed by his family were inseparable. To give up the former meant to deprive oneself of the latter. The education to which the level of literacy of the group bears witness – 95 per cent for the men, 87 per cent for the women – and their cult of appearances and leisure were thenceforth included in the budget of this group without any possibility of renunciation.

Knowing these budgets is thus doubly interesting. They prove the reality of a modernisation of consumer behaviour and the progress of the urban categories favoured by wealth and work, but they prove also, once again, the strength of the bond linking knowledge with those who use it. We have come a long way from the crushed situation depicted by Vauban and are not so far from the urban wage-earning class. The budget economy records new needs. The economic process of reproduction has entered a phase of transformation in which everyday life can serve as the means to understand how necessary needs are formed which, from now on, are no longer exclusively material, and, through them, the processes of accumulation.

To stay with our knowledge of these matters, we must go back for a moment to the fact that the budget equation greatly contributed to strengthen the idea that consumption was equal to production. *La Richesse territoriale de la France* here assumes emblematic value, in the reading of it advocated by J.-C.Perrot, which I shall follow.[39] In it Lavoisier presents a picture of consumption by Paris which, though familiar, is essential because it reveals a certain intellectual approach at the same time as it shows the capacity for transformation over a century and the specific character of the Paris market. It was at the request of the constituent National Assembly that he tried to evaluate taxable income, doing this less in the spirit of the political arithmeticians concerned to measure power and wealth of employment than in that of the economists of the second half of the eighteenth century, concerned to discover the capacity of the population to pay taxes or to contribute to developing investment and production. As Farmer-General he knew from the reports of the indirect tax administration what the general situation was, and he had also observed this on the ground. As an Academician he was at the centre of thinking about appraisal of inventions and interpretation of economic life. Since he could not proceed from a direct evaluation of production, for lack of complete statistics apart from the calculation of cereal output, he made the assumption that production was equivalent to consumption, as a function of this equation: consumption plus exports equals production plus imports. The second term could be calculated on the basis of average consumption, weighted for the country and for the towns, whose inhabitants he reckoned to number more than seven million (30 per cent of 25 million), and by taking account of the information acquired through various budgetary investigations.

The table of consumption by Paris gives us here an idea of the top of the hiearchy of expenditure. To establish this Lavoisier was able to consult earlier works, by Sauvat and Rousseau, by Lalande, by Hurtaut and Magny, the *Tableau des revenus du roi* (1774) compiled by the Abbé Terray, and, above all, the records of the Farm and of the tolls, where controls had been strengthened. The sources and information of this document are therefore exceptional, but it cannot answer every question. There are gaps in the sixty-six headings (milk, *fromage frais*), underestimates (vegetables) and omissions (quality of bread). The calculation of prices on the basis of an annual current price comes up against problems of conversion, e.g. of head of cattle into pounds of meat. For several products we have the value of the raw materials (wood, textiles) but not that of the commodities transformed and sold at a price increased by the added labour.[40] Nor can we know anything of the consumptions provided in a capital city by the service sector, which for many people were indispensable. And the final operation, to arrive at average expenditure per inhabitant, with all ages and both sexes lumped together, depends on the number of the population. Given 600,000 souls, Lavoisier revalues the figure for consumption per head – 250 million divided by 600,000, resulting in 416 *livres* 13 *sols*. For comparison, let us recall that the Lyons family of five or six persons had at that same time 1,800 *livres* and spent 2,049 *livres*, being at a social level that was already higher.

Lavoisier's approach is useful, since it enables us to perceive an average level and is not self-enclosed. Furthermore, it informs us with a fair degree of certainty about the distinctiveness of the consumption of the Parisians, whose diet was plentiful and varied: 460 grammes of bread per person per day, 90 grammes of meat, but also fish, poultry, cheese, sugar, wine, cider, coffee and cocoa. It has been possible to make a calculation of the equivalent in calories, optimistic, no doubt, but indicating probable improvement: 2,000 calories per day, not exclusively due to the cereals eaten. Bread represented no more than 16 per cent of expenditure, even though it still provided half of the average ration. We perceive, with the range of raw materials and commodities circulating in the capital, the role of increased demand for groceries, drugs, hardware, clothing, printed matter (10 million books per year), that the 'typical Parisian' was already a consumer who had gone beyond necessities and the mere need to reproduce life. We can appreciate also the difference from the rations to be observed in the country, or calculated for the poor, in which bread often accounted for between two-thirds and three-quarters of total expenditure.

The averages are only worth so much, and there were big differences between the expenditure of rich and poor in the consumption calculated by Lavoisier. Moreover, Paris, as the capital, enjoyed a privileged regime in respect of foodstuffs that were directly supervised by the police, and, thanks to the activity of its merchants, the city's population was supplied by a vast market well served by good roads. Quality and quantity combined in a formula which had perhaps less to do with the alienation of human beings than with their liberation. We were to discover all its merits in the nineteenth century, when the increase in population contributed to worsen the way it functioned.[41] Like other great capital cities, Paris was a field for experiences the meaning of which was plain: the context of the relation between productions and consumptions had evolved, everything was changing faster, needs of diverse quality had developed and the stranglehold of scarcity had slackened.

From scarcity to luxury

It is in these ways of thinking about its relation to economics and to things that we have to appreciate the movement which brought people out of a precarious age when their problem was how to live and survive into a society that was less fragile, perhaps more attractive, and certainly more secure. To give meaning to their life on earth the men of the seventeenth century turned towards Heaven, and it is the religious literature of the time that provides the historian with the markers needed to understand what transformed and what united things and men.

From among many authors the interest of whose writings had already been pointed out by the Abbé Bremond,[42] J.-C.Perrot stresses the symbolic significance of the book by Jean Girard de Villethierry, *La Vie des riches et des pauvres ou les obligations de ceux qui possèdent les biens de la terre ou qui vivent de la pauvreté*, published in Paris in 1712. The society it describes is not without wealth, but needs to justify its existence in relation to the mass of poor people who lack that wealth. We are familiar with the solution offered: true wealth is not where we think it is, its conquest is futile, 'no-one can serve two masters', and the end of all things will see the cards newly dealt. But over these principles on which one should always be meditating there hover two unavoidable questions. Since the goods at men's disposal are limited in quantity, according to what rules ought they to be shared? And, given that rich people exist, how ought they to behave?

To the first question correspond the entire functioning of a society of corporations and differences of status, together with the essence of the mercantilist economic culture, since the hierarchy of consumptions is in conformity to that of the powers ordained by God. To the second correspond both the moral economy, which binds the responsibility of the sovereign and the rich in relation to the public weal, and economic morality, which counsels moderate use of goods in conformity with one's rank. Thus we see extolled the stability of the world and the way society functions through the twofold mechanism of exchange and the gift economy. The rich class is identified mostly with the landowners and to a less extent with the leaders of commerce. They ought to possess their wealth not just without enjoying it but by redistributing it through almsgiving and legacies. Luxury can in this way be transformed into charity. In the market of spiritual goods superfluity is converted into spiritual riches for the giver and necessary goods for the poor who are helped. 'Almsgiving is a business in which we receive infinitely more than we give', writes Girard de Villethierry.[43]

In this transfer of values the income of the rich man is justified because through his consumption he provides work for the poor. The place of giving is central because it activates the circulation of goods and justifies rejection of hoarding and condemnation of its derivatives, such as usury. The ideal of the society of scarcity and the stationary state is founded upon four principles: reproduction of society in the same form, with little social mobility; primacy for redistribution of wealth, with capitalisation and accumulation rejected; luxury kept within the hierarchical conformity of the social authorities; primacy of being over seeming. Economy and consumption are not ends in themselves but means for making the world go round, with the act of giving making it possible to reconcile salvation with enrichment, justice with inequality, praise of work with asceticism in expenditure.

We see here how a doctrine can become a culture and make a virtue of necessity. The power of this model for conduct, in which economic and social considerations are combined, is due to its establishing of the religious domain and its means of spiritual conversion as the most general frame of reference for everyone in the sphere of material and economic life. The values of both are weighed in terms of religious and moral significances. We see these operating in economic discourse and practices, no less in the acts of administrators than in the demands of the masses, to maintain and justify the rights of consumers and just prices, with the principle of the market contradicting the way the market-places function.[44] We shall find the model persisting into the nineteenth century, from the pens of economists whose influence was not negligible, such as Say and Villeneuve-Bargemont. We can find some aspects of it in *Le Problème d'Adam Smith*, such as the formation of the metaphor of the invisible hand and the train of thought which led to the *Theory of the Moral Sentiments* and *The Wealth of Nations*.[45]

Other texts could serve as witnesses to the influence of this model and its variations in relation to social realities. For example, the *Vie du bon Henri* by J.-A.Vachet, which shows us what were the standards of the urban craftsman, or the forms of similarity and difference at work in Calvinist thought as analysed by Max Weber. If there is a spirit of the moral economy, as there may be one for capitalism and liberalism, it is simply a prompting to understand and organise the relation of mankind to the world and to things, to evaluate the complexity of the relations between material life and exchange, and to realise that the transition from the society of scarcity to that of consumption takes place in less linear fashion than is commonly held.

On this point the testimony of the persons involved is not without its uses, even if we need to be somewhat cautious with it, since they may exaggerate the changes they have noticed. Let us listen, all the same, to Louis Simon on change in the countryside of Maine: the coming of the royal road, the widening of familiar horizons, the accessibility of unfamiliar consumptions (printed calico, cotton), the role of information.[46] Or let us listen to ninety-year-old F.-Y Bernard telling us of the contrast between the abundance of food likely to be found in a rich farmer's family in Anjou and the relative absence of luxury in their furniture and clothes, the comfort where necessities were concerned and the lack of superfluities.[47] Everything had changed in the towns, more slowly in the countryside, between childhood and old age.

Other ways of life were possible, therefore, which had been unimaginable not long before. The progressive rehabilitation of expenditure, the praise of luxury, the transition from the watchword 'spend what you earn' to the command 'earn what you spend, so as to spend more', and the rehabilitation of entrepreneurs all tended in the same direction, shaping a different sensibility, giving rise to new standards and new intellectual consumptions. The new philosophy which united exchange and needs assumed several partings – from family and regional self-subsistence, from an economy in which money played little part, from the unchangingness of things.

And so the fundamentals of the Christian economy were turned upside down. Society was no longer to function with a view to redistribution, either benevolent or statutory, but to aim at interest and utility. The idea that the market was enough to harmonise particular imbalances and establish general equilibrium, thanks to the action of the invisible hand, was to take over, from Boisguilbert to Smith. Wealth was consumption by everyone, for everyone buys from everyone else. The landowner's rent provides him with a surplus over necessities, and that draws all the rest. 'All income, or, rather, all wealth, consists only of consumption' Boisguilbert affirms quite simply: the ruin of consumption brings disaster, its multiplication brings opulence. A new culture was to promote the value of enrichment and accumulation, change and mobility, setting individual choice above custom.

The dispute about luxury shows us that the new principles made their way only slowly into men's minds. It starts from the change from a conception of sumptuary expenditure which conforms to the economic ethic of the baroque and classical age. To be sure, it is superfluous, excessive expenditure, but it is a tolerated sumptuousness, made necessary by the very nature of the ruling powers in society. Norbert Elias sees in it the principal effect of 'the Court Society',[48] when the social being and the individual are mingled in representation and the increase in the power of princes intensifies competition for rank through rivalry in the signs of prestige: luxury has, first, a political function. It maintains cultural difference and imposes the respect due to the royal authority and to God, who is not grudged the sumptuousness accumulated for his service. Elias did not measure the economic capacity of the ruling classes to exploit their dependence on the monarch as well as their own power in order to avoid ruin through squandering (we know now what to think about the economic fate of the nobility) but he defined accurately the function of luxury. Luxury operated on the edge of things, being condemned by the preachers and controlled, at least in principle, by the sumptuary laws[49] and by mercantilist regulation of trade and production, an external means of enrichment which was the prerogative of a narrow internal elite.

The transformation which first of all affected England approached France only gradually, but we have observed the movement which spread from the towns to the countryside, and its reflection in the composition of budgets. The economists of growth through consumption, Boisguilbert and Cantillon, and observers of the Dutch miracle (Bayle) concurred in rehabilitating luxury. It was the way to measure the new understanding of men faced with expansion and invited to hedonism. 'The necessity of superfluity asserts itself through a new relation to the world and to objects which make life more secure, more beautiful, more reassuring. Virtue is no longer the fruit of renunciation but of moderate and reasonable use of goods and of the benefits they lavish. Self-love no longer separates the individual from the Christian community.'[50]

This rehabilitation stirred up opinion, and academies, newspapers, economists and philosophers argued over it for the whole century. A strong beat was given to the debate by the diffusion of the ideas of Bernard Mandeville, after the publication in 1723 of his *Fable of the Bees*. This allegorical poem, translated into French in 1740, owed its success partly, no doubt, to its assertion – scandalous for Christian thinkers – that private vices brought public benefits. Accepting the inescapability of the passions, Mandeville declared that societies can function by themselves, that morality and social utility are separable, and that it was time to de-bunk the conduct of the preachers of renunciation. Luxury became an obviously necessary fact of life.

Between 1736 and 1786 a good hundred publications echoed the discussion provoked by this cat set among the pigeons. Voltaire intervened, with *Le Mondain* in 1734 and with his *Observations sur MM Jean Law, Melon and Dutot*, dealing with trade, luxury, currencies and taxes. To the sanctimonious critic who blamed him for advocating luxury and softness the philosopher replied by setting forth the riches placed at the disposal of diners: wine from the Canaries, coffee from Arabia, porcelain from China, engraved silverware made from the metal of Potosi. The whole world had worked for his peevish heckler, luxury enriched the state, it was the certain mark of a happy reign: 'As we see in England, so in France, abundance flows along a hundred channels. The taste for luxury enters all ranks of society: the poor man lives by it, from the vanity of the great, and work paid for by softness opens gradually the way to riches.' Though Antiquity called poverty a virtue, the modern age should prefer work and the arts. Voltaire continued, let it be noted, to look at things in the mercantilist way, praising Colbert, state protectionism and spendthrift monarchs who followed King Solomon's example. He repeated in the *Dictionnaire philosophique* his defence of luxury, in the name of historical progress.

The Encyclopaedists would say much the same. Louis de Jaucourt, or perhaps it was Diderot, argued, in the name of the use made of riches, for the view that their increase was beneficial, on condition that the excesses of squandering to be seen in the luxury of ostentation be condemned and that one lived only in a luxury of comfort that was more egalitarian, less spendthrift, 'related always to what is useful' and incapable of degenerating into foolish emulation. The evolution of material civilisation and that of sensibilities seemed to ensure the triumph of those who praised luxury. In his essay 'On Luxury' (1752) [later re-titled 'On Refinement in the Arts'], Hume gave to Paris as well as London a manifesto of a liberated economy, the assurance of progress in political consciousness. It was then that there reappeared questioning of development and its consequences. This had not vanished from the collective consciousness, if we remember the steady success of reprintings of Fénelon's *Télémaque* or the echo given to Swift's satires. For the censorious there should be a return to the common good, consumption should be reduced to what was useful, and curbs should be set on the monetary imbalances and social inequalities resulting from the development of luxury. Those who wanted a return to morality in the economy were buoyed up by hope for a Christian reformation and dreams of a philosopher-king. To the excesses of the Moderns the philosophers opposed the frugality of the Ancients. The twofold condemnation voiced by the Physiocrats and Rousseau drew its strength from the same arguments about morality and society.

For Mirabeau, 'the friend of humanity', Quesnay, Baudot and their like, luxury was a brake on productive investment, an encouragement to the unproductive class, since superfluous expenditure destroyed capacity for progress. They all repeated the condemnations of aristocratic criticism and the idea that morals were being corrupted by material civilisation. Rousseau's intervention was doubtless more complex than theirs, being an aspect of a wider evolution of his social philosophy which followed a personal break that was painful. For him luxury was not just an idea, it was the concrete experience of inequality. To condemn it meant becoming able to perceive how a whole civilisation had gone astray, but also to perceive the solutions that would correct it, reconciling what was with what seemed, and man with things. Disappointed by the spectacle presented by the contradictions of progress and growth, he definitively cast out luxury from the categories of economic analysis. Adam Smith, in *The Wealth of Nations*, was to see in luxury only the spendthrift passion of an idle class, condemnable by moral and social criticism.

It would be wrong at this point to suppose that the debate was of interest only to men of letters, scholars and rich people. The *cahiers de doléances* sent up from Brittany in 1789 contrasted 'real necessity and fictitious necessity'. Those who compiled them presented well the way matters were seen by contemporaries, the state of society as perceived and imagined. They agreed in regarding corn, bread and salt as goods that were necessary for life and indispensable to everyone. They contrasted the opulence of the privileged with the poverty of the country-folk. But they revealed new habits of consumption when they demanded, on behalf of the boldest communities, that powder, braid, coffee and tobacco be taxed. The right to little pleasures constituted the other side of this condemnation of superfluity in clothing and food, superfluity in carriages and hearses and measures to beautify dwellings, all denounced in the name of the Christian heritage and of utility. A new pattern of cultural behaviour, made up of aspiration to well-being and dignity, had asserted itself.[51]

Luxury, which is by its very nature relative, is hard to define. The questions it provoked show clearly that here we have an interpretative key that enables us to appreciate the ambivalence of an age in relation to consumption. In many respects the debate broke out at a time when large-scale consumption was still confined to products of necessity, and luxury consumptions, both imported and made in France, were still reserved for an elite of rank and wealth, even though they reached a level, in volume and in quality, which had not been known till then. A slow movement was beginning. Changes in consumption by the privileged would gradually influence all society, making relative the notions of comfort and superfluity, which now became meaningful only in relation to individuals. The spread of luxury and opposition to the diffusion of baubles, trinkets and frivolous objects (to use Adam Smith's words) brought crucial changes to men's relation to the traditional view of the world. At the same time the disappointment engendered in face of this first abundance gave rise to many questions regarding man's material and moral condition.[52] By assembling the signs of change in the different domains of material culture we must now measure, as well as we can, tradition and innovation, so as to understand the many issues involved in enrichment, those of the movement which permanently drives onward everyday life and binds together needs and desires for things.

Part II

Ordinary life

4   Rural and urban houses

The house is for everyone the heart of ordinary life. In it we see coming together, and sometimes contradicting each other, technology, economics, collective culture, personal choice, constraints and compromises. In relation to both consumption and production it presents us with questions regarding the forces that organise reality, the agents who produce it – from architect to building-worker – and the ways of the inhabitants who are defined by their mode of appropriating space. Fernand Braudel, who devoted a chapter of his *Civilisation matérielle* to the house, places it between necessary and superfluous consumptions,[1] leaving us to gauge the respective share of permanent and changing features. The house is a subject to which there are no limits. We can find in it the influences of technical gaps and of the frontiers between geographical, historical and social factors. The history of building materials, which is being written by Denis Woronoff, Jean-François Belhoste and Andre Guillerme, introduces us to this huge domain wherein social rules prevail, for there are both poor materials and poor countries and rich materials and rich countries. The world of wood, earth and cob is not the world of dressed stone and brick. There are rich people living in traditionally built, unaffected houses while poor townsmen huddle together in 'machines for living in' which already belong to a world of technical and economic affluence.[2]

As time passed, functional divisions appeared and imposed different requirements on the construction of habitats, involving different forms of knowledge and skill. The contrast between town and country – which, however, should not be exaggerated – made itself felt increasingly with the speeding up of exchange and the differentiation of urban ways of life. There were transitional zones, outskirts and suburbs, and new urban developments that breached city walls.

The urban house is better known than its rural sister, even though the current efforts of the heritage services give us hope of change in this sphere. Behind the history of architecture and styles, thinking is becoming organised which brings together architectural changes and forms of private life, the mastery of domestic space.[3] Contemporary ethnology of everyday life, which carries forward the geographical tradition of regional and general studies,[4] encourages us to review what we know of these matters.[5] These changes will make it possible for the silent to speak and will show us how groups and individuals organised their territory, marked out its symbolic limits and imagined the frontier between the inside and the outside.

The solutions adopted for building and developing space can vary according to goegraphical setting. There is the rural site where stability of values dictates that the materials used, the dwellings and the way these are used must be long-lasting. And there is the urban site in which social changes and contrasts manifest themselves in another fashion and proceed ever faster, as in other domains between the seventeenth and the eighteenth century.

Habitat and everyday life

The house lies at the heart of human life, for historians as for anthropologists. From the earliest times, it has been the most visible sign of human occupation. Marcel Mauss said, jokingly, that 'ruins are the food of archaeology'. Since time past, the inhabited place has long tried to address the many problems arising from necessity itself not from luxury. Basic elementary functions find their response here; social and geographical divisions of labour diversify relationships.

The house was, first and foremost, the primary protected place. It was a shelter from the elements, from the seasonal variations of the climate, but also from the wild beasts that had not entirely vanished from the forests and fields, and from men themselves in regions of dispersed habitat and during troubled times. This role of accommodation and security runs through the ages and survives in men's consciousness. The house was also an instrument of labour, sheltering harvests and stock, carts and farm machinery.

Since long ago the ideal of the 'house in the country'[6] has sought to master the disorder of working and living, to shape a favourable environment through a system of arranged places which determines the aspect of the buildings, in accordance with the plans of the builders. The dwelling will, usually, look towards the rising sun in the months of March and September,[7] because the winds that blow from that direction are dry, and warm rather than cold, and the storms and frosts of winter will have less effect on the buildings. Similarly, the cowsheds will be open to the south, or the sunrise, while the barns will face the sunset. Within the logic of an ancient culture of medicine and learning, we perceive what the elites (brought up on time-honoured notions about air and morality, for which the house was the centre of a domain, a built-upon and cultivated space which was also a moral unit of living and management) were able to do in the face of the realities around them and so able to formulate a general programme of thought-out and mastered relations that could convince beginners seeking to build. Normandy, Picardy and the Paris Basin provide examples of the application of Charles Estienne's model, datable and provable, where systems of building have been adopted that conform to standards[8] established since the sixteenth century.

The function of work was not negligible in the urban house. Workshops demanded a way of arrangement which was not yet entirely separated from the sphere of private life. For a long time the merchant's house was a depot and a set of offices. In the aristocrat's town house was the workplace and sometimes the home of his clerks. The confrontation of these functions with family concerns, forms of sociability and religious demands enriched this structure of space, in which individuals would fashion their living conditions in accordance with their self-image.

While the house lies at the heart of everyone's life we must nonetheless distinguish between the dwelling, a significant element of human societies, and the habitat, which refers to the many practices and usages of the rural or urban house, the location of family life and social relations and symbol of power. Gaston Bachelard has called for a deciphering of this complex of ideas and realities concerning the house, the home.[9]

What is most real? The actual house in which we sleep, or the house in which, sleeping, we are faithfully going to dream? In Paris I don't dream in this geometrical cube, this cell of cement, this room with iron shutters so hostile to the nocturnal style. When my dreams are good to me I go into a house in the country or into several houses where the mysteries of happiness are concentrated.

In this story of images of reality to which the philosopher invites us we note that these are not concepts, that they are not isolated in their meaning, that they can act both for and against. The historian of the house, starting from a material element – the cellar, the roof, the loft, the fireplace – thus observes crystallising those values of sentiment and feeling which inspire everyone's conduct, together with the way in which they evolve in social relations. Bachelard's remarks encourage us to keep to the terms of a history of habitat which is bound up with time, the organising of space and the structuring of tasks.

Time, security, relations

The house is, first and foremost, 'petrified time'. It brings together and condenses the past and the future in the inhabited space which was built in the past and modified by successive generations which have unified the ways things are arranged in it. The objects contained and the lives of the occupants inscribe herein the lines of force of family life. Everywhere a form of organisation is imposed which is dictated by the general rise of the nuclear-family model made up of parents and children, rarely more than that. In towns this model provides the basis for 'the birth of intimacy', expressed in the hierarchy of means and social tastes.[10] The intimacy of the lower orders does not have the same reach or the same meaning, in their conditions of crowding and promiscuity, as the intimacy of the well-to-do classes.[11] In the country, 'household' signifies both the common life of a couple, the house and its interior, with their maintenance, mingling the biological and emotional dimension, community of life and work, in even stronger fashion. The household may embrace, though rarely going beyond the nucleus of parents and children, a domestic group enlarged through the coexistence of generations or the bringing together of couples. The residential group studied by demographic historians stays reduced almost everywhere between the eighteenth and nineteenth centuries.[12] It increases only in rich farms where domestic staff, shepherds, cowherds, carters and servants have to be accommodated, as also in mountainous areas such as the Massif Central, the northern and southern Alps, and the Pyrenees, where we observe traditional examples of extended families and 'big houses' that organise differently the evolution of the heritage and working life.[13]

The house, a product of time and a producer of various time-scales, is an integral part of all the economic and social movements that transform the world. Its construction and improvement develop when necessities, those of material life and of the land, do not sweep it away. The rural habitat consequently evolves slowly and by redistribution – the addition of new buildings, alterations. It is this historical tinkering that has to be understood in order to identify the mechanisms of variation, over and above the elements that do not change, the obvious comparisons and latent structures.[14] The morphology of the house which reveals a social history, the vocabulary of the constituent parts of the buildings, that of the materials used and of the building techniques, all have to be linked together.[15] Jean Cuisenier calls for a review in this sense of the 1,600 monographs on dwellings which were compiled under the inspiration of Georges-Henri Rivière during the last war,[16] so as to reconstitute the progress of the relevant forms of knowledge, those of the theoreticians, agronomists and architects, those of the builders and those, more empirical, of the occupants, so as to discover the relation between social logics and architectural composition. The historian, following the archaeologist, may hope to reconstitute, through deeds, contracts, leases and inventories, both the arrangements worked out in order to meet the demand for places to live in and the uses made of structures in their general relations with life.

The security-and-refuge aspect is fundamental here. It is of both symbolic and material importance, it implies the limits to control and it induces relations that affect the functioning of the family and relations with society. It establishes thresholds and orientations. In the rural houses of Touraine access to the dwellings which give on to the street, or to the small courtyards at their side, is carefully marked by barriers and gates; in lonely places, far from the villages, by hedges or what remains of thickets.[17] In the big farms of Normandy and the manor houses of the 'viceroys of the Beauce', access is protected by walls and big gates.[18] Everywhere, the front of the house takes on the task of representation, opening on to the street, expressing hospitality and rank, whereas the rear conceals disorder and private life. In the ambitious programmes of rural houses the main entrance is through the courtyard, on the sunset side, facing the master's dwelling. The approaches are disposed cosmologically and given value by the decor: the door between the west and the east is wide enough for the rites of the threshold – the reception of strangers and the poor – to take place there, and strong enough to withstand robbers. In the rooms the transitional spaces between outside and inside correspond to an ever-stronger frontier between private and public space. According to the social hierarchy, they protect, more or less effectively, intimacy and comfort, new values which are symbolised and realised by the furniture and the decor. The urban house, with its many activities, and the farmhouse or dwelling of the country towns and villages, stand in contrast to the disorder of the street.

All these types of habitat and residences have seen frontiers of new forms of behaviour become established in the modern period, modifying little by little 'the order of corporations, the order of manners and that of the family'.[19] This is why moral observers and reformers have difficulty in understanding the persistence of archaisms or the permanence of different ways of life. The habitat of townspeople, with its crowding-together, always seems to them reminiscent of animals' lairs. The huts, the temporary habitats, the shanties, the lodges in forests and heaths, the *bories* and *oustalets* of stacked-up stones that are lived in by shepherds on the Mediterranean coast, the *bourrines* of timber and thatch in the Marais Vendéen, the grottoes on the banks of the Loire, primitive dwellings on the fringe of civilisation, often seem to belong to a different species from the peasant house rooted in the soil.[20]

The difference between ownership and tenancy also determines the mode of relation to the habitat. In the rural world it depends on how the land is exploited – either direct cultivation or tenant-farming (or share-cropping) – and on whether the occupant is dependent or independent. Ownership dictates a strategy of conservation or expansion, favourable to a strengthening of the bonds between the household and the house. Tenancy may mean an attitude of waiting, a greater degree of mobility, a less constraining attachment. Rent is in any case a heavy burden on the peasant family of the labourer who has aspired to 'take a wife and a farm'. In tenant-farming or share-cropping leases the house belongs to the landlord, the lessee's means are usually slender, and housing absorbs less capital and labour than other changes. Nevertheless, the very large farms of the Ile-de-France, Perche and Normandy have seen the appearance of veritable manor houses. The diversity of the habitat is not dictated exclusively by the social hierarchy. The latter's role is obvious when we contrast castle with cottage, but it loses some of its meaning if we do not set it among all the components of the village organisation.

In towns – in Paris, Caen, Lyons, Rouen – a population of tenants, from wage-earners to bourgeois, occupy houses crowded into a narrow, carved-out tract of land. The aristocracy, both of wealth and of rank, takes suitable spaces for itself on which to build and rebuild town houses to receive the dependents and staff and these are re-appropriated in more and more various ways: lettings or transfers to the administration are often the fate of prestigious edifices.[21] It must be admitted that we know little about the relations induced, either betweeen owners and tenants – even tenants-in-chief who administer as sub-tenants the real estate of the owners – or between the form of management and the relations that it implies in the organisation of the space concerned or in the matter of private developments. The actual practice of sharing responsibilities and respecting customary undertakings ought to be confronted with an over-all evolution of housing. We know, for instance, that in Paris the proportion of reconstruction on the spot was greater than that of new building and that the property market was subject to bouts of speculative fever.[22] At the end of the eighteenth century new types of buildings, new ways of living, new districts built for profit and in accordance with principles of architecture and sociability that reinforced each other, extending west-ward on both banks of the Seine,[23] reflected changes in private space and public space alike.

Standard of living, life-style, manners, all played their part in the organisation of space. Openness, the threshold effects, verticality and horizontality – we know that the complex family dwelling on one level began mainly in the eighteenth century, as has been shown by J.-C. Perrot for Caen, A. Pardailhé for Paris and J.-P. Bardet for Rouen. With orientation on the street or on the yard the social significance and the relation to comfort without noise were not the same. The staircase and the landing are, in the urban house, along with the passage, the inner courtyard and the well, places which foster a specific form of sociability, favourable to all of life's activities – conflicts, friendship, love. The idea of *esprit de l'escalier* evokes noise and conversation.[24] Its mental images refer to aspirations for progress and personal realisation which evoke not so much the traditional hierarchy of occupations as the symbolism of the great monumental staircases where ceremonies were held, to welcome or to bestow honours, theatres of spectacular power. The builders' imagination could here spread its wings.[25] The service staircase to which, at the end of the eighteenth century, the movements of servants were confined appears as the culminating point in the general transformation of the passages in aristocratic and bourgeois houses, in the direction of separation and closure.

One of the major problems facing the population in this connection was that of the separation between residence and workplace. This has been seen as one of the clearest contrasts between the traditional society and the society born of the Industrial Revolution. On the one hand, proximity, the ideal of the craftsman's workshop and the merchant's shop united in a house where employers, workmen, clerks and servants live in relations which, if not more harmonious, are at least closer. A greater degree of openness of workplaces to the street, an interpenetration of public and private spaces, are supposed to have accompanied this set-up. On the other hand is separation of work from residence, with all its consequences: longer distances to travel each day, transformation of relations between classes and within families. This idea overlooks, first, the fact that definition of these spaces had long been the responsibility of the police of the cities and that they, reinforced by absolutism, had begun to evict unauthorised constructions such as shanties erected in public places. This policy formed part of a general putting in order of the town, the streets of which were cleaned up, swept, regulated and watched over. Overlooked also is the fact that the attraction exerted by the town, the renewal of its population by migration and the mobility of some of the workers dictated living conditions in which residence was already separated from work.[26] In the wage-earning and dependent society revealed by the records of criminal activity, looking for and paying for somewhere to live were problems all the harder to solve in that the instability of the labour market, the variations in the availability of jobs, bore heavily on the lower orders' incomes. Newcomers and older hands both lived wherever they could.

In Paris the map of furnished rooms was drawn, between the seventeenth and eighteenth centuries, by the increase in this demand. The level of rents for such rooms conformed less to a horizontal gradient between the centre and the periphery, as in Caen, than to variations in quality subject to a wide hierarchy of demand. At the same time we observe that this space where the lower orders settled was denser in the centre, where the concentration of their work was at its greatest, along north–south axes and towards the east of Paris.[27] Considerable distances between residence and work were established: the worker, especially if unskilled, 'went to work' in the ports, on the building sites, in the markets or even in the workshops in the city's outskirts. This separation brought new rhythms into private and working life, an element of discontinuity, a period already devoted to travelling, a contrast between work and leisure that had not been known to journeymen who lived with their master. Frequentation of inns and pot-houses established rules for living that were freer and less constrained and created a *de facto* solidarity, but also made the expression of violence possible. There was not complete separation between shop and inn, as the journeymen who were living-in were in contact with the others and the circumstances of his employment could oblige a man to change both situation and domicile.[28]

In the choice of somewhere to live, we find, very strongly marked, all the factors in the urban transformation: the integration of men and fortunes, the increase in prices and relative decrease in wages, the increase in rents and the utilitarian interventionism which altered living-spaces, subjecting them to other imperatives of aesthetics and convenience, economic functionality and guaranteed order. In country areas the pressure was not so strong, but other forms of control were operative, through the notables and their agents, to ensure the policing of morals and thereby also to change the relation between the public and private spheres.

Everyone's life depended very much upon the conditions for occupying the land and regrouping the habitat. The latter's evolution, the use of new building materials, the introduction of new models in the building-sites varied with the degree to openness, the existence or otherwise of intermediate categories, craftsmen, shopkeepers, schoolmasters, vine-growers, petty notables. The general organisation of the habitat and the state of the houses were doubtless closer to natural and regional circumstances, but they were not sheltered from the winds that blew from without and the effect of increased circulation. The history of modern building-sites has hardly been begun: from the prestige building to the utilitarian, from the dwelling-house to the workplace, they display a hierarchy of means and ambition, an accumulation of technology and influence of theoretical programmes, a functionality acquired or sought for, a diversity of builders and entrepreneurs.

The traditional rural house, between custom and innovation

The age of holiday homes has developed a taste for the traditional habitat and the stone house which, for townsfolk, embodies all the richness of old-time civilisation. This present-day way of looking at things strongly distorts our understanding of the past, because, over a long period and in numerous regions, the peasant's house remained cruder than that. It doubtless more often resembled those cottages with radiating roof-beams which observers described in Burgundy and Brittany during last century, with their facings of turf, their narrow vertical beams coming together at the top, their central hearth at ground level, or, more rarely, their fire-place, itself a sign of progress. The disappearance of all these old formulae that were kept alive by the precariousness of civilisation, but also by regional custom or adaptation to a certain kind of life – fens, forests, hill pastures – means that there is a certain amount of unreality in how we view this scene. The buildings that have survived from past ages, sorted out by the passage of time and preserved for their architectural richness, have always been modified. But the inventory of monuments enables us to list enough houses, farms and manors for historians to discover the main features of the habitat.

Where rural society is concerned one must never forget that a funda-mental split divides the world of the tramps without hearth or home from that of the villagers and inhabitants. Whether owner or tenant, the villager is settled in a home around which the life of a family group is organised, whereas the tramp lacks all this. The houses differ greatly, from one social group to another and from one district or region to another, in ways that correspond to their function, to the structures of local agriculture, to the size of families and to local building customs.[29] In their history all the motivations of human activity meet – religious life, social relations, juridi-cal customs, property, structures of exploitation, techniques of cultiva-tion, the attraction of the market, relations between town and country, input (quick or slow) of urban investment, and the local possibilities for innovation.[30]

Theoretical vision and overall geography

The three criteria that contribute to diversifying the rural habitat – regional, family and social characteristics – do not combine with the same effect everywhere. Typologies are consequently constructed which are at the heart of regional geographies. Albert Demangeon and Max Sarre sought to explain the arrangement of dwellings by comparing it with mode of life, forms of organisation of the landscape, constitution of tenures and aspects of the system of cultivation. They distinguished the 'elementary house' of the small-scale cultivator; the 'house in close order', bringing together all the vital organs of the farm around an enclosed yard, under the master's eye, as can be seen in Picardy, Brie, the Vexin, the Valois, the Soissonais and the Ile-de-France; the 'house in loose order', where the buildings are separated from each other, as in the stock-rearing districts of the West; and the 'house in depth', where animals, people, stores and tools are assembled under the same roof, as in the Midi, the Alps and nearly everywhere else.

The house constructed as a block or the house built round a yard, the house of the small or middle-sized cultivator, the house of the well-to-do peasant – here we see the historian being referred to contrasts which are simple and capable of inspiring numberless monographs on dwellings, villages and districts. Each level can engender a particular habitat, or even create a distinct architectural personality. We can perceive how the models offered to the builders provided a hierarchy by which to master heterogeneity and how, when pre-industrial civilisation was transformed, the overall map of the habitat recorded diversity. A number of regional examples illustrate these different changes and traditions.

Serlio's rural architecture

The rise of agronomic models in the sixteenth century is linked with the reconstruction of that period, one of economic and demographic advance. A new society, ennobled bourgeois, officials of justice and finance, townsfolk brought up within city walls, new landlords, had everything to learn about country life.[31] Jean Cuisenier shows how this new society was able to discover its principles in the works of Charles Estienne and a few others.

Sebastiano Serlio, a court architect from Italy, put forward in about 1550, in his *Books of Architecture*, the first published set of engraved plans for farm buildings and integrated gardens.[32] This was an important contribution to the works of reconstruction which had begun everywhere, since he offered ideas, based on his experience of cities and villages in France and Italy,[33] but also, what is more interesting in relation to this movement of society, because he furnished reproducible plans suitable for a variety of social uses. All the conditions were present for the ideal type to become real, wholly or in part, when it encountered the public of Estienne and Liébault. To builders he provided texts and plans that made possible a rural architecture which, in the main, needed no architect. To craftsmen who could read a little he gave a guiding thread for structure and capacity for adaptation on site. The portrait of the building, its representation, was made available to illiterate building-workers with a minimum of explanation. Responding as it did to a precise and explicit social demand, Serlio's manual evokes the stratification – social, cultural and economic – which ideally organised the habitat and which the France of the classical period interpreted and conserved.

His demonstration proceeds from one level to the next, from the worst hut conceivable to the most ornate of princely palaces, in country and town alike. Twelve models are offered to those who want houses in the country: the house for the noble-born gentleman, for the bourgeois, for the townsman going to live in the country (he distinguishes six examples depending on degree of wealth or on custom), for 'poor craftsmen', taking account of their degree of poverty, for the rich peasant (two degrees of richness distinguished) for the middle peasant (two levels distinguished) and for the poor peasant (three degrees of poverty distinguished).

From the nobleman to the bourgeois, from the rich farmer to the labourer, Serlio's plans were suitable for every level of society. When we put them beside the plans described by Charles Estienne and the realisations of those that have survived we can see the influence directly exercised by the solutions Serlio proposed, unifying residence and farm in lordly manor houses, arranging out-of-sight outhouses and noble buildings, already displaying the whole complexity of a social and regional hierarchisation of the layout of a habitat. At the bottom of the ladder, the poor peasant was entitled to a kitchen, with a fireplace at the side, and a living room, also with a fireplace. This is indeed a programme of suggestions intended for peasants and landlords engaged in reconstruction, but these suggestions no longer depict the oldest kind of house, with its one room, requiring an adaptation to necessity. The rich peasant was to be given a house proportionate to the needs of his family, organised so as to make the most of the central hearth. The ideal of the village notable took precedence here, no doubt, over observation of social reality, and the weight of the extensive patriarchal family over that of the limited family, but here, for the first time, a complete scheme was offered for modelling or remodelling the rural house.

Serlio's books of architecture began a traditon that grew richer and richer, from Philibert Delorme, with his *Nouvelles inventions pour bien bâtir à petits frais*, to Blandel's *Distribution des maisons de plaisance*, and from the *Encyclopédie* to the manuals of the nineteenth century. Houses for the poor are infrequent here, but we find in them the constructions of the great estates, and we can see how 'graphic reason' inspired in the modern period, closer and closer control of the relation between design, technology and functions. Mastery of the spatial field contributed to modifying the rural habitat and rural dwellings.[34]

The tax system and the peasant's house

At the beginning of the nineteenth century the rent tax enabled Gabriel Désert to construct a cartographical index which showed in broad outline the geographical distribution of habitats, because it brought together areas built on and the amount of usable space, quality of building materials and comfort – measured by doors and windows.[35] Two Frances were revealed. To the north of a line joining Geneva to Cherbourg, a France of modernised buildings, with the exception of the mountainous areas. To the south of this line, a France of backwardness and mixtures, with Brittany and the Massif Central providing the least satisfactory indices. This diverse regional geography needs to be further divided in accordance with three criteria, as these apply in the respective regions.

The criterion of height highlights the contrast between the civilisations of the South and those of the North, where the habitat lacks storeys. The influence of urban models and the diffusion of architectural plans, depending on wealth, may be felt here.

The criterion of roofing must not be studied solely from the standpoint of the contrast between riches and poverty, or between backwardness and development. Thatch, which may be made of straw, reeds or rushes, is, like wooden roofs, primarily an adaptation to local conditions: thatched roofs may survive development before surrendering to fashion. In Brittany they are more a sign of poverty than is the case in Normandy. Tiles, slate, roofing-stones, heavy roofs are, depending on cases, signs either of modernisation or of tradition. Tiles, machine-made according to different patterns, are making headway everywhere and their look and colour are a major feature of landscapes.

Finally, the criterion of the building material used relates, of course, to the resources available locally, but also to transport costs which, as they diminish, help to unify forms of building. The abundance of quarries ensures, of course, the presence of stone houses everywhere, but the geography of the nineteenth and twentieth centuries does not take account of the mixed composition of old buildings, in which wood may coexist with stone, cob with rubble, half-timbering with brick.

These local choices reflect variations in supply and demand, the hierarchy of means and the accelerated circulation of raw materials, models and aspirations for change. Apart from locally determining factors, the triumph of stone is probably encouraged by the striving for what is scientifically approved and for comfort, fear of fires, improved storage of heat, and, later, by the material's longevity. The stone house is a form of capitalisation, an investment which is costly but durable. The history of the reconstruction of villages destroyed by fire is still to be written: it would make perceptible, on the scale of the whole country, stages of change that would need to be compared with development in equipment, quarries, brickworks, lime-kilns, sawmills and tileworks. It would furnish a chapter in the triumphal progress of the heavy stone house, accelerated by the increase in land rent, by the need for reconstruction – as in the large villages of Lorraine after the Thirty Years' War – and by the diffusion of requirements observed or experienced in towns.[36]

The cottage-to-château hierarchy survived for a long time, but the differences between cottage and château changed. Nöel du Fail describes, in his *Contes nouveaux d'Eutrapel*, the cottage that he saw, perhaps in Brittany, in the second half of the sixteenth century. It was a hut made of mud covered with rushes and straw, 'seventeen feet square and twenty-eight wide, no more, because the villagers said that the nest was big enough for the bird', and all put together with material stolen in the small hours of the night. Poorly heated, littered with tools, meagrely furnished, this house reflected the hard life of its owners.[37] It fits well enough with the idea one is given of the main rural habitat throughout the seventeenth century and part of the eighteenth, as this was observed by Alain Croix in Brittany,[38] or Pierre Goubert in Beauvais and its surrounding areas.[39]

The cottage was gradually replaced by housing that was more expensive and more comfortable, in imitation of the dwellings of rich farmers of estates or other well-to-do cultivators. The contrasts were certainly more striking where the social hierarchy was more accentuated, as in the Ile-de-France, than where it was more homogeneous, as in Brittany, in the vinegrowing regions or in the mountainous areas. On the morrow of the Revolution travellers and statistically minded Prefects emphasised the permanence everywhere of the juxtaposition of an old-type habitat, a mark of archaism and backwardness, with a more adapted habitat, indicating modernism and development and, doubtless, a means of confirming a more general integration.

The eighteenth century thus bequeathed to the future not so much an overall transformation as a localised advance confined to certain regions and restricted socially by the peasants' capacity for investment, increased by the sense of distinctive success and the diffusion of models of decor and of lifestyle. In the North of France, around the towns, movement was faster. Yet the house of Balzac's peasant is strangely similar to that of Eutrapel's villein: a nest or burrow, yet enlarged, with two rooms, a loft, a cellar, a yard and sheds. The literary image never renders reality completely, except in so far as it shows direction of development. Here the peasant, freed by the Revolution, sometimes more comfortable, living better (to appreciate that, it is enough to compare the two descriptions of furniture) symbolises the taste for property which grows little by little, accompanied by concealment of increased wealth.

The vinegrower's house in Beaujolais[40]

Villages in the mountainous part of Beaujolais are organised in concentric circles. The first circle is that of the homes, with each one corresponding to a family. The second is that of the relations between the houses. Prevailing in the first circle are bonds of mutual affection, spontaneous relations marked by deep familiarity and free exchange. In the second circle we enter relations of power, rules of culture, commercialisation and the market.

The space of the house corresponds to the two domains. The historian defines this by adding principles. The home is a fiscal unit but also a demographic group, the centre of the farm and a *locus* of social relations. Nothing is superimposed, everything is mingled so as to endow the rural house with its security-ensuring power, both biological and economic, so as to shelter and embody these different relations. This feature depends primarily on the size of the house. Its dimensions vary in accordance with the owner of wealth and position in the community. At its lowest, with a small yard and garden, it is less than a hundred square metres, as in the case of Jean Rivoire's house at Saint-Genis-Laval. At its highest we find a barn, a hayloft, storerooms, fermenting rooms, cellars and something like a park – 3,800 square metres, as with Jean Brunet's place at Saint-Germain.

Most of the houses in Beaujolais were content with a *bas*, a ground floor containing a single, all-purpose room, sometimes divided into bedroom and kitchen, and an upper floor containing bedroom and loft. The notables and traders had more complex habitats. The smallest tenants, lacking property, and averaging ten per cent per village, paid heavy rents – 130 to 150 *livres* a year around 1750. Most people possessed one or more houses with some annexes, 59 per cent of them with gardens, yards and sheds. The house conformed to the social, family and agricultural system of life. In its architecture it reflected the social hierarchy without exaggerating this: the true stratification was based on cellars (capacity for storing wine) and land. Grouped in widely spaced villages with detached buildings, open to the soil, the houses of the Beaujolais vinegrowers were very homogeneous and adapted to the needs and capacities of the families who lived in them.

The pseudo-manor-houses of the Ile-de-France

Between the sixteenth and the eighteenth century a group of farmers established themselves in the great grain-growing plains adjoining Paris.[41] They conquered the local and regional space through their work and through the continuity of great dynasties of heads of enterprises, either as tenants or as owners, but all of them managing estates the structures of which changed with concentration of landownership and of the receipts from seigniorial rights. A good birth-rate enabled them to effect a minor migration into the clergy and the merchant class and also into official positions, and ensured a fair number of ennoblements through the secretariat of the chancellery.

The centre of these great estates – 234 hectares at Chaalis, 254 hectares at Choisy-aux Boeufs – was the residence of the farmer, built according to Estienne's formula for a house in the country. In the villages, grouped together but sometimes isolated, various buildings surrounded a rather extensive yard, with drinking-troughs and stables. A central residential bloc was reserved for the owner – two storeys, with cellar, loft, living-room and bedroom. The farmer's residence was more or less large, and included cowsheds, stables, barns and sheep-pens. The whole had been adapted or re-adapted. Since the sixteenth century tiles had displaced thatch, except for the roofs of small outbuildings, and chalky millstone material had taken over. The farmers' advance payments had often enabled the owners to maintain and sometimes to improve the buildings, which survived economic fluctuations but were more and more expensive to keep up. In the eighteenth century the owners tried to reduce their costs by re-structuring the buildings: the grouping of farms made this possible, through putting the burden of expense on to the tenant-farmers. Actual enrichment made improvement possible: the central living-room might have parlours and bedrooms added to it, and concern for interior decoration began to appear. The standard of living of the gentleman-farmers found expression, perhaps, more in the decor of their houses than in the masonry, the structures of which underwent little change, while imperceptible interior transformation indicated adaptation to new needs.

Improvements were made to agricultural buildings, but the farmers' habitat reflected this general evolution with delay. It had to be replaced by and large by the village or the big hamlets of the grain-growing plateaux and valleys. It coexisted with other forms in the Gâtinais, Hurepoix and Brie: the houses of small farmers, vinegrowers, craftsmen or labourers, owned or rented, which formed the principal fabric of relations in the village community.[42]

Country house and presbytery, models and contrasts

When we try to understand how it was that the traditional patterns of the rural habitat underwent change, several models come to mind: the lord's farm, the rustic house, the country house (*château*). The last-named constituted an enclave of luxury in the countryside, and the way it evolved depended much on the culture and the resources of the landowners. Consider Combourg, where young Chateaubriand spent his childhood. A place from where authority was exercised and agricultural activity directed, and where the landowner lived, the archaism of the house contrasted, in its size, with the withdrawn way of life and the reduced dimensions of the family. While the writer describes the paternal *château* with the vocabulary and the literary allusions of a period that liked gloomy novels and the Gothic, it remains the case that through the political significance of the evocation there shows the failure of the setting and decor to adapt to the life of the time. Practices no longer correspond to places, means to needs, a status unforgotten and unforgettable no longer conforms to society as it is.[43] Combourg can serve as symbol of the twofold effect of distance created by privilege and by the building which embodies privilege in the societies of the peasant world. It is not accidental, perhaps, that so many *châteaux* and abbeys have involuntarily served to improve the rural habitat by serving as quarries! The influence of a way of life was certainly more inspiriting when the nobility set the example.

We can measure the force of this with another model, invented by Pierre Gouhier in Normandy on the basis of the decrees of the King's Council authorising reconstruction, namely, the presbytery.[44] Being paid for by the parishes, it was an object of concern for communities wishing to provide the priest with a suitable dwelling while keeping down the cost thereof. This was also what the *intendants* wished, since they were interested in preventing increases in local indebtedness. This dual preoccupation has left us an extensive body of documents, which include estimates, plans and accounts. Several hundred buildings bear witness *in situ* to the scale of this campaign of development. At Longivilliers, near Caen, in 1783, the estimate amounted to 6,725 *livres*, adjudged at 5,250 *livres* net cost, without the land, 1,486 for timber, 2,806 *livres* for masonry, the rest for the construction of a house fifteen metres by six, with kitchen, parlour, washplace, cellar, servants' quarters, two bedrooms and lavatory on the upper floor, in fine dressed stone and roofed with thatch of 'wheaten straw'. This was unquestionably a level which testifies to real progress, by adapting to the standardisation of plans, all on the model of the house with a central corridor, arranged symmetrically, with its residential character predominant. It bears the mark of a kind of life improved by concern for comfort – heating and lighting are taken into account – and shows the permanence of utilisation of local building materials: Caen stone, Mortain granite, thatch. It reflects also the gap opening between the old traditional habitat and the new forms the longevity of which is based on stone and on constant maintenance.

In the history of the rural house the habitat of the non-peasant notables doubtless contributed, through its size, its materials and its signs of comfort, to the general evolution of distributions and arrangements. It combined with the bridgehead of influence won by the positivism of the agronomists and the hygienism of the notables, as demonstrated, between the eighteenth century and the beginning of the nineteenth, by the activity of the societies of agriculture and by publications and manuals. Here we see coming together the architects' mastery of space and the evolution of the peasantry's functions and structures.[45]

Density and continuity. The urban house

Several elements contribute to modifying the general conditions of the urban habitat. First, the density of population gathered in a more restricted space. In towns one does not move so easily from one circle of relations to another as one does in villages, and relations operate differently. Then there is the organisation of property in towns, which corresponds to a close parcelling out of the land: the houses are huddled against each other and the streets are laid out so as to respect this old division of the ground, being narrow and without views. In Rouen J.-P. Bardet calculated that 15 per cent of the streets were less than five metres wide, and this was true of 90 per cent of them in the old centre of Paris in the seventeenth century.

Ordinary life goes on within a confined space, in promiscuity and crowding, for town planning schemes come up against opposition both from landowners and from inhabitants disturbed in their routines. Urban equipment, the monuments of the church or of the state, the squares and palaces, the town houses of the aristocracy, with their outbuildings and gardens, bring into this crowded setting some breaks in continuity and breathing-spaces. The history of town-planning, which emphasises changes made in the course of centuries, shows how hard it is to develop the new districts which are made necessary by the spread of towns and the aspirations of new social categories[46] – as in Paris with the Faubourgs Saint-Germain and Saint-Honoré in the seventeenth and eighteenth centuries, and in Lyons with the nobles in the Ainay district or the big bourgeoisie of trade in Les Terreaux. The town as a whole, leaving aside major town-planning operations, openings-up and development of quays and squares, as well as localised enterprises of a speculative character, evolves more slowly. The changes undertaken bring into conflict the town's politicians and groups, municipalities, the Army, the Church and social classes – for or against a town that is more open and modernised, as in Caen. In Lyons, Paris and Rouen movement also took the form of reconstructions on the spot, heightening of buildings, fillings-in of back-yards. The area covered by dwellings had to be increased, the density of occupation in the renovated blocks had to be reduced, and new arrivals had to be accommodated. These operations resulted in exchanges of population, with the old occupants sometimes unable to pay the higher rents and the immigrants crowding together in a way the 'integrated' townspeople did not.

A third factor of differentiation follows from the very nature of town life, the complexity of which has already been mentioned. The town, the saying went, meant freedom, but it needs to be added that this was freedom under supervision. The Ancien Régime saw a decisive trans-formation in this sphere. A bourgeois, corporative and Christian concep-tion of a society which organises its relations in customary and organic fashion, with acknowledged inequalities experienced and displayed, for example, in the urban ritual of processions and festivals, was replaced by a vision at once simple and more complex introduced by the absolute monarchy.[47] Simpler, because the supervision of the social groups be-came tighter and bound them to the state in their definition and function-ing: a certain independence was lost, which resulted in changed relations for everyone. More complex, because the organisation of supervision of the towns-people imposed authorities without always solving all conflicts. Policy for the habitat, for town-planning developed within this general evolution in which, after the great reforms at the end of the seventeenth century and the appointment of Lieutenants-General, the police inter-vened more and more, supervising building work, property settlements and ways of life.[48] In Paris Commissioner Delamare depicted, in his *Traité de la police* written at the end of his career, all aspects of this conception of urban life in which the house, the neighbourhood, the street, circulation were factors active in the process of acculturating the townspeople. The towns, which had formerly been stuck in an unchangeable past, with their foundations no less firmly fixed than those of the ramparts, now stirred, emerged from their state of immobility, and adopted new forms of or-ganisation and new ways of dividing up space.[49] The towns, the centres of exchanges and services, included buildings and houses in which all func-tions and all types of towns-people found their places.

Relations between town and country nevertheless remained funda-mental. The town was still complementary to the country, but dependent on it for rent and population. If it was differentiated from the country, then this was through protection, freedoms and, in sum, way of life. The urban house was thus going to mark itself off through the strength and speed of growth of the urban organisms and by a progressive spatial differentation. The low height of the houses and the presence of cow-sheds, stables and gardens contributed to the urban fabric a rural charac-ter which was destined to last a long time, especially in small towns. On the other hand, in active metropolitan centres when former country-folk – gardeners, market-gardeners, farmers – reconstructed their homes, they built urban houses along the roads traversing the marshland which had been divided up and regrouped, behind embankments. This happened in the suburbs of Paris, which were turned into towns through the taste of the bourgeois for investment in land and for rural leisure activities.[50]

We must not forget that the town also depended on the country for its building materials, stone and the local roof-covering, and for its building techniques, the choice between a house of timber or of stone. The vertical timber-framing of Rouen's houses is found elsewhere in Normandy: the purlin timbering in which the rafters support the roof-covering is men-tioned in the customary of the forests. Transition from one model to another was slow, as we can still see today in the backyards of houses in Rennes that were rebuilt after the fire of 1720.[51] It depended on a number of factors and, everywhere, on the activity and culture of the builders, architects, entrepreneurs and workers in the building trade, masons, carpenters, roofers, joiners, glaziers, plumbers and engineers from the royal institutions.[52]

Clashes and agreements could take place in various ways between these levels of intervention. Architects often defended academic principles: the aesthetic of magnificence and convenience, mistress of regularity, sym-metry and order. Sometimes we see them engaging in more speculative undertakings, as in Mansart's case. The engineer in the service of the state and the public authorities supports the primacy of utility and the manage-ment of a productive space, governed by reason and geometry. Between the two, the entrepreneurs, the masters, were certainly the ones who exercised greatest influence on the ordinary habitat. Readers of surveys and summary plans, they were guided by profit and technology. They were the least-known of the actors in an architecture which very often lacked an architect.

For the rest, models circulated faster, reflecting new needs more quick-ly than in the country. From Philibert Delorme to Blondel, we are often in the domain of the masterpiece of magnificence offered to the Prince or to men of power.[53] With *La Manière de bien bâtir*, published in Paris in 1623 by Pierre Le Muet, a former collaborator with Salomon de Brosse and an engineer in Richelieu's service, we possess, for the modern town, a testimony similar to Serlio's. Le Muet's aim was to demonstrate a way of building on all the surfaces offered and imposed by the fragmentation of the land, between 27 and 1,000 square metres, by adapting his formulae to spaces, with all the distributions convenient to the landowners. A *vade-mecum* for a public of educated builders and their clients attracted by the prospect of investment in real estate, this treatise was directed at a market that was noticeably increasing. Four editions ensured its success down to 1685: in 1728 it was plagiarised by Charles-Antoine Briseux, and in 1764 by Charles-Antoine Jombert.

For Le Muet, who was thus read and re-read until the eighteenth century, narrowness and grandeur dominate the plan. For the small house of less than thirty square metres, there were four levels and three storeys, a fireplace on each floor and the same number of tenant households. When depth increases the plan can be diversified, height can be increased as well, and concern for privacy can grow. Beyond, main buildings are added on. Le Muet favours masonry and regularly ordains façades, roofs and ridges. The success of his work brought homogeneity to the buildings in Paris and subsequently to those in the provinces. His treatise idealises ordinary architecture: he does not mention the shops and workshops which everywhere occupied part of the ground floor. He targets the builders and their clients, financiers, lawyers, persons of talent who are the first to adopt an improved way of life. His influence was characterised by the normative aspect of the constituent elements, which reflected his experience as an engineer, and by his choices – stone, not timber. His ability as a teacher facilitated the use of these materials through provision of plans and bills of quantities.

Here we see again how 'graphic reason' was able to model space and offer programmes of domestic architecture for which innovations were introduced into established practices, making possible a living re-appropriation of the norms. The urban house does not exist as such: it is as diverse and complex as the rural dwelling because it results from the aesthetic and utilitarian logics learnt by the builders and expressed in their projects for housing, but also from the logic of the owners, and tenants and the way in which they live between the private and the public worlds.

Urban houses: diversity and functionality

While the urban space became increasingly a patrimony to be administered, the economy of the built-up area was echoing the movements in production and consumption, though without completely taking account of the debates engendered by the intersection of needs that were private and social, functional and symbolic.

The urban house responded to demands that were various and inseparable. It was a tool, harbouring as it did trading activities, shops and offices. In the Palais Royal, after 1776, Victor Louis organised around the function of trade the built-up area to which the financial problems of the Orleans family had given rise. Under the arcades of the buildings bordering the garden could be found all the ingredients of an urban society receptive to new forms of consumption: luxury shops, modistes, bookshops, theatres, bars, restaurants. Everywhere one recognised the signs of a mobile sociability that had undergone partial change. Elsewhere, workshops and means of production were set up wherever possible. The bakehouses of the Paris bakers occupied the back-shops on the ground floor, the basements or the cellars, to a greater or lesser extent depending on their activity.[54] The dressmakers' workshops were scattered through the upper floors while the enterprises of famous modistes decorated the ground floors of business houses, so that passers-by could see through their windows the *grisettes* busy at their work.[55] Attempts made by municipal and royal regulation to expel polluting and smelly activities from residential centres gradually took effect, getting rid of tanners, tripe-dealers, butchers and dyers, so that the relation to work and environment was changed.

The house was also capital, a commodity, a selected investment, the embodiment of representative and distinctive values. It was both profitable and expensive and saw its fate determined by the fortunes of families, changes in the appreciation of real estate, the 'freezing' of tracts of land by church ownership on rich aristocratic town-houses.[56] Finally, it was, with greater or lesser degrees of freedom, convenience and display, the place where private life met the collective or public space, between houses and streets, buildings and highways. Numberless relationships were present, even if only through cleaning, lighting, removal of mud and rubbish, and repair-work.

Only gradually, in the nineteenth century, did the municipalities win their struggle for ascendancy, causing buildings to close in on themselves. The pavement, as the pathway for townsfolk to use for all social communications and needs of trade, was to symbolise the new relation. Tried out at the end of the eighteenth century in the new districts of Paris, it became a dominant feature of provincial towns only after 1830.[57] The relation between the house and the town as a whole underwent change, through the progress of control over the common space and the triumph of that privacy which had begun to emerge in aristocratic standards and practices two centuries earlier.[58]

Urban policy, social appropriations

It was this general context which caused the building, distribution and uses of dwellings to evolve. The changes took place differently depending on the scale of the population, the proximity of authority, the social level, the acceleration or slowing down of measures of town-planning or policing, and depending also on the circulation of architectural models, bearers of aesthetic standards and requirements for comfort, which progressed starting at the end of the eighteenth century.[59]

Luxury and beauty were distributed unevenly but, if account be taken of representational values and social imperatives, we can see that three indices guided urban policy. The multiplication of building operations (which burst forth everywhere, in Paris and the provinces alike) favoured transfers of the technical solutions tried out in aristocratic houses to the dwellings of everyone at large. The general quality of building work, the nobler materials used, the better-ordered decoration, the improved ornamentation of interiors – grandeur, regularity, rationality – transformed old towns, which were 'de-Gothicised' and modernised. Finally, internal distribution, becoming specialised, separating the spaces where visitors were received from the private ones, provided, through cleverer arrangement, greater comfort and tranquillity. A habitat of the new classes came into being at the end of the eighteenth century, obliterating the distinction between town-houses and other premises. We can see the model for this in *Plans, coupes, élévations des plus belles maisons construites à Paris et dans les environs*, published in 1801, or in the plans for the Hosten apartments built by Ledoux in the Rue Saint-Georges.

Pierre Pinon suggests that there were three stages in this non-linear evolution that marked the great transformation of the town and the house.[60] First of all, isolated buildings were erected without any constraints other than those imposed by town-planning regulations and the petty divisions of ownership of the land the building stood on. Then buildings developed between yard and street, subject to the same regulations, but with the petty divisions disappearing, as can be seen from the regroupings of land-units due to the royal squares. Finally, more extensive operations appeared, in the building of *ilots*, small blocks in which the scale of constraints and monumentalisation was the same for all buildings and which necessitated very substantial regrouping of units of landownership.[61] From the seventeenth century the Ile-Saint-Louis provides, within the setting of a policy of extension and development, an example of the residential districts which saw the appearance of the 'stone-built town' of the grand classical style. Masonry and timber advanced together, making possible the creation of the typical Parisian house. This was a fine illustration of the power of Le Muet's model and the sworn surveyors. We discover it at Versailles, a new town for the King to live in, with unified layout, where the new habitat accompanied the palaces in structure, before it was overtaken by rented buildings and surpassed by development that was more extensive, more anarchic and less careful of town-planning regulations.[62] Other examples are to be found in the same great provincial capitals – Bordeaux, Nantes, Caen, Rouen, Toulouse – with nuances and variations due to the impact of the financial powers and local architectural influences.

The reconstruction of Rennes after the fire again offers a good illustration.[63] This operation, which involved the authorities, the *intendant* and the members of the *Parlement* in approving the plans of the architect Robelin, followed by Gabriel, resulted in the creation of some general amenities – bridges, squares, monumental palaces. The bulk of the task of reconstruction was left to private financing and to individuals, who preferred rented buildings to grand town-houses. The operation made general the house of two or three storeys, with a façade of stone but often with outhouses of timber hidden under their plaster. With a wide variety of innovations, Rennes established new standards of decor and comfort, as well as fireplaces.

The extension of Lyons gives us another example, richly documented by the analysis of the tax on income derived from renting houses which describes plots built upon and not built upon, distinguishes the sizes of houses, their situation, their surface area and height, and shows us the changes effected in techniques and the choices made by the entrepreneurs and owners. The criteria for the dwelling did not have the same meaning, given the same size, in the case of a bachelor's lodging and in that of a craftsman's family, or in the newly built well-to-do districts and in the old poor districts on the right bank of the Saône.[64]

Three types of dwelling appear in Lyons, The most frequently found consists of a single room, twenty square metres in size, which houses young families, single men working in the silk trade and working girls not living in with their employers. These rooms, lacking comfort, and situated on every floor, are very numerous in the overcrowded districts of the town centre. Most of the population, however, lived in a different type of house in which workshop or shop was combined with living quarters. The economic criteria coincided with those for construction and were little different from the ones which applied in Paris. A house with a frontage of 7.50 metres on the street was divided by a central passage, with two shops and a bedroom overlooking the yard on each side, and with two apartments on each floor – at least from the second floor upward – which gave an area of at least 50 square metres. This model, repeated from one district to the next, and from one occupation to another, with variations according to the requirements of the trade and the size of the household, is found in about 7,000 cases. Any extension of activity, for example, the purchase of a loom, meant encroaching on living-quarters. Privacy was obtained by the tenants themselves making closets and recesses or by putting children out to nurse. Finally, an almost bourgeois type of building appears with the more far-reaching town-planning of the seventeenth and eighteenth centuries. Both shops and flats could not be bigger. Higher than before, the building housed more people owing to the subdivision of the floors, from the roomy flats on the first floor to the garrets on the fifth. Thus, for many people, the quality of the habitat worsened, while for a minority it improved, as the town grew.[65]

Similar lessons could be drawn from Marseilles, a town which grew in extent as well as in population.[66] In both the old and the new districts the narrow house on a narrow plot was most frequently met with. Built in stone, with a façade of four or five metres, it sheltered all trades, all types of business and mingled all social groups. The two signs of change were connected with the appearance of town houses, as at Aix, and bourgeois residences that were not particularly uniform. Accommodation underwent little change in the seventeenth and eighteenth centuries. The rent that could be obtained for a house, and its surface area, were measured by the number of windows. It was less and less frequently the two-storey building and cost more and more. Marseilles became densely populated in the centre and thinned out in the periphery, without districts becoming segregated.

These provincial examples are not very different from what we find in Paris. The capital was in 1789 a town of tenants, so far as four-fifths of the wage-earning and domestic population were concerned, making up, doubtless, more than two-thirds of the total population[67] – three-quarters of the 3,000 inventories analysed in *La naissance de l'intime*.[68] Ownership of one's residence was rare, a class indicator. More than four-fifths of the Parisians lived in one room or two: where we find them living in more than four or five rooms we are dealing with the better-off classes. The aristocratic town-house was a scarce type of dwelling, doubtless numbering between 500 and 1,000 before 1789, and it housed a complex population. The lot of the inhabitants was therefore, most often, to be huddled together, except in the new quarters with larger buildings and in some parts of the outskirts. Rents increased just as in the provinces. Before 1700 tenants paid thirty-five to forty-five *livres* a year for a room, and certainly three times as much for two or three rooms, and on the eve of the Revolution the corresponding figures were 60 and 150 *livres*. The gaps grew between the comfortable and the modest habitat. This contributed to breaking up the social fabric, since choices were inevitable and linked with the size and capabilities of families. Most people were crowded into old buildings that had been adapted, and life spilled out on to the common spaces and the street. Specialisation of the rooms which separated the functions of the dwelling – kitchen, bedroom, living-rooms, etc. – had meaning only if there were more than two or three rooms. Imitation of the distribution found in the town-house or the rich family's apartment spread to the new buildings. Its success reflected, for limited circles, a change in culture, the appearance of a separation between what was public and what was private, the need for a more reliable refuge for the new emotional life of couples and families.

The history of the culture of the habitat remains a vast field of study in which we must be wary of the facts so far obtained and mistrustful of crude pictures or excessively simple conclusions. The varied documentary sources do indeed show, for the country as for the town, the importance of costs and of time. The rural house was never uniform, nor did the urban house ever correspond to a single model. It is the coexistence in time of different generations that is characteristic of buildings in modern France, yet nothing is unmoving or unmoveable. The transformation of the country districts brought about a slow evolution in habits and houses, a transformation that proceeded more quickly in towns, where things and values circulated faster. In order to know what exactly happened in the living spaces of past periods we need to understand more fully the mediations operating between architectural forms, ways of distribution, and the practices – heating, lighting, furnishing – which reflected different relations of dependence or different form of relations to space and perception of standards.[69]

5   Lighting and heating

The way that old-time houses were built and arranged responded, just as today, to essential needs, but the latter had then a commanding power which has been mitigated for us because these needs are now usually met by means of technical procedures that are easy to use even if not to instal. Our relation to heat and cold, and to light, whether this be bright or faint, no longer takes us by surprise, unless circumstances are exceptional: a severe winter, a burning hot summer, a protracted power-cut during a strike, a voyage that bears us far from our own climate, discovery of the world of the homeless in the midst of urban prosperity. As a result of a long history of struggle against the elements, our architectures incorporate features, nowadays commonplace, for resisting those forces of nature – heat, excessive cold or freeze-ups and the variation in natural light as the day goes by – forces which affect health and work and which depend on the rhythm of the seasons, the movements of the sun and atmospheric changes. Since the nineteenth century a general policy on planning both national and local has multiplied regulations and obligations, imposing upon builders in town and country principles of comfort and convenience which have totally altered conditions governing the healthfulness of habitats, improved insulation and ventilation, lighting and the penetration of sunshine. Relations to the world outside and the relation between private and public have been overturned and urban ways of life have been imposed on everyone, subjecting the rural world to fresh constraints.

Cold and heat, light and darkness

Traditional society, faced with all these problems, had recourse to a variety of methods. Insulation could be obtained naturally in the habitat of cavemen, hollowed out in the sides of chalk valleys where heat-storage and hydrometrical conditions were almost ideal without requiring much work to be done.[1] Most often the struggle against the elements and nature began with the construction of dwellings, with selection of insulating materials adapted to the local climate, provision of restricted openings, quest for methods of insulation against damp, arrangement of rooms, and utilisation of the body-heat of animals to warm human beings.

In this way the inhabitants of mountainous and stock-rearing regions were able to resist excessive winter cold. In Haut-Marche, above the 600 metre line, snow lies all through winter. It stays for forty days, on average. There are considerable variations in temperature: over 34° in August and below 24° in December and January, at Gouzon.[2] Only buildings that were solid and stocky, with walls of stone torn from the local quarries of schist or granite and roofs of thatch made from threshed rye (in 1850 70 per cent of the houses were still using this), with only one room, dark and unhealthy, small windows, stout, reinforced doors, a single fireplace and an adjacent cowshed, enabled the inhabitants to withstand the severe living conditions. People and animals lived together, following the same rhythm, in a time-honoured companionship which began to disappear only at the end of the nineteenth century.[3]

Steady warmth was thus secured at the expense of purity of the atmosphere. The microbe-killing rays of the sun failed to gain access to the traditional dwelling and the most common habitat, where animals and human beings huddled together, living in a relation to cold, heat, light, fresh air, smells, cleanliness and filth which it is hard for us to imagine. The environment of everyday technologies, the possibilities for creating a favourable artificial climate, were transformed by discoveries made in the nineteenth and twentieth centuries. Before that time peasants and townspeople alike had to manage as best they could, in accordance with old-established methods, if they were to get a minimum of protection. These methods were, of course, combined in their operation and their evolution, in parallel or separately, resulting gradually in cumulative effects on ways of life.

These minimalist solutions were based on the way houses were built and arranged, and therefore on the technical and cultural traditions of a given locality: the thickness of the walls; the size of the windows and where they were situated; the nature of the flooring – beaten earth, tiles, flagstones, floorboards, wood; the preparation of the walls – plastered and limewashed, panelled or papered, and with a variety of forms of protection. In the struggle against the cold anything and everything could be brought into play, depending on possibilities and requirements that differed within society. Clothing and bedding were important means to this end, and the way they were used reflects changes in needs.

In the eighteenth century a turning-point came when an increasingly large section of the population began to give greater weight to comfort (*confort*) in its ordinary arrangements. The word *confort* is old, in the meaning of 'consolation' and 'help' (today, in France, we say *reconfort*):

Furetière and the Academy's dictionary place it in the vocabulary of assistance and rescue. It came into use after changing its meaning, through the fashion for England and English ways, to signify the quest for material well-being. This semantic journey is symbolic of a certain type of material exchange with Great Britain, but what it shows, above all, is the retreat of a climate of austerity and scarcity, the spread of a notion that was needed to express ease in everyday life. Furetière saw in well-being (*le bien-être*) 'the situation of a person who lives conveniently, lacking nothing that is appropriate to his condition'. Elementary needs became means to refinement, 'conveniences' became more exacting, and the thinking of architects and inventors responded to a changing demand, more delicate, less crude.

Up to then the solutions found to requirements in respect of heat and light had not changed much for thousands of years, which does not mean that they had not changed at all. Fire and the mastering of fire are bound up with the very beginnings of human life. Measures to control it both so as to restrict the danger it threatens and so as to feed and maintain it were among the skills inherited from one's ancestors, and were directed to many purposes: cooking, heating, lighting, the work of very varied industries of transformation, textiles, breweries, smithies, dyeworks, food-production. Fire was everywhere present in town and village. From town to country the mastering of fire changed in scope and in the equipment used. In society it varied from the homeless poor, whom the cold could kill, to the rich, snug and protected by all available means of defence. The capacity of people to protect themselves against cold differed completely, from the single room of the common man's dwelling, in town or country, to complex residences with many rooms, more subtle conveniences and a more refined sociability. We shall refrain from making a value-judgement such as is made by reformers of all sorts, concerning these different ways of life: the common people were not animals.[4]

Sensitivity to cold and heat floats between the innate and the acquired: it is a profoundly cultural fact, like one's tolerance or intolerance of light. It is also a biological phenomenon, since men, women and children do not react to heat and cold in the same way. When promiscuity and crowding served as all-purpose remedy for cold, relations between the sexes, attitudes to children, use of clothing for protection, enclosing of beds and accumulation of coverings or feather-beds, all came together to define a protective microbiotype of which today's custom of separate bedrooms no longer gives us any idea. It was the combination of all these elements, the resonance of one in relation to the others that made for habituation or rejection, and body and intelligence were equally involved. The eighteenth century saw here one of its most interesting processes of change, because this drew upon the evolution of technology and the improvement in equipment no less than the less visible mutations in private and collective behaviour.[5] We observe in this case a progressive distancing from that basic dependence on nature and its rhythms which imposes fluctuations in life and labour, making the best of the season of fine weather and withdrawing when winter comes.

The annual procession of this life-cycle is portrayed in the autobiographies of the period. That of the glazier Ménétra, for whom mobility, work and leisure are governed by the sun's movements and the caprices of the weather.[6] That of Bordier, a peasant in the Beauce, whose work, punctuated throughout by the alternation of sunrise and sunset, foresees both the rhythm of toil and the level of reward, and is organised in accordance with a clear awareness of the succession of months.[7] In the season of fine weather, short and intense, are concentrated as many activities as possible – transactions, harvests, moves – and life is directed outward. The season of bad weather, prolonged and compelling withdrawal to the hearth, is as though directed towards waiting for the renewal of nature in the spring and summer. Life is closed in on itself and the need for warmth and light is at its greatest.

The traditional calendar of Christian and popular festivals took account of this organisation, punctuating the alternation of darkness and light, the retreat of the gloom and the coming of the new days. The offices and chants of the Church particularly emphasised the caesura about Eastertide. We can understand the spiritual resonance when, beneath the arches of cathedrals and famous churches, resound the lamentations of Charles Richard de Lalande and the musical exaltations of Couperin or Bach. In these rituals light has its place and the blessing of the Easter candle symbolises resurrection and continuing salvation. In popular and collective culture Christmas with its log-fires, Shrove Tuesday with its torches, Midsummer Day with its flames all bear witness to the attachment to rites involving fire, despite a clergy with a stricter attitude to superstitions and a social elite more utilitarian and hostile to the people's too-numerous holidays.[8] In the dialogue between man and nature in the modern world, the conflict between night and day endowed fire and light with powerful symbolic meaning, for it was also a confrontation between man and himself.

Feu (fire) which became a fiscal term, and *foyer* (hearth, home) incarnating the forces of privacy and the new kind of family relationship, express the centrality of phenomenological values in the material universe of the house. Nurtured by ancient philosophical theories, fed by myths and dreams, fleshed out and sometimes canalised by reasoning reason – think of the unusual history of the chemistry of fire, which did not meet its definitive rational destiny until Lavoisier and Priestley – these values are at work in ways of life and thought.

Here the history of material culture finds an ideal field in which power and complexity are revealed. Prometheus and the risks entailed by knowledge, Empedocles and the fascination of fires are fables which, as Bachelard says, show that with fire everything changes and vacillates. Thanks to fire, life is no longer the same. The definitions of private and universal, of good and bad, of cures and burns, of day and night,[9] acquire new meaning. In the seventeenth and eighteenth centuries men exercised their capacity for research and invention. They changed the 'deal' on this thousand-year-old terrain, developed another world of which we are the heirs and dependants both in material respects and in matters of intellectual analyses and sensibility.

Night and day

In 1698 Parisians used to sing, by day and by night, a song which left nothing unclear:

Le bout de Monsieur d'Argenson se raccourcit avec la lune,
Il devient un colimaçon le bout de Monsieur d'Argenson,
Mais il est plus gros et plus long quand il voit paraître la brune,
Le bout de Monsieur d'Argenson se raccourcit avec la lune.

['Monsieur d'Argenson's end shrinks with the moon, and becomes a snail. But it grows thicker and longer when he sees that nightfall is approaching.' The words *la brune* could mean either 'nightfall' or 'the dark-haired girl' – Trans.]

To the tune of a triplet, the singer and his public were laughing at a *Lieutenant de police* who was hard and pitiless towards the people. Behind the sexual joke we can make out some information which is to our purpose.[10] First, that there was public lighting in the streets of Paris. Its extensive network of lamp-posts was no small thing and technical prowess was needed to maintain it. The King endeavoured, through an ordinance, to have similar lighting provided in all big towns. Then the target changes. When M. d'Argenson cut down on night-time lighting in order to save money by clipping the 'candle-ends' on fifteen to twenty days a year, the Parisians, deprived of their lighting, protested. From this affair we can date exactly the expression of a collective need. Finally, this new sensitivity testifies to the shift that had taken place between what was 'day-time' and what was 'night-time', through the effect of measures taken by the city's administration. It had become indispensable to light up the night, even when the moon was shining.

This requirement expressed a cultural change which was profound and general.[11] It is reflected more clearly to our eyes through knowledge of the technical procedures and of their installation by regulations than by the manifestation of immediate, irrational reactions which eventually leave few traces. Very significant also is the ideology which gradually spread out from Paris. A task of setting the urban space in order, making it safer, cleaner and more orderly, fell to the *Lieutenants de police*, following La Reynie's example after 1667. Finally, comparison between the natural and social dimensions of this mutation, in which thenceforth the social was almost always dominant, reveals transformations which are interlocked.

In seeking to follow this evolution we shall be sorry to find that sources, other than administrative ones, are so few, or else interpreting them is such a delicate business, as is interpreting the iconography of the subject. Georges de la Tour is well known as a 'painter of light',[12] but to say that is merely to emphasise the difficulty. By what route was that flaring chiaroscuro arrived at, magnifying the inner life against very artificial backlighting? The aesthetic of a spiritual mediation is achieved by the most ordinary of methods – the flame of a candle, the trembling of a lantern's beam – as much as by the value proclaimed for new forms of prayer and worship, indeed of spirituality, as, for instance, in the association of the book with light.

The economic aspect of the phenomenon[13] has been little studied. Yet it is no trivial matter, for equipping a town with lights and (on a smaller scale) doing the same for a family is an expensive business. Maintenance and replacement pile up in budgets as expenses of consumption which come to a considerable amount for the kingdom as a whole. The service had need of specialists in metal to make the lamp-posts and specialists in glass to provide the panes, not forgetting the ropemakers for the hanging lamps. Several corporations were thus engaged, at the noon-day of the Enlightenment, in furnishing urban equipment. During his tour of southern France Jacques-Louis Ménétra made this a speciality of his. For every lamp, however, a candle was required, and that brought in other circuits: there was a need for tallow, a by-product of the slaughterhouses and butchers' shops which stank the towns out, and for the less smelly vegetable waxes which were bought by private individuals. In short, there was a need for many technical procedures and commercial channels, stretching from rural production to general consumption. At every stage these gave rise to problems of supply and of economic choices concerning quality. They called for decisions on quantity, which inspired inventive activity aimed at improving the instruments or the fuel used for lighting: the latter might be solid (tallow and wax) or liquid (oil). The town's consumption depended on either large-scale trade or local supplies, on whale-hunting and on the keeping of honey-bees.[14]

Moreover, the struggle against night could become a matter of pride and ostentation, not only because it was expensive but also because it formed one of the conquests of civilisation, one among a number of these that had not yet become commonplace. It is hard for us to conceive, in that world of scarcity, and of luxury without comfort, the abrupt contrasts between day and night which proverbs still strongly recall and which populate the imagination with so many phantasms. The eighteenth century brought into prominence the force of distinctions: easily available light was, first of all, something for rich people and for the town, but it was also a new and powerful relation which established itself between the development of a system of vision, of lighting that had been improved in quantity and quality, and the affirmation of the intellectual primacy of the sensualist system regarding cognition. From Locke to Condillac, nobody escaped this. The prime place in the senses and in cognition which the modern age gave to the sense of sight called into question the whole balance of sensations and the way in which these were apprehended. Enlightening oneself already meant bringing light, and reading, carried forward by the increase in printed and written material, amplified the phenomenon still further. We understand better the link that could exist between the collective action of the police and individuals' choices in this vast movement to promote clarity. By homogenising time it helped to drive away ancestral fears, and because it could provide a greater degree of safety it favoured a better mastering of spaces.

Similar questions arise in relation to heating. Struggling with a fire that is going out, reviving a flickering candle, protecting one's wax taper from draughts when one goes down into the cellar, are all acts that concretely humanise these questions, like thawing out the ink which, in winter, freezes in the inkwells of schoolchildren and of scholars with numb fingers. That world of chilblains, runny noses, illusory shadows and work that stops when the sun goes down has passed far from us who have known other technical triumphs. Yet, when we reflect upon its ancient structures and its capacities for change, we can test the spread of a new inventiveness and the workings, which were not futile, of a consumption on the march.

The reign of night

What strikes us about the old way of life is the inadquacy of the means to resist the tyranny of the hours of darkness. These means were very unequally available in society, and were also fragile and sensitive to bad weather and air-movements. Torches, wax-lights, candles, oil lamps, 'the thousands of ingenious methods of early lighting',[15] also failed to shed much light and could not be relied upon to last long. The same for centuries, they let life go on being organised according to the curve of intensity of natural light and in response to various needs.

The world of labour demonstrates this dependence, barely modified with the passage of time. The question arose directly in the statutes of the guilds and the regulated crafts, because it affected wages and the temporal and material organisation of work. The logic which mainly guided custom and determined the rules laid down was based on two principles: to adapt working time to seasonal changes, i.e., to lengthen or shorten the working day in conformity with the movements of the sun, while at the same time to make use of the wage-worker over a longer period, increasing production and profit with a minimum rationalisation of working hours. The needs of the economy clashed with custom and compelled master-craftsmen to get round the controls imposed by the authorities, who were above all afraid of the danger of fires which could result from an increase in night work.[16] Out of a hundred statutes of comparable Paris crafts between the sixteenth and eighteenth centuries, thirty contained clauses and arrangements for protection and supervision intended to facilitate the lengthening of time devoted to production.

All these precautions motivated by concern for urban safety and defence of the crafts were linked with desire to bring order into the town's spaces. The night had always been a time of disorder, favourable to thieves and robbers who were a danger to peaceful citizens. From Horace onward literary stereotypes testified to this way of seeing the night, and these filtered down from educated people to the masses. The *Bibliothèque bleue* and the popular literature of the towns found here convincing material with which to foster the phantasms and imagination of the townsfolk. Night was a supplementary factor contributing to urban disorder.[17] The records of the commissioners of police and the logbooks of the watch patrols show how much attention was devoted by the authorities to this aspect of urban troubles, which Boileau celebrated humorously, in the manner of the Ancients. All these manifestations testified, however, to one fact, namely, that the contrast between 'day-time' and 'night-time', though seemingly easy, was in reality less simple than supposed.

The uncertainty of day and night

There was no convincing frontier between work and leisure. Regulations imposed constraints but practice necessitated breaches of regulations. These were all the more frequent when the master lived in his workshop and did not hesitate to set his workers examples of such infringement.

Night-work went on by the light of candles or lanterns. In the printing trade journeymen paid fines if they let these burn too long. In bakeries the work, already hard and stupefying with a workday of at least sixteen hours, was all the more so because work was continued into the night. It was a slavery which turned the baker-boys into 'bats', cutting them off from normal society and ruining their health, since they lived, outside of time, in dark basements.[18]

Town life changed fundamental relationships in several sectors – the supply of food to the markets, textiles – so as to increase activity. Wages depended on this. Eighteenth-century regulations laid down a rate of twelve *sols* for winter, when days were shorter, and sixteen *sols* for summer, when they grew longer, but we know, through Michael Sonenscher,[19] that these figures had only abstract significance: actual wages could vary depending on numerous factors, including lack of respect for the rules on hours of work or on piece-work. Disputes about hours due or worked were a normal feature of relations between employers and workers, supervised by a police of the crafts which, in Paris, sought to restrict changes. What mattered here was that the clash over the length of hours of work, by day or by night, was bound up with the contrast between work and leisure. Part of daily or weekly resting time encroached considerably on the night, and, for a society policed and utilitarian, it was of decisive importance to control and reduce this fringe of time.[20]

In the towns, in Paris as elsewhere, habitual reference-points existed, therefore, but we see that they were blurred, though a frontier never disappeared altogether, on one side or other of which were people whose lives were governed by natural conditions, with meagre resources for lighting, people whose leisure had to be spent in the street.[21] This was also the case with the majority of people in the countryside, whose needs in the matter were not great. Some people, however, managed to free themselves from these constraints – those who could go to bed late and not get up in the morning, those who had the means to include artificial lighting among their possessions.[22]

Between these two worlds the struggle against darkness and the need for light could involve categories and individuals engaged in a variety of tasks or pleasure-activities: students, workers (think of Restif de la Bretonne, who was a printer working at night as well as the observer of *Les Nuits de Paris*), actors, dancers, office-workers pressed for time. Were we to list all the trades and all the tasks which, in the society of the Ancien Régime, had a propensity to night-work, we should find in it some of those which Adam Smith had difficulty in classifying along with directly productive tasks, together with a certain number of intellectualised occupations. The conquest of lighting was inspired by a particular aim, but it also reflected a quest for personal independence which operated variously in different social groups. Ability to control lighting techniques created a greater possibility for organising specialised and separate ways of life. It allowed for greater mobility, a different style of privacy, other forms of leisure and sociability, for reading (whether shared or not), for conversation, while inability to control these techniques contributed to confusion between public and private space.

The pedagogy of lighting

If one is to understand what was special about olden times, one must not forget that there were certain occasions when light and lighting conveyed messages, expressing by means of their pomp grandeur and power, the sacred and the divine. These occasions happened everywhere, though they brightened town nights more than country ones. They derived some of their intensity from the fact that in these demonstrations and these places the spectator was not entirely passive. When lighting in general was restricted and the night's share very great, these were exceptional moments in everybody's life. Festivals, theatres and churches provide three examples which are all the more convincing in that, in the course of the seventeenth and eighteenth centuries, their economy underwent changes.[23]

Festival and theatre: theatrical lights

In both Paris and the provinces the traditional system of religious and popular festivals provided a framework for time in which the repetitive alternated with the exceptional. Occasions for these events were many, from great political celebrations, ceremonial state entries, victories and funerals to customary manifestations like Midsummer Day. In Paris that festival brought the authorities and the public together in the Place de Grève. The King himself came to set light to the pyre on which, over a long period, foxes or cats were burned alive.

All of these festivals, which were marked to one extent or another by extensive and intensive use of light, disturbed habits and spaces. Illuminations figured among means of persuasion, and ostentation was a sign of political and social power.[24] Houses were lit up, monuments illuminated, great town-houses blazed in the night, torches accompanied the processions as they traversed the streets.[25] The nocturnal festival culminated in a display of fireworks. Because of these (organised by the town, by the great men or the ambassadors) 'the nights of Paris are sometimes the brightest in the world' (S. Rials). Spectacles of light presented publicly to the people formed part of a relation of symbolic exchange in which social pedagogy associated a profusion of light with that supernatural quality which still haloed all forms of authority.

The theatre also served. In many different forms it was a manifestation that both distinguished and brought together, by offering to the well-off, the middle classes, and increasingly also to the lower classes, another wizardry of light, another form of festival. Complete and established in Paris and the other major towns, the power of the theatre lay in its permanence and in the wide range of opportunities it presented. In the provinces, in the country, in the army it retained an energy that was more effective still because it was more rarely displayed, a spectacle borne by the strangeness and exoticism of troops of wandering players, from country houses to barns, from large villages to towns, from camps to fortresses. It showed the amazed peasants another possible world, wherein actions and things were sharply defined by light.

The theatre is also interesting in this context because it stimulated technical thought about lighting, with a view to controlling this better, on account of the risks involved. Theatre lights were the chief cause of big fires in eighteenth-century Paris. Organised lighting was essential for the stage, for the auditorium, for the actors' performance. For a long period the length of acts in a play was determined by the stage-managers' ability to replace the candles. The invention of footlights and modernisation of the theatre's apparatus on the Italian model made it a place for experimentation. Fair-ground theatres did not escape from this requirement, and the auditorium of the Opéra-Comique, built by Favart, was even destined to be taken as a model. The invention of the Argand lamp helped, around 1780, to free the stage, as also did the removal of the chandeliers from the proscenium. The magical quality of the plays was thereby made even more fascinating.

The history of play-production and that of theatrical architecture are here inseparable from the technical modernisation which, between auditorium and stage, helped to re-shape a form of sociability, a type of perception and a way of participation which increased control of the public and the fascination of play-acting. The tens of thousands of spectators who were drawn to the theatre and there discovered the light and shade of an artificial landscape were signal proof of a transient victory over the darkness which awaited them when they left the auditorium.

Lighting, faith and reason

The Church gave everyone an example of light in profusion. There was a direct link between its many ceremonies and the meaning of light. Fu-

nerals, *Te Deums*, festival services announced by peals of bells, and
ordinary masses set light at the heart of religious symbolism. It was made
to serve the dogma of a religion in which divine light came down to
enlighten mankind. Its use powerfully maintained the dialogue between
the visible and the invisible, the relation of God to nature and to men.[26] Its
prodigality was a way of involving the senses and convincing the intelligence. The lights of the Church proclaimed its power to lead the world in
the path willed by God. Candles paid for by the vestry had the task of
manifesting the presence of Christ, Light of the World.

Thinking about the beautification of churches, both liturgical and
architectural, questioned their decor and lighting. It extolled the fight
against darkness, it defended the whitening of temples that were newly
panelled and cleared of out-of-date material that was gloomy and darken-
ing.[27] One should read the story of the fight against darkness waged in the
face of imperatives that were super-devout and liturgical, technical and
economic.[28] In Paris this history shows us not so much the vandalism of
an epoch that was hostile to the Gothic style, and modernising in this
sphere no less than in others, as the part played by chance. Stained-glass
windows disappeared along with other features of old-time architecture
that were costly to maintain, or were considered impossible to repair, or
else cumbersome, such as pinnacles, crowns of arches and some rood-
screens.

Whitening was meant to beautify the sanctuary by an act of will that
was more constructive than destructive. The old stained-glass windows
then acquired an existence of their own as works of art, and people began
to regret the loss of them at the moment when their destruction became
irreparable and colourless glass triumphed in their place. Parish administrations favoured clearness because clergy, congregations and architects
were in agreement on the visibility that worship should have when reforms were being affirmed. The 'convenience' of congregations dictated
the taste for light as it did seating, heating and even the reading of
mass-books which became general.[29] Architects tried out on a grand scale
the solutions which were advocated for doing away with darkness, between 1650 and 1750, from the chancel of Notre-Dame to that of Saint-
Merri, from Saint-Germain-l'Auxerrois to Saint-Etienne-du-Mont, in a
rationalistic spirit enamoured of simplicity.[30]

At the same time, however, others such as J. B. Thiers and the glazier
P. le Vieil were defending darkness as being propitious to meditation and
prayer. 'We saw colourless windows more and more replacing stained-
glass ones even in churches. Their greater brightness was more attractive
to people who, less contemplative than their fathers, wanted more cheerful daylight in the holy places where a sombre light had edified their

ancestors and inspired that taste for prayer which their descendants have so rashly replaced with a dangerous itch to see and be seen.'[31] Here we see what was at issue where light was concerned. One had either to accept a worldly ambience, the new taste, or else to go back to the sombre light which corresponded to the modest use of means of lighting: chandeliers, lamp-posts, girandoles, footlights consisting of candles. This climate, in which artificial light retained all its pedagogical quality, seems to reflect a popular attachment which was echoed by the churchwardens of some parishes, conservative either by taste or from lack of means – Sébastien Mercier or the artisan Pierre le Vieil. Chateaubriand was to make of the luminous splendour of services held in the darkness of the nave one of the themes of his *Génie du christianisme*.[32]

The Church sought not so much to conquer the night as to appease it. These lighting systems, whether profuse or diffuse, doubtless helped to make congregations sensible to the new demands of convenience, as also to foster fascination with a darkness perforated by lights, and this all the more because its lessons of piety, like other moral teachings, redoubled the idea of useful clarity in the fight which, metaphorically, set the powers of darkness against the powers of day.[33] Very old stereotypes, ancestral ways of seeing things were in play here, placing on the dark side disordered morals, insecurity, social danger. Policemen and clerics thus made use of the same images and had the same interest in repressing illicit gatherings and nocturnal pilgrimages, places of leisure and entertainment, the excessive freedom of the dreams admitted to in confession.[34] They had to overcome what Gaston Bachelard called 'the Novalis complex', obsession with night sexualised by fire and light, a different kind of communion. When clerics and authorities lighted fires they were affirming the triumph of learned cultural logics and a way of colonising the nocturnal and its phantasms through moral practice.[35]

But nocturnal dreaming and distress were still present in the thinking of philosophers.[36] The final triumph of light was established if the night was lit up. That idea was expressed by Fontenelle and the poetic tradition which read, in the labyrinth of darkness, the harmony of the world, in which God kept his position. It is doubtless more interesting to observe how constantly eighteenth-century writers saw in the night the opposite of enlightenment, the world of ignorance and prejudice. Light was no more than a brief flash in a long night. Fear of darkness, the nocturnal vision of some permanent evil, is to be found in the work of the greatest novelists, from Lesage to Mercier and from Prévost to Rétif, who made it the central *motif* of his *Nuits de Paris*. Like Rousseau, 'the philosophers fear the night', because they identified it with the disorder of nature and the sleep of reason, a shadowy zone, hard to penetrate, in men's behaviour, the dark mysteries of which would be illustrated by Goya. That is why we find in *Emile* an apprenticeship to night aimed at killing imagination, fear of the passions, horror of darkness, at achieving a better mastery of the relation between men and nature.

In its own way the Century of Enlightenment lived on disquiet and fear of a reverse side of things that was obscure and uncontrolled. Night, which aristocratic festivals and the Church's regulated liturgies wished to abolish, thus took its revenge.[37] The Enlightenment did not resolve the tension which remained deeply rooted in collective impulses. It is against this web of sensibility divided between ordinary dependence, in which the relation to night is experienced as a sense of insecurity, acceptance of custom, and the limited independence of festivals, religious worship and the theatre, that we must understand the technical changes that took place. 'The practice of light and the expression of sensibility to light' have to be grasped together.[38]

The conquests of light, urban lighting

The battles between light and darkness soon involved administrative reason. Through a combination of thought and action by engineers, consuls, doctors, policemen and experts the eighteenth century sought to substitute reason for chaos.[39] It was in the cultural and technical dioptrics of the modern town that lighting came to embody obsession with order and transparency. This mutation did not spare private space, which it affected through remodelling interior decors even while the external and public space was being reorganised. The effects of the taste for the baroque and rococo aesthetic, very acutely sensualistic, came together in artists' efforts to provide their clients with enclosed places and to create in the heart of the town enchanted spaces that favoured the wizardry of light, the illusion created by mirrors, the unrestricted use of all the age's means of lighting.[40]

The story of the conquest of urban lighting is well known. A good idea of it is given by commissioner Jean-Baptiste Lemaire, in his memoir for the Empress in 1770, composed at Sartine's request. From the time of M. de la Reynie the link between lighting and safety inspired a policy which became general in 1697, and which was applied slowly in the provinces but more rapidly in Paris. Voltaire echoed this policy in a sonnet, *La police de Paris*, which seems to have been written to order, to celebrate its victory. 'A hundred thousand lanterns create a festival day in the midst of the night.'[41] We can follow the steps of this advance. In 1697, 2,736 lanterns with wax candles lit up the streets of the capital. In 1740 they numbered 6,400 and in 1766 at least 7,000. In 1789 the unit of calculation was changed, as each lamp-post carried two lanterns, with the wax-candle beginning to give way to the oil lamp.[42] Gas arrived in Paris, to light up the Passage des Panoramas in 1817 and the Odéon district in 1818. In 1830, 6,000 lamp-posts were lighting up the boulevards and main streets with the new fuel. This was a technical success achieved in less than 150 years, but, despite progress, concern for security had not disappeared.[43]

The victory won was expensive: 300,000 *livres* in the town's budget for 1702, 700,000 *livres* in 1789, or one day's wages per inhabitant at most. It was a disputed victory, as, in order to gain it, two conceptions of management had to clash: one, the time-honoured conception which entrusted maintenance and lighting of the lanterns to the bourgeois and landowners, making the inhabitants responsible through payment of the 'tax of mud and lanterns', for the infrastructures and material: the other, a modern, indirect conception, operating through taxation, excise or contract. Paris experienced both systems, one after the other, but the public solution came out on top, since everyone wanted to have the lighting without being obliged to light the lanterns every evening.

Two logics affected the cost of this change. The first was that of equality of lighting, uniform in time, homogeneous in space. It associated the increase in the number of street-lamps with the extension of the town and expressed the inhabitants' desire to enjoy light everywhere and all the time. However, the density of street lamps, in Paris as in Caen, decreased as one moved from the centre to the periphery.[44] The second was technical, entrusting solution of the problems to specialists and inventors, in order to perfect the devices and improve their output. In 1763 the Academy of Sciences created a stir by calling on the world of learning to find the best way to make public lighting better. Among the participants in this competition were Lavoisier (who was beaten) and Bailly. The victors were crowned for the *'lanterne à réverbère'* which was installed on the eve of the Revolution. This remained foremost in the field for fifty years, after which it was dethroned by the gas-burner.[45]

Encouragement by the authorities, passed on by the learned societies, excited the imagination of inventors with regard to lighting. In 'Floréal, An X', the printer Dondey Dupré presented a new project for illumination which clearly reflected the state of opinion and the hopes of the public.[46] The lamp-posts, 'equivocal by their nature' did not fulfil their purpose, since they left a cone of shadow before and behind them which was very inconvenient. They were rendered ineffective by the negligence of lamplighters or the activity of thieves, who were well aware of how to extinguish them. They broke, endangering the lives of passers-by. So much for the past. Now for the future. Experiments on lanterns should make it possible to reduce the failures of the lamp-posts, but, above all, Paris needed to be given an 'imposing, dignified lustre which, without ignoring the need for economy . . . would cause foreigners to know and admire its splendour and bring it into line with the immensity of its size and population'. Light-houses, inspired by the one in Alexandria, set up in the principal squares, would flood the town with their light and finally dissipate darkness. The author of the scheme kept secret the material and technology needed and was doubtful about the obstacles to realising it. However, he showed how hope in science and technology had come together with a need for comfort and for display which thereafter entered into the common fund.

The mastering of light, from public to private life

Was the same advance felt in the organisation of private space? It is difficult to give an unambiguous and simple answer to that question. There was certainly a gap between Paris and the provinces, as analysis of municipal budgets reveals. In the country districts, in Brittany, Brie and the Ile-de-France, inventories show that there were few lighting devices and those that existed were of poor quality. Night reigned over the villages throughout the seventeenth and the eighteenth century. There were not many notable changes in Bordeaux in the seventeenth century.[47] Fireplaces remained indispensable for the lighting of homes both urban and rural, especially where these consisted of a single room or a *basset*. Most families had taper-stands or candlesticks – at least one – made of metal or earthenware. The material used for these – from expensive bronze to copper, to brass, to cheap pewter – is a good pointer to social differences: in Paris, Bordeaux and rural areas expensive materials coincide with bigger dwellings. Silverware is distinctive of the upper classes.[48] However, we lack precise information for completing this picture of the past, even though the evidence confirms the scarcity of means of lighting and the role played by utility and by social differences.

It is certain that something did happen between the public and the private spheres. Condillac's *Traité sur les sensations*, Diderot's *Lettre sur les aveugles* and Mercier's *Tableau de Paris* invite us to discover this relation, proclaiming as they do the way our power of sight is doubly effective when lighting triumphs over darkness. Here as elsewhere what is needed is to compare sensations with what causes them and let experience speak for itself.[49] This new ambience was inseparable from architectural thinking and the evolution of technology, regarding glassware and windows and also decor, when the taste of amateurs and the cleverness of artists transformed this.

Three movements appear to have combined to favour the new ambience and stress the taste for light and refinement, in the transition from ostentatious display, as a way of affirming rank, to comfort and a quest for better living conditions which happened between the reign of Louis XIV and those of Louis XV and Louis XVI. In the first place there was the new taste for openness on to the outside world,[50] speculation on casements and large windows. Though familiar in the architecture of palaces, this was slower to affect the building of bourgeois houses and slower still to influence the simple dwellings of countryfolk. Its influence progressed with the advance of hygienism, concerned to let in fresh air and to light up neglected interiors.

The second dynamism brings together the history of glass-making techniques, that of carpentry and that of light. A progressive transformation of the product between 1660 and 1750,[51] the advance from 'French' or 'crown' glass, and then from 'Bohemian' or 'cylinder' glass, meant improved transparency and an increase in size, thickness and width. In one century, though at present we cannot give a precise date for this change, the glass market, supply and demand, came into line with the new values. From paper to sea-green Lorraine glass, from bluish 'French glass' to almost colourless 'Bohemian glass', the possibility of natural lighting grew nearer and nearer. The progress of an industry which changed in structure, technique and locations made possible in the long run the triumph of the large pane and the evolution of windows observable in the iconography and the plans of architects. In Boucher's *Le Déjeuner* the window with many small rectangular panes separated by sash astragals suggests larger bays and lighting increased through fairly transparent glass. This model became general between 1650 and 1750 in Paris and throughout Europe, from large town-houses to the rented premises which were not slow to follow. The modern window, more expensive owing to the carpentry needed, but easier to maintain since the glass was no longer set in lead and was more solid, made possible a new everyday relation to daylight. It was a factor in a change that was measurable in relation to the backwardness of the rural areas.[52] There remains to be considered the change in taste which we can follow, from the aristocratic retreats of the seventeenth century to the little closets of the eighteenth. The differentiation of rooms made possible a different philosophy of furnishing which found expression in experiments in wainscots, between magnificence and intimacy, in variation in decors which in different ways proportioned colours and monochrome, charm and rigour. There was increased concern for clarity and luminosity, and with the effects achievable with mirrors, following the example set by the enchanted palaces, like the Galerie des Glaces at Versailles and the Hôtel de Chevreuse.

Inseparable from the life of elegance, mirrors were to become ever more numerous, thanks again to technical success.[53] They were found in increasing numbers in the interiors of ordinary people's houses in 1700 and 1790.[54] Around 1760 Ménétra would have a bedroom fitted with mirrors such as, *mutatis mutandis*, Mademoiselle de la Vallière had had around 1668!

Windows, mirrors, colours of paint, even painted paper at the end of the century, many indicators proclaimed the rising value ascribed to daylight. The fight against darkness had been won, depending on different people's resources, by means of a profusion of devices: in 3,000 Parisian inventories, 8,000 pieces of lighting apparatus! The old methods were still predominant, for the most numerous means of lighting were mobile and very old, 63 per cent being simple candlesticks. Fixed instruments were rarer: 9 per cent sconces, branched candlesticks, brackets, 1 per cent chandeliers.[55] We see here the extent to which the progress of lighting in the towns was hierarchical, but we see, too, the complexity of the advance, associating technical improvements in matters of detail and generally, economic breakthrough and consumers' choice. Daylight had undoubtedly achieved its apogee before it became possible to dominate the risks of the night, in dreams and in reality.

Heat and cold

As between the outside and the inside, the struggle for light does not have the same importance in day-to-day and season-to-season life. The relation between cold and heat shows similar variations. Combating cold outside was a matter of clothing. Only the rich could have portable foot-warmers in their carriages, only the well-off could have fur coats in their wardrobes. Most people fought the cold by piling on layers of clothing. Blessed are those sunny climates wherein the poor have less to worry about.

The mutation in sensitivity to cold and seasonal inclemency was apparent less than in the case of lighting in public places. The changes took place more in private space, where the influence of the new family relationships was a major factor. Nevertheless, public obligation or the constraints of collective life also gave rise to revealing experiments in heating. The rules of monastic orders need to be studied as they changed over a long period: as time went by, rigour alternated with mildness, reform with relaxation, and attitudes evolved. From the collective plate-warmer of the Benedictines and the Cistercians to the individual fireplace of the Carthusians or the cells of the learned *congrégations* of the Catholic Reformation – Minimes, canons regular of St Geneviève,

Jesuits – we have an excellent field for examining collective choices and common conduct.

In public places the demands of reception, supervision and maintenance were equally important. From the sixteenth century the captains of the bourgeois militia of Paris were required to provide wood, which was very expensive, to thaw out the guardrooms at night and keep the soldiers alert.[56] Municipal buildings also served as places where methods could be tried out. On 24 November 1774 the office of the Town Hall of Paris made a contract with Louis Barbier, a hardware merchant, for 'supply and repair' of forty-three stoves, seven being made of faience and thirty-six of cast-iron. This was a sign of modernity. The stoves were installed in the Town Hall (two of them in its great hall), in the guardrooms on the ramparts between the Porte Saint-Honoré and the Porte Saint-Antoine and between the Gobelins and the Sablonnière des Invalides, eight altogether, and the rest in the guardrooms on the quays.[57] During the eighteenth century architectural and administrative thinking about hospitals, prisons and barracks included a new concern for improving the temperature enjoyed by these typical groups of people. In 1765 heating was installed in the women's dormitory in the prison at Caen, and in 1780 it was extended to the bedrooms of the nuns and the cells of those male prisoners who could pay for it.[58] In the barracks collective fireplaces provided the soldiers with a climate such as the town's population did not always enjoy. The military administration would very soon introduce stoves, and army doctors would ponder the consequences of this everyday luxury which improved conditions of service in town but spoilt the soldier for campaigns, when he would have only the fires of uncertain bivouacs to keep him warm.[59] Here we see drawn the curve of change in sensitiveness to cold.

The history of heating (I leave aside the struggle against heat, which presented different problems) involves all techniques and, in particular, that of fuels. Here we come upon all the preoccupations of science with fire and heat, the chemical and physical identity of which were revealed in the works of Lavoisier at the end of the eighteenth century.[60] This history is also connected with the concern of administrators with the 'dearth of wood', which was ascribed to changes in habits and the seasonal variation in supplies. Without establishing a causal link between these different developments – the problem of the forests, birth of heat-studies between 1780 and 1830, attention to seasonal comfort – we are able to observe some decisive changes made before the Industrial Revolution which were to reduce, as with lighting and sanitation, the influence exercised by seasonal variations.[61]

The royalty of fireplaces

During the seventeenth and eighteenth centuries and even in the early years of the nineteenth there was no revolution, but a stability in technique that was gradually shaken by the work of builders, the intelligence of architects and the demands of various clienteles and new ways. Actually, a long period drew to a close during which two technical trends clashed: that of the fireplace, which was dominant and that of the stove, which at first competed feebly with the traditional hearth but later gained ground upon it.

The lateral fireplace established itself in French houses between the twelfth and fourteenth centuries, with the features that are familiar to us: placed against the wall, its mantelpiece protected cooking activities while it gave light for the discussions which went on near it. It warmed the rooms where it was installed with much wastage of heat. The fireplace did not completely oust more primitive solutions, such as the brazier (we see this appearing on stage in Beaumarchais's *La mère coupable*) which used little fuel but was dangerous owing to the carbonic gas it gave off, or the central hearth in huts and shanties which could still be seen – nineteenth-century travellers were still coming upon it in the houses of Forez, in mountainous regions where it filled the common rooms with smoke. In Franche-Comté, in the huge farms of the Jura Mountains, the *tué* functioned with a central hearth with an open flame and a giant fireplace as high as the building itself: its hood, of ten metres and more, sheltered the whole family.[62] There was a smaller-scale equivalent in the *fucone* of the Corsican farmhouses. The lateral fireplace, doubtless an import from Italy, was a step in the right direction, because, to some extent, it freed the atmosphere from smoke. Nevertheless, it was a method that did not supply much heat, since experts in the matter calculated that two-thirds, or almost, was lost in the flues. For five centuries that was the main technical problem needing to be solved.

In both country and town the lateral fireplace with its chimney was a substantial job for builders. It called for masonry to avert the danger with which the permanent presence of fire threatened the house. In the towns the intelligence of chimney-repairers and masons began to solve the problem of loss of heat by clever thinking about flues. In the country, whether the fireplace functioned well or ill depended everywhere, as has been noted in the case of Touraine, on luck, or on the competence of the workmen.[63] The grate, the hearth, the mantelpiece were of greater or less size, depending on the shape of the room and its dimensions. Where people no longer lived with their animals, when the buildings were separated or the internal circulations were more complex, the fireplace became the sole source of heat. Its disposition governed draught and ventilation, the difficulties of which had been solved empirically by the craftsmen. The fireplace should not be situated directly opposite the door. The hearth was most often placed at ground level. The hood or the mantelpiece was equal in height with, or a little higher than, the actual fireplace which was a home for the fire and for cooking utensils. The choice of wall was important – no surfaces pierced by doors or windows, or encumbered by chain-bonds or breast-summers. Gable-ends had the advantage of thickness, but party-walls were most often ruled out. The lateral placing of the fireplace influenced the heat-giving power and the surface of radiation, creating an area large enough for someone to instal himself with his family, or with neighbours, for parties and gatherings. The style and decor of rural fireplaces gave evidence of urban and bourgeois influences, when financial resources allowed this.

In town there were regulations which obliged builders and chimney-repairers to take many precautions. The number and size of the fireplaces in a house varied with the size of the buildings. In those with four floors and an area of at least 28 square metres there was one fireplace per floor, with the flues of each superimposed on the one below. The number of hearths and flues determined the thickness of the chimneystack.[64] Around 1720 the general practice of building flues with an inclination made it possible to reduce the space occupied. When they were set against a party-wall the necessary thickness of the outer walls made it possible to arrange them espalier-fashion and reduce still further their excessive thickness. Le Muet and his imitators distinguished three types of inside fireplace: the 'living-room' fireplace, which was about two metres wide between its cheeks, that of the 'bedroom', between 1.65 and 1.80 metres, and the 'water-closet' model, less than 1.50 metres.[65] We see here a whole hierarchy of ordinary comfort, emphasising the advantage of living in town. In the richest interiors of the seventeenth century the construction and decor were bravura exercises asserting 'the primacy of architecture and concern for order. It is like another gateway, monumental and opening on to a wondrous world.'[66] Its role was to focus the gaze upon the centre, which was why this was adorned in a thousand ways and whole publications were devoted to it, abounding in models of ornamentation and composition which, from the end of the sevententh century, evolved in the direction of lightness and simplicity. Thereafter it welcomed pier-glasses, and ornaments appeared on its mantelpiece. Whether monumental or intimate, with its accessories, bed-plate, fire-dogs, screens, shovel, tongs, it appeared 'the heart of the house and of an entire civilisation'.[67]

The path of the stove

The existence of hearths with enclosed fires is proved by the presence of numerous industrial furnaces and by stoves. We know their geography, in general terms. The spread of the stove was concentrated in the north and east of Europe and in the mountainous areas of the centre and south. In the sixteenth century it was already in common use in Germany, where travellers noticed it. When Montaigne travelled to Italy by way of Lorraine and Switzerland he remarked on it as a characteristic feature of the inns he stayed at. This was the model of the Alsatian *stub* in which the stove warms the common rooms, but it did not drive the fireplace out completely, as we find this in the kitchens of houses with several rooms.[68] In seventeenth-century Holland, Descartes took refuge, to write his *Méditations*, in the room heated by the stove which sometimes came, as in Germany, to give its name to the room itself. The traveller Peter Munday described, in Danzig in 1641, stoves of various sorts, some made of faience, others of earthenware, some shaped like a tower, others square – the latter used less wood and the heat spread more widely.

A different civilisation prevailed between the Netherlands and Muscovy. There also the technical system differed. The potter's skill dominated when the stoves were made of fire-proof clay, that of the metal-worker when they were made of pewter, tin or cast-iron, using the methods of masons or chimney-repairers. Completely enclosed, these stoves allowed neither smoke nor smell to leak out, and they used a different kind of fuel – small logs or wood cut up small, which entailed variations in sawing, cutting and storing by individuals. This created a situation favourable to experimenting in new heat-producing products. The stove thus came to reign over a different way of life, other forms of sociability. When sitting in front of a fireplace one could easily have one's front burnt and one's back frozen; in the common people's houses one had to bend down in order to cook; and the hierarchy of age determined how close one might sit to the hearth. Round a stove the atmosphere was warmed more evenly, the furnace made it possible to work standing up, and everyone could sit anywhere he liked in relation to the fire, which was easier to maintain.

In the encounter between the fireplace and the stove we perceive anthropological contrasts. It was necessary to move from one style to another, which required resources and implied an increased taste for comfort. For that reason use of the stove spread slowly, even though its technical innovation and its cultural resonances appeared already in the sixteenth century. We find large glazed stoves in the inventories of some grand families who were sensitive to cold. It seems that in the seventeenth and eighteenth centuries the stove gained ground among rich people. The corporation of stove-setters and chimney-repairers began to popularise its use. In 1619 Franz Keslar, a painter from Frankfurt-am-Main, published at Oppenheim, in French, his *Epargne-bois* ('Wood-saver'), in which he set out the merits of what was, in France, still an invention for the future.[69] It was a way to keep warm in cold weather while economising on wood, and so to bring relief to the poor and the mass of the people. In France, following Germany, the public good was involved in this new skill at guiding fire and capturing heat, getting rid of smoke through pipes made of earthenware or metal, and warming rooms both large and small.

The model advocated by Keslar was a wood-burning furnace such as is still used today, several tiers high and 'magnificently' decorated, probably to make up for the loss of decoration due to the disappearance of the fireplace. It could be purchased in wrought iron 'which will not be very pretty but can be used anywhere'. Keslar expresses the satisfaction given him by his device: 'When, in winter, I often return home feeling cold, I like to warm myself beside my furnace (rather than before an open fireplace where one is often almost roasted in front while freezing behind) . . . [with] a glowing and agreeable heat.'[70] The publicity reveals the important fact that, though one loses the spectacle, one gains the liveliness of a fire that is not feverish. At the end of the eighteenth century Sébastien Mercier voices the same ambiguity, when the stove was making great advances in Paris: 'What a distance between a stove and a fireplace! The sight of a stove kills my imagination and makes me sad and melancholy. I prefer the sharpest cold to this tepid, dull, invisible heat. I like to see the fire, it stirs my imagination.'[71]

Fireplace versus stove: necessity and comfort

Study of inventories, both Parisian and rural, reveals a remarkable stability and scarcity where stoves were concerned. In the Ile-de-France there were none in the peasant *bassets*. In Touraine fireplaces were dominant as the main source of heat from the middle of the nineteenth century to 1920, except in the houses of notables who were responsive to the advocates of a novelty which had been around for nearly a century. In the Mâconnais stoves and furnaces were rare until the last third of the nineteenth century. In Brie, in the indices of standard of living calculated by Micheline Baulant, no change is to be seen through the seventeenth and eighteenth centuries. In Brittany, at Roscoff, in Anjou, the same situation. The presbyteries of Normandy were equipped with fireplaces. All over the countryside of France, North and South alike people lived in the civilisation of the open, free fire, with its habits, its repeated operations, its utensils, its need for constant maintenance in order to combat damp and cold, its ashes collected for use in major washing chores, for scouring pots and pans, and fertilising the kitchen-garden, its embers which had to be covered at night, its smoke which made one's eyes smart but protected hams, its pans hung from the pot-hanger and its pots entrusted to the fire-dogs.

Comfort progressed, following the town's example, by the increase in fireplaces in the bedrooms and the closets of the rich. A few stoves were to be found in the homes of innovating lords: e.g. in the *château* of Montgeroult, near Pontoise, in a beautiful eighteenth-century dining-room, a stove made of decorated faience enabled guests to avoid having the heat from a fireplace on their backs during the meal. At Combourg, in autumn and winter evenings, the Chateaubriand family spent its leisure hours in the great panelled hall painted off-white and decorated with portraits of ancestors and heroes.

When supper was over and the four of us had moved from the table to the fireplace, my mother sank with a sigh on an old day-bed covered in chiné. A little table with a candle on it was set before her. I sat beside the fire with Lucie. My father walked about. He was lost to view when he moved away from the fire, until he emerged from the darkness like a ghost.[72]

We observe here the literary effect based on the contrast in lighting and the lack of attention to heat, a sign of habit and familiarity, whereas the darkness impacts sharply. Cold is more bearable than darkness.

In Paris those notaries who did not include fireplaces in their inventories, though they listed their utensils – tongs, fire-dogs, shovels, bellows, screens, fire-guards, upper part of the fireplace and pictures – have left us a perception which, though indirect, is adequate. Fireplaces do frequently appear, in 3,000 inventories: on the average, two fireplaces per household, or a fireplace for two rooms. This meant comfort, even if crude. It provided some warmth and rest for the lower orders as for the bourgeois, the rest being obtained by piling on clothes and by pulling the curtains at night around well-covered beds.[73] However, the social contrast is seen in the degrees of intensity in use of the fireplace. In the dwellings of the lower orders it fulfilled all the necessary functions, just as in the country. In the homes of the well-to-do it diffused comfort everywhere, only 40 per cent of the annexes having a fireplace. It was the progress of the stone house and that of pipes that made possible these gains, which are demonstrated by the presence of accessories and the popularisation of auxiliary heating devices – warming-pans, braising-pans, braziers. We find these everywhere in Paris. At Caen their absence emphasises the social and geographical differentiation of the habitat. This situation improved over time. In 1730 34 per cent of the inventories for the centre of the town mentioned them, but only 13 per cent of those for the outlying parts: in 1790 the figures were 92 per cent and 33 per cent respectively.[74] While there was not an absolute correlation between the new sensitivity and wealth, the latter contributed substantially to it. Its victory was won, in the first place, through multiplication and improvement of the old-established methods of traditional France, and then later through the appearance of new devices.

Sébastien Mercier bewails this development:

Our fathers, more thrifty or more inured to cold, did hardly anything to keep warm. Three fires, including the one in the kitchen, were enough for a house in which there resided eighteen or twenty masters, and what masters! Men who occupied the highest posts in the state. With their legs enclosed in a bearskin they braved with equal courage the sharpest cold and the Royal Academy of Architecture.

The observer of this fact needs to go on to consider its causes. The blame lies with 'the luxury which has corrupted everything among us. It has lit inextinguishable fires in every corner of our dwellings and taken the axe to our forests, which soon became inadequate.'[75] The historian of Paris sees stoves and furnaces increasing in number, gradually revolutionising ways of life, even those of the people. They enable women to remain upright in their kitchens. They increase total heating capacity, even though there is still mistrust on the part of those who see them as merely a useful complement to the good old fireplaces 'because they would make one susceptible to cold', and for whom their proper place is only in ante-rooms, dining-rooms and cafés. In Mercier's protest we can see that supply is being increased by demand, production by consumption, and two problems follow from this – fuel and the art of heating.

Wood, coal, supplies and technical reflections

Combustion was based on wood, the fuel in ordinary use everywhere, even though anything at all might be burnt – e.g., seaweed and kneaded cow-dung, mixed with sawdust, as seen in Brittany. In the 3,000 Paris inventories we find wood mentioned in a third of the dwellings, but in only ten per cent of the inventories of lower-class people.[76] This means that they did not store it.

Wood was purchased regularly from a merchant who delivered to rich houses or supplied inns and hotels, which devoted to this item large and increasing amounts of money.[77] For lack of accounts the influence of seasonal changes does not appear to be very marked, so far as the poor were concerned, but it is apparent with the rich and with hospitals and collective institutions. A few bundles and a few logs constituted a store in which we find 'new wood', which had a high calorific coefficient but was expensive, since it was cut up and transported, in boats or carts, and also 'raft wood', which gave less heat and was cheaper.[78] A load of the former cost between twelve and sixteen *livres*, one of the latter between ten and twelve *livres*. Above all, the demand for firewood increased faster than did the population. In 1735, 400,000 loads were enough for Paris, but in 1789 the city needed more than 750,000, perhaps as much as 800,000 loads or 1,600,000 cubic metres, and doubtless the same amount of charcoal. The Parisians were warming themselves more and better, and everyone was doing it, which increased the demand for new wood 'because the fire is brighter and gives out more heat'. With the city's requirement standing at one cubic metre per year per inhabitant, more than a tonne, Parisians feared a shortage of wood no less than a shortage of corn.[79] The winters of 1709 and 1789 were particularly hard and Parisians plundered the woods of Vincennes and Boulogne despite the King's guards.

In the country, as we have seen, all the rural communities kept up pressure in support of local customs, so as to maintain the communal right to cut firewood. The forests were endangered by all the people who considered themselves commoners and who were engaged in violent conflict with landowners and lords right down to the Revolution. Altogether, six million cubic metres of wood were consumed in the towns, or a total consumption of nearly 38 million for the kingdom as a whole, and about 75 to 100 million *livres* was spent every year on heating (using Paris prices). The increased demand was an economic factor of great importance, and led to over-exploitation of forests, especially in the vicinity of towns, as well as competition between different holders of common rights and an increase in prices (63 per cent, calculated by C. E. Labrousse for the eighteenth century).

The shortage of wood in Paris became a matter of state concern. Throughout the century the supply of wood received attention from the Town Hall, and required the devising of a system which balanced the interests of merchants and consumers, arbitrated by the municipality. The latter supervised, organised and amplified the supply of wood by the foresters of zones old and new, and kept an eye on the rafting down the Seine, on which everything depended. Neither the need nor the policy to which it gave rise ended with the Revolution. Gloomy winters would revive anxiety about a shortage and would see logs being burned in the streets, for the poor to warm themselves by, as happened in 1794. Sébastien Mercier is a good witness to the crisis, its conjunctural and structural aspects, and its social consequences, which were shared unevenly. His view wavers between two temptations – to please his public by grasping the reality of the matter (supply is not without interest, new sources of energy are indispensable), but also to defend Parisian *bon ton* and a standard of comfort more traditional than innovatory.[80]

The crises made people think. On the production side, it was necessary to increase the output of the forests. On the consumption side, profitability had to be improved and fuel diversified. Gauger's *Mécanique du feu* was translated in 1714 and academic investigations progressed, in Paris and in the provinces, in the last quarter of the century, with Duhamel du Monceau, Hebrard, Croÿ, Lavoisier and Montalembert. Less well-known practitioners perfected new methods. Taking up this question meant looking at the monopoly of wood and charcoal. Advocates of coal had to wait until 1830 before this constituted a quarter of Paris's consumption of fuel – 1.2 million hectolitres, as against 2.4 million of charcoal, the rest still consisting mainly of raft-wood.

In 1774 Jean-François Clément Morand published *Les arts des mines* for the Academy of Sciences, a defence and illustration of coal in which he showed how important it was to develop its extraction and commercialisation, not only for the benefit of ironworks but also for heating, especially in Paris.[81] Morand estimated the annual supply at 7,200 loads, involving 200 boats, principally coming from central France, with fewer from England *via* Rouen, and for all purposes. He followed these purposes in detail, in workshops and homes, praising the medicinal properties of coal, its agricultural usefulness as fertiliser, its quality in the making of mortar, dyes and varnish, and as fuel in industry, on the basis of many experiments and observations.

Where heating was concerned the example to be followed in Paris and elsewhere was that set by the inhabitants of Liège and London. The advantages of coal had to be calculated, of course, by comparing costs, but could be appraised also in terms of its long-lasting quality, greater than that of wood, and of its more constant effect – a bushel of coal had as much effect as three bushels of charcoal: and, besides, it had profitable by-products. Coal fires were not dangerous, as was established by exposing a goldfinch for a whole hour to 'very thick and abundant smoke'. The possibility of suffocation could be avoided by ventilation. Fireplaces could be adapted to the use of it by means of grates. Stoves would be even more suitable, especially if, as in Liège, mixtures of caking coal and balls of clay were used. They burned non-caking coal, which elsewhere was not used. In the Lyonnais poor people had already applied this principle in their cast-iron stoves.

Morand lists the qualities of coal, established by evidence which it is hard to contest: prompt lighting of the fire, less smoke, fewer blazes (and so less risk of fires), greater evenness and uniformity, less smell, easier regulation in accordance with degree of cold or size of room, which one effects by deciding the number of 'balls' to put in the hearth. It is more convenient even than wood in the kitchen, adapts well to a traveller's use of his time, to use by individuals who have no servant, to use by day-labourers and to use by sedentary workers who need heating which is regular and unvarying. With stoves all these advantages are doubled, as could be seen in Liège, where the fire in modest households lasted for twelve or fifteen hours without needing attention and cost only half as much. Morand was certainly a persuasive apostle of a change in habits which, if attention was paid to them, re-shaped body and mind, freed and cleansed, preventing illness and making better hygiene possible.

This apologia for coal came at the end of the improvement obtained through the expertise of the chimney-repairers and the technology of travel, the reduction in the diameters of pipes through the use of better-quality fire-proof clay, and the supervised practice of chimney-sweeping. The *Encyclopédie* made itself a propagandist for the new fireplaces which, through improved flues and a reduction in the mantelpiece that was precisely measurable (in the inventories we find no pier-glasses in the homes of Parisian wage-earners in 1700, but in twenty-nine per cent of them in 1789), made comfort possible in the specialised rooms and the dissociation of domestic activities. Between the end of the seventeenth century and the beginning of the nineteenth technicians pushed to their uttermost limit the effectiveness and the profitability of the ancestral fireplace. Rumford calculates the gain as between five and ten per cent, which is not negligible, and that was achieved with simple methods: Franklin's smoke-consuming apparatus plugged into the pipes, the diffusion of chimney-back plates, the hood straight and smaller in size.

The stove passed on changes which were popularised by their adoption by aristocrats and bureaucrats and made widespread in public places. We see it established in the Jacobins' club, where the lighting was also provided by up-to-date Argand lamps. It was to be found in big hospitals and libraries, and it appears in the inventories of soft-drink sellers who kept a café (seventy four per cent) and those of inn-keepers (sixty per cent). Among the wage-earners of Paris, four per cent of the servants had stoves in Louis XIV's reign, but no journeymen or day-labourers had them. In Louis XVI's time the respective rates were forty and thirty per cent. Small or large, economical or costly, their prices varied between 10 and 100 *livres*. They were made of faience or cast-iron, of glazed clay or tinplate. They were a feature of a better class of dwelling. If to the stove was added a fireplace with a surround, not very deep, 48 per cent of the dwellings of workmen and 75 per cent of those of servants were affected by progress. Higher-up the social scale, and involving every category, new stoves and improved fireplaces showed the progressive arrival of a new sensitivity.

These changes, the destiny of which we have followed, transformed at first the lives of a minority, in the towns and then in the country. Sébastien Mercier, looking out from the towers of Notre Dame, writes of observing 'the chimneys of financiers and pontiffs which give out thick, oily fumes, while the frugal wisps from nearby dwellings tell us only of the thin steam rising from a pot on the fire'. The typology he sketches takes no account of the scales of income or rank, but is a way of noting various needs through emblematic models of consumption: 'We see through the chimney-flues the soup of the seminarist, that of the bourgeois and that of the prince, three very different soups, not to mention the soup of the pious lady. Eventually I would make out as many as seven, with different tastes and seasonings, if I did not have to conclude.'[82]

We regret the publicist's silence while retaining the method which juxtaposes way of life and symbolic values. The fact is that progress, neither wholly acquired nor wholly linear, has for its horizon a complex psychology in which abstraction gains on concreteness, homogeneity on heterogeneity, continuity on discontinuity, and this in relation to time and space that lighting and heating have helped to alter.

6   Water and its uses

Water-supply was installed in the village of Brantes, on the border of Provence and the Dauphiné, in or about 1950. Until then it had been neglected in all development plans, and some farms did not see water arriving in their sinks before the 1970s. When one old lady among the inhabitants encountered the new equipment she let her single tap run continuously. She had to be taught to perform new actions, to acquire new habits, turning off and turning on, something that was not obvious in a world in which the fountains ran without stopping (they needed only to be maintained), where springs, rare and abundant, were carefully looked after, and where wells and pumps required different methods for their use.

The coming of water into the houses and cowsheds changed everyone's life very quickly, relieving them of a centuries-old burden. For an entire generation progress broke with parsimony, while the old culture left a heritage of ultimate distrust, mobilised against the excesses of a consumption that was henceforth unlimited – the swimming-pools of the new-comers, plentiful showers, watering of summer visitors' gardens. The old conflicts over the sharing of water were never far away. After a third of a century they have diminished, but measures to protect and maintain the old sources of water have slackened. They are revived only during exceptionally sunny summers, when the levels of the communal reservoirs sink, when the pumps exhaust the last puddles in mountain tracks and holes in the river-bed and all, animals and people alike, are hot and thirsty. We hope then that rain will fall, to recharge the pools, soak the soil deeply and calm those who were made irritable by the drought. If there had still been a priest, we should doubtless have asked him to lead a procession through the fields. Not long ago he was expected to control storms and to ring the church bells in order to ward off disasters.

Exorcising nature's excesses and shortcomings is not a practice that dates from yesterday. People have engaged in it since ancient times, through witchcraft or through regulated worship. In this matter Christianity has done little to shake the old beliefs which, late in the day, it has been thought proper to classify as credulous. Water is at the heart of this religious attitude to the forces of nature, because it is essential for so many needs in life and work, because it is a good coveted by agriculturists and also by manufacturers who depend on it for transport and energy, and because the modern age sees its needs increasing. With some delay, Brantes has left, for good, one world for another.

The pressure on water

The early modern age was an age of scarce water. Antiquity and the Middle Ages had a different relation to water. Today the presence of water in daily life has become habitual and this benefit is continuous, regular and abundant. It is no longer a privilege to have water available: the natural and human cycles are experienced quite differently. The nineteenth century saw the coming of an age when water is common, having become an industrial and commercial product, mastered by technology and science.[1]

At the dawn of the third millennium we see returning the age of expensive and precious water, because industrial, urban and agricultural societies have reached levels of consumption without precedent in history. Already in 1946 statisticians calculated the needs of the population in towns of more than 10,000 inhabitants as 120 litres for domestic uses, including the watering of gardens, twenty-five to fifty litres for industry and agriculture, and another fifty for cleaning the streets and flushing the sewers, or, altogether, more than 200 litres per person per day, every year, a delivery of seventy-five cubic metres. By 1976 the figure was over 400 litres a day. At the end of the 1980s the big cities of the United States, Canada and Australia, champions in consumption and perhaps in wastage, were using between 1,500 and 2,000 litres. Experts are forecasting that in the twenty-first century this amount will increase to between 3,000 and 4,000 litres. In short, milliards of cubic metres of water are needed. There is consequently fear for natural reserves, ecologists watch over rivers and lakes threatened with pollution, and floods make us realise the danger of letting water run away uncontrolled. Manures and fertilisers that drain into the sources of water form part of the risks entailed by super-active agriculture.

The human pressure on water is very strong. For thousands of years people satisfied their needs without worrying about resources. Nevertheless, at the end of the Middle Ages the growth of towns began to cause changes and raise questions. As André Guillerme has shown,[2] water was the principal force for energy and everything depended on it: transport and the first industries needed it for their power, subsistence needed it for the mills and fisheries, and there were already requirements for domestic economy, steam-baths and baths, fountains and gardens. People became aware that their supply of water was threatened. At the end of the sixteenth century the *Complainte de la Seine,* a poem attributed to an obscure chronicler named Robert Vallée, or de La Vallée, spoke of this danger. The river of Paris was being spoilt: the workshops of the tanners and dyers and the rubbish thrown in by everyone were making it an uninviting river, full of refuse, so that everyone's health was endangered. This poem began, in a sense, the ecological awareness of the Parisians and led to questioning of the consequences of the growth of cities. A great transformation began in the ecosystem which can be understood only by studying the relative demands of systems of civilisation – material, techni-cal and spiritual.

From the Middle Ages to the industrial epoch the considerable variety of indispensable uses of water, for energy, drinking, eating (without water, no bread) and hygiene (the word was invented, in its present-day sense, in the eighteenth century) shows the wide range of issues and means. Three-quarters of the body's weight, most requirements for en-ergy and a big share of transport by land, river and sea all depend on this second of the four elements – earth, water, air and fire – the role of which in explaining our human nature and its relation to the great cycles of nature we recall. Water became everywhere a fundamental form of wealth and a symbol thereof. *Fluctuat nec mergitur* proclaimed the motto of the boatmen of Paris, which became the city's own.

The fact was that water entered first and foremost into the formation of cities and the construction of their space. It necessitated equipment and an entire machinery which grew in complexity, increasing a city's ex-penses. It became very soon an issue in the struggle between the authori-ties who shared control of the towns. In Paris the King, the town, the merchants and private individuals disputed the exercise of power over water-supplies. Their management figures in the web of social relations and provided material for political debates and for learned discussions. The consumption of water, the changes in its role and uses, were at the heart of urban politics. However, concerns for supplying and ensuring the amounts of water needed for all the purposes it served, for building and maintaining the equipment for its production and distribution, the major works of adduction or pumping were inseparable from more hidden movements which directly affected the horizons of moral and religious discipline, changes in the frontier between public and private, the rise of medical and hygienist ideologies and the revealing change in the thresh-olds of public tolerance regarding what was 'healthy' and what was 'unhealthy'. Conflicts began between entertainment needs, as seen in the grand scene painting of baroque gardens and fetes, and those of a society that was utilitarian and already to some extent under supervision of physicians.

The removal of waste, too, presented ever bigger problems. Throwing effluents out into the environment – the pond, the river, the street – became no longer possible with the increase in population and growth of industry. Regulations and police surveillance aimed at controlling a more artificial habitat. Different social strategies then resulted from new standards. The end of the eighteenth century appears, here again, as a fundamental moment coming at the end of five or six centuries of technical, medical and religious continuity. A series of slippages brought alteration in social mentalities and practices, challenging the customary criteria which until then had defined needs and resources. The town, with its conflagrations and its increased requirements, became the revealer of a transformation which did not spare the countryside. The cultivator needed water to irrigate his fields, the stock-breeder needed it for his animals to drink, and the forester needed it to float his rafts of timber, the specific answer found by pre-industrial society for supplying the ship-yards, the industries of transformation such as salt-works and mines, and also building work in the towns. Millers harnessed its regular power, fishermen organised fishing-grounds and sluices. In short, here also needs and conflicts developed through the increase in commercial demands, the diversion of resources to feed canals and the saturation of river-banks with industrial installations.

From utility to salubrity, the country districts followed, though doubt-less with some delay, the lead given by the towns, in respect, first, of their collective equipment (washplaces, wells, tanks and watering-places in rivers) and then of their public health arrangements. In Touraine it was only at the end of the nineteenth century that the doctors began to spread awareness of the danger from contaminated water. They were listened to in the country areas a few decades later and the struggle for hygiene continued from the 1920s to the 1950s.[3] Control of water went along with change of attitude.

The utility and the sacredness of water

Like fire, water is inseparable from the ideas which have been rooted for thousands of years in the symbolic power of the elements. Water accompanied people's lives in pre-industrial and traditional societies, from birth to death, from baptism to funeral. Women were its interpreters: ferry-women at the various crossing-points of life – midwives, mothers of families – they taught lessons that were of decisive importance for all. The

Church gave water an important place in its liturgies, and here, also, it found favourable ground for an attack on the peoples' 'superstitions', with a view to bringing these under control. We can see an emblematic illustration of this in the conflict between clergy and laity over the 'sanctuaries of grace' where the action of sacred waters could, through an unauthorised second baptism, restore to life newborn innocents who had died at birth.[4]

Water shaped the collective imagination, bringing together the thoughts of scholars with the inventions of poets and artists. Along with fire it defined an aspect of old-time medicine, a key to understanding of psychologies and forms of behaviour.[5] In his *Art de vivre longtemps* Lessius wrote that phlegmatics and melancholics dream of lakes, rivers, floods and shipwrecks: through dependence on water, old-time psychology half-opened the gates of hell and death. Charon and his boat reigned over the ghosts of the departed. The water of death doubtless expressed the violence of a world that men could not control. Contrariwise, water as mirror naturalises our image and describes a form of freedom to play: the myth of Narcissus weaves its links with the power of individualisation.

For poets water forms the decor of fragile love, of embarcations for Cythera and delights of fantasy. 'It is to the landscape what the soul is to the body' said Watelet in his *Art des jardins* in the middle of the Century of Enlightenment. In the Church's rituals of purification and blessing, in the myth of the fountains of youthfulness, in the widespread belief in the miraculous action of springs and woodland fountains, the power of water never belies its intense sacred energetics force, which is all the greater for being a sought-after good, getting scarcer and scarcer, less and less natural, and because people's idea of it is changing as a result of society's new demands.[6]

Three innovations were in fact, at work on ideas and ways of life. That, first, which was contributed by the doctors of space and topography who set water, like air, in a relation of appropriation of nature and culture. At the centre of their curiosity were marshes and the places of endemic pollution in the big cities, as with Lepecq de la Cloture or Vicq d'Azir. There were new attitudes, too, which induced practices and sensibilities which showed a threshold of intolerance in the spheres of the environment and of smells which, from having been bearable, now became intolerable. Those, finally, of moral judgement on manners, dirtiness and lack of water-borne hygiene which served then as markers to define the dangerous categories in society. In *Les Misérables*, Victor Hugo would dare to draw a parallel between the history of mankind and that of the sewers, the importance of which was shown in Paris at the beginning of the nineteenth century, when, between 1805 and 1812, the town's sub-soil was explored for the first time, when the salubrity upheld by Parent du Chatelet called for technical reforms that would make people and the settings of their lives healthier, and when the great cholera epidemics revealed the crisis in all its depth.[7]

This set of new problems made clear that it was necessary to take account of the water-cycle in its entirety, and so of the totality of ecological balances. At the end of the Middle Ages the cities introduced into the geographical setting a number of disturbances which, though doubtless not on the scale of the present-day's, had an influence big with consequences for the future. Urban life and the crafts brought about an initial transformation of the ecosystem.[8] Pollution and domestic and collective rubbish altered the balance of the river-waters, disturbed the ground-water-level and accumulated endemic risks. Most of the customs of the towns of Northern France included the first principles of urban control of hygiene, but salmonella and gilded staphylococci were already in the rivers and wells, invisible promoters of numerous incurable infections. The poisoning of the waters which in times of epidemic, from the Black Death in the fourteenth century to cholera in the nineteenth, was always attributed to the Jews, to foreigners, to marginal elements, to lepers and even to the socialists, was due, however, to poor filtering of water, lack of disinfection, difficulty in dealing with urban detritus, and the weakness of the measures of control that the authorities could apply.

The decline in the production of fisheries provides an illustration of one of the consequences of these disturbances, the underfeeding of part of the towns' population, or at least an important change in what they ate, leading to a different dependence. In Paris the community of fishers with rods and that of fishers with nets were not to stop, before the Revolution, their disputing over the carp, pike, barbel, sheat-fish and gudgeon that survived in the Seine despite the new oxygen-consuming pollution. For the feeding of the bourgeois and the people, however, fresh-water fish most often came from elsewhere, from the ponds and rivers of the upper basin of the Seine, and amounted to little as compared with the 50,000 casks of salt-water fish sold every year in the main Paris market: 3,000,000 *livres* for fresh sea-fish including 400,000 for fresh herring, 1,500,000 for salted fish, 1,200,000 only for fresh-water fish, according to Lavoisier's calculations.[9]

An important balance had undoubtedly been altered. One would like to be able to measure all the consequences, between the fourteenth and the eighteenth centuries, for the regime of the waters that resulted from urban and agricultural development. The clearing of forests and the increase in consumption of wood brought a change in the hydrous balance and a lowering of the aquifers, even if we allow that these events did not affect the delivery of the rivers.[10] In other words, the period when springs disappeared, with the problems that could ensue for towns concerned with water-catchments and the first worries for rural communities, began with mediaeval deforestation. The industrial era, with its deeper tillage and excessive pumping, would only accelerate the lowering of water-levels.[11]

Between these two moments, supply and consumption of both town and country were limited not so much by penury or difficulty in mobilising resources as by the exigencies and choices which resulted from a certain conception of the world and determined the specific uses that were made of water. Its scarcity and increased cost enable us to understand this particular moment when water was, if not insufficient, at least hard to obtain despite its abundance in nature, because techniques were stabilised under the aegis of the Vitruvian paradigm and the crushing superiority of hydraulic architecture, and because choices were torn between the wastefulness of the high and the parsimony of the low.

These attitudes have to be measured on the one hand in the way the problems of production and distribution were solved and, on the other, in the ways water was used and the types of consumption, the evolution of needs and uses in relation to that of ways of looking at things and of ideas.

The production of water

In the course of five centuries the ways in which rural and urban communities met their needs varied little, but they contributed differently to the organisation of the networks of equipment required for providing water and for getting rid of rubbish. In the towns the two things were inseparable, or almost, but in the country the former took precedence over the latter, which was left to nature to deal with. The former is well known, while the latter remains a vast territory still largely unexplored.

The inventory of resources offered three main solutions. Direct access to the utilisation of rivers, springs, lakes and ponds; the catchment of springs and their piping, chiefly to cities, through aqueducts or underground pipes; recourse to ground-water by digging wells. These three methods coexisted nearly everywhere, but it is not easy to discover what their capacity was or how this varied over time. Climatic differences and regional traditions could affect the balance between them, which was different in southern France from what it was in other parts – by the sea, inland, in the mountains. The recovery of rainwater, which seasonal scarcity might favour as a method did not result in the use of tanks everywhere, since these are directly associated with a type of roofing: with thatch one could not have a tank, but tiles and slates facilitated it. The big farms in the mountains had huge reservoirs for their animals to drink from. Citadels, castles and Vauban's fortresses usually had these, too, in order to withstand sieges. Tanks were less frequent in towns, except in the North and the South.

The article by Jaucourt in the *Encyclopédie* shows that the storing of water called for a complete technology. He saw this in the North of France, in Holland, in Flanders and in the South. Simple procedures of piping and filtering led the water from the roof to the tank of each house, which made possible a calculation of consumption which is worth whatever it is worth but is not without interest. A tank should hold 200 *pintes* for a household of twenty-five persons, or, per day, eight *pintes* each at 0.93 litre each (i.e. less than 7.45 litres), 'which is more than enough for all the uses of daily life' for everyone, from cooking to drinking, from garden-watering to laundering. Here there was a level of consumption, together with a certain reduction in the daily chores connected with watering, offering advantages over all the other ways of getting water. Some Paris town-houses built in the seventeenth and eighteenth centuries had their own tanks, which were very convenient for the gardens and for watering horses.[12] The tank implied ways of living and social relations that were different from those of regions where supply depended on sumps installed in a river, catchmented fountains and public wells or washplaces.

From river to fountains

Empirical and spontaneous access to watercourses made ease of supply possible everywhere with little equipment needed: drinking troughs for the cattle and horses, common or private flocks, *puisoirs* for the men who could be satisfied with an accessible strand. That was enough for the seven litres a day that Jaucourt assigned to a person, and even for the twenty or thirty litres required by a horse. Circumstances had to favour it. War often disturbed habitual practices: besieged cities cut off from their river might die of thirst and villages might burn without any means of fighting the fire. When the distances to cover every day were not too long there was no problem. The increase, in surface area and population, of towns built on rivers meant for many people separation from the *puisoirs* and dictated other solutions.

Conflicts developed around access to rivers, over freedom or continuity of use, as a result of competition between different activities and other constraints. In Paris, between the sixteenth and eighteenth centuries, the interests of merchants and boatmen demanded developments, and the policy of the town and the King made the banks of the Seine an area for high-priority intervention, the extension of which was paid for through a reclassifying of activities that proceeded not without disputes between the riverside population and the administration.[13] The construction of ports and controlled building-sites and the creation of monumental quays did not help the water-carriers, who were now obliged to fetch their supplies from spots reserved and arranged for them.

Disposal of waste from homes and hospitals into the Seine was not unusual, and the waste-water of the dyers, linen-bleachers, curriers, butchers and tripe-sellers also found its way into 'the River', either directly or via the Bièvre, which all accounts describe as a veritable sewer. All this called for action by the municipality, a policy of supervision which was expressed in ordinances and judgements by the King's procurator that were repeated again and again. The dyers, threatened with expulsion, fought against this new-fangled town-planning, and the dwellers beside the Bièvre struggled to defend its industrial role, which previously had been on the clear waters suitable for the scarlet of the Gobelins. A census carried out in 1748 recorded the presence of forty tanneries, twenty-one leather dressers, eighteen starch-makers, twelve bleachers, four dyers, a brusher, and some gardeners, butchers, curriers and morocco-leather-tanners. The complementary character of their activities favoured their establishment there, which gave employment to the rough workmen of the *faubourg* Saint-Marceau.[14] The water was permanently polluted by blood, offal, the waste from washing hides and skins, the bark from baths and vats, the lime and bran from the leather-dressers' workshops, and the ashes and soap from the laundries.

To all observers the Bièvre was a sewer which threatened to pass its contents into 'the River' and contaminate all Paris. For Claude le Petit, the author of *Paris ridicule*, it was the Styx. The hydrants and mill-leats brought the level down and in the summer the people who lived beside it were given a good idea of hell. The administration stepped in to protect the water, unifying the responsible authorities after 1732. The taxpayers were organised into an association for defence of their interests, regulations were promulgated and some works carried out. In August 1790 Hallé read before the Academy a memorandum which showed the permanent character of the difficulties and of the contraventions, the increase in 'putrid exhalations', the accumulation of mud and rubbish. Until the twentieth century the Bièvre reflected the link between industrial development and water, but showed also, in exemplary fashion, the progress of a requirement of public hygiene which clashed with habits and necessities.

Saturating the Bièvre meant protecting the Seine. The theme of 'the Seine as latrine' appeared in the sixteenth century, and did not disappear from pictures, topographies or the accounts of travellers who described the sanitary conditions of the town until the coming of the Third Republic. Down to the eighteenth century it was the Seine which provided Paris with the main part of its consumption, just as the Rhone served Lyons or the Loire served Orleans. Here as elsewhere – in England, Germany and Holland – batteries of pumps supported the work of the water-carriers in drawing from the river-bed water which the medical and civil authorities never stopped arguing about. Beaumarchais would say that Parisians drank in the evening what in the morning they had emptied into the Seine. The discussions reflected the loyalty to Hippocrates ideas that prevailed in those medical faculties in which the doctrine of fresh air had triumphed.[15] The Seine was a sewer from which anyone could drink. 'It supplies almost everybody's drink', wrote the doctor la Chaise, but optimistic chemical analyses revealed to him only tolerable laxative properties, a taste that was bearable, and obvious evidence that the movements of water and air acted as the best of filters. For lack of bacteriological analyses which were, of course, out of the question, no-one was able to prove the noxiousness of the water of that time, and Parisians' consumption of water never ceased to depend on the river.[16]

This was why Henri IV forced the pump of La Samaritaine, on the Pont-Neuf, on a municipality which was ill-disposed towards the Dutch, the leading technicians in hydraulic matters, and which was anxious to protect the interests of the boatmen, a matter of importance to the Provost of the Merchants (1608). Further down-river worked the pumps of the Pont Notre-Dame, installed in 1670–3, which Belidor, undoubtedly the best specialist of his time, repaired at the beginning of the eighteenth century. It was in the main bed of the river, opposite the Invalides, the Place de Grève, the Hospital and the ports of plaster and wood, that Vachette and Langlois obtained the privilege of drawing off more or less pure water which was filtered in reservoirs installed on the banks. And it was below Paris, at Chaillot, that the Périer brothers, convinced anglophiles, were to place their steam-pumps on the eve of the Revolution.

Like the Thames for London, the Seine remained the principal source of water for Paris. But as regards steam-engines France's capital was nearly a century behind the times, and around the Seine developed projects and initiatives which made of it an obligatory place of experiment in the equipment called for by town planning.[17] Controlling and mobilising the masses of water that passed through Paris and making it accessible to the greatest number of people in the largest quantity, were aims set themselves by all Parisian project-makers in the eighteenth century. This was a sort of prelude to the quest for mastery of water which other acute changes would make necessary.[18]

The conflicts over use of the river did not die down until priority, calculated by the engineers, was accorded to navigation. In the age of the architects, monumentality and aesthetics added another difficulty, and development of the river's banks had to be adapted to the requirements of traffic in a town which was trying to get rid of activities and products that were bulky and polluting.[19] The case of Paris is doubtless a guide to what happened to the other numerous cities situated on big rivers but whose equipment was less advanced. Nevertheless, other contradictions often appeared there.

Thus, at Louviers, a typical textile-making town,[20] the water was at a crossroads of appropriations and technical operations. It was essential for cleaning and scouring before carding. It figured again after weaving, in the fulling which pounded the lengths of cloth in baths of soap and fuller's earth. The Dutch mills introduced in the seventeenth century powered machinery, and high-quality hydraulic sites were sought for all these operations which were completed by the water-guzzling phases of combing and dyeing. The introduction of water-frames into spinning intensified a dependence which was already marked in the process of fabrication. It made it necessary for workplaces in textile towns to be located on the river. In 1700 there were in Louviers three corn mills, seventeen factories, four dyeworks, thirteen tanneries. In 1770 there were forty factories on the different canalised branches of the river, sixteen dyeworks, fourteen tanneries, four linen-mills. The conquest of the waterside sites by the laundries and the dyers had begun. The transition from wool to cotton after the Revolution did not halt the drift towards the river and the lower part of towns, with de-industrialisation of the upper part. Thenceforth, everything depended on the waterway, but the supply of energy took precedence over navigation and fishing. The technological improvements in water-wheels which had taken place in former times favoured the multiplication of uses by adapted solutions, either on the banks or floating, sometimes as alternatives. Paddles were as suitable for fulling as for paper-making, and, as they functioned continuously, they were polyvalent. We get an idea of the saturation achieved from the *Statistique du département de l'Eure* in 1803, which lists 628 water-operated factories, including more than 500 corn mills.

By improving and surviving more costly developments, the water-mill became the instrument of a powerful capitalism which dominated the small-scale industrialists. After 1808 a thousand dossiers of proceedings show how conflicts which had been going on for two centuries had accentuated. In town and country alike direct access to water is a way of showing the social production of a good through uses and conflicts, needs and consumption.

Well-water, sociability and consumption

In a village it was not so much the household as the community that was directly associated with water. It determined totally the difference between grouping and dispersion. The big, isolated, fortress-like farms of the Ile-de-France had their own wells. Villages and hamlets maintained communal wells. On plateaus, rivers were the sources of water, at the bottom of the valleys, while on their slopes the sources were springs that were carefully protected, and that had been the case from the sixteenth and seventeenth centuries. Some springs fed fountains and wash-places that were looked after by the communities.[21]

Whereas fire individualised people, except when conflagrations needed to be put out, water brought people together, in its production as in its consumption, because it necessitated regular encounters, conversations and conflicts. In his *Essai sur l'origine des langues*, Jean-Jacques Rousseau saw in the relation of countryfolk to water one of the best examples of communication, at the starting-point of language and civilisation.[22]

Natural circumstances compelled family groups to live together and obliged them to collaborate if they were to survive. Like the historians and the Scottish economists around Adam Smith, Rousseau believed in a close connection between the means of providing subsistence and the needs which gave rise to societies. Around fire, meals and water festivals began, changing people's lives. Rousseau saw in the shepherds' world of the dry regions the fable of the origins of the formation of the Southern languages. People had to assemble in order to dig wells, agree on how to use them, and, in a splendid image, he shows the link between the spurting-forth of the first common language and the adduction of water. The thirst of flocks timed the trysts of young couples. 'The substance of the invented languages is both leisure and ardour, the fire of love and thirst assuaged by beneficent waters.[23] It is there that the first links were formed between families. There occurred the first rendezvous between the sexes. Young girls came to fetch water for their households, young men came to water their flocks . . . Water became unnoticeably more necessary, the animals became thirsty more often, they were quick to arrive and sorry to leave . . . It was there that the first festivals were held, feet jumped for joy, the eager gesture was no longer enough, the voice accompanied it in passionate accents . . . There, finally, was the real cradle of the peoples, and from the pure crystal of the fountains sprang the first fires of love.'[24]

We should be careful not to apply to the villages of modern France the terms of an explanation of the birth of humanity. But the infectious warmth of Rousseau's very language, its inner power, cannot but evoke comparable truths regarding rural civilisations: how the tasks connected with water were shared between the sexes, the major role played by women through the ages, the natural rhythms of the repeated actvities, the sociability kept up in village life and the common obligations which still weighed upon the rural collectivities of the Kingdom.

Thus, the civilisations of the North could resemble those of the South in possessing common features and an increasing tendency to treat the sources of water as sacred. Springs, fountains and village wells were still connected with a cult. In the country there was no great incompatibility between a concentrated habitat and the presence of sacred waters. At Sainte-Bazile, in Haute-Vienne, the miracle-working fountain was close to the houses, and stock-breeders brought their animals to it so as to put them under divine protection. In Brittany the fountains were often situated close to churches and many sites of mediæval cults were everywhere located on sacred springs, primeval and Christianised. No doubt the mistrust felt by the reformed clergy, in the seventeenth century and after, contributed to push the cults far away from the habitat, into the bush or the waste-land, but they survived despite their remoteness, and regular pilgrimages helped to keep them in being into the twentieth century. Both people and flocks benefited for a long time from the mediation of the waters.[25]

Springs and fountains might be cared for as a result of more utilitarian and everyday concerns. They required an investment, in labour and money, contributed by all, if they were to be safeguarded. Wells, too, entailed costs. Urban euergetism sometimes found here a way to express itself, creating a memorable place, as in Paris, on the slopes of the Montagne Sainte-Geneviève, the Puits de L'Ermite, dug in the sixteenth century at the expense of the local notable after whom it was named. In villages the necessary equipment was sometimes donated, but probably more often it was through *corvées* and taxes that catchments were organised and *puisoirs*, drinking-troughs and washplaces built. This is a little-known page of rural history, which has shown more interest in large-scale water-supply enterprises such as the drying-out of marshes, the digging of irrigation canals and drainage works.

Study of the architecture of water in Berry shows that most of the existing structures date from after 1800.[26] This, however, does not affect the presence of an earlier network of wells, arranged in direct association with the habitat, country-houses, monasteries, manors, big farms, hamlets and grouped villages, with an intensity corresponding to the difference between cultivation and stockbreeding. Practices regarding water had been established long before in the rural communities of Berry. At Ineuil-sur-Cher a contract of 1650 shows how expenses were shared and the role played by joint ownership. The well was situated in the midst of the dwellings, near to the animals and the garden, sometimes also within the house itself. A strong sociability surrounded the well, where the village women assembled at least twice a day, this being the first and last task of their daily routine. Children were sent there after school, but men rarely, except when there was need for large amounts of water. In the Berry village as in Rousseau's fable, the well and the fountain were at the heart of the many relations that wove the web of village life.

In towns it was doubtless the case that wells were dug more often and at less cost than reliance on a fountain which needed to be fed by adduction. In Paris, when dwellings were built far from the river banks and in great numbers, landowners and bourgeois dug wells so as to have water easily at hand.[27] André Guillerme found evidence of this particularly in cities of the second rank, after the thirteenth century, when the more important cities were establishing artificial fountains which used the water of catchmented springs. Place-names often recall the habitual use of collective wells: rue du Puits-Mauconseil, rue du Puits-qui-Parle, rue du Puits-de Rome, rue du Bon-Puits, rue des Puits-Mauvais and rue Puits-Mauvais, rue du Puits-de-Fer, rue du Puits-Certain, rue du Puits-Notre-Dame, rue du Puits-du-Chapitre, rue du Puits-de-l'Orme, or du Puits-d'Amour, which disappeared in the eighteenth century.

The hydrology of Paris was not one of the most favorable, given the level of technology. Well-sinkers could easily dig down to the layers of water at medium depth, but the major levels were for a long time out of their reach. The water they discovered was tainted by all the things that the townspeople threw out, but it was essential nevertheless. The common well, among the houses, formed part of life just as in villages. About 1833 the engineer Girard calculated the number of wells that reached the water-level of green plastic clay at 25,000 or 30,000, which meant nearly one for every two houses. On the first day of the siege of 1871 Belgrand, who was in charge of the town's water-supply, caused more than 30,000 wells to be visited, and 20,000 were repaired.[28] That was doubtless the largest number ever of private bore-holes. It is hard to know what contribution they made to daily consumption, but very likely the housewives, craftsmen and tavern-keepers of Paris drew some of their everyday supply from them.

For the bakers the well-water was an essential ingredient, 'the soul of the bread'. Its quality depended on the nature of the water, which had to be light and pure. That was what made the reputation of the bakers of Gonesse who put their products on the market. Parmentier, however, supported the opposite view, charging the bakers with faulty work. The well-water used in three-quarters of the bakehouses was 'heavy and salty', but the quality of the loaves was no different if river-water or rain-water was used. His experiments were conclusive, but they did not convince either all the specialists in food or the public authorities, who urged the bakers to give up the well-water in favour of the water from the fountains or from the Seine, which, be it noted, found in Parmentier their greatest defender.[29]

The dispute about the bakers' water reveals clearly how people were increasingly aware of the problem of the quality of what was available in the ground-water beneath Paris, polluted through the centuries by cesspools, latrine-ditches, the water from rain-washed streets, the rubbish dumps and the cemeteries, which meant that it was not very healthy and had to be boiled, or else kept for external uses only – washing, watering gardens – or for industrial purposes. Contaminated as it was by these many infiltrations, the well-water would seem to us a filthy mess, like the water of the Seine, but in the eighteenth century they argued over the curative or unhealthy qualities of both. The movements for sanitation and hygiene and the progress of major drainage schemes would gradually doom the well-water, but for several centuries its contribution, in Paris as everywhere else, was not negligible. The great cholera epidemics of the nineteenth century, along with quasi-endemic typhoid, showed the danger clearly through the map of their incidence.[30] They turned well-water into a suspect given respite.

Two important features of the consumption of water in the old town can be perceived through the constant use of boreholes and wells. On the one hand there was a social topography of uses which set the districts in contrast with each other (in Paris the left bank, with the university, being high up, had fewer wells than the alluvial right bank), as also types of house – public buildings, hospitals and prisons possessed their own wells, as did aristocratic town-houses and religious communities, which had special need of water for their gardens, whereas private houses and tenements often shared the use of a well. The individual pumps installed on all these wells made it easier to draw from them, as we are told by Bernard Palissy in the sixteenth century and by the *Encyclopédie*.

These different ways of access to water were associated with as many different ways of life and types of sociability. The collective wells in streets and squares, the private wells in urban courtyards brought together every day, just as in villages, neighbours of both sexes, servants, users of all kinds. News both true and false was exchanged and assignations fixed. People quarrelled and made up. These were, everywhere, monuments raised to scarce water and collective urbanity. They entailed sharing of responsibility between the landowners who paid for the borehole and the masonry, the pullies, chains, windlasses and wheels, while the cost of the ropes and buckets was often borne by the 'principal tenant', who was usually the craftsman who lived on the ground floor and was the main user. Drawing water from the well was not always easy, which was why, for farm animals' or horses' water, the river was preferred. Accidents were not infrequent, lids and curbstones being provided in order to prevent them. In all this the town retained many characteristics of village life.

On the other hand, the wells of the monasteries and convents, the public buildings and the great town-houses showed a different social space, more reserved and less utilitarian, with access under greater control, less noisy and disordered. This was, all other things being equal, a world with different demands, wherein the regularity of the supply of water and its easier accessibility for a small group did not correspond to the same immediate or deferred uses.

Water from aqueducts, utility and the heritage of Rome

We come again upon this division when we consider the contribution made by the aqueducts to the town's water supply. An expensive means of catchment, they presented everywhere the image of a Roman and monumental fidelity, in the antique style, with an urban grandeur and aquatic liberality altogether out of proportion with the amenities they provided. Their disappearance, between the fifth and twelfth centuries, from the territories of ancient Gaul was due much less to the brutality of the barbarian invasions than to the disappearance of town life and the ruralising of civilisation. Their gradual reappearance was connected with the combined efforts of the authorities, lay and ecclesiastical, who sought to meet the needs of the new agglomerations, supplying water to the districts distant from rivers and combating fires, much to be feared in towns built of wood.

The monumental fountain fed from the channels of the aqueduct manifested the attractiveness of town life and the grandeur of the city.[31] For learned men and travellers returning from Italy this was one of the major themes in the evocation of a civilisation in which the magisterial skill of the builders raised up in the towns of the Empire monuments to the glory of water, baths and fountains fed by gigantic aqueducts. In Paris the water was catchmented on the heights of Arcueil and flowed fifteen kilometres down to the baths of Cluny. In the hinterland of Nîmes the Point du Gard was already attracting a crowd, limited as yet, of sightseers. Rome's sacred water provided the foundation for a way of life which the townsfolk of the modern epoch could barely imagine, let alone copy.

At the end of the fifteenth century the Paris municipality controlled the distribution of about 300 cubic metres a day, brought within the walls by the canals of the Pré-Saint-Gervais and Belleville, the sources for which emerged in the marls and screes of the hillsides that supplied the neighbouring villages. A dozen fountains *intra muros* were managed by the municipality and gave a few dozen privileged persons the supply they needed for their 'household', on the basis of free and usually honorific concessions. The sixteenth century brought few changes in the system of adduction and distribution. It was under Henri IV that the most important transformations appeared, following the sieges which had left the capital entirely dependent on the Seine and the wells. On the one hand the King decreed the construction of the pump on the Pont-Neuf and the great aqueduct at Arcueil, a tribute to ancient Lutetia and the first example in modern France of a water-conduit contained in a gallery. It was to supply the capital with a mere thousand cubic metres, when conditions were favourable. On the other hand, the King inaugurated the supervision of the water-supply by royal officials and the provision of paid-for concessions. He also found a clever way of financing the works by means of a tax on wine entering the city, so that, from that time on, wine paid for water. These main features established at the beginning of the seventeenth century lasted, with minor changes, until the last quarter of the eighteenth.

From these various fountains – sixty in 1700, eight-five in 1785 – and from the private taps plugged into the pipes there flowed about 2,000 cubic metres of water every day when Louis XIV's reign was ending. That meant barely four or five litres per inhabitant, but the Seine and the private wells supplied the rest. Merely for the 40,000 or 50,000 horses in Paris 800,000 litres were needed daily, even more than a million litres, or seven million pails of fifteen litres each! The amounts actually consumed are impossible to evaluate.

The response made to needs and the system of appropriation show how important, in the period when the quantities concerned were stable, were the conflicts of authority around the management of the water-supply. In Paris in modern times – but some works done on the great rivers of France, the Rhône, the Rhine, the Garonne, the Loire, the Dordogne, presented a similar picture – the principal contenders were the municipality and the King, the local communities and inhabitants and the central administration, its agents and its experts. One defended the needs of navigation and sought to control initiatives and projects based on the river, together with the right to intervene in town politics, while the other initiated works and granted concessions which created a paradoxical situation, insofar as these were paid for out of all the receipts from the tolls and contributed to accentuating the social tensions around the sharing of water.

The three or four hundred concessions, some free and some paid for, and the King's own water which supplied the Tuileries, the Louvre and the Luxembourg and was administered by the Intendant General of the Fountains, took a substantial share of the output of the public fountains: a minimum of 1,056 square metres for 200 concessions around 1715, together with between 500 and 600 cubic metres for the King, accounted for more than half of the catchmented public water. This Parisian aristocracy of water consisted for a good third of religious and educational establishments and hospitals, for a good quarter of great court nobles and ministers, forty per cent of private individuals, members of the *Parlement*, former magistrates, administrators and lawyers. Geographically, there were not many hydrants on the Left Bank (twenty-five per cent) and these served principally the religious communities and the colleges, together with some great families in the Saint-Germain district, while on the right bank they were concentrated in the old central districts: Saint-Denis, Saint-Martin, the Temple, Saint-Honoré. The social topography of water still conformed to the social structure of the old districts which were as yet not very differentiated.

Almost all the people of Paris were without direct access to running water, just as they had no taps. They depended for their daily supply upon their own strength and that of the innumerable servants, for whom fetching water was one of their chief tasks. The daily supply depended too on the strength of the water carriers who fetched water in casks from the river and in pails from the fountains. Armed with fifteen-litre pails they carried thirty litres on each journey and delivered the water to people's homes, storey by storey, at a rate of payment fixed by the authorities. Around fountains which gave out little water quarrels broke out that, for three hundred years, set one against each other, men and women of the people, bourgeois and servants, and water-carriers who were rowdy and argumentative, practising their hard trade with intimidation and insult to protect their territory. The police arbitrated these quarrels, which occurred more often in districts where a well-to-do population attracted the water-carriers, sure of finding enough customers, whereas in the poor parts of the city the inhabitants drew their water themselves from the public fountains or were content with the polluted water from the wells.

The problem of the amount of water available was always present, but it was not equally acute or significant for everyone. Scarcity was common to all categories as regards availability, but in different degrees depending on habits and on wealth. Inequality was always present where quality of water was concerned, along a fundamental frontier which it is difficult to trace through the whole of society.

Natural and social constraints

The old regime of the water supply was trebly dependent – on nature, on technology and on a certain model of civilisation. The disparate and inadequate supply reflected the weighty bonds that linked the material culture to the environment.

In town as in country seasonal variations upset all schedules. Summer dried up the rivers and the ponds. For the townspeople this was a hard time, when the water-carriers had to supply a thirstier population from scarcer water. The police watched over consumption and the fountains. Smart crooks stole water by selling inspection holes and pipes. The jets spurting forth in the gardens of the powerful were a provocation for poor people suffering from lack of water. The King and the municipality revoked the concessions at this time. The output of the aqueducts and pumps sometimes fell by half, the water in the wells stank and all Paris was dying of thirst. In the country this was also a time of restrictions and measures of supervision by the rural police.

In winter, freeze-ups could affect traffic on the river. Pipes cracked under the pavements when heavy wagons passed. In the badly heated homes of the poor, ice covered the water in buckets and pails, so that it had to be warmed by the fireplace, first thing in the morning. Lumps of ice blocked the paddles of the pumps and obstructed the boats used for drawing water. The drinking troughs and *bateaux puisoirs* became inaccessible, horses lost their footing on frost-covered slopes. Fear of fires made the policemen and firemen more tense. The great floods at winter's end brought disaster and interrupted supply. From the end of the seventeenth century the scale on the Pont de la Tournelle showed the level to which the river had risen: in 1740 it reached nearly eight metres. For the water-supply this meant total disturbance, since the pumps gave out more than was needed and were at the same time under threat, because the ground-water was polluted all over by the overflow from the submerged latrines and the discharge of the sewers. In summer and winter alike precariousness and rationing prevailed.

However, the shortage of water was due also to the inertia of technology. The skill of fountain-makers and master-spring-finders made little progress between the Middle Ages and the Enlightenment. The pipes made of wood, lead, iron and earthenware were crude and fragile. The system of gauging remained very archaic until the seventeenth century. Hydraulic science was at that time incapable of taking account of variations in the volume of water coming out of fountains through its speed, inclination and distance travelled. The water in a conduit would be sufficient for the diversions drawn from it, provided that the sum of these diversions did not exceed the cross-section of the main pipe. The concession-holders and the fountains were therefore connected directly to the main pipe between its upper extremity and the first reservoir of the principal fountains, and if all the taps were turned on then all the water would pour away before reaching it, and in fact they never stopped night and day.

The fountain-makers of the seventeenth and eighteenth centuries, better informed about the law of hydraulics, dealt with these leakages by establishing the starting-point of the pipes in the basin situated at the lower end of the main pipes, but without stopping the wastage from continual flow. The fountains were thus better supplied and supervised, and the private concessions participated in the seasonal variations in the output of the adductions. This technical mini-revolution effected between 1630 and 1660, under the stimulus of drought, altered the context. The introduction of pumps on the river also helped, but their output was slight and they were expensive to maintain. Between 1626 and 1777 ten projects for improving the old installations or creating new ones were rejected. A technical limit had been reached at that time for hydraulic pumps.

This was of course the technology of the classical period, the golden age of water-driven mills and machines, of which hydraulics was the dynamic, and which would survive the triumphs of the thermodynamic revolution at the end of the eighteenth century and the beginning of the nineteenth.[32] For several centuries water was at the heart of the architecture of the engineers and of the mechanics of the architects. It subjected them to its laws, in accordance with the great Vitruvian model. It was no coincidence that modern hydrology was born with Pierre Perrault's *Traité de l'origine des fontaines* in 1674, and in 1673 his brother Claude translated Vitruvius's *Ten Books of Architecture*. Hydraulic architecture mobilised the energies of craftsmen, fountain-makers, mechanics and engineers together with those of the theoreticians of nascent hydrodynamics, Bernouilli, Euler and Clairault. Theirs were problems, theoretical and practical, of maritime navigation, canals, sluices, water-clocks, fountains, water-wheels and water-pumps. We find them brought together in the monumental work of Bernard Forest de Belidor, *L'Architecture hydraulique, ou l'Art de conduire, d'élever, et de ménager les eaux pour les différents besoins de la vie*, published in Paris in 1736.

The apogee of Vitruvian hydraulics and needs

A technical system cannot progress without a quantitative and qualitative leap. The means for supplying water cannot increase unless the pressure of needs forces research for new solutions. These appeared in the urban dynamic and in the context of a profound change in ways of thinking, when the provision of water ceased to be a privileged and aristocratic conception and became a dimension of collective appropriation aimed at social, sanitary and economic control. From this standpoint what was important was not so much the innovatory use of the steam-engine as an alternative solution which solved all problems, as the conflict which developed in the development of the towns' territory, the economic exploitation of the kingdom imagined by the engineers, and the exploitation of nature.

Watt's engine, even if it entailed a more complex economy through its supplies and costs, was a 'mill' like any other that could be listed among the machines of hydraulic architecture, which was what the engineer Navier did in 1819 when he published an updated version of Belidor's work. The debate ranged the supporters of a passive hydraulic mobilisation of resources in order to catchment springs and supply towns[33] against the defenders of pumping by machine within the city walls. In the years 1770–80, Deparcieux, Perronet and de Fer, advocates of large-scale passive equipment, confronted the brothers Périer, anglophiles who advocated machinery that was costly to maintain. Mirabeau supported the former, Beaumarchais the latter.[34] We can perceive in this confrontation the battle between the Roman model and the British example, distribution from the periphery or supply at the centre.

The opposition between canal and machine involved two contradictory conceptions of urban politics and economy. In both cases plentiful supply was possible: ten of the British machines could provide as much as the French canals and, in the long run, the redistribution was the same. The machines were solutions expensive to make, though less so than the adductions. Above all, they required care in use, renewal of parts and sets of parts, transport and storage of fuel, and so, for the mass of the population an ultimate cost, when receipts and expenditure were compared, and inevitable rationing. Canals, passive and indestructible systems, needed little maintenance and were more or less stable in cost, without great charge. The equipment provided plenty of water for almost nothing: it had, ultimately, no exchange value.

The public weal was once again in conflict with profit, for the initial investment would have to be borne by the state. In the end, 'the liquid network has to disappear, leaving to the habitat the trouble of developing without remembering that omnipresent water was one of the conditions for its existence'.[35]

Royal, bourgeois and popular water

The warm world of thermodynamics and steam-engines was to see the victory of the passive equipment dreamt of in the cold civilisation of hydraulic architecture and water-mills. This symbolic limitation of the power of fire characterises the transfer which took place in connection with water in the civilisation of towns. In modern society and in the period when water was scarce, an aristocratic model was dominant which was based on riches, the employment of numerous servants and, often, the grant of an individual privilege, but which did not necessarily imply a rigorous social frontier. Nobles and rich people drank the same water, of the same bad quality, as the less well-off. Their real privilege was to have it in quantity and regularly, to be able to filter it more easily, and to add ice to it in hot weather. Toilet measures were as perfunctory in both groups, and indulgence in baths, at a barber's where there was a steam-bath, or even in the river, was due to age, sociability, leisure and health as much as, if not more than, to concern for hygiene.

Water was above all an element of decor in the aristocratic civilisation of appearances. It served primarily for fetes, for aesthetic purposes and for the embellishment of parks and gardens. When Henri IV planned bringing the water of Arcueil to Paris he reserved more than half of it for watering the grottos of the Luxembourg and the groves of the Tuileries. The Francines, mechanics and fountain-makers from Italy, developed the royal parks at Saint-Germain, Fontainebleau and Versailles. Their achievement at Versailles was gigantic and amazingly inventive. They provided the park with the hydraulic devices required for the royal entertainments, fed through a system of pumps and canals with water drawn in by these Voluptas machines. Catchmenting the pond at Clagny, the reservoir, the grottos, the partial catchmenting of the upper Bièvre, the flower-bed, the water avenue, the theatre and pavilion on the water and the basin of Neptune swallowed up, before the construction of the machine at Marly to raise water from the Seine (1687), the huge sum of 40 million *livres*.[36] The Arcueil aqueduct had cost, in 1634, 460,000 *livres*, and Belidor proposed to equip the capital with two fire-engines for less than three million around 1730! At the end of the seventeenth century and the beginning of the eighteenth technological dependence seems to have been less restrictive than the constraints of nature, still poorly mastered and, especially, the preferences of society. The scarcity of water in Paris and in most of France's cities conformed to the political, social and cultural system. We can thus appreciate the backwardness of Paris relative to London, and understand why research served the ruler rather than the people. Versailles was a technical laboratory in which the most effective conduits and machines were compared and tried out. Court civilisation promoted a model of needs and uses which protracted the economy of scarcity into the last quarter of the century of Enlightenment. The rural areas were not touched by the court.

To realise what this meant it is enough to calculate what was available in this domain to the little people and to try and see the principal uses to which it corresponded. In theory the water of Paris furnished, in about 1700, less than five litres per head and ten litres in about 1789, with a population of between 400,000 and 700,000. Post-mortem inventories enable us to calculate what was available to the families covered, assuming that they filled all the pails recorded. In Louis XIV's reign that figure was forty-nine litres for a wage-earning family and twenty-eight litres for servants who could use their employers' water and often had two domiciles. Under Louis XVI the figures were still forty-three and sixty-one. Water was scarce, a luxury for lower-class families. At the beginning of the century an average of about ten litres per head was not fantastic, but such provision had to last for several days.[37] On the eve of the Revolution less than a quarter of the inventories of wage-earners showed a family average of fifteen litres. The situation had worsened, or at least had not improved much, while the public equipment had made possible a distribution which advantaged only the rich. Here is another indication of this probable deterioration: in about 1700, copper fountains holding drinking-water were not rare, even though expensive, but they had become so by 1780, and had been replaced by cheaper models made of stoneware and faience, and by miscellaneous jars, buckets and pails.

For most of the population managing water was not very easy. In towns some practices were inconceivable, or almost. One's washing was very soon entrusted to the washerwomen,[38] though the well-off also had it done by their servants, using water from the well or the river. It was not possible to take baths except in the river in summer, and then despite the prohibitions (men and youngsters did it), or else in a few, not very numerous, establishments. In 1789 Paris had fewer than 300 bathtubs in the bathhouses in the town and on the Seine. To these can be added a good thousand private bathtubs in aristocrats' houses, and one or two hundred more with the coopers, who hired them out as required and for medical use. Two thousand is a generous estimate of the number of baths, public and private, in Paris. For drinking and bathing thirty litres (*une voie*) were needed in the upper floors, and this cost two or three sols, depending on how high up one lived: one cubic metre cost three or four days of wage-paid labour. In the country water was more economic and was conserved in pails and casks kept filled by the servants.

Clean and dirty, wholesome and unwholesome

Scarce water implies a different culture which must not be judged according to present-day theories of hygiene[39] or from the viewpoint of the old fashioned medical practices. The customs of cleanliness or uncleanliness associated by all well-informed observers with the way of life of the lower orders were above all the expression of a different culture of the body and other acceptable habits. This was, it seems, an old *habitus* in which familiar smells and tolerances of dirt, even notions of what was and was not wholesome, were different from ours.[40]

For a long time, if an individual smelt, that meant that he was strong and prosperous, as many proverbs testify.[41] Plague was combated with the mustiness of night soil, dungheaps at the door did not inconvenience anyone and showed how well-off a household was – a good sign for knowing what a fiancée's expectations might be. People feared losing their strength in the bathwater if they washed too much, and babies grew all the better if they had a thick crust of dirt on their heads. Taking warm baths was linked with lasciviousness and condemned by the moralists of all the churches. To conclude, the French, associating a strong smell with good health, kept up a long-lasting collective distrust regarding all ablutions. The interiors of the dwellings of the people of Paris showed this tolerance of the nauseating and suggested a specific ambience which offended modernistic doctors and could only be changed through control of water.

For most people, therefore, in town and country alike, availability of water was limited, and so were needs. It was necessary to be sparing in the use of water for washing up, housework, a modest amount of laundry and limited washing of the person, except in the case of rich peasants and nobles. While all these facts underwent change as one rose in the social scale, that happened without great variations either in quantity or quality. We know what smells prevailed on the seamy side of the Grand Siècle and what tolerances there could be beneath the gold and the mirrors in a civilisation of appearances.[42]

Two great movements are observable simultaneously in rural and urban societies between the seventeenth century and the nineteenth. On the one hand the civilisation of manners gradually imposed on everyone some new constraints in bodily habits, which were inseparable from sartorial practices.[43] On the other, the consumption of water remained stable for a long time, whereas that of linen increased in line with the standards of the new propriety.[44] The two aspects of behaviour are inseparable and the social demands which ordered the old attitude to bodily hygiene were no less powerful than those of the hygienists of the nineteenth and twentieth centuries.

Historians of behavioural values describe a watery Middle Ages, with frequent baths, steam-baths that were indispensable in the public space of the towns, mingling the use of water for pleasure with a comparative concern for cleanliness. We are shown rivers frequented by bathers, bathers in the *bagnos*, which were both bathhouses and brothels, and the first fountains. The picture is too beautiful, and the documents are too few for us to know how everyone actually behaved. However, let it be admitted that the elites of mediaeval society had values which maintained hygiene through the use of water. As for the majority we may have our doubts. What is likely is that in the Middle Ages water was not used, or not primarily, for washing bodies that were dirty and soiled, but was associated with the pleasures of the body, with encounters that were courteous, amorous and friendly, whether venal or free. It was an aristocratic and urban use of water.[45]

Modern times, after the Renaissance, saw indulgence in the pleasures of the bath grow less frequent, there was a flight of the elites from the baths along with an increase in interest in water-connected monuments. Needs were reduced to bare necessities – drinking, some limited ablutions, the upkeep of linen. In classical civilisation, under pressure from the church, separation of the body's demands from those of the soul contributed to a change of attitude regarding care of the body, a hitherto unused distinction between the clean and the dirty, and led to a transfer of investment from one's body to one's linen, clothing, adornment even.[46] The cleanliness that mattered was no longer that of the body, in the Roman fashion or in pursuit of pleasure, but that of the soul. We can follow the formation of this normative discourse through sermons, education both religious and secular, morality, medical treatises, the philippics of priests and the indictments of doctors. The body, conceived as being exposed and agape, was constantly threatened by intrusions from without. Hot water, by opening one's pores, prepared the way for all sorts of danger. Cold water might be allowed, in order to close up the opened pores and also calm sexual desire. One ought, therefore, to avoid the humid and prefer the dry and cold. We see, too, how the imperatives of the medicine of humours could be applied to these moral systems. The scarcity of water could thus fit in well with praise of sparingness in the use of it. Its impact coincided with that of the static economy and of morality.

We perceive here the basis for the rhetoric of the manuals of 'good manners'[47] in which everything to do with clothing is concerned both morally and socially with a type of behaviour, civil decency. 'It is the body's body and gives an idea of the soul's dispositions.'[48] 'Agreement between what is within and what is without' reveals agreement between being and seeming,[49] while at the same time serving to express the social hierarchy. Cleanliness is expelled to the exterior and to linen.[50] Attention is concentrated on the extremities, the hands, the neck, the face, which one may wipe carefully with water, and on one's linen, the whiteness of which embodies virtue, so that it must be changed and cleaned with the means at one's disposal.

This was the principal dilemma of the invention of linen. It was the bearer of the new moral and social hygiene because, when dry, it soaked up sweat, screened intimate filth and protected the body against illness, yet at the same time increased the chores of cleaning, if it was not to lose its effectiveness.[51] Care and cleanliness did not march at the same pace where the body and its linen were concerned, while at this time a new epidemiology paid attention to them. In opposition to this, the plagues which still troubled the realm before the 1720s set off repeated denunciations of linen, which was accused of carrying the miasmas of the epidemic and which might certainly harbour rats and lice, the true plague-carriers. Unless one changed often the danger would grow but this did not necessarily entail a requirement of cleanliness through washing oneself. The persistent vermin expressed corruption of the humours, secreting fleas, scabies and mites, which were combated with bleeding, emetics, purges and dieting.[52] Scarcity of linen fostered illnesses, abundance of it caused them to retreat. By becoming widespread, especially in the form of shirts, linen made possible a cleanliness that was wholly superficial.

This cleanliness was achieved through the labour of women as laundresses, and was proportionate to the capacities of households. Water and linen were central to the social construction of new feminine personalities, which made their way down from the landed aristocracy to the popular classes and were passed on by schools and families. In the country the wisdom of proverbs and good manners was not offended in the same way as in urban practices with smells, stains, dirt and parasites, which one had to put up with and which popular medicine frequently associated with wealth and fullness.[53]

This was why there coexisted 'little laundries' and 'big steamings': it was a question of means, of riches and accumulation of tradition and rural ritualism. The one was more a family affair, domestic, repetitive ('only the vermin-ridden wash their clothes'), the other more collective, festive and convivial, experienced as transition from dirt to cleanness in the cycle of the seasons, the victory of life over death. The water of the wash-places and tanks crystallised both, in different spaces, internal and external, from the farm to the wash-places, from the precarious clothes-lines to the meadows where the linen was left to flap.[54] Until the end of the nineteenth century the rural communities did not possess the equipment to make the water-festival less crude and less niggardly. This was to be the great century of linen and the triumph of large-scale laundering. Until then, happy were the villages and market-towns that happened to be situated by a river.

The town had assembled other ways of proceeding, because the accumulation of people amplified there all the material constraints and obliged poor and well-to-do alike to move away from house and family. The economic and physical obstacles to responding to social proprieties and the precepts of the hygiene of good manners were considerable.[55] Doctors thought it reasonable to change one's shirt every two or three days: a little more often in summer, more frequently in the case of rich people. That meant, for a town of 600,000 inhabitants, a daily pile of 200,000 shirts, not to mention other garments. There were several co-existent ways of meeting such needs: uncertain home washings in hovels or in yards with common wells, abundant washings in the Seine or the Bièvre, repeated laundering by families, professional laundering by washerwomen, laundries of communities, hospitals, convents and prisons, and industrial bleacheries which were promoted by shrewd chemists like Chaptal on the eve of the Revolution.

Paris was never to see the washerwomen give up the river, despite the wishes of the administration. Between the seventeenth and eighteenth centuries the boat-wash-houses numbered between seventy-seven and ninety-four, or about 2,000 places. The washerwomen and their ways were part of the landscape. 'Anyone who possesses only one or two shirts acts as his own launderer, and if you doubt that, cross the Pont-Neuf on a Sunday at four in the morning, when you will see on the river's bank several individuals who, naked under their overcoats, are engaged in washing their one and only shirt or handkerchief', wrote Sébastien Mercier.[56] This was also the case with the poorest housewives and workers, but most of the population, from the marchioness to the water-carrier, from the courtier Abbé to the lady's maid, made their way to the laundry shop because neither the insufficient amount of water available nor the organisation of the poeple's dwellings facilitated large-scale home washing. This fact is witnessed by the account-books of the laundresses and the liabilities shown in post-mortem inventories, the interest of the economists who calculated the economic capacity of the businesses, the motivation of the inventors of methods for washing linen 'whiter still', the attention shown by the town hall and the police, who saw in this a cause of more and more frequent conflicts by the Seine, the soap riots which broke out during the Revolution, and the snobbery of the great, 'whose custom it is to send their linen to the American islands for laundering'.[57] The need for white linen and the morality of appearances increased the need for water. This was a conquest of the eighteenth century, which came more than a hundred years later than the promulgation of standards.

The dream of pure and plentiful water

At this same moment a second cultural break began to become apparent. The rejection of water in medical and educational literature was followed by its apologia. In *Emile* Rousseau echoed this new advocacy. Cold water, it was claimed, would strengthen the body, harden the character and help to form citizens worthy of Antiquity, of whose benefits aristocratic softness and monkish filth had deprived them. Water – cold, lukewarm and hot – found a place in 'the art of keeping healthy'. It extinguished neither 'the capacity of genius', seeing that Demosthenes, Cato and Caesar were water-drinkers, and even swimmers, nor sexual vigour: 'Tiraqueau, who drank nothing but water, had thirty children and wrote as many works.'[58] A new bodily hygiene which generalised breathing through the skin by cleanliness through washing challenged popular prejudices and the precepts of the medicine of temperaments.

In his *Dictionnaire de la conservation de l'homme*, Louis-Charles Macquart found, in Year VII, lyrical accents in which to proclaim the many virtues of water, which brought richness and fertility to the earth, ensured the health and growth of human beings, protected them from gout if they drank three litres of it every day, and prevented the agitation of highly strung people who were excited by liqueurs and coffee. 'It is the most health-giving of drinks.'[59] It was the basis of hygiene, the regulator of health, and taught men how to keep at bay the ills that threatened them and how to live longer. Its merits should be taught in the schools so as to ensure happiness for people and states. Modern legislators, following the example of the ancient philosophers, should use it to reconcile public and private hygiene. 'They ought to establish, for the general health, public baths and artificial lakes which, while honouring the arts by the beauty of their construction, would do good to individuals, especially the poor, who deserve the benefits of a government active, just and great.' In these words we hear the concern for the reform of ways of life which ran through the Revolution, and the appeal to philanthropy. We note the transition from a civilisation of aristocracy and amusement, in which water was scarce and hygiene incorporated in concern for appearances, to an age that would be more egalitarian, more civic, in which plentiful water strengthened the idea of a universal capacity for happiness. From the cleanliness of what is visible to the hygiene of what is not visible, a movement was beginning here which would continue into our own time. However, manifestation of the new standards would have to wait, if we look at people's actual practices.

Habits evolved collectively at a slower pace than the moral or medical discourses which sounded their appeals in the last quarter of the eighteenth century. Ability to respond to these appeals varied in accordance with social groups and their education. There are several indications of a tremor. Among the people of Paris inventories taken around 1700 reveal that among wage-earners about 2 per cent had water-pots, washbasins and accessories needed for cleanliness. By 1789 the proportion had reached twenty per cent, and in the population as a whole it stood at more than a quarter. Chamber-pots and commodes were rare: barely 10 per cent at the beginning of the century, 30 per cent at its end. On the basis of several thousand inventories this shows that the hierarchy of practices still prevailed. Among the aristocratic town-houses, Dominique Massounié's surveys attribute to the most luxurious habitat one bathroom in ten buildings in 1750, but by 1800 the proportion had risen to thirty per cent, one in three.[60]

These figures enable us to compare with reality what was being written and to show the extent of the possible transformation, in relation to types of dwelling. Space reserved for the toilet was a feature of the architecture of palaces. Versailles had several bathrooms, as the Louvre had had between 1650 and 1680, when Anne of Austria lived there. This was not solely due to medical considerations, as we know that the young King also liked the Court to bathe occasionally in the river. Although, as the King grew older, this summer pleasure declined in appeal, the fashion for bathrooms continued to progress in the precepts of architects.[61] Of ninety-six buildings Mariette, in 1727, assigned such amenities to seventeen per cent. In 1752 Blondel assigned them to 16 per cent of 30 buildings: Kraft, in 1802, 42 per cent: Percier, in 1833, 40 per cent. We perceive here an effect of fashion borne forward by the victory of intimacy and a new care for the body, even though these old aristocratic bathrooms corresponded to a wordly familiarity rather than to total privacy. It was a progressive luxury, driven by the taste of high society and that of the Court. Louis XVI provided Versailles with six bathrooms, each with a refined decor. At the top of the new society hygiene and new practices could combine their effect. Down below, the gap was still there, and in the country it perhaps grew wider.

We must not over-emphasise the contrast and easy antitheses. At the very heart of the system of scarce water some acts testified to the possibility of living differently. Thus, bathing by the lower orders was tracked down and persecuted from the seventeenth century onward, not for medical reasons but for the sake of modesty, offended by the masculine nakednes of boatmen and boys of the town which gave pleasure to the washerwomen. As a cause of accidents in a period unpropitious to the art of swimming, bathing was forbidden every year in notices put up by the town hall. They were not effective. Bathing went on, regardless, for two centuries. Need dictated it, along with the pleasure that hard-working folk took in cleaning themselves up during hot weather. In *Les Nuits de Paris* Restif de la Bretonne[62] testified to the liking for bathing which became common, 'It was beginning to get hot. The bathing boats were in place. The extreme heat attracted a crowd to them as evening fell, and this for two reasons: because people were more at liberty then and because a sort of modesty still prevented women from going there in the daytime.' Restif made the round of the baths, from the Place Maubert to the Cité, from the Pont-Marie to the grain port, from the Pont Neuf to the Quai des Théâtier and the Quai de l'Horloge.

It was very late. Children and apprentices were bathing in the little branch of the river that runs in front of the Augustins and separates them from the Quai des Orfèvres. I noted how much these paltry bathing places, which were like those that poor savages might use, proclaimed the filthiness of the greatest city in the world. Five or six cabined baths for Paris! The fact is that hardly anybody baths here, and those who do confine themselves to once or twice, in the summer, that is to say in the year. While I was thinking about that and wishing that the practice of taking baths was more widespread, I heard a noise coming from the little branch of the river. It was some children running away. There was an order forbidding them to wash in the river . . .

Everything comes together in this passage from Restif: scarce water and filthiness, religious and moral prohibitions, and the affirmation that change is on the way. Bathing is a good thing, and it will lead to people learning to swim, to cleanliness and to health.

At the end of the eighteenth century two intellectual phenomena expressed the rise in expectations, the dream of pure and purifying water. First, the crisis of the town and its pathogenic and criminogenic effects. The townsman was losing his profound quality.[63] For the neo-Hippocratic doctors bodily hygiene, food, drink, clothing, linen became cures for urban illnesses. Control of water figured in this programme, which aimed at rehabilitation of individuals and of the town. The urban organism needed a grand clean-up which could be accomplished only if plenty of water was available. Action would be focused on the centres of multiple infection – hospitals, cemeteries, prisons, butchers' shops, sewers, tanneries – and would sweep away the black tide of slush. The slippage from medical to social took place imperceptibly, and while we must not confuse reality with what these observers imagined, it does enable us to understand how the town's pathogeny became pathology. In 1830 the increase in crime, proved by statistical and literary analysis, was identified with a biological crisis which was best revealed by the cholera epidemic. The sanitary movement desired and initiated in the Century of Enlightenment culminated in a general vision of social conduct. The poor man ought to be clean. Running water available to everyone was the instrument of this action, at the end of the great works begun in 1800 and completed in 1830, with the Canal de l'Ourcq.

Secondly, however, awareness of this group of needs, which made what was a special luxury into a universal necessity, presumed a deep-going revolution in sensibilities, the crossing of a threshold of tolerance.[64] That which had been bearable for centuries was so no longer. Thenceforth the sense of smell took first place among the senses, attacked by the harmful effects of a town without water. Signs of the pathology of smells reinforced those of the town's pathology. The weakening of tolerance led to a twofold transformation: withdrawal by the individual, who isolated himself when he washed or defecated, the concealed toilet, the private and individualised use of water, while, at the same time, a war was waged against unacceptable smells. Ventilating, disinfecting, draining and irrigating, cleaning up the town and its inhabitants, the practice of putting all waste in the sewers and the installing of the toilet-flush would create cities that were clean and bodies properly cared for. The city of the Enlightenment completed the work of the civilisation of manners so as to control the affects. The installation of equipment helped forward the silent domestication and liberation of people, implying self-control and greater attention to others.

At the end of the eighteenth century, in the writings of Jean-Noël Hallé, inspector of the banks of the Seine, physician and Academician, in those of the killers of stench, Macquer, Parmentier, Malouin, Mercier and Béguillet, in the projects of the architects and engineers Patte, Moreau d'Esproux, Poyet, Girard, de Fer and de Parcieux, the strategies of this great purification were determined. Water was, for them, not yet entirely the instrument of individual hygiene but the means of combating endemic nuisances and the risk of epidemics.[65] The catchmenting of springs and the digging of canals were at that time intended not so much to make running water available to everyone as to clean up the points of exchange where the concentration of human beings created a critical situation. Water drew a new frontier between the wholesome and the unwholesome, first in the town and much later in the villages.

7 Furniture and objects

Furniture and decors hold a special place in the tour in which we set necessities, conveniences and luxuries against Society's means and capacities, consumption and production. From the end of the Middle Ages they underwent a slow and many-sided evolution which speeded up in the eighteenth century. Even if, in this domain, fashion moved slowly,[1] changes are observable, stimulated at first by urban demand and the rise of new requirements.

There is a strong temptation to be satisfied with talking about the stereotypes based on the evolution of furniture or decoration in the grand style and to describe, from Louis XIII to Louis XVI, the march of taste and manners, the progress of what are called the minor arts. This is especially so because the century of Enlightenment lends itself easily to such an exercise, since it saw a profound transformation in the decor of life and a moment of exceptional refinement in furniture, decorative elegance and goldsmith's work. In those days all Europe copied French models and fashions, giving employment to our workshops and our artists, our decorators and our architects. English cabinet-makers imitated French creations, and their language preserves evidence of that: the easy-chair called a *bergère* became, on the other side of the Channel, a 'burgair'. These accepted and seductive images dominate the realm of conversation, from the hieratic and courtly style of the age of the Great King to the ingenious elegance of Louis-*Quinze* rococo, ending with the aristocratic sobriety of the immediately pre-revolutionary period. To repeat them would not be to betray entirely the spirit of the age, its thirst for happiness, its taste for intimacy, its search for well-being which guided the elites of society and which the painters of the time illustrated with such talent: from the dazzling fete of the Regency, breaking with the brilliance, restrained by crisis, of Louis XIV's reign, to the rococo detour and, beyond, to the austerity of neo-classicism, we should, without much trouble, have covered the essentials.

This continuity made up of discontinuities the truth of which we perceive immediately, with its creators – was it, in fact, as obvious to the mass of consumers outside the circle of the Court and the town? Clearly, it does not enable us to understand the domestic space, the interpenetration of family life and work which was typical of the majority of both country-folk and townsfolk. Study of these configurations implies analysis of the functionality of things in relation to uses, of an instrumentality which is to some extent in conflict with the frivolity of taste. It is a way of thinking about the strange relation between the material, on the one hand, and, on the other, what was felt and thought. Furniture mingled the heaviest constructional material of olden times, wood, with the most lively ideas.[2] Decor made concrete in everyday life the encounter between tradition, the archaism which necessity imposed on everyone, and imagination stimulated by the example set by a few, the adventure of the boldest and most enterprising in peasant society and among the lower orders in the towns. We cannot, alas, like Mario Praz, dream of transforming the existence of everyone into an object and discovering, in the commentary of a tour of the house, the colours of life, the joys and sorrows that things awaken in the heart.[3] But we can at least hope to discover the informative role of things and the spirit of a long period which, for the most part, was one of 'traditional furniture'.[4]

To define it, two criteria have been proposed by Georges-Henri Rivière and Suzanne Tardieu. First, let us look at articles of furniture shaped by town and village craftsmen. We pass from a time when furniture was rarely to be found in modest dwellings, and was reduced to a few types 'of a functional simplicity that almost signified poverty', to the time of an upsurge, datable between the eighteenth and twentieth centuries, which saw the multiplication of models and progress in their decoration. Thereafter we are concerned with the totality of the goods belonging to the occupiers of a house, depending on their respective situations, ways of life, technological needs, social behaviour, customs and conception of the world, which were characteristic of a stratified society that was mainly agricultural, artisan and urban to a lesser degree and scattered among villages and towns. Paris, like the great provincial metropolises, was then only a lighthouse whose light was distributed meanly over a territory preoccupied with local affairs, yet open to a limited, gradually increasing extent. Souvenirs of that time and that society are not infrequently to be found in museums or in our dwellings. The taste for old-fashioned peasant stuff multiplies them through copying and industrial reproduction to meet other demands.

The demands of usage

Traditional furniture belonged among the various devices conceived in order to conserve products, things and goods. What solutions were found to the problems of reserves, garnering and siloing, the conservation of foodstuffs, transition from farm to market, from fair to store, from factory to shop, from there to the homes of various customers? This is a network of uses whose history is little known, but the circuit already suggests, by its successive breaks, that there were changes of scale in behaviour and means, and that it would be hard to reconstitute its many aspects. But should one overlook this history of microscopic and everyday technologies in which one can read, through bags, packs, parcels, baskets, boxes and carts, a common modification of exchange and of the rationality of actions? It would be possible to write the history of the scrip or the suitcase, of the crate or the hamper-frail, of the trunk or the chest. In the historical adventure of storage what is shown is a formation of our present-day social personality. The mirrored-wardrobe in the bedroom illustrates the rise of the European bourgeoisie no less well than the increase in the rate of profit. All methods and procedures of storage deserve our interest, because they throw light on the rhythms of life, the ordering of possibilities, the strategies of the circulation of goods, their hierarchical organisation between the intrusions of the functional and those of the aesthetic.

Furniture is conveniently classified by its relation to living conditions in the family setting, when each piece is useful each has its own and multiple use. Its diversification depends on the improvement in living conditions, but what is essential, for the rural and urban population assembled in a communal room (the most frequent situation, as we have seen) is to meet simultaneously the needs of work, rest, sleep, preparation of food and sociability.

In the geometric place of family life people sleep, receive visitors, eat and perform most of the everyday domestic tasks.[5] The items of furniture symbolise the course of life: the chest, the bed, the table and chairs, the kneading-trough, the clock. From modest interiors to many-roomed houses they can grow in quantity and improve in quality, respond to needs of storage developed by wealth and accumulation, and change in significance. The evolution we perceive in objects that have been preserved leads to a certain degree of specialisation, but this is not immediately perceptible: the bed is sometimes a chest, the chest is also a seat and may serve as a table. The late specialisation of items in accordance with use accelerated the development of the functional link, but this was limited and unknown before the nineteenth century so far as the peasantry were concerned: 'they gathered into one room all the items of furniture needed for their life'. In 1870 50 per cent of the rural dwellings in Touraine still consisted of a single 'principal room with a fire', in which everything was assembled in a space of thirty or forty square metres, and in the eighteenth century 75 per cent of the homes of the lower classes in Paris consisted of one room.[6]

The phenomenon was massive. It imposed a way of life in which were organised, in adjacent circles, private life, with its bed or beds, communal life with the fireplace, the furniture for meals and for rest, the furniture for preparation and conservation, life turned to the outside where were found the entry and the reserves of water. Between these three zones disparate objects unified the space, such as the poles on which hung hams, baskets, sickles, hats, guns (rare among the poor). It was necessary to use to the utmost what surface was available. The communal room was less congested. It lent itself to a greater degree of functional diversification. Free space was sought by way of a calculated arrangement (furniture was placed against the walls), the surface area was shared by partitioning off the beds and wardrobe so as to obtain some autonomy for the members of the family, certain functions were removed to an annexe wherever this was possible. A study of the living-room is not to be confounded with recognition of the fact of overcrowding, primitiveness and promiscuity, in contrast to the freedoms enjoyed by the nobles and the rich. It had its own logics and capacity for imagination, even taste. Nevertheless, down to the nineteenth century it was the place where the old-established practices of polyvalency were preserved.

The history of the bedroom is equally favourable for demonstrating that the power of usage is connected with the transformation of objects, inspiring social habits and the technical capacities of manufacturers. Behind appearances and maintenance there operate overlapping chains of logics. Here four systems of use and value come together. The material conditions of heating and arrangement free the bed from its role as isolate and protective draught-proofing. Nightwear relates to practices of comfort, taste and manners. Lighting operates between utility and modesty. The body's economy and biological necessities dictate the presence of a chamber-pot when latrines and toilets are often non-existent or are outside the house or other dwelling, as was so in most cases. We can appreciate that displacement of any one of these parameters modifies the rest – clothing and heating in the first place, followed by water. The example of the bedroom thus reveals clearly the overlapping of choices, the encounter of strategies of struggle against necessity with those of improvement of one's condition, indecision between the cultural and the technical.

Far from being trivial, the history of the people's furniture and decor is a sphere of discovery. Its complexity is also due to our way of ordering facts. It belongs to the history of the minor arts, seeing in the evolution of furniture the major indicator of an advance in the technical capacities of the manufacturers and in the taste of consumers, linked with the conservation of a patrimony of fine objects.[7] These objects have already been selected by use and by time. Our actual knowledge of them, *de visu* (and not merely through the iconography of the subject, which is deceptive, or the reports of notaries, where one has to question the relation between words and things and between vocabulary and the nuances of experience) is inversely proportionate to the hierarchy of goods and usages in earlier times. We are better informed about the King's furniture than about that of the peasantry and we can wish to see develop the study of furniture in regional and social groups.

The space of a material art

At every level what matters most is the disposition of the furniture, its relation to space and its use, the world of the practices of everyday luxury, in which three forms of knowledge converge – that of objects and styles, that of production and commercial circuits, through which the hierarchy of receptions is formed, and that of consumptions, where we find, as ever, stability confronted with change.

From this standpoint the encounter between the material and the perceptible is immediate, since furniture illustrates a 'philosophy of possession'.[8] In the same way, the storing of things in their proper places, in artefacts created for this purpose, expresses a spontaneous theory of needs of classification, of the orderly organisation of the undifferentiated into rationality, which involves the powers of memory and awareness of comparisons and similarities. In furniture are embodied ways of ordering things assembled, histories marked by the ordinariness of everyday actions, the need for privacy, the valorisation of what is contained by what contains it.

This is reflected in different ways by poets, novelists and painters. The first proceed from the actual to the imaginary: 'At night I shall break through the curtains of your bed' (Agrippa d'Aubigné). The second use the language of things for the purpose of a romantic intrigue without aiming to provide a documentary illustration of reality.[9] The last transpose various materials through aesthetic effects and contrasts of colour, design, pigmentation that reveal the play of light. What they give us is more than a testimony, it is a metamorphosis, as with Crébillon's sofa or the pleasure-machines of the Marquis de Sade, the paintings of vanities or the still lives of a Chardin. But a like chain of associations strengthens the meaning of things in their relation to a whole: symbolic values of the imagined, ritual configuration of usages and actions, weight of a relation to the material form, confrontation between the actual and its norms. The historian cannot treat objects solely as signs and art as a language. He is obliged to give them back, between art and usage, a place that conforms to a complex role, going from dominant instrumentality to aesthetic valorisation, from the banal to the prestigious, up to the capacity to deliver a message, information in symbolic form, to serve as model and reference for a period.[10]

From functions to forms

Furniture and the ordinary objects of life correspond to a certain social conception of the division of labour and of the hierarchy of activities. As Aristotle's heir, the classical city contrasted the domain of the liberal arts, the sphere of intelligence and of *otium cum dignitate*, with the vulgarity of the useful, the mechanical and technical: the scholar was contrasted with the craftsman and the work of art with the manufactured object possessing no social nobility in itself.

Between the seventeenth century and the eighteenth an important change regarding that contrast took place in economic and moral thinking, which culminated in the *Encyclopédie*. Useful work was rehabilitated, though without, as yet, definition of its value for its own sake: human products – objects, furniture, tools and machines – were praised as manifestations of a creative genius. To Antiquity's contrast of the liberal with the mechanical there succeeded the opposition of the intellectual to the physical, adapted to a situation in which the crafts were undervalued socially while being extolled economically for their usefulness.[11] The outlook of the Enlightenment criticised the prejudices against labour, and called on the liberal arts to enrich the mechanical ones:

Let us give to the artists the justice that is their due . . . It is for the liberal arts to draw the mechanical arts out of the debasement where prejudice has kept them for so long. It is for the Kings' protection to guarantee them against the poverty in which they still languish. Craftsmen are thought to be contemptible because people have held them in contempt. Let us teach them to think better of themselves. That is the only way to obtain better products from them.

So wrote d'Alembert in the article 'Art' in the *Encyclopédie*. That was a positive work of rehabilitation, even though it remained ambiguous regarding the dualism of hand and brain.

At the beginning of the nineteenth century the creative value of craftsmen's work was given recognition, with the notion of a 'minor art'.[12] The great creative artists involved a variety of arts in their achievements, maintaining very precise relations of dependence and influence with furniture and decor. We can perceive how furniture and decor illustrate 'the phenomenon of recurrence by which an art extends itself to the entire framework of existence'.[13]

Furniture and its uses

Need is a major element in the chain that links objects together. Furniture is characterised by its mobility [*meuble* → *mobilité* – Trans.] This is a property which has become, by opposition to the *immeuble* (building) that cannot be moved, essential for designating whatever it is that ornaments and fills the house. As means, furniture responds to necessity (sleep, eating, work): the table for eating, the bed for sleeping, the chairs for conversing, the secretaire or work-bench for work intellectual or material, these are what orientate space and activities.[14]

	Action	*Storage*
Physical needs (e.g. eating)	table	sideboard
Intellectual needs (reading)	armchair	library

Articles of furniture are placed as intermediaries between the internal setting (needs and habits of the group) and the external setting (which provides the materials required for satisfying these needs). André Leroi-Gourhan points this out, situating these articles in 'the expression of the techniques of consumption'. They make concrete a relation to nature, their purpose being to 'enable man to live' by satisfying a primordial need. Directly, the bed is for sleeping in and the chair for sitting on, but at the same time they both modify the needs they are destined to satisfy. Moreover, they cannot be isolated, but enter into a network of material and sensible relations. Understanding of practices depends on the classification and selection of furniture, for there is no useless article of furniture.

Anthropology makes a convenient distinction between articles of furniture that support and those that contain. These two functions may combine, but one of them is always predominant. In each case subdivisions reveal aims that are more precise – the storing of particular objects, support for the body or for something else. This typology becomes more exact with the passage of time and functions variously in the regional nomenclature of patrimonies, as can be seen from notaries' documents.[15] Articles of furniture play a complex game of interrelations and reciprocities the organisation of which serves the purpose of man's existence, but also the way in which each person, collectively or individually, responds to that interrogation. The global purpose of an article of furniture affects its form and structure and the material of which it is constructed.

This is made clear by a history of chairs or seats.[16] For Roubo in the eighteenth century, in *L'art du menuisier*, the seat is determined by man's verticality, and this posture, unique in the animal world, makes it possible to rest the muscles by relaxing the legs and trunk. The inclination and depth of the seat offer a greater or less degree of comfort. Man has shaped his furniture as he has cut his clothes. But this result has a history. To some extent the Middle Ages did not know the chair, which was an attribute of the sacred, reserved for Kings and holy images. The common people sat anywhere, on the ground, on the ledges of the fireplace, on cushions, coffers or benches, depending on rank and in striking proximity to each other. In the fifteenth century the chair appears, standing on three legs, not yet on four. It is less honorific and coincides with various uses – writing, eating, conversation. It comes close to the table and, between the sixteenth century and the eighteenth, conquers the social space. Then a veritable creative fury breaks out around the chair, which expresses best of all the quest for comfort and relaxation.

The history of the chair is also that of posture, which is not the same everywhere and which we see varying between hieratic dignity and lack of constraint. Knowing how to sit became a polite art, as we see from the paintings of de Troy or Boucher and the engravings of Moreau the Younger. The design of seats expresses a need which is not bound up with a static posture, since it requires slight movements. Shifts in sitting position reveal in portraits, through greater or less tension in the legs, a more or less marked degree of withdrawal. One sits without rigour and without constraint. Roubo codified the formal principle of the new art, which found application in innumerable models: the easy chair (*bergère*) which envelops the body, the duchesse, the gondola chair, the settee, the ottoman, the sofa. A whole society that loved pleasure and sought happiness here below could recognise itself in this luxury which would shock the adherents of a more fined-down aesthetic, one more rigorous and less restful, in the age of neo-classicism. The eighteenth century novel could draw from it an evocative power to illustrate a situation, animate an action, demonstrate a way of life, and express the desire felt when 'everything converges towards the article of furniture wherein reposes the body that is desired'.[17] We see already a cultural relation being expressed through an object's function.

Furniture, decoration, significances

Furniture reveals to us a state of society through its significance, giving material form to needs and referring to the silent language of symbols. There is no more everyday intermediary between us and our needs. It is hard to trace here a hierarchy in the exercise of functions, from use (the table) to culture (the desk): all articles of furniture bring out cycles of behaviour the understanding of which is made concrete only in objectification.[18]

With the table 'man lifts his food to himself in a setting which adorns it, disguises it and almost makes him forget it', says Maurice Pradines. Lebrun's *Benedicite*, engraved by Duflot at the beginning of the eighteenth century, illustrates this idea. We see the family assembled, the father and the children seated, the mother standing, in a spiritualised atmosphere, probably hinting at the Last Supper. Ordinary feeding is not to be separated from the outlook which gives thanks to God for everything.[19] The table, a modern creation (for a long time people were able to do without it), combines thenceforth a number of social situations. To be at the Prince's table is a sign of high distinction, if not of gastronomic taste. Among the aristocrats who had themselves painted, the well-furnished table of mediaeval banquets was replaced by refined instruments. They organised dining-rooms fitted by architects into small apartments, the decor of which followed the evolution of taste. They surrounded themselves with an ever-increasing number of supplementary articles of furniture and with accessories – dishes, cutlery, linen. Usage dictated tablecloths, either plain or figured, which served to conceal wooden planks, trestles or folding-tables, and which unified a decor by displaying the wealth of the hosts. From the sixteenth century, the table imposed forms of good manners. In the eighteenth century it was the place that expressed a different pleasure in eating. From the peasant's cottage to the aristocrat's house the jump is great, but in both cases the table responds to a need in the relations between persons: eating was transfigured into social relations.[20]

With the bed and its function as a place of rest a dual mediatisation appears.[21] The bed raises the individual off the ground and protects the sleeper from cold, but, above all, it ensures for the intimacy of a couple and for sexuality a degree of enclosure which could not be created in a space of traditional cohabitation. In the communal room the bed contrasted the private and nocturnal space to the daytime and collective expanse. Its transfer to a bedroom was to mark the tendency to privatisation, to withdrawal into conjugal life. This twofold value – protection and isolation – is expressed in the article of furniture itself: the Bretons' wooden bed enclosed by sliding doors, perforated and decorated,[22] or the bed enclosed by an architecture of pillars, curtains and canopy which predominated in Parisian interiors – and also in the beds' equipment, accumulated with varying levels of luxury and wealth: sheets, coverlets, pillows.[23] The separation signified by the bed which confers secrecy on the sexual relationship, introduces people to a new sphere, making sacred reproduction through love, something inseparable from a new conception of the family.[24] Around the bed a pomp is displayed which is exceptional in the ordinary world, and the green of its hangings, the colour which predominated until the seventeenth century, is a symbol of fertility and of joy.[25]

Seats responded, as has been mentioned, to a need for rest obtained by sitting down. Notaries' inventories show that two types coexisted in the countryside of the seventeenth and eighteenth centuries. Movable stools and chairs made it possible to clear areas in the organisation of the space of living-rooms. Fixed benches were attached to the table or, in some regions (Brittany, the Alps), to the bed. In the Vannetais the farmers had chest-tables that they could not put their legs under. Around the table they had benches which were also chests, serving both for rest and for storage. Rich families who had several of these put them alongside the enclosed bed, for which they acted as steps.[26] The multiplication of chairs expressed wealth, freed the polyvalent space and constituted a normal furnishing of the second room. We sense here a different meaning of confrontation than that evident in the use of benches and we are already on the way to the 'conveniences of conversation', to use the language of Molière's *précieuses*. The armchair would become a mark of distinction.[27]

Seats expressed, in town and country alike, a technique of the body wherein relation to the object reflected a need for rest less obviously than in the case of the bed. 'The charm of the seat', says M. Pradines, 'is that it works on the impulses of fatigue, subjects its movements to a plan, encloses them in a framework, and thereby offers, symbolically, an ideal perpetuation thereof.' A person seated is still raised for social interaction, in which seats express orders of precedence. At the court of Louis XIV everyone sat according to his rank: the King had the right to an armchair, the Dauphin to a chair with a back, the princes of the blood to raised stools, the *ducs-et-pairs* to ordinary stools, the dukes to folding seats, the courtiers to cushions. Circumstances might, of course, modify the hierarchy. Above all, comfort and elevation were regulated in relation to the royal person to whom one was more or less near. 'Seats receive the imprint of rank rather as clothes do.' Hierarchy appeared also among mere individuals: to a lawyer of the long robe one offered not a chair but a folding chair. The presence of one or other feature – an elbow-rest, ornamentation – ensured the social destination of these articles of furniture.[28]

Rank was reflected less visibly in the furniture used for storage. Chests, sideboards, cupboards, chests of drawers, dressers had an unsurpassable functionality. In the countryside of modern times the chest predominated, a piece of furniture that was low and able to accommodate anything: agricultural produce, stocks of food, clothes, linen, cloth. The order of accumulation reigned in the chest, and, to insert or extract the objects within it, one had to lean, to bend oneself towards the ground. The sideboard, of which Suzanne Tardieu has analysed the use, appeared along with the multiplication of objects – pots, faience dishes – which could no longer be kept merely in the open air, on planks or hung up. Closed by doors, it marked progress in the protection of things: low, it was nevertheless higher than the chest: high, it provided greater convenience for storage and, above all, testified to a quest for symbolic verticality. A rustic piece of furniture which is opened by two doors, separate and one above the other, constructed similarly to a sideboard, was charmingly called a 'standing man'. The sideboard reached the French countryside in the seventeenth century, being followed more slowly by cupboards and chests of drawers.[29]

Each phase saw an improvement in storage capacity and in specificity, while verticality increased or was maintained. The urban chest of drawers in which one stored, at first, precious objects and clothes without any confusion, saw its name (*commode*) emphasise its function to the detriment of its membership of a semantic family. It lifted the need for clothing above need, giving a sacred quality both to order and to adornment. Like the sideboard, the cupboard and the dresser, specialised containers, the chest of drawers evoked or revealed what it contained, symbolising a family's wealth.

In their production, all these articles of furniture followed the changes in taste, style and fashion. Thus, art won ascendancy over the companions of people's material lives and was reflected there in a specific way, in creative independence, without, for all that, following in the wake of the major arts. This was the domain in which regional identities would find expression – identities that were all the stronger because they affected not structure but ornament. The use of locally available woods often entailed special techniques and decors. We can see this if we compare a Breton kneading-trough of the eighteenth century, undecorated and destined to serve every day as bench and flour-chest, the work of a village joiner who made it out of a dark and rustic wood, with a Provençal kneading-trough in the style typical of Arles, in the time of Louis XV, with its decor and its jigsawed bread-box which, in the main room of a farmhouse, already reflected a distinctive striving for refinement.

In the seventeenth and eighteenth centuries the break was expressed not only in the quality of the objects produced, their technical excellence, but also in the acceleration of creative capacity: the synthesis of decorative aspirations which mingled themes and sources of inspiration, the continuity we can perceive in the transition from the classical style to rococo, from baroque to neo-classicism. Forms freed themselves from the constraints of display of the grand taste, curves took over from straight lines, then the latter recovered their authority under Louis XVI, but, above all, forms broke with their subjection to architecture. This movement expressed not so much the transformation due, as is constantly said, to the change in manners and life-style, symbolised in the intimacy of the boudoir, as to the capacity for independence and the choice of a new aesthetic language. Starting with ornamentation, furniture separated itself from the art of building. Design, sculpture, execution made forms and structures converge towards a linear tendency which culminated in neo-classicism. The art of furnishing became one of design in space.[30] Its evolution showed the influence of the cultural demands which united the world of the producers with that of the consumers. Its diffusion – conveyed from the centre to the periphery by trade, by copying and by fashion – testified to the progress accomplished by new ways of feeling, submission to a nature at the very height of artificiality.

Production and consumption of furniture

In the production of furniture and in its utilitarian and economic purposes, techniques play an important role, because upon them depend forms and values. The creative explosion of the eighteenth century presents us with the problem of the routine of the pre-industrial age. The possibilities of production were closely bound up with equipment that was inherited from olden times. It was, first of all, the axe that made the making of furniture an art of the woodcutter and the carpenter, limited by the availability of local woods and trees, with variations that depended on urban wealth. The sixteenth century saw exotic species conquering Europe from Flanders and Antwerp. New woods and new tools: mechanical saws became common after the fourteenth century, driven by mill-wheels. They made possible finer work on planks and panels, and ensured the triumph from the fifteenth century to the seventeenth, of joiners who worked brushwood, on which the plane and the jointer conferred new mastery. At the end of the seventeenth century and during the eighteenth artists in ebony introduced even greater virtuosity. The equipment had settled down, as Roubo noted: saw, plane, chisel varied from one work-shop to another only in the quality of their steel and in their style. There would be no decisive change before the nineteenth century.

The art of furniture-making depends on mastery of geometrical design, the art of drawing and the making of joints. The cabinet-making joiner who inspired Roubo was, in the first place, a geometrician, which enabled him to base the making of furniture on a reasoned system, to carry out its reproduction and to attain perfection in the art. This configuration already indicates the geography of a consumption. It corresponded to a progressive refinement of methods and of tools which departed from the 'heavy and crude' furniture of the past. The progress of joining – with mortises, tenons, dove-tailing, dowel-pins, and, in the eighteenth century, with screws – was facilitated by that of the tools used – axes, hatchets, chisels, hammers, planes, mauls, lathes. This made it possible to create a new style which triumphed thanks to the virtuosity of the crafts, the diversity of the clientele and the geography of the workshops and the consumers.

In Paris, where all the tools and all the techniques had been present since the sixteenth century, the important innovation was marquetry, as a result of the diffusion of techniques for inlaying on wood set in panels. The quest for contrasts and the preference for the decorative and the luxury of precious woods were reflected in the system of production. Roubo describes all that, dividing joiners' work into two main types: that of large-scale work, where wood was used for buildings and vehicles, and that of the cabinet-making joiners engaged in making furniture that was joined (cupboards, chest of drawers, secretaires) or of simple structure (seats and beds). These crafts cannot be isolated from other occupations on which they depend for their raw material and supplies – sculptors, workers in bronze, chasers, gilders, painters, all play their part.

In the furniture world the division between joiners and cabinet-making joiners was both technical and sociological.[31] The joiners were a solid corporation, with powerful masters. Around 1700 they had nearly 900 workshops (300 making furniture, 150 to 200 cabinet-makers, 200 to 300 for the rest). The cabinet-makers arrived later and were often of foreign origin – German, Dutch (think of Oeben, Riesener, Van der Cruyse). They founded robust dynasties. They sometimes allied themselves with French craftsmen but more often remained on their own. The joiners, mostly natives of the country, were strongly united through intermarriage, with fathers, sons, uncles, nephews forming an active network through three, four or five generations, as with the Foliot, Tillard and Collet families. They were not all established in the same part of Paris. The joiners lived and worked chiefly in the centre, the Bonne-Nouvelle district, Rue Saint-Denis. The cabinet-makers installed themselves in the *faubourg* Saint-Antoine, a favoured area where they could get round the corporative controls. However, members of both groups could be found everywhere.[32]

At the top of the hierarchy of enterprises a few big businessmen were linked with the world of the mercers who sold works of art: Delanois and Jacob from the joiners, Cressent, Leleu, Riesener and Gandreaux from the cabinet-makers. Despite differences in way of life or origin, all were driven by the same capacity for invention. The hierarchy was created on the basis of creative capacity, level of clientele, and the family's reputation regarding use of the new woods, lacquers and ornamentation. Thus, luxury production eclipsed ordinary production, which was never large-scale, for the leading workshops managed to produce a hundred items a year and the leading cabinet-makers rarely put out more than a score. Production of a small number of items satisfied a more ordinary clientele, with specialisation, even separation, making possible a wide range of qualities.

The provinces and rural areas lived at the same rhythm, as regards corporations and techniques, but with an interval. In Lyons the joiners predominated and there were few cabinet-makers, and this may have been the rule in most big towns. In the villages the system of production was a little different. Many peasants, still being woodcutters, were able to make a simple piece of furniture. Workshops were established in the villages in proportion to the clientele and the craftsman often went to work in the farm, country-house or presbytery of his client, performing on the spot the task required. In this way supply and demand met directly. Only the higher categories enjoyed the benefit of indirect access, through the channels of the large-scale furniture-trade carried on by the mercers, or, and doubtless more often, through orders from the towns of the region where the journeymen circulated.

Furniture was everywhere a means of expressing one's affluence. This tendency was present even among the poor.[33] But who guided taste, between the necessary and the superfluous? There are many answers to that question. At the top, the capacity for innovation of a great clientele of rich amateurs came together with the creative independence characteristic of the great cabinet-makers or joiners. The role of the Court and enrichment at the top of the state were two factors of acceleration. At the bottom traditions persisted, with furniture belonging among customary practices and ritual beliefs. There, the craftsman was more conformist, construction changed little, but decoration was cleverer. It is difficult to go beyond this outline which is not contradicted by the organisation of production in accordance with a dual hierarchy – that of wealth and that of acculturation thanks to proximity to information and to the circulation of things.

The ordinary people in town and country were content with fairly crude furniture: a few pieces, the basic household utensils were enough for them. The value of all that depended on the correlation between level of income and capacities, nature and quality of goods. In Paris among the wage-earners, the frontier ran at about 500 *livres* of capital at death, before 1789.[34] Below that line poverty and mediocrity of living conditions prevailed, while above it there appeared signs of progress and comfort.

For all peasant families in the realm investment was limited and furniture changed little, for everything had to last. The example of Alsace shows, nevertheless, that necessity did not rule out a certain variety, which included the use of hierarchised and distinctive woods – from pine to deal, from walnut to oak and the woods of fruit-trees, which were the most sought-after and richest – and the transformation of the sculpted or polychrome decor.[35] The richest peasants, the farmers of lordships, the rural petty-bourgeois acquired showy pieces, just as in Paris. Rich journeymen and well-off servants adopted chests of drawers and easy-chairs, following the example of higher circles. In the countryside near Paris a slow movement got under way. It was marked among the big commercial farmers, but slower in the Vexin, among the peasants who were less rich and less oriented towards Paris and its fashions: they had few sideboards before 1770 and no cupboards before the nineteenth century.[36]

When, in this connection, we come to the Court and the aristocracy we find profusion. Versailles, the King, the grandees, the princes of the blood who took their lead from Marie-Antoinette, such as the Condés, the Penthièvres, the Fitz-Jameses and Montesquieus, Madame de Pompadour, the du Barry, the farmers-general – these were the big spenders who appear in Lazare Duvaud's *Livre journal*.[37] Furniture was a considerable item in prestige expenditure. Impelled by the culture of appearances, it asserted one's status, but it was also influenced by the quest for intimacy and comfort. Here we notice transversal behaviour. There were society people who were conservative where furniture was concerned such as Louis XVI, whereas the Queen was in the vanguard of taste. *Mesdames*, the sisters of Louis XV, who had been thrifty and somewhat stingy down to 1785, thereafter indulged in prodigious expenditure: the Duc de Croÿ feared that building costs would be too much for the budget of the households. The decoration amd furnishing of the town houses of the Paris-based aristocracy brought wealth to the world of the craftsmen[38] who contributed to the establishment of the new districts in the *faubourgs* Saint-Germain and Saint-Honoré. In the Marais, and among the men of the *Parlement* generally, the tone was less disposed to ostentatious expenditure, and a certain conservatism prevailed in the interiors.[39] Lovers of old-style things were already disturbing the hierarchy and bringing success to great artists like Boulle.

There was a real contrast between Paris and the provinces, but account must be taken for the provincials' capacity for innovation and of their ability to follow the fashions of the capital. The gap between styles, which is perceptible in the furniture which has been preserved, varies a great deal, through the importance of relationships and social life. Some provincial capitals were quickened by the presence of high-level consumers. In Bordeaux, Richelieu, the Archbishop Mgr de Rohan and the great intendants engaged in reconstruction were fond of 'the mahogany which is plentiful in the port', and that gave their furniture an original touch. In Dijon, the Princes de Condé did a lot for the cabinet-maker Demoulin. In Lyons Pierre Nogaret demonstrated that this city could create light articles of furniture – seats, small tables – that were just as original as anything produced in Paris. However, the ordinary joiners built cupboards and sideboards of rigid and massive structure, with luxuriant decorations and stiffer rococo. Lyons had few cabinet-makers and many joiners. As with regional costumes, we lack an historical analysis of these variations, bringing together the local ways of life, the level of technique, the capacity for acculturation and the permanence of a tradition in decoration which was slow to take in sophisticated styles.

It was undoubtedly at the beginning of the nineteenth century, when furniture-making craftsmen had attained better mastery of their trade and their customers wanted furniture that was more adapted to the new standards of comfort and taste, with the new-rich classes showing themselves more demanding, that there began to appear all over the place a traditional type of product which popularised the *style Louis Quinze*, with its jigsawing and fined-down lines. The *style Louis Seize* did not become popular except in certain regions: e.g., for cupboards, in Normandy. Regional studies reveal everywhere the heterogeneous features of the art of woodworking.[40]

Return to function, utility and change

Kant, more correctly than Descartes, was to maintain that the *ego* is more dependent on the object than vice versa: 'Our internal and, to Descartes, indubitable experience is in itself possible only under the previous assumption of external experience.'[41] This experience has a history in the adventure of things which, by themselves, create nothing but which, when brought together, reveal a set of relations, show forms of behaviour and either reject or welcome changes. The art of the tapestry-worker and that of the mercer provided rich people with the ensembles they wanted, when their wealth made possible complex combinations, usually connected with the aesthetic celebration of authority and at the expense of the net profit. Ceremony, the fete, display of lavishness formed part of the civilisation of appearances, endowing luxury consumption with a fragile and dazzling coherence.

In the ordinary lives of the largest number, peasants and townsmen, the precepts of distinction and consideration initially affected dress. Expenditure on furniture was certainly governed by necessity, utility and means, but also by the taste and culture of individuals, the tradition and style of consumption of families. The inventory of chief domestic functions which we can try to compile on the basis of social and regional examples – sleep, storage, sociability – brings out the diversity of behaviour, despite the necessity common to all.

The hierarchy of sleep

As we have seen, the organisation of rest varied according to whether or not a person possessed an independent space, a single room or a complex and hierarchised dwelling. The bed then became the symbol of the sleep of the just, symmetrical with the hearth and the fire. What, for millions of couples in town and country, for millions of children and single persons, could be simpler than to go to bed? From the pallet of the poor to the luxurious couches of the rich, everybody spent there a large part of his or her life. One was born there and died there, and in the seventeenth century one still received visitors there. Capacity for sleep and insomnia gave one either good nights or bad ones. The bed was the special place for sexual relations. In short, it was neither insignificant nor simple, because there was no equality in the matter.

We are no more equal where sleep is concerned than we are in sexual performance or in health. La Fontaine's rich financier and poor cobbler know something about that, in their own way: for the fabulist the quality of sleep depended on wealth, which was an argument for moderation, dear to the moral economy. Let us dream of a social history of sleep in which we should find the choices and obligations of society, the time of rest gained or lost, and at what price, the role of intimacy, the struggle against cold, the right to be lazy: *descansar es salud*.

In Paris beds were to be found in all dwellings. In *La manière de bien bâtir* le Muet includes a bed in every plan. In a room fourteen square metres in size he allots to it six square feet (four square metres) to serve comfortably the sleeping needs of two or even three adults. Space is organised around the bed, which is separated by the ruelle from the nearby wall. In the eighteenth century the bed-area advocated by architects declined in size, or else lent itself to arrangements that were less central and less symbolic: Jombert and Briseux allot to it 140 by 110 centimetres – less than a metre in the case of a folding bed.[42] In inventories of all social categories in the seventeenth and eighteenth centuries one model predominates, namely, the crib on legs, with curtains (75 per cent of the mentions in inventories). Even the lower orders had proper beds, this comfort having been acquired by the end of the seventeenth century at the price of great financial sacrifice: the bed represented 25 per cent, at least, of the value of the furniture possessed by the wage-earner, and 39 per cent in the case of a servant.

What made the difference in means and tastes was the cost of bed-clothes, their quality and quantity, which were so many means of combating cold and the environment.[43] These needs could vary the cost by a difference of one to five among the lower classes. Around 1700 a good bed cost at least twenty *livres*, and could run to fantastic amounts in rich bourgeois and noble interiors – up to 500–700 *livres*! What caused the change and revealed the innovating spirits and the households alert for new fashions was the increase in variety, the unburdening, the quest for mobility in cluttered interiors. What really made the distinction was possession of an individual bedroom with a fireplace. However, the Parisians succeeded very soon in winning the individualised bed for themselves.

This article was no less essential in the country. For longer than in Paris the word for 'bed' could mean bedclothes, or a litter without a wooden frame, and the appearance of wooden beds and cribs on legs, high or low, reflected prosperity. The enlosed bed, already mentioned in connection with Brittany, and which was also to be found in the Alps, the Pyrenees and the Massif Central, can also be considered to be one of the symbolic formulas of the life of families who were reduced to a single room. In Brittany, where it kept the heat in and protected a minimum of privacy, it was arranged traditionally: this bed for the grandparents, that one for the parents, the other for the children. Elsewhere, when cribs on legs were used, the best was assigned to the parents. Children and servants had to be content with bedsteads, pallets or mere straw mattresses. In this case too it was piling up, accumulating sheets, coverlets and eiderdowns upon superposed mattresses that protected the sleeper best from the nocturnal cold. The lot of the poor was straw or maize beard, while the rich had goose- or chicken-feathers, and, later still, wool.

The evolution took place first in the towns, as the example of Bordeaux demonstrates.[44] There, at the end of the sixteenth century, 95 per cent of beds had feather-filled mattresses, and at the end of the seventeenth 95 per cent had mattresses of mixed wool and straw. In 1600 there were 10 per cent woollen coverlets, in 1700 100 per cent. Seven per cent of the households owned bedwarmers. For the lower classes of provincial towns conditions were still similar to those of the peasantry. Among them a culture of poverty prevailed in which to display coloured curtains or wood that was of an unusual kind and coloured was to proclaim a certain degree of prosperity.

A bed was an expensive investment for a newly-married couple, its average cost in Bordeaux in 1675 being 50 *livres*. A fifth of lower class dowries failed to cover the expense, and people economised on the curtains, which were a mark of prestige. The evolution was similar among the peasants of Maine who were studied by Anne Fillon.[45] The enclosure and bedding changed, eiderdowns of twill replaced rough cloth, goose-feathers gave way to chicken-feathers, the single coverlet of a rough fabric made of a mixture of wool and hemp gave way to coverlets of green or white wool, supplemented by pelisses of sheepskin or dogskin. The curtains were complete. The sheets, standard until 1730–5 also changed: 4.8 metres long, they were reduced among the poorer sort to 3.60 metres while among the rich and the bourgeoisie they exceeded 6 metres. This reflected increased wealth and investment in linen.

In Alsace[46] the bed strongly symbolised the transfer of powers and the passing of generations. It figured importantly in marriage contracts as in space. In the seventeenth century the rural bourgeoisie adopted the bed enclosed with curtains, a mark of luxury. A bed for two was general. In the eighteenth century well-to-do peasants and craftsmen slept in beds with sloping canopies, which imitated the beds '*à la française*' in the towns. In the south of the province enclosed beds survived, as in Brittany. Privacy and sleep had become expensive products: a good bed could easily set one back fifty or sixty *livres*, the price of an average horse. Two features were characteristic of sleeping arrangements in Alsace. On the one hand, the German style, without sheets under the duvet, coexisted with the French style: on the other the specialisation of beds progressed. In the case of one of every two families the records mention children's beds, rarely distinguished as such elsewhere. And this was in an area where heating by stoves was more common.

Close to Paris, in the Vexin, in the Ile-de-France, the Parisian style predominated, with 75 per cent made up of cribs on high legs, but with the short-legged kind gaining favour with the lord and the rich farmers. The fight against cold was won, here as elsewhere, by piling on bedclothes and enclosing the bed. Pillows were rare, but were making notable progress in the eighteenth century. Social contrasts persisted, but a bed was sometimes the poor man's luxury: Nicolas Langlois, a workman, devoted to it eighty of the 365 *livres* in his inventory of 1749. Who used the bed remains partly a mystery, interesting for measuring, together, the share of privacy and the growth in concern for children. In the Vexin village two-thirds of the families had more than one child, yet the notary recorded only a single bed in two-thirds of the homes. This meant, consequently, priority given to the marriage-bed and improvisation for the children who could make do with straw mattresses, bales of straw or hay from the stables. The cradle was a piece of furniture that practically never appeared before the notaries. Only the families of well-to-do families had beds in every case and for everyone. Lords, priests and officials had beds for visitors.

The means provided for rest point to an evolution, but analysis by regions always presents problems that are hard to interpret globally. The progress to be observed everywhere was based on several criteria. There was the general increase in the number of beds per household. The acquisition of individual beds was connected with a reduction in the number of persons living under the same roof. The symbolic significance of the bed declined if heating improved. Quantity and quality advanced together and the value invested in sleep increased. The individual bedroom alone made possible privacy as conceived according to the new standards.[47]

Storing, classifying, receiving

For the novelists the space for privacy underwent a change. It narrowed, it was furnished, it was divided 'into bedroom and closet, and most often a great deal more – into dressing-room, wardrobes, various nooks and corners'.[48] At the end of his *Amours du chevalier de Faublas*, Louvet describes it as a journey to be made, 'in the morning in the dressing-room, after dinner in the boudoir, and when evening comes, in Madame's bed. I see nothing there that a well-born young man cannot honorably perform.' This space underwent furnishing and became cluttered: dressing-table, mirrors, sofas, easy-chairs – so many objects that were 'functional because as favorable to boldness as suitable for willingness', wrote Crébillon in *Le hasard du coin du feu* (1763), a novel the title of which was thoroughly in the spirit of the new culture.

Imagination evokes the multiplication of things and furniture to serve as markers in an advance to proximity and intimacy: the bed becomes a space in itself. The novelists needed a whole set of places to indicate the distance of the relations orienting the intrigue: dining-room, receptions, conversations on the border of the public and the private, the passage, the ante-room, the stairs, evocative of the vertical organisation of the house, relations of nearness, advance and retreat. The furniture and objects, the decors and the things are urban, but the use made of them reveals the new social divisions between the private and the public. Emphasis is placed above all on circulation. The furniture and so on are inciting, they are agents of pleasure or of manipulation. Beyond the correlation noted between the evolution of practices and novelists' observations, this is the purpose that can be grasped: the multiplication of objects in the novel affects all the senses, for nothing can escape the effect of the things that are sometimes described in the form of a catalogue of objects classified according to the order of sensations. In the ordinary domestic world this order exists, in its own way, since it is needed to avoid cluttering by objects which have to be put away and this makes possible the organisation of (either close or extended) social relations.

The increase in things, the improvement in incomes, the specialisation of spaces led to noticeable changes regarding the way of life of traditional society. They modified the rhythms of acquisition for both the necessary and the superfluous, they created a new relation between having and being in the revelation of riches which one either ought or ought not to display. Here, too, the economy of scale had decisive effects since, as in the novelist's perception, analysis of interiors and of their consequent furnishing reveals the progress of privacy and comfort. The Parisian system of storage shows at once features of adaptation which are proportionate to wealth and specific manifestations of the life huddled together in common rooms.

From the seventeenth century to the eighteenth the general decline of the chest in all social categories was thus the sign of the decline of a rural feature which was characterised by mobility and functional polyvalence.[49] When the space was divided up, the chest was relegated to the kitchen, the closet or the lumber-room. It was found much more often in the lower-class districts than in the bourgeois ones: thus, in the *faubourg* Saint-Antoine, among the servants, there were plenty of them on the eve of the Revolution (75 per cent in the inventories).

The relative decline of the chest had as corollary the rise of, first, wardrobes and then chests of drawers. The former are already found at the end of the seventeenth century in three-quarters of the homes of wage-earners. There was a slight decline around 1780–90 which may well be explained by a diversification of means. In all other circles the wardrobe progressed in accordance with means. In the middle of the eighteenth century a cupboard might cost between fifteen and a hundred *livres*, even more, the price varying with the quality of the wood – white pine predominates over oak and walnut in the inventories of lower-class people – but also with decor and style. The wardrobe can, in its way, testify to the conquest of linen and clothing among the Parisians. This was the article which made it possible to store more numerous textile products, while the sideboard played that role for the dishes or the kitchen utensils, which also multiplied. Already it was facilitating classified, selected and rational storage. Its grandeur and majesty endowed it with a role of representation.

In this sense the chest of drawers marked a different direction. At the end of the seventeenth century it was a novelty which the art of the cabinet-making joiners provided for prestige and show among the rich. After the Regency, it spread more rapidly among other categories. Unknown to the poor around 1700, at the end of the century it was turning up in a quarter of the lower-class inventories. Furniture could serve as a symbol of the creative capacity of the Enlightenment, through its workmanship, through the research into forms which it inspired, the quality of the woods of rare species that it necessitated, and the variety of its marquetry decor and ornamentation. Also, however, it reveals a need for storage that is more reasoned, more secret, more intimate. There are no doubt cases of disorderly use of the drawer, but it does suggest a different way of sorting things and storing them than does the wardrobe (vertical) or the chest (undifferentiated). The chest of drawers was destined to follow the movement of diversification of the habitat, along with other furniture of use or show that we find only in town-houses and homes of the elite: chiffoniers, secretaires, desks, book-cases. The revolution in Parisian intimate decor organised itself around the chest of drawers. A tour of the provinces brings to light gaps, delay in the diffusion of novel forms, hardening of the hierarchy of possessions as between town and country, rich and poor.

In Alsace we find the same sequence as in Paris, but at a lower level:[50] general survival of chests (89 per cent in the pre-Revolution inventories), slow increase of wardrobes (20 per cent around 1700, 54 per cent at the end of the Ancien Régime), rarity of chests of drawers and other articles of furniture which appear mainly among the rich. The chest symbolises in another way the home and the kind of life of everyone: in it are piled up linen and clothes, cloth and thread, provisions and papers. Progress shows itself in the specialising of these roles, and so in its multiplication. While it was not supplanted until the nineteenth century its character underwent change. Feet were added to it, making it something like a chest of drawers. It was restricted to the storage of provisions and old records, while the wardrobe held clothes and precious objects. The wardrobe of the Rhenish peasantry reflected a certain *embourgeoisement*. It made possible a form of storage that ended the promiscuity of things of different kinds. One no longer heaped things up, so that it was always necessary to rummage in order to find something. Instead, objects were arranged in orderly fashion, on either the vertical or the horizontal principle. The chest of drawers was rare in Alsace, more so than the sideboard, which benefited from its close link with the kitchen.

On the borders of the realm fashion advanced slowly, but the picture was not greatly different in the Ile-de-France, the Vexin, Brie, Burgundy, Brittany and Touraine.[51] Everywhere the chest held out, the wardrobe advanced, and the chest of drawers was a sign of refinement among the well-do-do peasants and notables. There was one chest of drawers at Nangis-en-Brie around 1700 and ten at the end of Louis XV's reign! At Roscoff, in Brittany, one chest of drawers was recorded at the beginning of the century, and barely more at its end. The system of storage was based on coexistence of the chest and the wardrobe, which symbolised refinement through its West Indian hardwood and its price.

Even in the towns the spread of these things was not altogether a straight-line and steady affair. Not a single day-labourer in Angers possessed a wardrobe.[52] For a long time traditional country people and some townsfolk were to look unconcernedly on the piling-up of objects. It was their accumulation, the new values that they embodied, that expressed both intimacy and social hierarchy. Thus, in nineteenth-century Touraine the wardrobe and its contents symbolised what was private and concealed, as against what was left exposed to view, set out on the ground. It manifested the prosperity of households.[53]

Sociability was different in all classes of society, but, in its most developed formulas, it is this that symbolises the Century of Enlightenment, its taste for conversation and the art of receiving. Look at *La Lecture de Molière*, painted by Troy at the beginning of the century. Here we see the permanence of a collective activity, bringing men and women together to read, listen and discuss. At the same time it shows the selection of an appropriate decor and setting, that of the salon or the closet around 1730, among the Parisian aristocracy: an inlaid floor made up of square pieces, a marble fireplace in the new style, with lowered mantelpiece, a costly mirror, lighting brackets, armchairs that are low and deep, with high backs, covered with damask or petit-point upholstery, walls hung with damasked silks, book-cases, draught-screens, a Boulle clock – here we are at the top and amid the brilliant affirmation of social comfort.

Parisian reality does not contradict the picture, but puts it in its proper place: the eighteenth century was the century of the seat. The hierarchy of means appears clearly in the inventories. In 3,000 inventories, 7,000 seats: but in the house of *le sieur* de la Grange, which accommodates ten persons in forty rooms, there are 173 pieces of furniture available for sitting down on, whereas in the home of Henri Lemaine, day-labourer (one room, four persons) there are five chairs and a poor threadbare armchair stuffed with straw. Of the seats of this period 63 per cent are chairs, 24 per cent armchairs, the remaining 13 per cent embodying the novelties of the joiners' art as well as archaism. As for the bench, now increasingly rare, it is found in taverns, pleasure-gardens, rooms for collective use, refectories in colleges and convents, hospitals and barracks.[54] Even among the lower orders the chair predominates: only 5 per cent of the inventories mention benches. In the communal room seats are huddled around the table or form a barrier in front of the beds: the space is thus unified by circulation between sociability and intimacy. Armchairs are rare – one for every three or four chairs – and are turned towards the fireplace. In most lower-class homes they are modest articles, made of white wood and stuffed with straw, rarely upholstered. The general change is carried forward by a threefold movement: increased disposable income, directly correlated with prosperity, seen among the well-to-do journeymen and important servants; progress connected with the division of space; specialisation in accordance with activity made possible by wealth and taste, with sofas and settees, all the products of craftsmen's creativity reserved for the rich. These transformations point to a twofold demand: from the bench to the chair one goes from a squeezed-together situation to sustained repose, from forced proximity to an individualisation of relations. At the same time the uses of seats may be enlarged or specialised. We are entering the world of suitable uses (for reading, for relaxation) and more extensive forms of sociability. The space is no longer oriented solely by relation to the table but by a variety of choices.

In peasant houses the equipment remained more faithful to tradition: benches broad and narrow, stools, straw-bottomed chairs were what was common everywhere. White wood predominated, as for the tables, the size and shape of which – oblong, round or square – already reflected an advance in wealth and taste. In the Vexin *français*, at Genainville, the lord and the priest had their comforts: in the home of the former there were seventeen chairs (of which six were of straw-bottomed ash), two narrow benches and five armchairs.[55]

In Touraine benches and chairs were set together at table down to the end of the nineteenth century, but with the chair advancing at the expense of the bench: there were 427 chairs, sixty armchairs and four settees for a hundred families, 180 of them in the communal room and 120 in the separate bedrooms.[56] Greater rarity could also be compensated for by greater mobility in case of need. At Nangis-en-Brie the chair competed slowly with the bench. At Roscoff there were sixty per cent chairs, but still 40 per cent benches, which were usually associated with the table. Armchairs were rare – none to be found in inventories of less than 1,000 *livres* – but two noble bourgeois had a canapé and a sofa 'of oakwood, covered with chintz, blue-based'. Among the Alsatian peasants there was a gradual movement from group furniture to individualisaion. Around 1700 there were 10 per cent chairs and 3 per cent armchairs : around 1789 the proportions were 59 per cent and 6 per cent. The chair was winning, because it offered more mobility and independence in the communal room. It made possible a re-composing of the space in terms of the rhythms of utilisation, around the hearth, the table, the stove. The rare armchair was a mark of prestige, the total effect remaining modest and utilitarian.[57]

From Paris to the countryside we observe a different situation, factors which orient possibilities for change, access to the forms worked out by the cabinet-makers' skill being reinforced by wealth and openness. Everywhere the evolution of intimacy and sociability dictates the choice of furniture, in a progress towards individualisation of behaviour. Everywhere, the specialisation of rooms coincides with other ways of distributing furniture and makes possible a little more rationality in ways of storing objects and goods. The rhythms of town and village life, so far as we can reconstitute them today, were different from each other. In the latter, rarity and uncertainty necessitated solidity, the need for things to last, a slow rate of replacement. The furniture was robust, progress was to be seen in marginal aspects, in decor, in wood that was more or less rich. Storage and consumption were made uniform by the functionality which to some extent erased social divisions and local particularisms. In the former, movement affected all groups, progress was expressed in forms which allowed of less homogeneity, more individuality. The economy of action and fatigue due to the new distribution of spaces and furniture advantaged only a minority of privileged persons, but provided an accessible model. The distance between townsfolk and peasants increased, but community of symbolic values still united them around furniture that expressed a plurality of attachments – those of the continuity of generations and the virtues of transmission, those of the family community, whose framework for living they constructed, and those of the individual and the family.

Painting, rather than acting as a witness through painting, enables us to understand the representations that were involved in this evolution. In the middle of the seventeenth century the brothers Le Nain composed several pictures depicting the rural family, more especially in the Ile-de-France, but in *Le repas de paysans* as in *L'interieur campagnard* stress is laid not on the furniture shown but, primarily, on the clothing. When they depict religious scenes these pictures emphasise the rough and gloomy tone of the clothes of the poor people who give meaning to the expressive intentions of the artist. The elements of the material culture and the furniture are reduced to essentials: the fireplace, a window, in which the glass is set in lead, a few chairs, the table, a bench covered with a tablecloth. So much for rusticity, but the elegant and delicate glasses in the hands of the characters come from another world. The affected style makes plain that they were not yet in everyday use in rural interiors. Similarly, the white cloths thrown over the table or the bench were not to be found widely: they were brought out only on special occasions. The painter wanted to show the simplicity of humble people, the strongly symbolic sociability of the meal or of the exchange between neighbours, the poverty, the religious virtues, the contrast between the absence of refinement, the general artlessness and the fleeting brilliance of an object that was rich and enriching.

Now let us look, less than a hundred years on, at *Le déjeuner*, by François Boucher. Are we going to find here illustration, in the Dutch style, of the material world which, through the Paris inventories, we see being transformed?[58] Actually, what we see displayed is a bourgeois art of living which draws its inspiration from aristocratic models but breaks with their ostentatious pomp. It is a definition of the Parisian ideal, wherein we see the appropriation of fashions and the circulation of modernity. The picture's subject points to the new taste for exotic beverages – here, chocolate, since coffee is not being served to the children gathered round their parents, in line with the new requirement of family feeling, and the father is holding a chocolate pot, not a coffee pot. However, a teapot does appear in the picture. On the same theme, we can note the exotic character of some objects: a porcelain service in the centre of the composition, a Chinese grotesque figure on the what-not, a precious vase. The decor materialises the rococo style of the interior, the light from the window made of small panes separated by astragals, the mirrors, the fireplace with its surround. The family is assembled under the sign of light and warmth. The curtains and portière ensure the right temperature as well as enclosure. Some showy furniture – a console table, a vase, a hanging wall-clock, a cane-bottomed chair – typify a room dedicated to sociability. The space is ordered and calm, the arrangement of things logical and without crowding. The furnituire is that of the world of luxury, it answers to comfort and display, with armchairs, cane-bottomed and upholstered, granting rest and relaxation. Not everything is in fashion: the seats are in the taste of the day, the years of the Regency, but the gilded console table, through a certain stiffness, still belongs in the seventeenth century.

There we perceive what is essential, the overlapping of objects and time-scales, heritage and the appropriation of new styles, intimacy and the life of richly endowed urban families, idealisation of a social group and its values, between moderate innovation and tradition. We find a more modest expression of this in the work of Chardin, though this is still located among the well-off bourgeoisie. A visitor to the annual art exhibition in 1741 wrote: 'There is not one woman of the Third Estate who goes there that does not believe that it is a representation of her own appearance, that does not see here her domestic round, her frank ways, her bearing, her daily concerns, her morals, the mood of her children, her furniture, her wardrobe . . . ' The silent compositions by Chardin and those, richer and more eloquent, by Boucher, speak in the same way of the acceleration of demand and supply, when there is a brisk movement of objects and values, affective values and the value of the individualised allocation of space, everything inseparable from everything else. For rural France this silent revolution was barely beginning at the dawn of the nineteenth century.[59]

8   Clothing and appearances

Charles Darwin's son George (later to be a scientist himself) suggested that the evolution of costume should be seen as similar to that of organisms: 'The law of progress holds good in dress, and forms blend into one another with almost complete continuity. In both cases a form yields to a succeeding form which is better adapted to the then surrounding conditions.' Thus, knee breeches and boots gave way to trousers when it ceased to be requisite that a man should be ready to ride at any moment. Again, the ulster, an ample and cumbersome overcoat, was fostered by railway travel. Following the example of natural selection, the historian could judge the degree of progress in the scale of clothing by the progress of specialisation of the 'organs'. The red coat, once a gala costume, is henceforth reserved for huntsmen or provincials. Items of costume reveal their utilitarian or decorative origins, selected and banned by fashion, 'like remnants of former stages of development': hats, turn-ups, buttons, cuffs, high boots provide the naturalistic philosopher with examples of those many survivals which he would like to explain in the spirit of the doctrine of the natural sciences that 'nothing exists without a cause'.[1]

Beyond its caricatural aspect, Darwin's analysis invites us to pay attention to the little facts which express clothing's capacity for conveying information. The most talkative of social facts may also be the most universal, and analysis of the evolution of dress, or even its description, doubtless turn out to be less fruitful than its interpretation.[2] Ways of dressing evolve according to their own rhythms, and their variations belong not merely to the history of fashion, because in modern society there coexist groups and ways of life that are affected by mobility to different extents.

Words and things in the history of clothing

This history of ways of dressing presents several difficulties. The first is that of the relation of words to things and thus of the sartorial vocabulary.

We have to distinguish between *attire*, something individual, which appropriates what is offered by the group, and *costume* or *clothing*, elements of a formal and normative system consecrated by society. The primitive facts of protection, adornment and modesty become facts of clothing only through recognition by the different groups in society, and through their language. Fashion itself has not always had the same meaning. In the seventeenth century it meant custom, conformism in usages and ways of behaving, and only secondarily everything that changes with time and place. It was also a way of characterising the social hierarchy, at once fixed and mobile. It was, finally, a moral practice for denouncing 'the world's inconstancy'.[3] Fashion taught one to play on all the possibilities of the language to speed up consumption, and the variations of a very specialised vocabulary followed change while helping it to evolve. Measuring innovations or changes depends partly on our capacity to understand this multiplicity of meanings.

The second difficulty lies in the fact that clothing brings together various functions which come forward disguised under social usages. Its function of protection remains fundamental everywhere, adapted to the natural milieu – to the warmth of the South, to the cold of the Northern regions, to the rainfall of the Western provinces. Clothing certainly played a part in the struggle against cold, a part that was more important then than at other periods of history, and in a more permanent way in the life of every day and of ordinary nights, because there were hardly any other means of protecting oneself.

Clothing speaks of many things at once, either in itself or through some detail. It has a function of communication because it is through clothing that everyone's relation to the community passes. Costume reveals, in the first place, what sex one belongs to: adoption of the other sex's costume was a subversive act, a disturbance of all order in old-time societies.[4] It reveals one's age-group, one's rank, occupation, social position. This language must generally be understood by all, despite its variations depending on level of fortune, way of life, age, and the evolution of the social mobility of families.

Costume also informs about the social division of space and membership of national and regional communities. From the Renaissance onward this has been one of the principal features of the history of costume and of the collections which offer a picture of the world through 'portraits of clothes'.[5] Collections of costumes can be compared to collections of curiosities, but their task is to make clearer how people objectivised their relation to appearance through the diversity of places and sartorial customs, as an invitation to compare the ways of readers with those of other people.[6]

We must therefore pay attention to the whole as well as to the parts, the signs which indicate minorities (such as the Jews), the colours that can characterise social functions and membership of different groups, the cut, the material, the types of jewellery; the head-dresses and the way of wearing them, the slant of the hat which indicates the bachelor or the settled man. This silent language can be followed, as Nicole Pellegrin invites us to do, through the iconography, the documents of notaries, judicial and police proceedings and 'even more, through the declarations made by the men of the Revolution, who were so hostile to diversity, whether linguistic, sartorial or ideological'.[7] Behind these observations lies the question of the existence of regional costumes and their history. The best-known of provincial costumes belong to 'a periphery of the realm which is not so much geographical as mental': Brittany, Alsace, Arlesian Provence, the Pays de Caux, Auvergne and the Pyrenees, places visited by travellers and antiquarians. Here the influence of women plays a growing role, through head-dresses and adornments, through their talent for putting together not a unified set of local usages but variations that mingle inherited items, elements from fashion, and personal additions. Regional costumes did not become numerous until the nineteenth century, despite the unifying tendencies, thanks to exchanges and to a certain improvement in conditions, and thanks also to movements among historians which endowed the provinces with a new importance.

In all these manifestations the sartorial function responds to codifications which avoid the arbitrariness of signs, teach and inform in accordance with situations and interests, and impose constraints, though without absolute determinism, for usurpations by signs sometimes confuse the answers to the questions that one can put.[8] Connected with religious convictions, faith and powerful symbolic expressions, clothing is a prop to beliefs and observances, as it is to social representations. At every moment clothing expresses links with authority, suggests the sexual hierarchy of roles in the family, points to the power of beliefs both in its details and in its totality. A history of uniform and of the standardisation of dress in accordance with circumstances lends itself to demonstrating political customs. A history of the button, such as Lucien Febvre dreamt of before the war, would reveal the geography and the hierarchy of a way of fastening things in which the *sewn* is contrasted with the *draped*. The button is a mark of masculine power, for women and children fasten their garments with pins and laces. The woman is always held back 'by the great paraphernalia of fabrics and haberdashery' that make up her clothes, and this justifies the domination by one sex over the other.[9] A history of the dressed statues of the Virgin would show the ways in which various ideas of the sacred were conciliated through sartorial rituals, their secret or processional display, and their frequentation, which favoured manifestations of very ancient attachments to the sexual wizardry of holy bodies.

Hierarchy, fashion, totality

This history of social ways implies a change of attitude from that which is usual in history-writing.[10] The learned and anecdotal study of costume concerns itself above all with forms, sartorial taste and fashion, linked with a political dichotomy that lacks real meaning, and is busy above all with the history of clothing in the social categories which were privileged by rank, wealth or proximity to the ruler. However, we must also study general practice, that of the peasants and townsfolk, the lower orders and the elites, and show the contexts of production and consumption, because clothing is connected with all cultural, economic and social phenomena. It has its place in the history of acquisitions individual, sexual and social, in the many procedures for shaping and controlling the body, down to individualisation and recognition by the family and local group. In the pedagogy of sartorial knowledge and usage a world-order is transmitted in which, in pre-industrial society, the central ideas are 'modesty' and 'moderation'. They teach the virtues of adaptation and are thus at the heart of the economy of scarcity.

Costume cannot be isolated from the whole system of material civilisation. It follows the transformations of that civilisation and plays an essential role in them, in three ways. It brings to the front the topographies of society and their different consumptions. It distinguishes between society's ordinary and extraordinary situations, between everyday and holiday. It reveals the influence of circulation and exchanges, both through vertical movements (sartorial habits can move from below to above in society, but also in the opposite direction) and through horizontal ones, involving commerce and industry. Being a universal social fact, clothing presents the question of production – capacity in relation to demand. In *L'art du tailleur*, published in 1769, Garsault invited his readers to understand this complicated process: 'From the need to cover ourselves we have arrived at elegance in clothing under different forms, at distinction between peoples and, within each people, distinction between different orders and conditions, which has given rise to ornamentation and magnificence.' From the social to the individual, this is an excellent sphere in which to grasp how practices which are identified with possessions have to be situated within a totality. Here, once more, Diderot can be our mentor and guide. Let us recall that Madame Geoffrin presented Diderot with a splendid dressing gown. The philosopher regrets the loss of his old garment.

It was made for me: I was made for it. It fitted every fold of my body without chafing. I was picturesque, I was handsome. The other, stiff and starchy, makes me look like a tailor's dummy. There was no demand to which it would not respond: poverty is almost always obliging . . . Now I look like a rich idler: no-one knows who I am.

At one level, we see here evidence of the material and the intellectual coming together through the shaping of appearances and the effect of clothes. The writer, the man of letters, the son of the cutler of Langres, had exchanged the private garment which did not contradict his plebeian origins too much for a garment that belonged to the bourgeoisie and social recognition. Sartorial aesthetic always unites morality and consumption, and the effects are interconnected.

Where is my old, my humble, my comfortable scrap of calamanco? My friends, hang on to your old friends. My friends, fear the onset of riches. Let my example be a lesson to you . . . Hear the ravages of luxury, the consequences of a consequent luxury. My old dressing-gown was at one with the other tatters which surround me. A straw-bottomed chair, a wooden table, a Bergamo tapestry, a deal shelf which held a few smoke-stained, unframed prints, nailed at the corners to this tapestry, and three or four busts hanging between them, used to form, with my old dressing-gown, a most harmonious indigence. Now, everything is out of tune. No more cohesion, no more unity, no more beauty.[11]

Here are proclaimed the unity of material culture and the aesthetic of the moralised decor, here are denounced the ravages of luxury and its propagation. How are we to reconcile need and necessity, reason and sensibility, artifice and nature, Diderot asks. The anxiety that the 'intruding scarlet' provoked in the philosopher, who liked to compare himself, jokingly, to Diogenes, was that of a whole epoch. 'I have left the barrel where I was king, to serve a tyrant.' Clothing, more than any other element in material culture, embodies the values of society's mental image and the standards of reality as it is experienced. It is the obligatory battlefield for the confrontation between change and tradition.[12]

Reconstructing that moment means, for the historian, trying to overcome certain gaps. The deficit in our knowledge where the clothing of the peasantry is concerned, that is, the clothing of the majority, is substantial. Moreover, we know more about the eighteenth century than about the sixteenth and seventeenth centuries.[13] An essential problem, that of different temporal economies and of the actual rate of accelerations, thus remains unsolved. In towns, in Paris, we glimpse how the improvement in the standard of living and the opening-up of trade which began very soon contributed at the same time to the integration of sartorial production and consumption into a wider economy.[14] In the countryside, where isolation, conservatism and even stagnation prevailed, more stable sartorial systems could survive. The entire circuit of the acquisition of clothes is involved and, with it, the operation of the capacities for distinction and communication which are inherent in sartorial culture. This entire history needs to be illustrated, from traditional consumption to the first transformation we perceive in the development of towns and the brilliance of the Court, down to the great urban ruptures of the eighteenth century and the debates to which they gave rise.

Did the sartorial Ancien Régime exist? Yes, it did, if by that expression we mean the ability to unify forms of relationship between clothing and appearances in a productive totality dominated by scarcity and restricted exchange. It was indubitably one of the ways in which a regime of production for subsistence expressed itself. No, if we see in it a close correlation between the translation of social hierarchies and the revolutionary break. Sartorial freedom was already existent in 1789, even if somewhat marginally, well before anyone thought of proclaiming it in legal form, but its space was restricted by capacities for change and by the codes that governed it.

The culture of consideration, permanence and re-use

Descriptions given by travellers and administrators, notaries' inventories and judicial documents reveal the inertia and immobility that prevailed in the villages where clothing was concerned. This was, all other things being equal, the same situation to be found among poor people in the towns who had come from the country, before they wiped off their rural dirt. The slight difference between everyday and holiday costume was dictated by lack of means, clothes for special occasions being handed down perhaps even more often than others.

Almost everywhere there was a marked contrast between the dress of men and that of women. The peasant woman possessed some typical articles: the shift which could serve as either an inner or an outer garment, a petticoat, a skirt, a pair of stockings, and often, still, an apron. The countrywoman's wardrobe lacked the gown, an urban article. It becomes more comfortable when we see that it also contained a corsage, a stiff bodice, 'short under-petticoats and flat shoes', as in la Fontaine's fable. But it also contained some head-dresses that mark the differences between ages and conditions of life – singleness, marriage, widowhood – and between places, villages or districts. The multiplication of articles corresponded to wealth: in the seventeenth century the number of petticoats possessed by the girls of Chambéry clearly indicated the increase in their dowry. Fortune was sometimes expressed in other ways: quality of fabric, possible variations, traditional symbols such as the velvet ribbon on the hem in Pont l'Abbé, the width of which showed gallants what the girls' expectations were.[15] Not much linen, wooden shoes, a few ornaments, that was all that can be observed throughout. The male peasant had not many more and not many fewer articles to wear. In the seventeenth century he wore, over his high hose, a doublet, which was a sort of waistcoat, long and with or without sleeves, a shirt, stockings, sometimes a jacket, a mantle and an overcoat, more or less lengthy. At the beginning of the eighteenth century he was still wearing breeches, hose or knee-breeches, with a short jacket or a smock. To this can be added sabots – leather shoes in the case of the well-to-do – and hats fit to withstand any wind.

The poverty of the countryfolk forbade variations in dress, because undoubtedly it was on clothes that they could cut down when successive crises, increased taxes and repeated epidemics and wars reduced their resources. In 1634 the states of Normandy described the destitution of their province: 'The burden of *tailles* has grown to the point of wresting away the shirt that was left to cover the body's nakedness and this has prevented women in several places, through shame at their nakedness, from going to church.' At the end of the century Vauban, too, emphasised the people's sufferings and their sartorial consequences. In some regions, he wrote, 'not one of them has enough to buy a decent coat'. The quality of coats worn distinguished those parishes that were exempt from *tailles* from the redeemed villages in the neighbourhood of Rouen. For the latter a good coat would infallibly serve as pretext for adding to their tax burden in the following year. In Louis XVI's reign Arthur Young's description of the wretched areas of the countryside he travelled through was not much different. Rags, clothing of men and women alike reduced to essentials, bare feet were all additional indicators of the economic backwardness which he sometimes exaggerates. Seventeenth-century painters of reality confirm this picture, more or less, while those of the picturesque or the sentimental *à la* Greuze invalidate it a little.

Everywhere clothing was made from local raw materials: rough wool spun at home and woven in village workshops: hemp from local hempfields: flax less frequently because it was often produced for sale to urban linen-drapers. Rural upper Poitou was in the eighteenth century a civilisation based on hemp. This fibre, which supplied a considerable sector of the economy, was the basis, either by itself or mingled with other things, of all the household linen and a big proportion of the clothing of the peasantry, who were thereby confined to what was dull and coarse.

Textiles played a part in the social and customary relations of the village in the rites of passage and their pedagogy, in spheres of work, in the ordinary lives of families, in the ways in which economic hierarchies, behaviour and morals were judged. Proverbial wisdom bears witness to this.

However, this 'culture of consideration',[16] in which the elements of costume, its colour and the way it was worn were closely observed, if not watched, did not have the benefit of an extensive language. The range of colours – mostly dark, black, brown, grey, unbleached whites turning brownish – was limited, and more brilliant colours often bore a strong symbolic or regional significance: the green of the coats of the hill people of the Vosges, the red of the late madders of Provence, the indigo of the Indies which figured in the palette of the village dyers.

It was owing to this inertia of the sartorial economy of the countryside that work done at home survived for so long in association with that of professionals in the villages and market towns. Similarly, the women were for a long time to play a considerable part, especially in the preparation of yarn, which could be done in the meadows while they were guarding flocks and herds, or in the evening, in company. From the spinning stage the market was dominated by exchange. Peasants' clothing was no exception to the general rule of goods produced locally. The weavers made the fabrics of all kinds, sheets and rustic cloth. The making-up was partly done within the family, especially where linen for household use or wearing was concerned. 60 per cent of households in Brie in the seventeenth and eighteenth centuries lived by producing for themselves. Tailors and seamstresses sometimes worked at home, so as to mend or make clothes for the whole family, who might also buy at their village stalls. Production was at that time exclusively masculine, while preparation of brides' trousseaux and the maintenance of linen was mostly women's work. Rural civilisation remained strongly attached to the separation of roles between the sexes. Everything was discussed around the wash-houses or while sewing. When stains, tears and holes were noticed, tongues wagged.[17]

Few clothes, then, and those made from rough and crude material, dark in colour, and not often renewed. Rural inventories, where they have been studied, show that clothes were often re-used. This was a civilisation where the threadbare was usual, after years of washing and cleaning with locally available means, with no effective detergent except the ashes used in the wash-houses, or, rarely, soap, the use of which gradually spread. In Poitou and western Limousin 50 per cent of the wardrobe of linen or clothes was described as 'threadbare'. In the best cases the very bad state of a garment did not mean, as it would today, that it would be discarded.

Its re-use formed part of a set of actions and values, in that transmission which was effected by gifts, inheritances and markets for second-hand goods, and which we observe happening between parents and children in wills, between rich and poor in alms-giving and works of charity, in marriage contracts, between employers and employees, between farmers and labourers, masters and servants, in wages, and even in professional gratuities, which could consist of an article of clothing or a remnant of cloth. The purchase and sale of second-hand clothes passed through many circuits: barter between individuals, losses at gambling, auctions after death, purchases from itinerant pedlars of second-hand goods who kept prices down, or purchases from shops, which helped to circulate urban products, and the sale or re-sale, in secret, of stolen goods.

The sartorial and textile culture of the peasantry was thus a matter of continual improvisation. Observable in it, also, was an increasing importance attached to the marks of distinction reserved for the rich and the well-to-do. Social difference was shown in sartorial differentiation. It was visible in the value of wardrobe contents (a hundredfold difference between the labourer and the well-off farmer), in the accumulation of linen to be found both in the rich manor-farms of the Ile-de-France and among the prosperous share-croppers of the Gâtine of Poitou. F.-X. Besnard in his *Souvenirs*, like Mistral in his *Mémoires*[18] could deduce from this the distance between new and old ways at the end of the eighteenth century and the beginning of the nineteenth. Colour belonged to the rich and powerful. If everybody's clothes were beginning to assume other shades, that was the sign of a twofold transformation: agricultural production was improving and was better distributed, and new patterns of behaviour allowed contraventions of familiar practices.

Codes and principles, manners and sumptuary laws

Rural society wore dark clothes but dressed up for holidays. When means increased, the number of garments and the quality of materials and workmanship began to show a difference. The harshness of agricultural work, which demanded solid clothing, together with the inelasticity of the peasants' budgets, allowed little room for fancy. Lack of money was made up for in part by investments in time, which were based on work by the womenfolk, the difference showing itself in details, with a lower valorisation for the men.

Propriety dictated coincidence between moral being and status, appearance and social consideration. The principles of this culture of distinction were expressed in codes of good manners and in sumptuary laws. Starting with Erasmus, codes of good manners laid down rules for a discreet and moderate appearance which avoided drawing attention to oneself by its form, and which advocated making clear what one's rank and condition were. At the top of society each order had its distinctive sign. For the clergy there was the tonsure and, after the Counter-Reformation, the cassock. For the nobles there was the sword and appropriate dress of gentlemen. Magistrates wore a gown, either long or short. The pressure of Court society and its ceremonial was expressed in its rules, the importance of which we have seen for explaining and motivating the new practice of wearing white linen, in the context of a hygiene both social and moral.[19]

Between the sixteenth century and the eighteenth, the discourse of good manners expressed sartorial conformism in the choice of fabrics, colours and adornment. The notion of propriety encapsulated the essence of an attitude which treated costume as the body's body and an expression of the soul's disposition. Suitability and cleanliness of clothes revealed the character of a man or a child. Judging people by their sartorial appearance entailed the obligation to teach and learn the correct way to dress in order to present a just and good idea of oneself which corresponded to the real person. The manuals of good manners would transmit the values which daily example and practice would foster, 'since the shortest road to becoming a decent person is to frequent decent persons and observe how they behave, because example affects our minds much more than words can', wrote, in his preface, the author of the treatise on good manners published by Oudot in Troyes in 1649.

In all the standards governing care of the body, facial expression, conduct in church or at home, at table, at games or in company, clothes were made subject to a rule of moderation under which everyone could find what was appropriate to his condition. They always recommended modesty in the choice of fabrics, colours and ornaments. For Erasmus 'wearing clothes that are striped and multicoloured means wanting to look like mountebanks and monkeys', and Jean-Baptiste de la Salle thought that 'clothes with trimmings are suitable only for persons of high status'. Order, cleanliness, the way of wearing were thus regulated for everyone, and the rules circulated in widely distributed texts, for manuals of good manners were used in schools for teaching the alphabet, letters and propriety. The texts were adapted to social groups and age groups, from court circles to the urban and rural schools where little townsfolk and little peasants haltingly recited the same maxims. From direct diffusion (there were 176 versions of La Salle's *Règles de la bienséance et de la civilité*) in 1703 to examples explained, we can see how moral value and social reputation were involved in all of these practices. The processional order in towns proclaimed these principles in the manifestations of authority and, similarly, sumptuary laws imposed there the idea of a social order whose prohibitions and exceptions they codified.

These laws, which were part of European civilisation from the Middle Ages, survived in Switzerland, Germany and Italy down to the nineteenth century.[20] In France as elsewhere they affected all forms of consumption, clothes being one element among others that was likely to increase 'splendiferous expenditure'. Between 1485 and 1660 we thus see taking shape both an economic policy and a defence of noble appearance. For two centuries the monarchy struggled to restrict silks to the nobility, to define a hierarchy of colours and to prohibit the use of gold and silver in the fabrics and adornments of common people – in brief, to restrict the merging of conditions through appearances. When monetarist justifications prevailed at the beginning of the seventeenth century, the sumptuary laws conveyed the impression of a nation wherein the extravagance of consumers was diverting precious metal from useful circuits and from the state's coffers. The policing of expenditure now affected every subject as if, with everyone's consumptions being unified, it was necessary to combat all the superfluities that could ruin the economy. Thereafter the King despoiled the nobles and the bourgeoisie so as to reserve luxury consumption for the Court, the supreme enclave of social distinction. Legislation confirmed what was in the manuals of good manners, with the sumptuary laws focusing on and striving to control the mechanisms which recorded social mimesis.

In effect, court practices gradually took shape and brought in their wake the display of luxury that could be seen in spectacles or else dreamt of and imagined by the ordinary reader of pamphlets and newspapers. These displays strengthened condemnation of the sumptuary order by all who denounced squandering and its threat to the social order. They thought the social order would be endangered as a result of imitation by the *nouveaux-riches* or in general by the vanity of appearances. The Christian economy called for stability. But the air of the Court unified the common language of appearances, for the idea and the prohibition of luxury also kept going a movement of publicity which engendered innovations and imitations. Here occurred a major breakthrough of early modernity: the gate was opened for 'confusion of ranks'.

The sumptuary laws, like the manuals of good manners, found their coherence in the affirmation of an ideal of consumption which reserved manifestations of luxury to the forms of power and regulated the use of wealth by transforming it into charity. The order of appearances was experienced more intensely in towns than in villages, which it reached in weakened condition, as France's sumptuary laws never descended to the minutiae that comparable laws dealt with in Germany or Geneva. This hierarchy of appearances shows how display ruled reason.

Our magistrates have well understood this mystery. Their red gowns, the ermine in which they swaddle themselves like furry cats, the palaces in which they give judgment, the fleurs-de-lys, all this pomp was precisely necessary, and if doctors did not wear cassocks and slippers and lawyers did not wear square caps and excessively ample gowns four times too wide, they would never have duped the world, which cannot resist this so convincing display.

Pascal confirms here that the sartorial hierarchy corresponds to a proclamation of authority at the same time as it extends the power of the civilisation of manners and its symbolic domination. The magnificence of display subjects to itself the violence and disorder of the affects.

Moral and economic thinking marched at the same pace, defining the stationary economy in which everybody was dressed in accordance with his rank. Being and seeming were dictated by conformity, with luxury reserved to manifestations of power, and precedence assigned to giving over accumulating. The culture of appearances was primarily an apprenticeship to the proper use of riches. It is therefore not surprising that it was challenged, from within, so to speak, at the very moment when its principles were codified in laws, in manuals of good manners, and in sermons and works of moral theology. The thing was that everyone felt that the habit no longer made the monk. The sartorial consumption of country-folk was never totally frozen, and that of townsfolk still less. A chorus of lamentations rose up, denouncing infractions and falsifications of appearances. Molière denounced them in *Le bourgeois gentilhomme*, on behalf of the Court, to which he was close. He was a good observer of the prohibitions which Monsieur Jourdain and his tailor set out to defy. Ranks perverted, morals weakened, servants corrupted, all redoubled the harmful consequences of disorder. The world no longer ran true. The warning had general application, being aimed at all who supported declassing at a time when the monarchy and court usages were making more rigid the scale of social values of appearances. Nobody could with impunity assume the clothes of public personages and masters of display. The bourgeoisie, who launched themselves into imitative competition and sometimes put on, as in the United Provinces, the luxurious austerity of fine cloth that was black and fine lace that was white, were ordered to keep their place.

This wind did not blow only in towns. Here we have Madame de Sevigné, at Les Rochers on 15 June 1680:

The other day I had a visit from a pretty little farmer's wife of Bodegat, with fine sparkling eyes, a very handsome shape, and dressed as spruce as hands could make her, in a white holland gown, as fine as cambric, with ruffled cuffs, and trailing on the ground. Good heavens! thought I, when I set eyes on her, I am ruined: for you must know, her husband owes me 80,000 francs.

In Brittany where, in sartorial matters, 'there is great thrift' and where 'the utmost negligence' prevailed, here was the wind of luxury blowing, the rich fabrics and fashionable styles that could be displayed by a rich peasant woman, the wife of the farmer of the lord's estate.[21] Again, twenty years later, at the beginning of the eighteenth century we find the priest of Rumegis admonishing his parishioners, the young men who wore hats trimmed with gold and the girls who wore elaborate bonnets. And in 1720 or thereabouts, here is Jamerey Duval on his way to Sunday mass: 'and, a moment later, I had the pleasure of seeing arrive a crowd of peasants dressed in cloth [not to be confused with the rough local fabrics], most of them having their wrists adorned with silver buttons and cuffs. For the neatness of their attire the women could have appeared along with the sprightliest bourgeoises I had yet seen . . .'[22]

The discourse of remonstrance would never cease thereafter. It inspired the zeal of preachers and the treatises of the last defenders of the Christian economy, such as Abbé Reguis, in his *Traité contre l'amour des parures et le luxe des habits* in 1780. These laments show the effect of the social mechanisms which were subverting appearances and their display. At the top was the court, which until the beginning of Louis XIV's reign, moved around, imposing its parade of ostentation and luxury and the stir created by its servants, soldiers and merchants. In everyday life there was the visiting of their domains by landowners, lords, grandees and nobles. During these comings and goings the air of the town blew for an instant through the village. From time to time troops of travelling actors displayed before the peasantry an unimaginable wealth of costumes. Furetière has left us a realistic and critical description of such occasions. Ordinary clothes were no longer adequate for Sundays and holidays. When material conditions improved, from passive spectators the peasants became active agents. They went to fairs and markets, while pedlars toured the countryside, offering ribbons, needles, handkerchiefs, buttons, little articles from the world of fashion and gallantry.

Towns and prosperity, a first change

Hierarchy and stability in sartorial matters began to be upset from the end of the seventeenth century. Consumption of clothes increased in the towns first, with the country following slowly, though without a complete break in continuity. Furetière's *Roman bourgeois*[23] shows how expenditure grew among the middle classes. Lucrèce, a young bourgeoise living in the Maubert district is courted by a marquis. When a passing coach splashes her with mud she rushes into her house to change: 'She came out soon afterward in fresh linen and a different dress, and it was no small matter of vanity for a person of her sort to show that she possessed several dresses and could assume so quickly a *point de Sedan* that could put to shame the *point de Gênes* she had just taken off.' This novel, which is wholly inspired by the contrast between the old ways and modern politeness, evokes here the confrontation of sartorial capacities with the demands which gave rise to them.

The same can be observed in the accumulation of clothes in Paris. The patrimony of the different categories of society was already considerable at the end of the sevententh century. Among the nobility linen and clothing together amounted on the average to 1,800 *livres,* or thirteen per cent of their movable fortune. The corresponding figures for the artisan and shopkeeping bourgeoisie were 344 *livres* (twenty-eight per cent): for the bourgeoisie of officialdom and the non-noble professions 148 *livres* (thirteen per cent): for wage-earners, casual workers and labourers 42 *livres* (eight per cent): and servants 115 *livres* (twenty per cent). These averages certainly conceal differences within each category. Most of the inventories of nobles varied between 300 and 1,000 *livres* for clothes, but a few great court families boost the figures. This expenditure represented between fifteen and a hundred *sétiers* of corn at the current price.[24]

Among the wage-earning population the sartorial patrimony accounting for eight per cent for their goods in constant use does not represent an expenditure. It is an average calculated on the basis of the accumulation effected over the years: when a man's fortune increased the percentage going on clothes did not follow at exactly the same pace. Servants were the best off, because they enjoyed the advantage of being housed and (partly) fed and, above all, of being clothed by their masters. Among the Parisian bourgeoisie mediocrity and sumptuousness coexisted, the driving force of trade being certainly more effective in this respect than the traditionalism of the law and the world of letters. Above all, analysis of wardrobes reveals a population whose sartorial habits were homogeneous. Women's clothing was dominated by the set of skirt and petticoat, mantle, apron and stiff bodice. Gowns were still rare (only 16 per cent among the nobility). For men the usual purchases were: jerkin, waistcoat, breeches, mantle, hat. Formally, there was nothing to distinguish these townsfolk from the inhabitants of the countryside, apart from social differences that were clearly marked by contrasts in quality (the value of garments) and quantity (capacity to replace). The hierarchy of clothes was like that of labour, leisure and sociability. In all categories it was the women who were in the forefront for expenditure.

While parsimony and moderation were still characteristic of most purchases of clothing, with the solid, the durable, woollen cloth and dark colours predominant, indices of acceleration were perceptible among a minority (perhaps ten to twenty per cent of the notarial sample). Three tendencies guided supply and demand for a market of 450,000 people. There were, first, those who possessed only the indispensable minimum of garments, in accordance with religious, social and economic requirements. For the poorest, their practice where clothing was concerned was dictated solely by necessity. Secondly, there were those who sought to make of their clothes a sign of social distinction. This tendency was found especially in the middle sections of the merchant, artisan and liberal bourgeoisies, that is, the profound social armature of urban life. Neither poor nor rich, they were comfortably off and, desirous to rise in the world, they wished to reconcile religious and moral rules with the civilisation of the manuals of good manners. Thirdly came the circle of the big spenders, individuals or small groups who were alert to changes, to the values of imitation and fashion which they tried to follow in general or in detail. This social aesthetic might, with some, caught in the circuit of ostentatious expenditure, bring them close to excess and squandering. In this world of appearances servants had the task of reinforcing their masters' affirmation of omnipotence. Menservants and maidservants were drawn, through the double use of clothing and livery and the proximity of their masters, into paths of consumption into which they, in turn, attracted other sections of the population who came into contact with them. Taverns, the pleasure-gardens of the faubourgs, theatres, fetes and fairs were the most obvious places for such transfers, but others, and not the least important, occurred in people's homes and within families.

These three sensibilities existed independently of economic reference-points. The sartorial system in Paris in Louis XIV's reign consisted not so much of a series of strata corresponding to economic and social levels as of a continual interweaving of choices and forms of behaviour which could affect simultaneously the rich and the less rich. This phenomenon assumed a collective dimension at the end of an accumulation resulting from multiple individual choices. Clothing mirrored the lives of men and women. The latter played a dynamic and driving role, but lost this among the wage-earners, where the equality of necessity ruled both sexes, and also among the aristocracy, in which the men were impelled to assert their rank and prestige by means of sumptuary expenditure symbolic of social status. They invested in clothing at least as much as, if not more than, did their womenfolk. Courtiers and the King's intimates were drawn by the logic of etiquette into a sartorial super-consumption in conformity with the aristocratic ethos, which was essentially different from that of the bourgeoisie of the professions.

In the capital, and perhaps also in the large towns, the sartorial system was connected with consideration, calculation of economic chances and necessity. No logic coincided exactly with any one social stratum, but all were linked together, across all the groups, with each having its constraints and its reasons which intersected in the space of the town. It was thus both in average value spent and in capacity for affirmation that the inhabitants of the towns differed from those of the country.

This first transformation was due to the development of the textile industries, which were in the forefront of production. The famous major centres of cloth and silk manufacture started on a process of growth that was destined not to halt. Lyons, Tours, Rouen, Amiens, Reims, Beauvais led the way for luxury fabrics and silk, while Languedoc, Picardy, the Cambrésis, Normandy and the North increased their workshops serving the ordinary market for linen and cloth.[25] Versailles, Paris, the Army, the cities with *Parlements* and the capitals of commerce were largely supplied by the drapers and merchant mercers of Paris. The expanding current market enjoyed support from the state, which granted monopolies and privileges, while the Inspectors of Manufactures watched over the products whose quality ensured their sales.[26] Through supervision and information the textile sector – woollens first, then silks – unified and encouraged the producers after the years of difficulty. A first process of growth began, a first technical consciousness came into being.

The means of transformation appear to have followed in the corporative world of the towns. At the top were the great guilds, the clothiers, mercers, male and female linen-drapers, who everywhere propelled the trade in raw materials.[27] At the bottom, modest and effective agents reproduced and invented, within the framework of an economy in which division of labour did not exactly keep step with growth. To the variety and multitude of crafts, infinitely specialised in the making of all or part of a costume, which were busy in the mediaeval town the Paris of Louis XIII and Louis XIV contrasted the strengthening of three great crafts organised in guilds. These were the tailors, who provided everyone's new clothes and controlled the home-workers: the second-hand dealers, who sold old clothes and might 'make up on spec', using poor-quality cloth costing less than ten *livres* the ell: and the dressmakers, who clothed women and children. Among the mercers there were a few men and women who were already co-ordinating the work of the other crafts and inspiring the pursuit of fashion. The shop-window of fashion was located at Versailles, amid the gold and mirrors of the absolutist celebration, but also in Paris, whence emerged the prints, the news and the fashion-dummies that were sent to the capital cities of Europe.

Paris, which attracted a ceaseless flow of visitors, was already spreading the directives for change everywhere. The testimony of the de Villiers brothers,[28] representative members of the Dutch aristocracy who were drawn into France's diplomatic orbit before the conflicts at the end of the century, bears witness to this for the 1650s:

> On the 24th, a Sunday, we stayed at home, as we did not have apparel in which to show ourselves, especially on holidays, when every idler takes note of all that passes before his eyes. All we had was our travelling clothes, old-fashioned garments trimmed with gold and silver and loaded with that mass of ribbons which has just gone out of fashion. While propriety would not have prevented us from appearing in that condition, the strict edict in force against this excess obliged us to keep indoors. We summoned the tailor, first, to alter our clothes. He did his best to make us look fashionably dressed, and our clothes served for our first visits while he was making new ones for us. On the 25th he brought them: they were adorned with rather long ribbons which were tied in the form of aiglets, and there were tags at the end which made them fashionable.

Everything is said in those few lines about the society of the rich, the world of the urban salons, the aristocratic riding academies attended by young foreigners, beyond the Court. The demands of decorum, the control of sumptuary consumption, here a new edict against gold and silver trimmings, issued on 13 November 1656, which upset usages and gave a fillip to trade and, finally, sociability with its rules. Clothing made it possible to classify and to know: it imposed a homogeneity of practices. The first rule for a foreigner was 'not to make himself stand out but to dress like everybody else', as the German Nemeitz confirmed in the 1720s:[29] 'as regards everything to do with dress, what is best is to imitate the French'. The town was already setting the tone for the foreigner visiting France, but the rest of France was not inert.

Avignon, or ostentatious penury

Between the capital and the countryside, Avignon provides us from now on with an excellent observatory in the form of the archives of its Mont-de-Piété.[30] The pledges that we can follow through two centuries enable us to measure the sartorial choices made by everyone, though mainly by the lower classes when affected by want during crises. More than 600,000 inhabitants of Avignon pawned a little of everything – kitchen utensils, linen, fabrics, jewels, costumes, toys, tools. Here we perceive the appearance of temporary poverty, such as could strike families when they were short of work, and which could cause movements both upward and downward, since there were winners as well as losers among those who had recourse to the pawnbrokers. The establishment of the Mont-de-Piété in the 1610s aimed to ease the lot of impoverished people, combat usury and, as in Rome, to restrict the role played by the Jewish money-lenders.

A selection from 59,000 objects (or 17,000 pledges) shows that the public which used the Mont coincided with the lower orders of the population. The lenders do not include members of the urban elite, nobles, bourgeois, merchants, lawyers or clergy, but those who were outside the political and economic leadership. Officially, talk and regulations spoke of the 'shamefaced poor', which meant deserving de-classed persons, the unlucky and, especially, those whom the temporary distress of the time brought to the attention of the charitable confraternities. Persons who possessed nothing or were homeless were shown the door of the Mont. Most of the pledges deposited were reclaimed within a period of one to three years (ten per cent were never reclaimed). The clientele were loyal, since the receipts issued by the Mont were almost equivalent to money, being circulated and exchanged. Seventy-six per cent of the objects deposited were worth between one and ten *livres*: in 1610 that was equivalent to between one and fifteen days' consumption of bread by four persons. What we have here, therefore, are short-term consumer loans which remained the same in real value all through the seventeenth and eighteenth centuries.

Between 1610 and 1626, the only period in which the registrars recorded the social position of the borrowers, we find that, out of 250 cases, seventeen per cent were engaged in agriculture, sixty-one per cent were wage-earning craftsmen and twenty-two per cent were servants or persons in various services. This is a piece of sociology which reflects the activity of Avignon, a textile town where the silk and woollen trades employed 10,000 people. It was a regional capital for redistribution, with shops, carriers and street-porters, which also had a garrison and included within its walls a good number of gardeners, market-gardeners and agriculturists. The silk workers – ribbon-makers, lace-makers, taffeta-makers, velvet-weavers, silk-throwers, dyers – were well represented at the Mont. They worked for a sensitive sector of the economy, subject to competition from the rising centres of Lyons and Nîmes and restricted by the export duties to be paid, but a sector which nevertheless was hardy. However, the clients of the Mont consisted above all of women, mostly married ones (75 per cent). Their pawning was connected with work and the management of families. The woman was in charge of the household: it was she who, in case of need, chose the objects to be pawned – which were usually clothes, jewels and linen, i.e. whatever belonged to the domestic sphere, the body, appearances.[31]

The objects deposited bear witness to consumers' habits. We find neither footwear nor bedding, which were indispensable, nor books, these being rare among the people, but, instead, things that were marginal to necessity, things one could do without for a time. Tools are rarely included, but household objects are numerous. Jewels account for half of the deposits around 1610, after which they tend to decline slightly and steadily. On the other hand, clothes (a quarter of all pledges at the start) increase regularly, exceeding domestic equipment in the eighteenth century. Deposits of textiles – yarn and unfashioned fabrics, cloth, woollen materials, silk and cotton goods – are well represented. A remnant of printed calico was deposited for the first time in 1673. This was, in a way, a reflection of Avignon's textile culture: increased use of the new fibres, silk and cotton, declining use of wool, steady use of local fibres, especially hemp.

The principal item among the deposits was shirts – undifferentiated, unisex, long and heavy (1.50 metre, 900 grammes). These were products of weaving and dressmaking, without collars or buttons, and in various states of wear and tear. We see here evidence of the town's conquest of linen and the new attitude to cleanliness. The Avignon shirts, already worn, already made supple, lacking stiffness, belonged to the intimate sphere of households. Forty-seven per cent of the clothes deposited in the seventeenth century were shirts, 30 per cent in the eighteenth, and in the same period deposit of single items gave way to deposit of batches (of three, six or even twelve items at a time). 'Dry toilette', which meant merely changing one's linen, had become established after 1673. Deposits of shirts increased hugely after the ending of the plague in Provence in 1722. In contrast to this, the poor representation of other underwear, night-gowns, for example, is striking. In the eighteenth century the shirts become more luxurious: they have collars and are more varied, which shows both the triumph of a certain pattern and its improvement owing to increased means.

The women's clothes deposited at the Mont conform to the old sartorial style until the middle of the seventeenth century but what we observe is a costume made up of separate items. At the beginning what predominates is the combination of jacket with corsage – in Provençal, *ganachon* and *gonelle*, often worn one over the other: to these are added petticoat, skirt, stiff bodice and apron. Neither head-dresses nor stockings were deposited, nor were the shoes which we see appearing in the dress of women in hospital.[32] The clothes are, up to eighty per cent of them, described as shabby or of mediocre quality. After 1650 the silhouette changes. It is not 'long-line' any more, but split in two in the association of skirt with corsage, or stiff bodice, so as to show off one's waist. The petticoat and skirt ensure the progress of cotton: though all tissues are represented, cotton surpasses silk after 1700. Also, dark or natural colours give way to yellows, and common rough blues, less frequently to expensive reds. We also note that multicolouring and fantasy come to the fore, with stripes and checks at the end of the Regency. The Parisian garment, the gown in two pieces, advances, accompanied by numerous objects both ornamental and utilitarian: corset, short gown, tippet, apron. Two features of a regional nature appear: embroidery and stitching, which makes possible the use of 'ends' and is associated with cotton, and the braid which ornaments skirts and petticoats. In the course of two centuries women's dress has thus become more supple, coloured and diversified, in association with the new textiles. Paris did not have a monopoly of changes.[33]

The men's clothes deposited at the Mont are less numerous (only twenty per cent of the pledges). The old rural style predominates, a basic costume at first consisting of doublet, trunk-hose, shirts and mantles. The hospital deposits show that the men of the lower classes have hats, shoes and stockings enough. The silhouette is heavy, and the colours are dark, the materials rough, mainly caddis and wool. Around 1670 doublet and jerkin disappear, being replaced by breeches and waistcoat. The transformation is slower than in the case of women, the clothes are less variegated and the formal features of the old style, stiff and dark, survive longer, a sign that the men have less money to spare.

Besides, the women have an additional trump-card, in their jewellery, which, when necessary, they deposit in great quantities (50 per cent of deposits around 1610, 9 per cent in 1789). Most common is the wedding-ring, then, in equal amounts, cross, belt, necklaces. Here we discover a taste for adornment to a degree that has no equivalent in the Parisian household. The tone of *dorure* and *bellure* is that of the local sartorial style, illustrating a certain tendency to show off one's success as the nuptial symbols of wealth. Avignon's consumption of clothes reveals the diversification and lightening of dress, the role of women at the centre of the system, the possibility of showing off even when short of money: jewels and clothes serving as reserves, almost as instruments of exchange, while retaining substantial use-value and symbolic value. A real desire to make an appearance is obvious where the public of Avignon's Mont-de-Piété is concerned.

Clothes were not subject to one set of circumstances only. Between 1630 and 1660 the styles are fifty years or so behind Paris, for the first change: after that, the changes that occur are more limited in nature and proceed at comparable speeds. The fabrics have a different life. The end of domination by woollens comes earlier than in Paris. The rise of cotton is quick, carried forward by the movement of Mediterranean imports.

The presence of silk goes back a long way. There are, in quantity as in quality, spin-offs of production: after 1680 the people of Avignon were won for printed calico even before calico-printing workshops had been established in any number. The chronology of the deposits shows the progress of this material. Between 1679 and 1690 the registers show the arrival of domestic equipment, curtains, fabrics; between 1680 and 1700 indoor clothing, dressing gowns; after 1700, all kinds of women's clothes, together with neckerchiefs and waistcoats of piqué. The costume of the women of Avignon's lower classes was not based on passive imitation, since it was expressed in a liking for jewellery, printed calico, with its exotic decoration with plants, and for piqué. The forms of the garments were the same as in Paris and elsewhere, but the detail and the combination were individual and local achievements.

From Paris to the provinces, the change in the eighteenth century

Change and fashion progressvely took over the capital and began to affect the provinces, where the peasants' consumption started to diversify. At the end of the eighteenth century the people crossed the frontier of necessity. With greater or less speed they took part in the presentation of sartorial appearances, the decline of culture, distinction and good manners. The breaks in these movements and their extension can be measured. The forms of clothes, both men's and women's, were fixed in Paris at the end of the seventeenth century, then they came into line and differentiated, influenced by fashion which only the rich could afford.

In all the inventories we note the increase in accumulated expenditure on clothing. The average amount spent, taking all social categories together, is 2,500 *livres*. Linen and clothes reached 7,700 *livres* in 1789, a nominal increase of 300 per cent, or, in real terms (reckoned from the price of corn), of 80 per cent. In all social groups the value of wardrobes increased faster than that of goods in common use taken as a whole, or than the increase in patrimonies of moveable goods. The increase in consumer goods was general, but everything that related to the expression of appearances, both social and private, increases still more.

Of course this advance varied from one social group to another. At the top of the list were servants (an increase of 321 per cent, with an average of 293 *livres*), then came officials and professional people (272 per cent and 699 *livres*), nobles (6,000 *livres* and 163 per cent), wage-earners (115 *livres* and 148 per cent) and craftsmen and shopkeepers (587 *livres* and only 35 per cent). The intervals in the social topography had widened. Among the masses the share of the conquests was greater for the lowest patrimonies (less than 500 *livres*) than for the fortunes (bigger than 3,000 *livres*). In relation to goods in common use as a whole it was 16 per cent as against 7.5 per cent in 1700 for the former and 1.6 per cent and 0.6 per cent in 1700 for the latter. The doubling of the figure was, moreover, due to purchases by women. Among servants the increase was greater (from 10 to 30 per cent of goods in common use), and the sexual dimorphism continued. Among the nobility a ceiling of consumption was reached which could hardly be surpassed. Expenditure no longer increased systematically with the level of wealth, and behaviour was greatly unified by access to the market of fashion. On the other hand the bourgeoisie seem to have lagged behind, even though, in the worlds of trade and officialdom, they were already far removed from wage-earners' expenditure.

Another sign of change was the unification of sartorial habits. It had won over the population as a whole, for numberless intermediaries, the rich among the poor, attractive bachelors, servants, whether obedient or insolent, and women in all categories of society caused to circulate, wholesale and retail, the results of modistes' work and the novelties from the manufactories. That the woman of the last phase of the Century of Enlightenment spent twice as much as her husband, except, perhaps, among the high nobility, is a fact of major anthropological interest: this was, indeed, a general attitude which transformed the female body between the seventeenth and eighteenth centuries and which had consequences for the conduct and demeanour of men. The movement of sexual differentiation began well before the nineteenth century.[34] Everybody's habits were much more homogeneous under Louis XVI than in Louis XIV's time. The wardrobes of both men and women conformed to the change in clothing begun in the seventeenth century, with, everywhere, an increased number of objects. For men there was the triumph of the costume *à la française* and for women that of the gown and the bodice, these main items being accompanied by many accessories – corsage, short gown, tippet, apron, in the case of the women, and, in that of the men, mantle, especially in winter, and hat. The intervals were still there. The average number of items of clothing possessed by a male member of the nobility was eighty, and only fifty-five for the women, each item costing more. In the wardrobe of a lower-class person the average for men was five items and for women about ten. For the women of the bourgeoisie and the merchant class the accumulation was similar (ten items), a little less for their husbands. It was twice that amount in the case of the men and women of the official and professional classes.

The new consumption, both masculine and feminine, thus diffused widely an ideal of change and renewal, the faculty for seeing the trifling and agreeable come to terms with the usual and the solid. Everywhere shoes were worn by the lower classes. Linen had invaded wardrobes, retaining its role of substitution in hygiene. A lower-class mother of a family could now change her shift every day, her husband his shirt almost as often, and a reserve remained for dressing up or looking good in the evening and on holidays. Even the lowest figures show the progress made by the lower orders, while the richest men were even better supplied under Louis XVI than in Louis XIV's time. Finally, the range of textiles was more diverse. Wool, which had prevailed for several centuries, was being rivalled by cotton and silk, hemp by flax – all much faster among the rich than among the poor. Colours, like fabrics, became lighter. The lower classes dressed more lightly, but what they gained in diversity they lost in solidity: they found themselves obliged to speed up the rhythm of their purchases, to struggle against wear and tear. With a wider palette of colours they breathed an air of fashion. The silhouette changed. It lost its stiffness and adjusted to English or exotic ways and more frivolous styles. The 'civilisation of manners' won more ground at the same time as conflicts over precedence increased and observers agreed in speaking of the confusion of ways of behaving. The elegant borrowed from the man of the people – hence trousers – while the man of the people imitated the dandies – look at *Monsieur Nicolas* or Jacques Louis Ménétra's *Journal of my Life*. The more earnest and gloomy saw in these transfers signs of probable impending catastrophes. Like M. de Ségur, who wrote: 'In ceasing to respect the public one lost sight of all differences in society.'[35]

It is difficult to judge how far this sartorial revolution went in the provinces, as the sample for comparison is too small. A few towns and a few rural samplings do allow us, however, to recognise a similar effect of influence, with, in every case, wider gaps between social groups. At Versailles the value of wardrobe-contents increased less quickly than in Paris, but the average increase was, nevertheless (as calculated from several thousand inventories, both bourgeois and lower-class), from 95 *livres* to 230, between 1700 and 1789. The evolution of textiles was considerable, the progress in colours and the diversification of objects worn following the same rhythm as in Paris.[36] At Auxerre the situation was similar (93 *livres* in 1700, 282 in 1789). At Chartres it was about the same in the higher social categories but somewhat behindhand in the lower ones and among the peasants of the town's periphery. At Limoges linen, the new textiles and colours appeared fifty years later than in Paris,[37] a gap that was even bigger in Brittany. At Besançon there was the same gap where men's clothes were concerned, but this was out of step with the progress in women's wear: linen had been acquired by practically everyone in the middle of the eighteenth century.[38] The triumph of luxury and finery was reported elsewhere by travellers and observers. At Montpellier one such illustrates the progress made, but aso the social implications of urban appearances:

Finery is the rule in this town. The women and girls of the first and second estates have gone overboard for it. The most beautiful silk fabrics, made up in the best of taste, are used for their clothes. Fashion or taste requires that they have several, for the seasons of winter, spring and summer, so that they can change for each season. They must also have elegant déshabillés and mantillas of every type and colour. This is matched by fine linen and lace. Footwear generally consists of shoes of white damask. Head-dresses are, at the moment, small, since they curl their hair, which they pull back and up to the top of their heads, a style which is most becoming: in particular, it gives an air of youthfulness which enhances the beauty and the softness of the face. To this are added plumes, ear-rings, necklaces, bracelets, rings, diamond buckles, a gold watch, a gold snuff-box, the case also of gold, a muff and a fan. This is what shows on the outside and is the rule for women with rich husbands . . . The men are no less enamoured of finery. Coats of velvet in winter and silk in summer, and waistcoats of cloth of gold and silver are very common, to the point where they make a sort of large surtout or redingote of velvet to be worn over coats of broadcloth. Bag-wigs are the most common. Lace cuffs and fine linen are becoming general: they are changed every day, which means you need to have a lot of them.[39]

At Montpellier as at Avignon the gaps were still there, between the top and bottom of society, but requirements were greater. In town there were now two ways in which one could behave: as required by traditional social relationships, though this was no longer prescribed by the sumptuary laws, now abandoned, or as dictated by personal choice, that is, by the public, for whom appearance ought to reveal estate and moral being; and the private way, in which the values of the intimate could correspond to one's personality. Sartorial usages and codes were in confusion. The ladies of the Court dreamt of dressing simply, in the English manner, as shepherdesses, in town as among their family. Provincial people imagined that they were copying aristocratic airs. Servants everywhere imitated them, and triumphant bourgeois put on an appearance of nobility.

In the countryside the conquest of linen preceded that of clothes and the changing tastes which imposed urban fashions. We notice this delay quite close to Paris, in the Vexin *français* or in the big farms.[40] Women had about a dozen shifts (between six and ten, on the average) and the durability and stoutness of clothing were still very substantial: a lot of woollens and rustic cloths, not much in cotton, or only late in the period, few gowns, many skirt-and-corsage ensembles, not so often the stiff bodice or corset. The wives of well-to-do peasants possessed several luxury items. The men possessed the essentials, of lower value than in Paris and not so diverse. A few notables engaged in ostentatious expenditure, characterised by elegance of fabrics and designs. The three coats mentioned by F.-X. Besnard in his *Souvenirs* had been acquired for everyday wear, for Sundays and for ceremonial occasions. The scene was similar in Brie, around Meaux, at Nangis.[41] In 1665 one-third of the inventories make no mention of a shirt, but seventy per cent of the population already have more than five. With the same fortune the Brie peasant possessed more linen than a lower-class person in Paris! In 1750 spare linen is found everywhere: forty-five per cent of the inventories list more than twenty shirts. It was the same among the Burgundian vine-growers and farmers in Franche-Comté.[42]

In all these examples the content of the woman's wardrobe is already more varied than that of the man, but the fabrics are everywhere more traditional – wool, serge, broadcloth, hemp, not much cotton – before the end of the century. In Brittany, at Roscoff, the diversity of the objects is less and progress is confined to the rich. Printed calico is entering the scene slowly, but cotton has arrived. Colours are evolving slowly, too:[43] in 1700 we find fifty-eight per cent dark colours for men's clothes, forty-two per cent for women's: in 1789 the corresponding figures are forty-one and thirty-seven. Alsace shows few innovations, either in value (10 per cent of the moveable patrimonies of the peasants was made up of clothes) or in quality. Clothing both masculine and feminine is stout, even rustic, though the designs are those realised in Paris in the seventeenth century. Eighty-five per cent of the inventories mention breeches and waistcoats and as many skirts and petticoats. Accessories and colours are making slow progress. The costume of the Alsatian peasant evolves little: 'he conveys a sense of belonging to a world that is stable and almost unmoving'. The values of a modern world, of diversified appearance, concern for the decorative would take more than a century to triumph there.

The distances between the rural and urban world were still there, but not as in the seventeenth century. In the 1750s and 1760s we observe everywhere the same revolution in the design of clothing. In the case of women, the silhouette that was austere and stiff, dark and without fantasy, is replaced by a figure that is supple and coloured. In that of men, unmatched clothes made of broadcloth and brown holland, dark and stiff, are replaced by the *ensemble à la française* – breeches, waistcoat, coat. In his autobiography, Louis Simon, tinsmith, weaver, sacristan, tavern-keeper, describes changes that he dates from the 1770s when the highroad from Paris to Le Mans was opened.[44] 'I saw the beginning of cottons and cotton goods. At first the richest ladies wore them, then the ladies in trade, and finally the servants and even the poor. After that, *toiles d'Orange* and printed calico also became fashionable with the great ladies and then with the other women, as we see today' – meaning, at the beginning of the nineteenth century, which was when he wrote these memorable observations.

In the country the values of stability, identified with the solidity and repeated wearing of clothes, did not disappear, nor did the re-use, darning and mending which gave the peasants' clothes their specific aspect. The taste for rustic cloth and solid fabrics might indicate an outlook that was not governed by mere imitation of the great and rich or by financial capacities. Taking part in the spectacle of the privileged and in renewal was less easy, but there were already opportunities, on Sundays and holidays, for putting on clothes that were new and less often worn. The culture of respect survived better than in the towns, and everyone kept an eye on everyone else. One's condition ought to show itself in what one wore: but visits from pedlars reinforced the shop-window effect of the town. Meanwhile, tastes were beginning to be individualised: tastes for ribbons, for lace, for shawls, for neckerchiefs, a more elegant garment, a less rustic fabric.[45] While some women were able to invest in superfluities, the general transformations expressed not so much the self-assertion of a class as a greater capacity by society to consume and to produce.

Manufacture and rural industry followed, accompanied or preceded this movement. Entire sections of the textile part of the economy adapted themselves to demand and the new needs, bringing the victory of the 'light materials'. Printed calico, which threatened the old forms of cloth production, gained ground despite the resistance of the makers of silk and fine woollen cloth, who succeeded in forbidding its production until 1759. Cotton goods enjoyed success first through smuggling, then through the development of workshops.[46] The woollen cloth manufacture of Languedoc began to convert to silk, partly for exporting ordinary fabrics and partly for selling these same less expensive fabrics on the domestic market.[47] This ruralising of textile production helped to intensify the production of cotton, wool and silk. Diversification of change and of trade followed, and in the sector of more luxurious products dictated the changes. Tailors, dressmakers, second-hand clothes merchants, linen-drapers, modistes provided access to the Paris market, but all these various products also circulated outside market relations, by way of gifts and thefts.[48]

Theft and re-sale were subject together to the same reproof, in the eyes of good society, but they convey something precious to the historian – the creation of illusions and the effectiveness of marginal diffusion. Cases of stealing of clothes made up a quarter of those judged in Paris in 1710–35, and 37 per cent in 1790. This illustrates well the evolution of opinion regarding this crime, the object of which, rare at first, became common, and also the importance of a means of credit which enabled a person to appropriate the appearance of someone else. This form of criminality was rooted in the new habits of consumption: it emphasised the social caesuras in them and speeded up their circulation. Cartouche would become legendary for his red coat, Mandrin for his elegance and Marion du Faouët, whose band of brigands disguised as travelling mercers went from fair to pilgrimage, for her blue doublet, her big black hooded cape and her English-type overcoat which she hid in her baggage.[49] The second-hand clothes trade, re-sale of clothing, worked in the same direction, though less marginally, emphasising the frontiers between the new and the used, between made-to-measure and ready-made, between repairing and re-appropriating. The 'sartorial revolution' would have been inconceivable without the beginning of the empire of distribution and of commercialised maintenance in the towns.

Good manners and consideration were thus being challenged, without it being possible to call the new balance egalitarian. The gaps between social groups remained and were reflected in greater or less capacity to renew quickly the contents of one's wardrobe, and so by a more or less steep social gradation in the obsolescence of things. These gaps showed themselves in ways of following the changes of the seasons, in the indicators of refinement and quality (of fabrics, colours and ornaments) as well as in the increasing number of accessories. The values of accumulation and re-use by several generations gave ground to the values of fashion, of continually reactivated taste and of change. It was at the moment when the *civilisation of manners and of the court* attained its apogee that it was questioned by the valorisation of the artificial, for fashion, which both unifies and distinguishes, constructed thereafter as many individual identities as collective personalities. The divorce betweeen being and seeming became, with Rousseau, a commonplace of philosophy. In this de-structuring, struggles of representation were organised in accordance with the new configurations that corresponded to needs, capacities and aspirations, and so to sensibilities. Down below were the excluded and the poor: receiving as gift, charitable or from the poorhouse, or taking by theft, they constituted the reservoir of occasions and traditions. Tatters and rags enabled them to combat necessity and the weather. At the middle level were the supporters of standards or of indifference, who showed no haste in following the incitements of novelty, with greater or less dynamism. It was this category that ensured, among the Paris bourgeoisie, the constant triumph of black, thanks to which Protestants had been able to recognise each other, as also, later, members of the Third Estate. Their tacit refusal might correspond to a choice, religious, moral and ascetic, but it could also have an economic value, wisdom recommending moderation in consumption as against other, more effective choices. Or it could correspond to a superior indifference and detachment.[50] At the top we find the activists of competition, guided by their interest in the struggles for precedence: courtiers and *nouveaux-riches* followed the dictates of the latest fashions out of aestheticism, from convenience of hygiene, or through the passion for elegance that makes dandies and the great creators of fashion. This pattern could be modified according to age and gender, time, good or bad luck. Social commands were followed to a greater or a less extent, and their mimetic values were not confined to the rich, the privileged and the townsfolk. The importance of the sartorial revolution in the economic and social debate which overturned the values of the Christian and moral economy lay in the fact that it substituted, in everyday life, a number of values for the old ones which it erased. Instead of obligation to redistribute, the power of accumulation and enrichment. Instead of the weight of custom and tradition, the force of individual choice and renewal. Against belief that luxury should be reserved for manifestations of authority and rank, dictating sartorial appearances, the liberal assurance of capacities, the economic and moral utility of consumption. Thereafter, fashion inserted itself between constraint and freedom.

9   Bread, wine, taste

For a majority of the population, food was the number-one preoccupation. Response to this concern, and the cost entailed, determined everything else. If, however, we stop at that, we risk seeing in means of subsistence only an imperative – the struggle for life, eating in order to survive. To satisfy persistent needs and escape from the burden imposed by environmental constraints, men have invented a variety of solutions.

Adaptability to food is both physiological and cultural.[1] In it there come together the setting, the quest for new recipes to respond to need, the invention of a science of cooking which is at the origin of the conquests of taste and gastronomic inventiveness. The natural setting, it must not be forgotten, plays an essential role here. Until the eighteenth century, cooking and eating meant profiting by the supplies which followed one another as the months and years went by, according to regions, that is, with an irregularity that it is hard for us to imagine. In the forefront stood the painful problem of survival, conditioned by unpredictable weather:[2] exceptionally cold winters, spoilt springs or summers, rainy autumns that devastated wine-harvests, but also changes of intervals, manifested in repeated seasonal accidents, which alternated periods of rain, chill and warmth, resulting in very diverse conjunctures of production.[3] The setting had its effect also through modifying caloric needs in relation to climate, seasons, altitude, and also depending on the level of activity dictated by the technical capacities of the epoch. Everywhere, consumption had to adapt. It put off the utilisation of harvests in relation to their production and acquisition – here we again come upon the problem of stocks and reserves. It was organised, too, very differently as between the sexes, the age-groups and the social categories.

Foodstuffs are not only good to eat, they are also 'good to think about and imagine'. They occupy a considerable place in religious and symbolic life. They imply forms of social behaviour, in private as in public, and even inspire regional stereotypes. In the seventeenth century the Breton, drunken and quarrelsome, was contrasted, in the imagined geography of the realm, with the sober Provençal or the civilised Tourangeau.

Travellers made these types of conduct generally known and drew a lasting map of the peoples on an all-Europe scale. They applied to culinary habits a pattern of interpretation that was drawn from the lessons of the manuals of good manners and governed by the imperatives of the civilisation of manners which were themselves drawn from the ways of the Court and of cultivated circles. While these images give us only a relative picture of usages, they nevertheless do bear a certain relation to reality, indicating what was available locally, specific products and particular ways of consuming. Similarly with drink, which is closely linked with nutrition in the strict sense: everywhere, people drink to refresh themselves while taking nourishment. In the North, drink was consumed in the setting of a social relation, away from meals and away from the family circle of private life. The attention paid to drunkenness allegedly general in Germany, Poland or Brittany, was due not so much to actual drunkenness as to a real difference in the ordinary expression of needs.[4]

Need, labour, symbol

The history of food is therefore special in more ways than one. It is a history in which nature and humanity meet, a nature transformed, already historical and cultural, associating mind and matter. It is a history in which can be read the result of immense toil over thousands of years during which vegetable and animal species have been gradually domesticated and eating practices have become unified on a continental scale. Finally, it is perhaps the domain in which needs, symbolic forms and class oppositions intersect with the greatest intensity. Marc Bloch saw this clearly:

Old-time eating is an expression which may be useful in that it emphasises a contrast with present-day conditions. But it is certainly too simple. Along with differences of periods and regimes it also diminishes differences between classes. We cannot conceive past societies without this antithesis: the lower orders in the countryside in a state of perpetual undernourishment, the rich overfed. How many kings and princes were obese in their old age! What irritability among the most gifted! The carousals of the good old days have become legendary only through contrast with the everyday regime . . .

To what extent can we speak of traditional eating? To be sure, eating practices were greatly unified by dependence on harvests and on difficult transport conditions which for a long time doomed the market to dullness. Inadequate capacity to store grain, and the basis of taxation, which was too wide until the eighteenth century, restricted commercialisation, with some exceptions, in particular in Paris.[5] Security of food supply dominated everything else, inequality of resources was still great, and monotony in the choice of food prevailed in the sphere of production for subsistence. It involved, to a huge extent, a basic consumption of grain, which served Vauban as his term of reference when calculating his budget.

However, the towns set exchange going and created the market, which had local repercussions on the food supply. Above all, between the seventeenth and the eighteenth century the spectre of crises and famines tended to fade away, undoubtedly because cultural practices evolved. Gardens played a part in these changes. According to Olivier de Serres, in the sixth book of his *Théâtre d'agriculture et mesnage des champs*, at the beginning of the seventeenth century, it was 'the gardens that furnish for the useful adornment of our households an infinity of roots, herbs, flowers and fruits, with much that is marvellous'. Kitchen-garden, flower-garden, medicinal garden, fruit garden, arranged according to rules or left in disorder, this was a reservoir of many resources in which people learnt to cultivate plants that were delicate, frail and as yet little-known. An artificial creation, it required much toil, much natural fertiliser and water, but 'it gives forth all the time in every year', whereas arable land could yield a crop only once annually. These modest laboratories of culinary experimentation made it possible to vary the monotonous consumption of cereals. The gardens and kitchens of their owners were thus the first to welcome such novelties as cabbages, cauliflowers, turnips, carrots, parsnips, early peas and, in the eighteenth century, potatoes – also, perhaps, in the sixteenth and seventeenth centuries, the maize of the South-West.[6] However, whole phases of the history of the conditions of food-supply are still but little or poorly known: stock-breeding, meat and dairy products, cheeses, the products of fishing,[7] the scale of storage and the rhythms of purchases by urban families, the simultaneous variation in capacities for production and in tastes.

From this angle the evolution of the objects and of the ways of preparing them is important, because it either maintained or created differences between the poorer people's ways and those of the bourgeoisie. Cookery books, which recorded the evolution of the science of cooking and the science of appreciating food, brought about culinary revolutions. The classified list[8] showed how one proceeded from the products to their treatment and then to the ways of sharing the meal. Bread, wine and water were central to a traditional *savoir-vivre* and its ideas, the value of which cooking and taste progressively modified. From nature people passed to art and science, and from hunger satisfied *a minima* together with gluttony, which was defined as a deadly sin, they arrived at last to 'good taste' and its cult of gastronomy, an invention of the last years of the Century of Enlightenment.

A traditional savoir-vivre *and a traditional* savoir-faire

In modern society there were three types of cookery and feeding: family cookery, everyday and private, making use of female labour (in the aristocratic town-house the formula expanded and tended to involve males); collective and utilitarian cookery, in poor-houses, convents, armies, prisons and colleges, but also by caterers and in the restaurants which appeared in towns; and festival and display cookery which, on special occasions, religious or social, anniversaries, calendar feast-days, family or public receptions, brought table-companions together in more or less large numbers. In these different types of cookery the relation to nourishment was not identical. The ordinary meals of the great and of princes were not like popular banquets: the economies of scale were not the same and neither the principles nor the choices of consumption were completely analogous.

The information we possess on these three types of cookery is not equal. Records of private cookery are rare, except for the tables of the rich. On the other hand, we have abundant records concerning communities, and these have enabled us to calculate the earliest types of caloric rations. It must be admitted, though, that these records are skewed: the cookery books tell us what was possible but do not reveal the reality of everyday meals. When one of them sets forth a menu, it suggests that in those days they ate quantities larger than we take in nowadays.[9] Thus, the *Ménagier de Paris*, at the end of the fourteenth century, offers four dishes made up of five or six ingredients: 'meat broth, beef hash, lamprey pie, roast meat, fish both sea-water and fresh-water, roast young rabbit and small birds, pies, crackling, slices of bread, blancmange, milk sprinkled with crust, boars's tail, duck *à la dodine*, capon, paté of bream and salmon, cream and cheese tartlets, frumenty, venison, *froid-sauge*, eel *renversée*, capon paté, fish jelly'!

This list suggests a quest for refinements, sauces, spices, infatuation with meats, game and fish, but it is hard to know how much of it all went to each participant in the banquet. It tells us, in fact, less about tastes than about spectacular organisation of meals and the way in which social prestige was established.[10] The contrast between the quantitative (the abundance of the old-time menus was a characteristic, for both ordinary and extraordinary occasions, of the tables of rich people) and the qualitative, meaning the modern ways that we have inherited, refers us to the change in social relations and to the relation between giving and redistribution. Luxury was here easily materialised as charity. Well-known pictures of banquets, kermesses and carousals illustrate these festivities – royal, Christian or pagan, local or regional, urban or rural. We see expressed in them at once a different relation to the body, to the expression of plenty when scarcity is usual, and to other people when the community is drawn into the spectacle. Down to the beginning of the seventeenth century, at least, people seated at the same table were not supposed to eat the same things. Olivier de Serres advises a country gentleman to lay in some poor-quality wine for his guests of 'little worth', keeping his good wine for distinguished visitors and for himself.[11]

Consumption, food products and expenditure on them

Seventeenth- and eighteenth-century budgets reveal the predominance of expenditure on food – between half and two-thirds of the total, and the importance of cereals as basic foodstuff. This was the case, even if we do observe some diversity beginning to appear. Cereals were consumed mainly in the form of bread, less frequently as porridge: wheat, rye, buckwheat, barley. We find bread on all tables, but it is blacker and more mixed in composition among the poor and whiter and purer among the rich. The proportion of one grain or another varies according to the result of harvests, but also in dependence on the seasonal or holiday calendar.

Paris was privileged to eat white bread almost all the time, either because the town enjoyed the economic advantage of a market reserved for itself or because it considered untouchable its right to eat corn and the status that followed from this. In the eighteenth century experts on cereals agreed regarding the qualities of wheat as a foodstuff. It gave the body everything it needed, in quantity and quality. The flour made from it rose better and nourished better than that of any other cereal. 'This delicate refinement' of which Voltaire spoke found expression in rejection of substitute foodstuffs and the protests of the people of Paris when a shortage occurred. White bread was a criterion of taste in which some perceived the corruption of the lower classes in the capital, since the whiter the flour the fewer the consumers who could be fed with a given amount of grain.[12] In any case, cereals in bread form were the least expensive item in the people's diet, costing eleven times less than meat and sixty times less than fish[13] (1,200 grammes of bread gave between 2,500 and 3,000 calories, depending on the quality of the flour).

The calculations made by the composers of budgets, like those of historians, emphasise the monotony of country people's food as compared with townspeople's. While quantity and quality were still beyond the reach of the poor, certain categories possessed resources which ensured for them an intake equivalent to that of the rich, without always guaranteeing the same quality. These were destitute persons in receipt of aid, the sick and infirm in hospitals, teachers and pupils in colleges, soldiers and sailors.[14] We have several examples of food rations, documents which enable us to calculate the different items in the food budgets and to attempt an evaluation of the caloric intakes. We arrive at some impressive figures: 4,000–5,000 calories per day for sailors, 3,000–4,000 for soldiers, 5,000–6,000 for schoolboys and the young ladies of St Cyr. But to what extent are these calculations precise? No doubt we ought to set them within a broader system of redistribution, integrating in these groups family members and servants, small groups of personnel and larger ones.

In the army, in 1757–62, about two to three million *livres* a year had to be spent on keeping the soldiers alive: at least 20,000 to 30,000 sacks of grain were needed every month.[15] As a result, each infantryman could reckon on 24 to 28 ounces per day of baked bread, together with half a pound of meat and a *pinte* (Paris measure – about a quart) of wine. Non-commissioned officers and officers received, in theory, larger rations: six times as much for a sergeant, twenty-four times as much for the Inspector-Commander-in-Chief. Of a soldier's pay in 1771, which was five *sols* and eight *deniers* per day, two-thirds went on food. As a food ration the intake of 3,000 calories was adequate, but this diet of bread, meat and wine obviously implied a lack of fats and vitamins. This is a theoretical evaluation: in practice the soldiers' diet was doubtless more varied than that, since to it must have been added plunder during campaigns and also various individual expenditures while the men were in garrison. Calculations carried out on the basis of supplies delivered in particular situations (the provisioning of a besieged town in 1748, the sustenance of the Saint Malo forts in 1759, of the military hospitals in Lille in 1771 and of the troops in Canada in 1756) always show an adequate intake, in quantitative terms (running from 4,900 calories to 3,000 or 3,500 calories, or to 4,100 calories) with carbohydrates predominant (50 to 75 per cent).

The navy gives similar indications.[16] The crews of the King's ships received about 4,000 calories, obtained from biscuit, cheese, beans and wine, including an intake in carbohydrates of about seventy per cent. Without discussing problems of method,[17] we can accept that the navy's headquarters had worked out what was necessary and possible, given the objectives of conservation and volume, which meant 730 grammes of bread or 550 grammes of biscuit; 250 grammes of salt beef or bacon, 0.5 litre of wine, or one-and-a-half of beer; dry vegetables, peas, baked beans or haricots; sometimes rice, and olive oil as seasoning. This reflected a general effort to improve the nourishment of the sailors, combat scurvy, and overcome manifest deficiencies the causes of which in insufficiency of vitamins were not yet known in the eighteenth century.[18]

We thus have an evaluation of the needs of a category that, broadly, was close to the bulk of the male peasants.[19] However, whereas, in principle, the sailor, the soldier, the hospital inmate received their ration regularly every day, the peasant was sure of nothing – neither of the number of days' wages he would earn, nor of the natural conditions, and so of the outcome of his labour from which would be drawn the cost of his food and that of his family, together with the amount of tax and tithe he had to pay. On the other hand, basing oneself on the single criterion of food adequate in quantity but inadequate in quality would mean forgetting people's capacity to diversify or to increase, regularly or occasionally, their basic food intake. In the rural world diversity, ingenuity, irregularity and inequality were the order of the day.

Furthermore, as B. Bonnin has shown, a product mentioned in a document was not always consumed, especially if it was something that could be sold, or that was required by the landowner or the lord as dues. Similarly, current products might be underestimated: we cannot calculate how much wheat, wine, vegetables and products of the garden or kitchen-garden were consumed by those who grew them. Quantifying the peasants' consumption is thus a highly delicate exercise, since we need to take account of family and servants, the ages and sex of all concerned, and the amounts that were available for consumption after deduction of taxes and dues and of the indispensable portion set aside to be sold.

From table to diet

If we are to understand what the majority of the population ate we need to take into account also the 'herbs' from their gardens, the eggs and small creatures from their farmyards, hunting (whether authorised or forbidden), fishing and items gathered in the woods, as well as geographical diversity and social inequality. Everywhere most peasants and peasant craftsmen, workers and day-labourers lived in a state of uncertainty and economic dependence. They were all the less sure of eating regularly in that they had to buy a considerable part of their food. Attachment to collective usages and common goods was a form of homogeneity and security. They were also in the front rank of the victims of crises.

At the top of rural society the well-to-do, landowners, notables, farmers, well-established cultivators had in normal times enough to eat. All of them lived from the soil and found in it what they needed to provide them with adequate sustenance or with the means to buy whatever was lacking. At the foot of the ladder, vagrants without resources depended on charity or their own ingenuity to rout out a meagre food-supply, and were the first to take to the road when difficulties arose. While irregularity was general it was even more so for the majority than for the rich or for those who were integrated into the circulation of goods.[20]

Consequently it was cereals in one form or another that reigned on the tables of most peasants: huge loaves baked in the lord's or the family's own oven, and made to last, porridge, gruel, pancakes and flatcakes, usually made from rye or maslin – in the case of the poor, from barley and oats, and in that of the rich from wheat. In the South-West people were already eating maize, and, in regions with thin soil, buckwheat and millet. Rice made timid incursions along the frontier with Piedmont. The herbs and roots used to complement the cereals varied from region to region: cabbages, carrots, turnips and *fines herbes*. In times of crisis regions not dominated by cereal monoculture stood up better, because they offered a variety of resources. In the mountains of the Massif Central the chestnut, in various forms, might thus be substituted, to some extent, for bread.

Meat was undoubtedly less rare than has been supposed, but the situation varied widely between regions. Where animal husbandry was practised – in the West, in the mountains, in the areas where sheep and goats were reared, the South-East and South-West – 'flesh' was common, but it was rarer elsewhere, especially in the great grain-growing plains. Pork certainly played an important role, owing to specific habits and rituals: *la tuée*. Several occupations gathered round that fascinating and cruel moment: examiners of pigs' tongues, castrators, sellers of *cresto pouares* (pigs' testicles). The pig is easy to rear individually, but, above all, it holds a special place in everyone's mythical and mental universe. It plays a part in the beliefs surrounding one's childhood: it was one of the incarnations of the antagonism between Christians and Jews. The 'peculiar creature' that the peasant killed and salted every year before Christmas illustrates a way in which the cultural and the culinary were connected.[21]

Other products might be added to all that – those from the farmyard or the dairy – but we know hardly anything about how important they were. Fish, obligatory during Advent and Lent and every Friday, arrived sometimes on tables in the form of salt-fish. There is little reason to doubt that people fished in their spare time wherever they could, and thus the coastal regions provided a share of basic foodstuffs. As for fats, these depended very much on people's means and customs. Northern France and the cattle-raising areas ate butter, either salted or unsalted. In the South olive oil was used, and Central France, from Auvergne to Anjou used walnut oil. Salt was indispensable for preserving food. People had to buy it, and its consumption varied in accordance with the regimes of the *gabelle* and the resources of families. It was important in the animal-husbandry regions.

Drinks were highly regionalised. To the water he drank every day the peasant added a variable proportion of cider, perry, beer or thin wine and *bevande*, i.e., wine watered and of inferior quality. This was a usual practice with almost all. The well-to-do bought better quality wine, which was also kept for sick persons who needed to 'have their blood restored'.

The picture remains abstract and uncertain because we are ignorant of the most routine practices. The reality, in fact, was infinitely diverse and difficult to know. To us it must seem only monotonous and coarse. Monotony due to the repetition of the products consumed – cereals and dry vegetables basically, the rest exceptionally, depending on season and occasion. Monotony, too, in the way the food was prepared: bread soaked in broth, rubbed with garlic and oil, undistinguished soups. Soup dominated the morning and mid-day meals as well as the evening supper: more or less thick, more or less enriched and improved with herbs and vegetables. Into them were put all kinds of farinaceous foods, a little bacon, a litle meat. Feast-day meals, at which there was more on the table and when wine flowed freely, were occasions for forgetting these repetitive diets.

The monotony was certainly accompanied by a certain coarseness of taste, due to the conditions for preservation. Bread was baked for several weeks ahead. Meat, the nutritive quality of which is hard to judge, was always salted or smoked. The dairy products eaten could easily cause disease. Eating in those days meant taking a risk. It wavered between deficit and excess, certain chronic illnesses being characteristic of these imbalances: diabetes due to carbohydrates; gout, gravel, high blood-pressure, but also the deficiencies due to lack of vitamins or mineral salts.[22] The intake of proteins was reduced because vegetables lose their vitamin strength when boiled. In normal times most of the population attained easily the 3,500 or 3,000 calories needed daily by a working adult, with lower rates for women and children. But, outside the well-do-do categories, food intake was always unbalanced, and living uncertain from one day to the next. This situation did not change from the sixteenth to the seventeenth century. It improved somewhat in the eighteenth century, less perhaps through an increase in the amounts consumed as through a reduction in the repeated risks of famine, and thanks also to better organisation of transport and of administrative intervention.

Diversity and reality: Périgord and Auvergne

Two regions can help us to understand better the ordinary differences in a diet of which it is difficult to give a uniform picture.[23] In Périgord, which was not then the gastronomic paradise we know today, the descriptions given were often apocalyptic. 'Here people are dying like flies.' This was a region of modest agriculture, dominated by the chestnut and the association of poor areas (Cosse and its forests) with richer valleys, those of the Dronne, the Isle and the Dordogne. The diet made possible by this subsistence agriculture was monotonous in the extreme, because the range of products consumed was narrower than that of the products grown. Two foodstuffs succeeded each other as the year went by: maize in summer, chestnuts in winter. The whole of rural life was defined by the cultivation of chestnuts: 'Our help, our chief food, with it we feed our families, our servants, our animals, cattle, poultry and pigs', wrote the inhabitants of Rouffignac in 1709. 'Spanish corn' (maize) held a similar position in the form of porridge, soup and flatcakes, accompanied by various vegetables, rape, haricots, beans. The diet of the people of Périgord was poor in bread, which for them was an extra foodstuff or one for feast-days. The consumption of meat was a good criterion of the social hierarchy. Priests and nobles ate plenty of it throughout the year, but peasants less often. Everyone raised chickens and ducks to pay dues, goose and duck, pickled or salted, being reserved for the better-off. Bacon and pork, however, were in current use. A pig would feed seven persons. It was sold at fairs and killed in spring and autumn for the family's reserves. Finally, walnut oil was in general use. Fruit was eaten in summer and autumn. Dairy products were rare. Eating what one had grown oneself and concealment were the rule, signs that there was little available in normal times.[24]

Nevertheless, denutrition was infrequent in eighteenth-century Périgord, although there was still a series of crises of mortality to which, no doubt, both underfeeding and epidemics contributed. Distributions of rice were made frequently (in 1747–8 and 1778), but the peasants refused to eat this unfamiliar food. We may suppose that if there had been serious famine they would have known better where their interest lay. On the other hand, malnutrition was general. The high predominance of carbohydrates, the insufficiency of fats and proteins, the shortage of vitamins C, D and PP were written in the physical appearance of the Périgord peasantry, 'small and ill-formed'. La Servolle, a correspondent of the Société Royale de Médecine, quoted examples of rickets due to a diet based on maize and chestnuts. Pellagra was reported as the seasons changed. This diet, which existed almost identically in the Landes and the Confolentais, shows the importance of food intake in the physiological powers of resistance of the rural populations and that of the variations due, of course, to social differences, but also to the possibilities of exchange: access to Périgord by the Dordogne was at first limited, with wine exchanged for salt and dried fish, but it grew as time passed.

Auvergne provides another example of the complexity of the regions.[25] Being a region lacking unity, eating practices varied a lot from one district to another. Limagne, grain country; the 'cut-off district' of the Allier hills, wine country; Montagne, grass country – each had its own habits. The Clermontais was dominated by bread made of rye mixed with spring wheat, vetches, barley (not very digestible), together with beans and walnut – or hemp-oil. Thin wine was imported. Though there was not much meat on the tables, cattle being rare in Limagne as on the slopes of the 'cut-off district', the dues that were paid show the importance of farmyards and so of eggs, chickens, ducks and, to a less extent, rabbits, scarce here as everywhere else. The family pig was a mark of social distinction. Milch-cows or goats were almost unknown. Sheep-breeding might be carried on in the vine-growing areas, together with the cultiva-tion of fruit, which doctors denounced when epidemics of dysentery occurred. Altogether, it was a diet with little variety: coarse cereals, monotonous vegetables, watered wine, cheese, fruit and, depending on occasions and individual resources, a greater or smaller amount of meat.

In the mountains (Montagne) greater diversity prevailed. There was no lack of milk, from which porridge and cheese were made. The forests provided grazing for large herds of pigs, raised on acorns or chestnuts. Sheep, goats and the odd milch-cow were tolerated by local custom. A wider variety of cereals, different herbs, more plentiful vegetables, very soon the potato ('food for animals and the poor'), resources from fishing in the streams, together with a little poaching, made possible a diet that was richer in sources of energy, proteins and even vitamins. The hillman was more robust, the plainsman frail, ambushed by deficiencies and illnesses, and the difference was measurable from earliest youth.

Between the two diets and geographical areas there was not much exchange, apart from cereals going to the towns, cheese to the plain, wine to the mountains and the grain-growing districts. In every region cooking was done in a pot which hung from a hook. The fire in the hearth was kept alight all the time. A few cauldrons and stoves and numerous bowls made up the utensils which everywhere constituted the equipment of the people's kitchens. In the homes of the notables, rich cultivators, mer-chants, lawyers, collectors of lords' dues, priests and minor nobles there were to be found dripping-pans, spits, stew-pans, miscellaneous dishes, fish-kettles and more complicated utensils. The hierarchy of equipment suggests a hierarchy of diets and also one of capacity for modernisation and innovation.

Between the problem of survival and the problem of how to live, a tour of the realm shows that response to the general precariousness took many forms. Two examples of deterioration and two of amelioration did not make the period from the sixteenth to the eighteenth century either winter or springtime for all concerned. Only the towns escaped from this domination by natural causes which made so frail the existence of communities, families and individuals.

The townspeople's privileges: regularity and diversity

As regards food, the town consumed while producing little. It depended entirely, as J.-C. Perrot has shown, on its local sources of supply, and the larger a town's population the larger those became. In the case of Caen we thus see appearing areas which corresponded to specific supplies: the market-gardens (the area closest to the town), the grain-growing area (the biggest one), the area of cider, cattle, fishing and spices reaching to the sea.[26] In the case of Paris the entire kingdom was placed under contribution. First, the grain-growing basin surrounding the city with its haloes of dominant monoculture, then the livestock-raising area (the animals were driven from the pastures of the West, or, where sheep and pigs were concerned, from nearer parts). Fish came from the Channel and the North Sea, brought fresh down the fish-cart roads, along which galloped the Boulogne mares of the fish-sellers. Fruit and vegetables arrived in the markets from the city's outskirts. Cheese was supplied by Brie, Touraine, Normandy, Picardy, Auvergne, even Rouergue. Ordinary wines were bought from nearby vineyards, while fine wines came from Bordeaux, Beaune, Epernay and Rheims. At the beginning of the century the Orléanais and the Blésois supplied fifty to sixty per cent of Parisian wine consumption, Champagne fifteen per cent and Lower Burgundy twelve per cent.[27] Spices and luxury products arrived through the major ports, the routes leading in from foreign countries, and the colonies.

This list alone shows how various were the products that the townsman could find in the markets and testifies to their regularity, for, in the event of a crisis, the public authority established reserves and endeavoured to keep prices down through requisitioning. While the inhabitants of towns were better supplied and better nourished than the country people, it is not certain that this plenty meant that everyone was equal as regards consumption or that most people's diet was very different from what it was in the country. Everywhere, as in Paris, diet was dominated by the bread produced by the bakers. In provincial towns – in Strasbourg, in Chartres, in Brittany – the quality of bread was less varied and it was darker in colour. Everywhere, too, the price of bread determined what a family could spend on other foodstuffs. In Chartres a day-labourer with a daily wage of thirteen sols could buy fourteen pounds of bread, equivalent to two days' consumption by a family of five, when the price was fixed at eight *sols* for an ordinary nine-pound loaf.[28] At Bayeux between 1765 and 1792 the wage-earner could buy 10.2 pounds of bread.

In the capital 'everyone buys bread on credit' noted Abbé Galiani: this was, for the baker, a way of keeping his clientele loyal, and it enabled customers to regulate their purchases in accordance with their means. Prices were fixed and supervised so as not to upset the public and to prevent 'commotions'. Despite the difficulties and the criticisms of liberal reformers, the current price was a tendency around which revolved supplies that varied in amount. The crisis price was a maximum fixed by the *lieutenant de police* at a level that took account of the people's poverty and the danger of speculative excesses. The price changed, yet, in a way, stayed always the same. A whole view of the world and politics operated around the just price of bread, particularly in the 1760s and 1770s. Consumers in Paris and the chief towns were as much dependent on the police as on the bakers: this was the consequence of a contract which the liberals wanted to break and which endowed bread with its true socio-political weight.[29]

Townspeople's plates also had meat on them more often than those of the country people: 70 kg per year in Paris around 1700, 60 in 1789. The sanitary rules, the supervision of slaughterhouses and the price-ceiling were effective everywhere. The Paris pork and veal market was well organised. Pork was eaten in winter especially, veal in the spring. Mutton was eaten in summer and, increasingly, beef throughout the year.[30] Here we note a twofold change. For most people meat had ceased, to some degree, to be exceptional, while the good cuts had become habitual with the social elites. The social frontier of consumption no longer ran between bourgeois, eaters of butcher's meat, and aristocrats, eaters of game, but between the elites of the nobility and the bourgeoisie, partial to the good cuts, and the masses who ate the inferior cuts. In Grenoble the annual consumption of meat grew from 26 kg per year in 1743 to 31 kg in 1774. This was less than in Paris, but the weight given here should be raised because the farmers of the town excluded pigs and goats from their calculation. Grenoble stood at the same level as Caen (32 kg per year) and above the national average, which Lavoisier estimated in 1789 as 23.5 kg. Above all, taste for beef caused consumption of mutton to decline in a market in which competition was increasing along with the dependence common to all luxury trades.[31]

Lavoisier's calculations illustrate the independence of Paris, but they cannot be applied across the board to all the towns.[32] For a population of 600,000 the average caloric intake was 2,000 calories, of which 208 came from the daily 50 kg of proteins (30 kg is the figure accepted nowadays). The Parisian ate a lot of meat: carbohydrates made up fifty per cent of his normal diet, and fats one-third. As we see, bread continued to be essential. Besides meat, Parisians could eat or drink milk, butter, eggs, cheese, oil, sugar coffee, cocoa, fruit, vegetables, wine, liqueurs, cider and beer. Thirteen per cent of the caloric ration came from meat, eggs and fish, ten per cent from fats, eleven per cent from alcohol and three per cent from sugar. The toll records present a picture of a balanced modern diet. We must, howver, modify this picture in the light of the value of the caloric elements designated and also because the calculations are based on a certain figure for the size of the population. Actually, we do not know what that figure was: for 500,000 people the ration rises to 2,500 calories, for 700,000 it falls to 1,700! Where Lavoisier put 78 kg or even 90 kg of meat per year, the records of supplies show only 60 kg with a decline from the beginning of the century. Moreover, there was a substantial floating population of immigrants from the country whose diet consisted mainly of bread. Finally, we must allow for marked differences in diet due to financial capacities and ways of spending wages, but also to status or rank.

At the head of the townspeople's diet there remained still the bread of the poor. Then one moves gradually towards the diet of the rich, with increases in calories that were slight, on the average, but entailed greater expenditure, devoted to the purchase of more varied foodstuffs. Between the poor person and the rich one the difference lay less in quantity than in quality, the subsistence of the poor being more vulnerable to the effect of dearths than that of the rich. But the supervision of food supplies benefited everyone. New products, such as inferior cuts of meat, were acquired by the lower classes, and demands increased generally. Furthermore, there was perfusion between the diet of the rich and that of the poor. By making their purchases from the dealers in second-hand food, who redistributed leftovers of meals bought from noble and bourgeois households, the poor people took a step towards a new type of consumption. Observers like Sébastien Mercier could see in this only a sign of urban pollution and disorder. Again, new ways of life advanced with frequentation of taverns and, at the end of the century, of restaurants. The feeding of Paris was based on these new habits, which made it possible, in Restif's words, to 'live at all prices'. This adaptation of consumption to the life of day-to-day, which defies caloric calculations, permitted an infinity of forms of behaviour and choices, regardless of the fundamental attachment to the more traditional foodstuffs and those with greater symbolic value, in town and country alike, namely, bread and wine.

Bread and wine: from Holy Communion to good manners

If bread was unquestionably a fixture in the people's lives, this was also because it had not yet lost its spiritual significance. Christian tradition, grafted on a pagan culture devoted to the worship of Ceres and grain, had endowed it with wonder-working power. The Gospels and the entire liturgy are full of images that illustrate this attribution of a sacred character to bread. Jesus was the bread of life, and the institution of the Eucharist, Holy Communion in the form of the consecrated wafer, was central to worship and piety.[33] Private and solemn communions were rites of passage and integration into the community of believers, like the annual communion at Easter. Besides union with God, accord with other people was what was achieved through taking the sacrament, and doing this again and again. For many, acts performed in the family were analogous to those of the Eucharist: breaking bread involves and unites the family and its members.

This model could doubtless strengthen conviction that bread alone was able to keep life going, that nourishment possessed fullness and power, its providential status in the form of bread alone. S. Kaplan has reminded us of the quasi-liturgical practices that accompanied the consumption of bread: reserving its distribution to the head of the family, tracing a cross on the loaf before making the first cut; not wasting bread, which one ate when it was stale and hard; not letting bread fall to the ground; not allowing its 'bad side' to be exposed by turning it over; distributing consecrated bread in turn (a subject of discussion among the enlightened). This essential food could symbolise work itself ('earning one's bread') and one's whole life ('losing the taste for bread'). Christian wisdom and popular tradition concurred in placing in the forefront a consumption that was both sacred and egalitarian.

It was the duty of the King, the foster-father, to ensure the availability of this fundamental means of subsistence. The traditional idea of the monarchy tottered when the eucharistic logic of the common good was made to give place to the economic reason of the market, or when the police, the right arm of the father, failed in their duty as protectors, something that rarely happened in eighteenth-century towns. Bread was thus at the heart of the collective life of a people-consumer united with a prince-provider. Identity, morality and politics were indissociable from 'the sovereignty of bread'.

Wine played a role symmetrical to that of bread. We find it endowed with the same power in theology and in the liturgy, in religious history and in popular practices.[34] In both the Old and the New Testaments wine and the vine are used as metaphors for divine wisdom and God's people. The pruned vine symbolises the Resurrection and eternal life: *vitis et vita*. In Holy Communion the ritual use of wine is like that of bread, and transubstantiation changes both of them, into the body and blood of Christ. Sacerdotal dignity reserves for the priest and the King the chalice and wine of Communion. Under these two expressions wine is at once egalitarian, a pledge of community, and hierarchising, a sign of the distinction possessed by the Lord's Anointed. More than bread, in art and literature wine was to signify the way of salvation, but also that of sin, drunkenness, and what this leads to.

Wine would long retain its role in sociability. It gathered and united table-companions and friends. The medicine of humours took hold of it: wine was mingled in its cures, because wine eliminated evil fluids, restored strength, 'opened the pipes', multiplied the 'subtle spirits' that are the strength of intellectuals, and reconstituted fundamental warmth. A whole civilisation thought, along with Hippocrates, that it was 'a thing wonderfully fitting to man if, in health as in sickness, he is given it to drink at the right time and in the right dose'. Down to the eighteenth century drunkenness remained sinful and moderation was good form. The *philosophes*, who cared little for the Eucharist, conferred upon wine a power of social communion which brought consumers together across the distances created by rank and fortune – thus, Rousseau, lover of the white wine of Arbois, and Voltaire, drinker of champagne. The taste for wine brought people together: 'As a general rule drinkers are cordial and sincere', we read in the *Lettre à d'Alembert*.[35] Wine, which featured more than ever in the consumption of the worker in town and country, might be looked on with suspicion by the civil and religious authorities, but it kept the effective power which made it preferable to the polluted water of the towns and wells, and its efficacy, symbol of the instrument of life and of sociability. From the cradle to the grave it accompanied the events of family life and the great feast-days in the calendar. Giving strength to the body, it kept its value as earthly food along with its cultural and social power, manifested publicly by festive gifts to the people and privately by the refinement and expression of joy and fervour. In church it remained, for all, the symbol of Redemption.

Wine and bread were two major elements in a system of consumption which was also a way of conceiving the world and society. In times of shortage this view gave a perspective of salvation to the way things were used, marked by moderation and the respect due to what was essential. These practices were progressively gnawed away by plenty and diversity, but during several centuries they were kept up and taught through the literature of good manners, just as were sartorial usages, for comparable purposes and with similar targets.[36] In the codes of good manners eating was a matter for regulation and ritualisation. From the sixteenth to the seventeenth century, from Erasmus to Antoine de Courtin; from the seventeenth century to the eighteenth, from Jean-Baptiste de la Salle to the 1749 'manual of manners for boys', the authors of guides to good manners took up and insensibly corrected established usages, which stayed put, essentially, with modifications of greater or less importance. In order to tame a natural bodily spontaneity and instal a better social and personal way of eating and drinking, three apprenticeships were taught: in mastication; in learning that the body must confine itself to the space of the table; and in respect for social relations and companionship at meals.

Effacement of the body was the first rule which created distance between the biological function of eating and drinking and social conduct. To this end, the body must become silent. Noise from lips, throat and nostrils was banned. 'It is very bad manners to make a noise with one's lips when drawing breath as one puts the spoon in one's mouth, or with one's throat when swallowing. Soup must be taken into one's mouth and drunk with such great discretion that not the slightest sound is heard,' La Salle prescribes. Banning noises meant overcoming those affects which betray gluttony, greed, carelessness in eating and drinking. For the lower classes, voracity: for civilised people, discreet behaviour. The manuals of good manners condemn whatever reflects bulimia as well as whatever expresses satiation. What they aimed at, after all, was to blot out human hunger, everything that might recall the fear of famine and the anxiety created by scarcity. Chewing slowly, swallowing without mishap, as quickly as possible and in silence, formed a part of the panoply of actions which set nature and animality at a distance, bringing closer culture and restrained bodily pleasure. The manual of good manners disowns aversions and preferences, advising the reader above all to accept, to eat anything put before him, so as not to be thought too fussy. 'It is a most unseemly failing to say out loud: I don't eat this, I don't eat that . . . Such aversions must never be made known', is Antoine de Courtin's advice to decent people.

A table procedure took shape between the seventeenth and eighteenth centuries. It is then that we see becoming defined the role of the cover, the use of the spoon and the napkin. La Salle's manual of 1782 devotes an entire chapter to the things that should be employed at table: napkin, plate, knife, spoon, fork, goblet. The modern cover was constituted, and established a different relation to the food: breaking the bread, putting one's hand in the common dish, those old actions which effected the communion of meals, were replaced by individual use of cutlery. In Erasmus the old customs are still present, though accompanied by warnings: do not lick your finger, wash your hands before eating, do not dip big pieces of bread in the pot, do not play with your food. In Courtin and La

Salle the covers individualise the sharing of food and establish rules of cleanliness which forbid contact with fat, sauces and syrups. From now on one must show respect to the space of the table, sit upright at it, in a disciplined way, without disturbing one's neighbours. The table and chair, the role of which in furnishing we have seen, define a space of tension and reserve. The verticality of the body keeps the diner in his place. His gaze should not wander and reveal too much desire or interest.

The code of prohibitions draws its references from the animal world (lick like a cat, sniff the meat like a dog, drink like a stork) and prescribes restrained actions: bread must be treated with respect, cut properly, eaten with discretion, without tucking it away or taking the crust off: soup is to be consumed with delicacy. Ultimately, this means that a new relation to other people is being prescribed by the rules of good manners. The child or the decent person, must observe these rules from one end of the meal to the other, washing his hands and saying the *benedicite* and graces. The Christianising of the table belongs in the general movement of reformation of mores and affirmation of hierarchies and ranks. Taking one's place, serving, clearing the table are all parts of a common apprenticeship, in which new ways of eating go along with politeness in conviviality and conversation at table. Checking on the cleanliness of the body, exercising discipline in gestures: we find in the culture of eating and drinking principles of propriety, moderation, and decorum which modify through individualisation and intimacy all the forms of consumption.

Knowing how to eat, knowing how to live

'How does one eat?' In normal times, and increasingly, this problem was as important as 'What does one eat?' because the alimentary codes were as serious as the sartorial ones, the way to eat counted no less than food itself. The manuals of good manners were one of the instruments of this setting in order which emphasised the importance of time and of things. For most people the division of the day by meal-times provided the usual framework of ordinary life.

In the country the seasonal rhythm of work dictated a change between winter, when, as a rule, three meals brought the family together, and summer, when the longer days made four or even five meals necessary. The peasant in Alsace, Auvergne or Touraine began with breakfast at dawn, about five or six o'clock: this was a hot meal, with soup more or less flavoured with meat. At eleven or twelve, another meal – dinner or a snack, hot or cold, depending on the season. At four or five p.m. a little cold snack with bread and vegetables. When night fell, between seven and eleven, a hot supper which gathered the whole family round the table. Preparing all these meals was a task for the mother of the family, sometimes alone but often, in big farms, with the help of servants. The same dishes appeared regularly and at harvest time they were repeated several days running. Variation between seasons, Sundays, fast-days, feast-days brought a little variety.[37] Except for the rich, the daily meal was not so much a bond of sociability as a repetitive necessity. It was usually eaten in silence, with nobody speaking unless called upon by the head of the family. The master served himself first, the women last: they were busy serving and looking after the small children. It was a break in work and, on some occasions, an opening into the social world, which it stabilised, fixed and explained.[38] Each person found there an image of society, a hierarchical family, the civilisation of manners having encroached upon country people's ways less rapidly than in the towns. Proper behaviour at table progressed slowly, being expressed first, no doubt, in the handling of utensils and instruments, and later in a profound alteration in everyone's conduct. 'At table as elsewhere, after all, one should think of one's neighbour' observed the Marquis de Coulanges, a contemporary, in the 1670s and 1680s, of the great transformation of manners at court and in the town:

> Jadis le potage on mangeait
> dans le plat sans cérémonie,
> et sa cuillère on essuyait
> souvernt sur la poulle bouillie
> Dans la fricassée d'autrefois
> On saussait son pain et ses doigts
> Chacun mange présentement
> Son potage sure son assiette
> il faut se servir poliment
> et de cuillère et de fourchette
> Et de temps en temps d'un valet
> les aille laver au buffet
> Tant qu'on peut il faut éviter
> sur la nappe de rien répandre
> Tirer au plat sans hésiter
> le morceau que l'on peut prendre
> Et votre assiette jamais
> ne serve pour différents mets.
> Très souvent il faut en changer
> Pour changer elles sont faites
> Tout ainsi que pour s'essuyer
> on vous donne des serviettes
> À table comme ailleurs enfin
> il faut songer à son proclain.

[Formerly one ate soup from the dish, without ceremony, and wiped one's spoon often on the boiled fowl. In the fricassee of those days one dipped one's bread and one's fingers. Now each person eats his soup from his own plate. One must make polite use of spoon and fork, and from time to time a servant will wash these at the sideboard. So far as possible one must avoid dropping anything on the tablecloth, and likewise refrain from grabbing from the dish the piece one wants. Never use the same plate for different courses, but change the plate frequently. That is what plates are made for, just as you are given napkins to wipe your mouth. At table as elsewhere, after all, one should think of one's neighbour.]

This behest by the Marquis de Coulanges situates the spread of the new ways in a conjunction of the moral and the material.[39]

Peasants' inventories show how slowly progress advanced in this matter. In the Maconnais, Brie, Brittany, Touraine and Alsace we find the same picture. They cooked in and ate from the same utensils. Tureens and cooking-pots passed from the hearth to the table, and their contents from the fireplace to the bowl. For a long time these peasants ate with their fingers and dipped their bread in the pot. They drank from the neck of the bottle – a recent invention, apparently introduced from England in the eighteenth century – or else from the pitcher. The tureen and the dish did not appear in the peasant home before the eighteenth century. Peasants still ate standing up, or with a trencher of bread or wood, the first individual support for food to appear amid the collective practices. The covers and crockery known to us – plate, spoon, knife, fork – made possible that invisible line of separation between table-companions which the manuals prescribed. The first stage in this individualising of table manners was the possession of personal bowls, distinguished by a decoration or an inscription, as we find in the Pont l'Abbé country and the Maconnais. The plate, when already widespread in towns, reached the country areas in the nineteenth century, rarely earlier, except among the rich. The materials from which all these utensils were made reflected the social hierarchy: the most common were of wood or in earthenware, plain or glazed, while the better-off had faience, pewter, copper and even silver.[40]

The fork began as a royal whim. King Henri II imposed it on his Court, along with the plate, in imitation of Italian practice. This fashion was at that time condemned by moralists. In the eighteenth century it made its way into the rural world: one household in ten owned a fork in Alsace, where it advanced after 1730–60. The commonest instrument was undoubtedly the spoon, even though Goethe said of the peasants that 'if it were to rain porridge they haven't even got a spoon'. The table-knife was rare, and men normally used their pocket-knife. The glass and goblet appeared late in the day. In Alsace they figure in 5 per cent of the inventories, while in Brie these show the most remarkable progress, with forks in 95 per cent of the homes of rich notables and in about half of those of the well-do-do peasants, while 40 per cent of the mass of the peasantry had them. They turn up in the Ile-de-France, too, in proportion to peasants' means. However, the presence of one object does not mean that another has been abandoned. The economy of scarcity demanded that old and more recent items be used together, and the latter at first met with a certain reserve. Urbanity and circulation exerted a decisive influence in the spread of the new usages.[41]

It was between the seventeenth and the eighteenth centuries,[42] in the towns, in Paris first, that ideas about consumption underwent change. The rules proclaimed by the manuals had not triumphed by the end of the seventeenth century, even at Court, where Louis XIV ate with his fingers at the start of his reign. At the end of the eighteenth century we have evidence that the new instruments were being used, but while the courtier had his plate, his cover and his napkin, he did not yet have a glass before him, and sometimes several table-companions still drank from the same glass. The values of intimacy had created privileged moments, but also a simpler organisation: while the spectacular aspect of the royal and aristocratic meal did not disappear, the spectacle was henceforth focused on the table rather than on external manifestations. The 'grand dinner' at Versailles was open to the public: this ceremony of the cult of monarchy survived for a long time, but bored the performers themselves. The habit of eating in public needed to be acquired in childhood, 'lest so many unknown eyes directed at you should take away your appetite', wrote Madame Campan in her *Mémoires*.[43] In townspeople's dinners and suppers, among the rich and the rest alike, manners followed the example set. The spread of objects bears witness to this: pewter dishes were replaced by pottery and faience and the elements of the cover appeared in evergreater numbers in all social categories.[44]

Among ordinary folk we note more and more objects with specific uses – bowls, sugar-basins, egg-cups, teapots and coffeepots – which, with glasses, covers and plates mark the advance of the new manners. Noticeable among the elites in the seventeenth century, they are found a century later among the lower classes, through which they spread at a rate proportionate to wealth. Above all, we observe the decline of the noble materials: silverware, cup, goblet, personal or grand crockery have ceased to be representative, and are no longer to be found among the very rich. The progress made by ordinary, cheap materials which break the retreat of the solid and prestigious, shows that the loss of real value of these objects coincided with changes in sensibility. The world of ephemeral consumptions and rapid ageing of needs had begun. Among the rich it was symbolised by the triumph of porcelain, which finally freed luxury from the tyranny of usefulness, reflected the bursting forth of more rapid successions and confirmed, by its exotic origin, a domination which announced also a civilisation of manners.

New knowledge, new consumer goods

A widely circulated print produced by Pellerin at Epinal shows *La fête du village* at the beginning of the nineteenth century. A table beneath a tree, broached casks of wine, cooking-pots doubtless filled with soups and stews convey the atmosphere of plenty characteristic of a special meal which nevertheless does reproduce the excesses of old-time village fetes. If we look closely at the table we see the utensils of the individual cover: plates, knives, forks. The itinerary followed by the wine in order to arrive at the table is easy to follow. From the cask it passes into pitchers, from them into carafes, and it is from carafes that the glasses on the table are charged. The print shows the trilogy of everyday meals: bread, wine, soup. To be sure, simplification is imposed by a picture which cannot show the succession of dishes served, but the choice made has symbolic value, too. What we have to see conforms to the usual and is not a display of extraordinary crockery. The iconography here is not behind the times, indeed, it may be ahead of them as regards common habits, for the new knowledge advanced cautiously, together with the dictates of good taste and the possibilities of new consumptions.

On the transformations that took place between the seventeenth and eighteenth centuries we have plenty of information from cookery books, confirmed by the observations made by travellers. First, the code of practices changed when *Le Cuisinier français* and its imitators broke a century of publishing silence in 1651. Comparison between these works and those of the sixteenth century shows that everything was changing at the same time: the composition of meals and the organisation of courses, the arrangement of dishes, the behaviour of table-companions and ser-vants. On every plane the science of the table was being formalised. The new culinary style was characterised by three main features: a decline in spices, with use of aromatics and locally produced condiments, shallots, onions, scallions, garlic, capers, anchovies; the choice of good-quality butcher's meat, replacing game (the cuts were hierarchised and the ways of cooking adapted); the rise of vegetables and cooked dishes, which was to lead to increased use of kitchen-gardens and of hot-plates set beside the hearth.

All sorts of variations of this pattern were possible: regionalism in details, but also standardising from above, as shown by the *pot-au-feu* becoming the national dish, according to Brillat-Savarin, in the course of the eighteenth century. The religious imperatives that were imposed by collective standards also played a role, but were strongly hierarchised by social usages and personal preferences. Eating wild fowl during Lent was not a proof of asceticism, and the table kept by the Carthusians was one of the best-reputed in Paris. Along the calendar of works and days more refined dishes appeared, satisfying tastes for food in accordance with financial capacities. The gastronomic discourse of the rich became more complex and more opulent. It grew more demanding in the matter of colours, but also more subtle in distinguishing the effects obtained by the culinary art, in the treatment of soups and dishes made less artificial (*blanchir* did not mean making whiter, but treating a foodstuff with water and fire). Vision and taste shared in the changing of gastronomic sensibility, just as they organised sartorial perceptions differently.[45]

In short, we see the birth of the *gourmet*. The multiplication of dishes in *le service à la française* aimed not so much at filling bottomless bellies as at enabling each person to choose according to his taste. The imperatives of superior taste gradually became dominant as a result of the skill of cooks and their patrons, a classical taste, as in literature and aesthetics, triumphing over 'basenesses' and 'beggarlinesses'. In cooking as in appearances, a manifestation of merit united distinguished patrons. Being and having were there to the same extent, defining an individual as a consumer, because luxury and usages were the domain wherein 'the various classes that made up the social elites in the seventeenth and eighteenth centuries were able to communicate most easily'. This was a translation into the community of the new relation to things.

New consumptions made possible a wider range of sensations, while pushing back the frontier of constraint imposed by the sole principle that dominated the economy of scarcity: one must eat to live. In the modern period France, and Europe as a whole, was, in that domain, neither stable nor closed: between the sixteenth century and the eighteenth the range of foodstuffs available expanded. The adventure of the humble potato serves as a symbol, in the slowness of its journey on the way to popularity. This happened faster in Holland and Northern Europe generally, than in France, where the potato's presence is reported here and there, about 1650, in some border areas of Flanders. Three reasons account for its success. One hundred grammes of potatoes contain only ninety calories. The same weight of bread provides three hundred calories. But, on the same tract of land, one can produce, in potatoes, food enough for five times as many people. The potato can be grown on small pieces of land, which made it attractive to poor peasants, who showed themselves more disposed than the others to substitute it for bread (the rich ones saw it as a foodstuff fit only for pigs). Finally, the potato was loaded with progressive values, being defended, propagated and eventually imposed by the best agronomists, of whom Parmentier was only the best known. Cultivation of the potato advanced wherever the population was increasing rapidly. The Massif Central, Auvergne, Périgord, Alsace and Lorraine made it welcome: but it was still a poor man's food that Parmentier persuaded Louis XVI to taste.[46] *Solanum tuborosum* would complete its course by graduating from the status of something to be added to soups that were too thin, and to satisfy the appetites of bellies that were too empty, to the rank of a recognised vegetable. The American cultivator Saint John Crèvecoeur made himself the propagandist for the potato, in which he saw, from the example of the Irish, a national manna that could solve all problems.[47]

Between the sixteenth and the seventeenth century a crucial period began in our acculturation to new foodstuffs, bringing to French tables eatables that had come from Asia or America after journeys that were sometimes long and the acclimatisation of which alone made possible their widespread consumption and the organisation of their supply in sufficient quantities for their prices to come down and a large market to open for them. The path from botanic gardens to kitchen gardens and from them to the open fields was not always straightforward, as the arrival of the novelties gave rise to suspicion. Asparagus, artichokes, rice and pasta, from Italy, and tomatoes, pimentoes, sunflowers, maize, Jerusalem artichokes and turkeys, from America, followed particular itineraries with greater or less success. The melon that Pliny knew came, no doubt, from Persia: it returned through Spain, passed through Italy, and owed its success in France to the Italian entourage of Catherine de Médicis. There were fifty ways of serving it. Doctors found it 'aggressive' and demanded that it be 'tempered with wine'. Devotees ate it with salt, pepper or sugar, making the melon a prestigious dainty at the end of the seventeenth century.

The haricot's trajectory was not simple. Le Roy Ladurie sees it arriving in Languedoc in 1594: from Italy and, later, America, it reached England under the name 'french bean'. There were also, however, local varieties, among them *vigna unguiculata*, which conquered Mediterranean Europe, having come from India well before the sixteenth century. Others were *faiols, faisols, mougettes, mouesettes* and *doliques*, similar to the beans used to thicken soups. European and Italian haricots later shared the people's favour with the American variety, which drove out the old foodstuff of the poor and took its place on their tables and in the rations of prisoners and sailors, eventually contributing to the folklore of the *pétomanes*.

During several millennia the alimentary field increased hugely and the selection of social choices was formed progressively, between necessity and quality.[48] The new consumptions were inseparable from culinary styles and ways of life.[49] Take the case of sugar. For centuries people lived with sweeteners derived from honey, and in the Middle Ages cane sugar became a spice much sought after. From North Africa to the Canaries it reached the West Indies and America, where the colonialism of sugar was to reign. The slave-trade and the refineries gave life to the great ports and the towns that were centres of this business, such as Orleans.[50] When the price of sugar fell it was eaten more widely, competing with local honeys. But sugar was also a product of distinction the fashion for which inspired the fantasies in cakes and confectionery of the gourmands of the Court and the town. Cakes, *compôtes* and jellies opened for sugar the gate to the art of dessert, and it ensured the success of ices and sorbets. It gave rise to a multiplication and refinement of the utensils for its preparation, in copper or other metal, in glass or in porcelain: from the cooking-pot of the confectioner to the sugar-bowl it conquered the Parisian domestic scene.

The *Encyclopédie* conferred a festive quality upon sugar, associating it with a celebration of cheerful talk, while literature linked its consumption with happy sociability, decent joy, in contrast with the dull bulimic coarsenesses of the peasantry and the effete profusion of the baroque Court celebrations. Sugar was the totemic food of the Enlightenment civilisation, the two faces of which it displayed: one, sombre and expensive, associating the production of and trade in sugar with slavery and its horrors; the other, bright and merry, associating it with knowledge and the civilisation of manners, even with pleasure. In novels, sugar and femininity were linked with lightness and delicacy, in contrast to the rich and gross content of the menus of the people and the bourgeois. Sugared, light and delicate collations went with well-born heroes.[51] When novels praised food that was frugal, natural and vegetable, a way of condemning town-life, luxury and the decline of manners, sugar was absent. The literary effect here joined with philosophy, which preached a return to nature, as in the *Encyclopédie* and *L'art culinaire*, which recommended going back to natural and vegetable foodstuffs and simpler recipes. The inanimate has much power over the animate.

Coffee was even more exotic than sugar, which it accompanied on the journey from the East to Italy and France.[52] Like sugar, which softened its bitterness, coffee expressed modernity and the triumph of trade. Like sugar it gave rise to much discussion among doctors about its power to enliven the humours or to weaken them, and for that reason it caused milk to be used widely. It was a triumph of intelligence that Montesquieu celebrates in his *Trente-sixième lettre*, because 'it makes those who drink it witty'. The century of Enlightenment would ensure its success and that of the products and conduct associated with it: 'Martinique, Mocha and China furnish the breakfast of a servant girl', said Voltaire. Economics and intelligence were thus reconciled. The café was contrasted with the ignoble and plebeian tavern. The soft-drink seller was a man of taste, his clientele was more elegant, with manners under better control. In his shop there was less noise, more concentration, and one could read, converse, play chess or flirt with the ladies, like Rousseau and Ménétra, Rameau's nephew or Philidor. The café, Parisian or provincial, offered its customers an ordered decor, free warmth from the stove, a civilised space. Two kinds of life became organised – lively and festive in the tavern, less tumultuous, a realm of controlled leisure, in the café. In the former a warm society, integrated in the space of 'fragile life' and everybody's habits: in the latter a world colder and more fluid, organised for silence, decorum, appearance.[53] From products to things and from things to persons there circulated a comparable influence, expressing the tensions that structured social relations, the materialisation of intelligence, the capacity for abstraction of things.

In France coffee emerged victorious from its battle with chocolate and tea, which, more than in Spain, Italy and England, remained the rich person's beverage. Lavoisier calculated the annual consumption of chocolate in Paris at 250,000 *livres* – two hundred grammes per person per year – and that of coffee at 2,500,000 *livres*, or 50 kilogrammes per year. Tea does not appear in his list, but was perhaps included among drugs and spices. Because of its price and its ritual, tea did not enjoy the success that coffee had, despite medical or gastronomic advocacy.[54]

Coffee, tea, chocolate dictated conditions – at first secondary, but eventually indispensable – for their consumption. The Paris inventories show that these utensils were to be found among the better-off and middle-ranking sections, especially after the Regency, and among the people before 1789. Debts left with suppliers illustrate also the rise of the new needs for which the chocolate-merchant or the grocer catered. Boxes, coffee-containers made of tinplate, stoves or pans for roasting the coffee, hot-plates, cooking-ranges and, especially, coffee-pots, table-services and little spoons appeared everywhere. The coffee-pot, which was a sort of big kettle, cost between fifty and two hundred *livres*, if it was made of silver or porcelain, but only a few dozen sols if only of pewter. Among the nobles and clergy stocks of Mocha were to be found. Around 1760 thirty-seven per cent of the inventories in the parish of Saint-Germain-l'Auxerrois and forty per cent of those in the parish of Saint-Sulpice mention a coffee-pot, whereas they figure in less than 20 per cent of the inventories in the lower-class districts in the east of Paris. Tea left fewer traces, but these do show up in a few inventories: 10 per cent in the parish of Saint-Eustache, two per cent in the parish of Saint-Germain-l'Auxerrois. Tea-caddies, pots, jars, teapots, in porcelain, in pewter, in copper, in tin-plate, in silver (in which case it was worth between a hundred and two hundred *livres*), cups in porcelain or faience; complete services decorated *à la chinoise* in the houses of the rich, who, copying the ways of English good society, indulged in serious expenditure,[55] showing thereby their magnificence and their ability to keep up with fashion. At tea-time the young were to the fore. The new way of life was animated there less by family intimacy, as with coffee or chocolate, than by sociability, meeting others, politeness – all functions that are symbolised by the well-known painting *Le Thé chez le Prince de Conti.*

At the edges of Paris, in the farms of the Ile-de-France, in the houses of the Vexin, these objects were present, though less costly, and only among the rich. Such luxuries reached the provinces but slowly: 20 per cent of the inventories of Angers mention a coffee-pot around 1780. True, one can prepare coffee with other utensils, but this was a sign that the effects of distinguished refinement were advancing irregularly and less quickly. For the poor, sugar and coffee were welcome complements in a diet that was subject to precariousness.

The progress of the art of cooking triumphed only slowly over the old conception of eating which combined medical knowledge with popular customs. The commented aphorisms of *L'Ecole de Salerne*, the *De conservanda bona valetudine*, enjoyed, indeed, a long-term success after they were included in the *Bibliothèque bleue*. Of this work 240 editions published between 1474 and 1846 have been preserved! It was a breviary of health compiled under the auspices of nature and common sense. In the modern period eating was always a way of taking care of oneself. For a long time the stomach was thought of as a sort of pot that, boiling with internal heat, cooked the substances one had ingested. In those days each kind of food could show itself now beneficial, now harmful, depending on humours, seasons and ages. Each month had its planetary sign, its work to be done, its ways of eating to be respected. Religious metaphors and the terminology of the Gospels conveyed this cosmic symbolism: fishing, harvesting, the wine-harvest, the bread and wine of the Lord. The liturgical calendar intervened in the cycle of feeding, imposing a fast at the end of winter, during which people had, if possible, eaten fat or salted food. For a long time the thing was to unite sympathetically particular foods with the body's needs. Olivier de Serre, from Ardèche, Liébault, from Burgundy, and Estienne, from Paris, integrated these principles of healthy and balanced eating into a catalogue of the virtues and norms of domestic economy. Lists of products and plants were drawn up, their use being dictated by botanists and doctors: Liébault was a professional physician. While the art of cookery made little showing in these treatises, it was not independent of them, for it also registered the transformations of the economic and alimentary potential recorded by the scientific literature of botany, medicine or agronomy.[56]

The conquest of taste proceeded quite differently, being visible in the rise of a specialised and independent literature, and it reached the reading public without difficulty. An initial series of works appeared in the middle of the seventeenth century: *Le Cuisinier français*, *Le Confiturier français*, *Le Cuisinier royal*. With over 230 editions recorded in the seventeenth and eighteenth centuries, 68 per cent of them after 1700, there was a potential public of 300,000 persons, broad and diverse, for the huge output of works on gastronomy published in Paris assumed every form and every format.[57] Baron Grimm exclaimed 'Science and philosophy then took hold of the cooking-pot.' From *La Cuisinière bourgeoise* by Menon, we get the impression that this book was to be found in the servants' quarters, in the living-room and in the dining-room of both aristocratic and plebeian houses. People learnt from it the new table-manners from Court society, with their modulations. It ennobled plebeian dishes and promoted new resources. To the grand style of the seventeenth century succeeded a taste that was more refined and more varied, a quest for the quintessence of dishes along with a praising of simplicity. Good cuts of meat and good wines, and especially the ability to appreciate them, were at the heart of a new sensibility in which bourgeois simplicity could become the height of chic. As the debate about luxury died down a new dispute set the partisans of natural food, like Rousseau, against the oppressive discourse of the lovers of superfluities, who, in the theatre, mocked them as lettuce-eaters. The new medicine of Tronchin and Tissot argued, in its turn, for a return to natural sources and for a social and personal codifying of diets. Soon, reason and chemistry would, with Réamur and Spallanzani, enter into the realm of eating.[58]

The Century of Enlightenment ended with a dream that the old anguishes and the iron collar of subsistence would disappear. Liberal economists preached against the tyranny of just prices. Scientists and agronomists, botanists of field and salon, carried out experiment after experiment so as to endow man with greater mastery over nature: for example, the principles of fertility were studied in order to understand the diseases of corn. The *Encyclopédie*, like *La Cuisinière bourgeoise*, gave prominence to the potential wealth of supplies and their great diversity. In this way eating in the Enlightenment reconciled the mastery of a foster-mother nature which had long been at hand and drawn upon with the contributions of long-distance trade, exotic or familiar, from sugar to cheese and from rice to citrus fruit. The economy of scarcity hovered over these forms of liberation. It was the lot of the majority and knocked at the gates of the towns. The new needs, sugar, or soap for cleaning clothes, were not the last to provoke defensive feelings. Though neither the monotony nor the crudeness of most people's diet had been overcome, it ceased to be irregular and began to diversify. Urban instability contrasted with rural stability, which was maintained by consumption of one's own produce and too hesitant an opening to exchange and the market. It was at fairs and markets, at inns and hostelries that people acquired a taste for the new ways. The spread of literacy and increased reading of manuals of good manners and almanacs helped the simultaneous advance of the civilisation of manners, improved taste, and the sense of the individual and the private. In the nineteenth century Feuerbach could declare that, more than ever, man was what he ate and that obeying one's senses pushed back religion and philosophy: but the materialist principles of the Manifesto were, in fact, only a confirmation of the old postulates of medicine and theology, in the service of a new art of living, turned inside out, wherein the subject had for his body a care that was just, necessary and adequate.[59]

Conclusion

It is easy to perceive the limitations of this 'history of everyday things'. First, because the results presented leave aside decisive factors in modern life: the organisation of private and family choices of ways of life; the essential role played by women, which should be analysed separately from the general principles of an economy of roles in the family or in work; the evolution of practices concerning the body, and everything that has to do with health and hygiene. For lack of studies, or because too many studies have already been published, as with the history of women, a selection has to be made. But also because the chief guiding idea in this book has been to follow the successive phases of the principal devices of material culture, in their context. However, it is easier to reconstitute a circulation of things than to restore their individual appropriation or their real status, which is closely dependent on the biography of their owners. To achieve that one would have to attempt an ethnography of the minute in which the process of creation of the value of the objects would at last become visible.[1] The history of consumption as production is still, to some extent, waiting to be written.

What has been established appears, nevertheless, in the transformation of the perspectives from which we can grasp the cultural history of consumptions and consumers. It was necessary to break with historians' indifference to the world of objects other than those that are usually focused on by our culture hungry for artistic consumptions of all kinds. The picture I have drawn breaks systematically with the methods and descriptions, the ways of classifying and the categories that are often adopted: the popular and the scientific, the dominated and the dominating, the poor and the rich, town and country, creation and passivity, the real and the imaginary. It breaks also with the traditional accounts of everyday life in that it gives prominence to the organisation of the facts into a system. It tries to discover, at the heart of the consumption process the simultaneous action of intelligence and sensibility, of the material and the symbolic, and shows that the causes and effects of the changes do not operate in a simple manner. An innovation may itself signify something different as between social categories or individuals. It does not erase all at once the consequences of past time. Finally, this picture shows the limitations of the contrasts generally accepted in the study of consumptions – supply and demand, to explain the models of consumption, material analysis or study of behaviour in order to understand the culture of consumptions, whether private, which belongs to the cultural sphere, or public, which relates to the social sphere, in order to define the identity of consumers, the market or distinction in order to analyse the significance of goods. The modern habits of rapid using-up of objects were born in a heterogeneous world wherein several modes of consumption and different spheres of merchandise coexist.[2]

The study of eating, if we stick to the conclusions of the historians of economy and agriculture, shows clearly the general unification of behaviour due to necessity and the importance of 'alimentary security'. The symbolic value of bread and wine confers on this old regime of subsistence a power that it would retain right into the nineteenth century, because the economy of salvation and moral and political responsibility coincided in the concepts which ensured day-to-day order and inspired consumers, the governed and the governors. The liberal break with all that, the logic of the unregulated economy, deeply undermined confidence in the government and in the King.[3] At the same time, the alimentary regime was more complex at the margins – for eighty per cent of peasants and landowners the unknown factor constituted by their consumption of what they themselves produced confuses the picture. Ingenuity and regional diversity permitted the introduction of various foods – meat, fish, vegetables, fruit, dairy products – which modify the notion of an alimentary regime uniform in space and time. What people ate during crises upsets everything, while long-term changes in their eating brings fresh possibilities. All the time the advantage enjoyed by the townsman made itself apparent in less monotony, less crudity and more choice. The gap between town and country grew steadily wider, not only in the food eaten but also in table-manners, which slowly altered objects and actions. These manners spread through society not so much vertically as horizontally, with mobility, intermediaries and centres of exchange playing an active role. The new consumptions could come together at the top of society around social distinction, and at the bottom because they responded to needs, as with coffee and sugar. The economy of scarcity hovered over all forms of liberation.

The history of appearances followed a similar process of transformation. The passage from the seventeenth to the eighteenth century saw a freeing of needs and a growth in the superfluous. Poverty and parsimony still prevailed among most of the peasantry and townsfolk, but for all of them the culture of appearances was not that of under-development. Already at work was the symbolic and social efficacy of the linen revolution and the increased capacity of individuals, who were informed by the movement of people, supplied by the trade in second-hand clothes, and led on by the offers of pedlars and fairs. Everywhere confusion was to be observed, to such a degree that the authorities ceased to be able to control equalisation and standardisation. Through comparison of being and seeming the first consumers acquired a greater independence that was confirmed by the confusion of signs. Clothes, which are certainly the most general and most pertinent indicator for measuring the transition from scarcity to relative profusion, show at one and the same time the dream of an order based on hierarchised consumption and the dissociation of that order, the points at stake in distinction and communication, the power to lead on that was wielded by demand and by commercialisation. The revolution in linen and clothing was of essential importance in the economic, social and moral debate, because it overturned the values of the Christian and stationary economy, initiating people into the economy of circulation, personal change and individualism.

The habitat and the dwelling, from the house to its decor, from its setting to its furnishing and the practices connected therewith in respect of water, heating and lighting, demonstrate the functionality of things in ordinary life. Living space for two-thirds of the population was confined to a single room, with at most a few annexes that defined the domestic territory in which there reigned the strongest relation to persons and things. This constraint weighed differently on country-folk and towns-folk, but it united them in an identical awareness of the family and affective space. Above all, it dictated principles of organisation that drew a real social and cultural frontier between themselves and those who benefited from a freer and more generous disposition of things. Way of life, process of appropriation of space, capacity for changing a relation with places were not to be compared between these groups. The hygiene which was becoming established among the educated elites, modesty, the relations between the generations huddled together, the contrast between dirty and clean, healthy and unhealthy, the capacity to withdraw into oneself, separation between tasks – everything was bound up with that fundamental condition.

The evolution was usually slow. For the majority we note the overlapping of signs and values which combined in the struggle against cold, the role of clothes, that of lighting, or care of the body. Progress in the control of affects was linked with the spread of objects and ways of using them: bed, table, chairs, tidying and storing utensils. Town life, improved income, social status brought other possibilities, a different scale of effects produced by space and the possibility of using it in. The accumulation of things is reflected in the inventories, which, unfortunately, present us only with a picture of a stock and not that of a flux of possessions. It is harder still to know the way people behaved in relation to these objects, which was not necessarily the same with everyone. We have to relativise consumers' access to the forms elaborated by the skill of cabinet-makers and the work of joiners. The autonomy of town life could find a rural echo only in the homes of the privileged – nobles and notables, priests, rural bourgeoisie, rich peasants escaped at that time from the realm of utility and modesty in which progress could appear only marginally, in decor and choice of materials.

The values of fashion and the change of style it dictated were much slower to spread in this sphere than in sartorial habits, which were more fluid. Practices and the norms that governed them were expressed more visibly. Old and modern forms of lighting both manifested a religious and secularised symbolism of man's mastery of nature and of himself. Illuminating the public space and private interiors became, well beyond necessity, the expression of a need for order and control of social and domestic relations. The technical triumph celebrated by the academies belonged both in an economy of display and in a logic of rationality which modified relations to work and leisure, drawing their power of conviction from the spectacles of the theatre or the Church or the time of festive profusion. Certainty of life and experience gained from this. In the same way, in the struggle against cold, a frontier of sensibility was moved thanks to urban inventions in heating. It led, through thinking about convenience and comfort, architectural changes, modifications in night life, questionings by scientists and moral observers concerning the variability of habits, to the diffusion of technical inventions.

Going from town to country, we can re-examine family relations and sociability on the basis of the new devices installed. Among countryfolk, because winter dictated long evenings devoted to work or relaxation, this was a time for story-telling, for telling jokes, later on for reading and discussing the news in the papers: lighting and heating were undeniably important in that connection. In town, frequentation of collective places, cafés and taverns, led to different habits, and the progress of equipment accelerated. In both cases a revolution began, the revolution of the place assigned to the hearth in cooking and in family relations, but its symbolic position was not yet devalued.

The uses made of water provide a comparable lesson. While the urban and scientific dream of water pure and accessible to all made progress in the towns, destroying the old traditions of ostentatious consumption, in the country the possibilities increased only at a slow pace. The peasants were less well-equipped for the conquest of water lagged behind the towns. Crossing the threshold of sensibility which in traditional society linked incomplete cleanliness, the value of a powerful smell, and the use of linen took place much more slowly in the countryside. The pathology of signs advanced, but the availability of means was behindhand. This reflected the lack of interest that men, who had always taken charge of collective means, took in a sphere and an occupation that were essentially feminine.[4]

At every level of these transformations, geographical or social, it was the first possibility of change that arose: how had constraint, necessity, need lost ground? The answer is to be found beyond the indicator provided by the growth of population, in the capacity for acceleration of the conversion of goods and things into objects and wealth, in the possibility of rejecting stability, in indifference to the status quo and tradition, in the power to refute the philosophies of asceticism and contempt for the object that were taught by Christianity and Christian stoicism. We therefore perceive the importance of the economic thinking of the Enlightenment and its discussion of the principles of the moral economy, along with those of mercantilism, which restricted and hierarchised the distribution and circulation of products and riches. The luxury which displayed the power of the superfluous remained therefore a major problem in the old society, in both its economic dimension and its moral depths. It illuminated the mechanisms of the demand economy, while it questioned the pedagogy of standards of consumption.

Condillac, theoretician of perception, economist of language and linguist of economics, provided a unified view of this movement: 'All our needs are interconnected . . . Associated with a need is the idea of the thing that can assuage it.'[5] The history of consumption, from Antiquity to modern times, can thus be interpreted like that of a script which everyone understands, in which the abstract and the sensible, the natural and the artificial are inseparable. From the moment when artificial needs take precedence over natural needs the nature of nature is changed.[6] 'When a society starts to enjoy things of secondary necessity it starts to be selective in its food, its clothing, its housing, its weapons: it has more needs, more wealth.[7] The circulation of wealth begins with increased consumption, as we see with the whole problematic of budgets and their role. The arts and education crown the edifice, which is based on the wealth of the towns. In a state which is isolated and stationary, needs are equivalent to means, the imagination is restricted, 'every person will wear the clothes appropriate to his estate'.[8] In the developed and urbanised state the order of exchange is established and the dynamic of all consumption moves it forward. Luxury can then threaten the balance, for the logics of the economy of consumptions which are linked with the concentration and division of labour and power, the accumulation of desirable objects, urban expenditure and luxury, the theatricalised idea of appearances, come into conflict with the necessities of politics and morality in the city.[9] 'We need riches but not rich individuals.' This dilemma is still as acute as ever, on our scale, the global scale.

The way this thought has developed can serve as testimony for all who lived in France before the second revolution[10] of the 1960s, those who were between fifteen and twenty years old before 1950. Whatever the social level of their family, with some exceptions, they knew the world of scarcity. The winter which descended upon Europe and our country, in 1940, was the occasion of an ultimate experience, that of cold and hunger which were but poorly cheated by the ingenuity of heating by wood or by a stove fuelled by sawdust, balls of paper coated in damp coal-dust put in the grates of fireplaces, and the elementary rations offered by the food cards for categories J2 and J3. Everything came together at that time to motivate the vigilance of housewives, to hunt everywhere in order to supplement, however meagrely, the official allowance and to invent substitutes.

This book is, in a sense, dedicated to those who suffered from chilblains in winter, who could not read at leisure because the power was cut off or petrol hard to find in the hardware shops, those who wore clothes handed down by their elders and relatives and cut down to their size, and who had to learn to mend them: to those also who still detest cold water and the reactionary morality that it justifies or accompanies, to those who, in Paris, were able to see inequality in all the forms of consumption reserved to the privileged by wealth and the ruling power of that time, the customers of the black market.

On the road which has led my generation from those dark days to the society of growth, it would be naive to suppose that a certain kind of progress has banished inequalities or that our society has ceased to function through exploitation, but it would be just as unintelligent to mistake our adversary. That adversary is not to be sought in things and in the contrast between the intellectual and the material, but in our collective inability to conceive solutions for ensuring to everyone more equal access to the wealth that our society is always able to produce, and to reduce the social inequalities which are organised on a planetary scale. On this matter history and the historian can offer neither lessons nor remedies. They can, together with the other social sciences, invite to reflection, dissipate some prejudices, show examples of the spirit of enterprise and freedom which have been able to overcome habit and custom, encourage optimism, and argue against exclusion and stupidity.

Notes

INTRODUCTION: CULTURE AND MATERIAL CIVILISATION

1 K. G. Schelle, *L'art de se promener* (1802), French trans., Paris, 1996, pp. 19–20.
2 F. Dagognet, *Rematérialiser, matières et matérialismes*, Paris, 1985, pp. 8–16.
3 J. Brewer, N. MacKendrick and J. T. Plumb, *The Birth of a Consumer Society: the Commercialisation of Eighteenth-Century England*, London, 1982; J. Brewer and R. Porter, *Consumption and the World of Goods*, London, 1993.
4 K. Marx, Introduction to *A Contribution to a Critique of Political Economy*, in *Collected Works*, vol. XXVIII 1986, p. 28, and *Capital*, vol. I, in *Collected Works*, 1996, vol. XXXV p. 91.
5 D. Roche, *La France des Lumières*, Paris, 1993.
6 F. Dagognet, *Eloge de l'objet. Pour une philosophie de la marchandise*, Paris, 1989.
7 J. Le Goff, R. Chartier and J. Revel (eds.), *Nouvelle Histoire*, Paris, 1978.
8 N. J. G. Pounds, *The Culture of the English People: Iron Age to the Industrial Revolution*, Cambridge, 1994.
9 F. Braudel, *Civilisation and Capitalism, Fifteenth to Eighteenth Century*, vol. I, *The Structures of Everyday Life: The Limits of the Possible*, London, 1981, Preface, p. 27.
10 D. F. McKenzie, *Bibliography and the Sociology of Texts*, London, 1986; R. Chartier, *L'ordre des livres*, Paris, 1992.
11 D. Roche, *The Culture of Clothing*, Cambridge, 1994, pp. 501–19: 'La culture des apparences entre économie et morale, XVIIᵉ–XVIIIᵉ siècles', *Bulletin de la Société d'histoire moderne* 17:2 (1990), pp. 14–17.
12 Roche, *Culture*, pp. 450–2.
13 Dagognet, *Rematérialiser*, pp. 36–43.
14 The 1970 catalogue of the collection (*La Vie quotidienne*, published by Hachette), lists some two hundred titles, arranged in rubrics: Ancient Worlds, History of France, Provincial Life, Crafts, Religions of the World, Peoples and Societies (Africa, America, Europe, Asia), Groups and Classes.
15 Paris, 1983.
16 L. Febvre, *Pour une histoire à part entière*, Paris, 1962: 'Civilisation matérielle et folklore' groups articles published before 1945–50; R. Mandrou, *Introduction à la France moderne*, Paris, 1961, studies culture with the approach initiated by Febvre, using the concept of 'mental tools', time, space and perceptions in order to analyse the scale of humanity, social groups and activities; Braudel, *Civilisation:* mankind faced with everyday life; special issues of the journal

Annales, Economie, Société, Civilisations assemble investigations and discussions: 1969, material life and biological behaviour: 1970, the history of town-planning, and the history of food; 1975, the history of consumption; 1976, anthropology, and the history of diseases; G.Thuillier, *Pour une histoire du quotidien au XIXe siècle*, Paris, 1977, pursues Febvre's programme from the standpoint of a 'reconstruction of experience', and opens up a list of questions which have been taken up by historians – the history of water, air, smells, hygiene, noises, colours, gestures. This pioneering work urges the creation of new sources, the meeting of psychology with the object and an archaeology of behaviour.

17 Braudel, *Civilisation*, pp. 27, 83–8.

18 M. Mauss, *Cours d'anthropologie*, Paris, 1947, brings together lectures given between 1926 and 1939; M. Douglas and B. Isherwood (eds.), *The World of Goods: toward an Anthropology of Consumption*, New York, 1979.

19 H. Lefebvre, *Critique de la vie quotidienne*, II: *Fondements d'une sociologie de la quotidienneté*, Paris, 1961, pp. 25–35. See also A. Lüdtke, *Alltagsgeschichte*, Frankfurt, 1989 (French trans. 1994).

20 R. Chartier, 'Le monde comme représentation', *Annales, Economie, Société, Civilisation;*, 1989: 6, pp. 1505–20 (quotation from p. 1509).

21 D. Miller, *Material Culture and Mass Consumption*, Oxford, 1987: *Acknowledging Consumption: A Review of New Studies*, D. Miller (ed.), London and New York, 1995.

22 A. Hirschman, *Shifting Involvements: Private Interest and Public Action*, Princeton, NJ, 1982; A. Hirschman, *The Passions and the Interests*, Princeton, NJ, 1977; C. Borghero, *La polemica sul Lusso nel settecento francese*, Turin, 1974; W. Sombart, *Luxury and Capitalism*, Ann Arbor, MI, 1967; A. Morize, *L'apologie du luxe et le mondain de Voltaire*, Paris, 1919; P. Perrot, *Le luxe, une richesse entre faste et confort, XVIIIe–XIXe siècle*, Paris, 1995.

23 J. Baudrillard, *La société de consommation*, Paris, 1970; J. Baudrillard, *Pour une critique de l'économie politique du signe*, Paris, 1972.

24 Dagognet, *Eloge*, p. 12.

25 P. Perrot, 'Notes pour l'élargissement d'une notion et d'une histoire; la consommation', *Bulletin du Département d'Histoire Économique*, University of Geneva, 1987, pp. 14–19.

26 G. Simmel, *The Philosophy of Money*, London, 1978.

27 G. Simmel, *Tragédie de la culture et autres essais*, Paris, 1988.

28 J.-C. Perrot, *Genèse d'une ville moderne: Caen au XVIIIe siècle*, 2 vols., Paris, 1975.

29 J.-P. Séris, *La technique*, Paris, 1994.

30 D. Roche, *The People of Paris*, Leamington Spa, 1987, pp. 36–63.

1 THE NATURAL FRAMEWORK AND THE HUMAN FRAMEWORK

1 This chapter is greatly indebted to the discussions in the seminar I conducted along with J.-C. Perrot, though I am solely responsible for any shortcomings. On the precautions that have to be taken where the production–consumption relation is concerned, cf. G. Levi, 'Comportements, ressources, procès: avant

la "revolution de la consommation" in J. Revel (ed.), *Jeux d'échelles: la micro-analyse à l'experience*, Paris, 1996, pp. 187–207; C. Baudelot and R. Establet, *Maurice Halbwachs: Consommation et société*, Paris, 1994.

2 A. Heller, *The Theory of Need in Marx*, London, 1976.

3 A. Corbin, *Le miasme et la jonquille. L'odorat et l'imaginaire social, XVIIIᵉ–XIXᵉ siècle*, Paris, 1982.

4 X. de Planhol, *L'eau de neige, le tiède et le frais*, Paris, 1995, especially pp. 204–307.

5 J.-Y. Grenier, 'Consommation et marché au XVIIIᵉ siècle', *Histoire et Mesure*, 1995, vol. X, nos. 3–4, pp. 371–80.

6 D. Roche, *The Culture of Clothing*, Cambridge, 1994, pp. 5–6.

7 Grenier, 'Consommation', p. 374.

8 H. Vérin, *Entrepreneur, entreprise, histoire d'une idée*, Paris, 1982; Roche, *La France*, pp. 476–81.

9 F. Angiolini and D. Roche, *Culture et formation négociante*, Paris, 1995.

10 Levi, 'Comportements', pp. 196–7.

11 Grenier, 'Consommation', pp. 376–7; C. Berthomieu, 'La loi et les travaux de Engel', *Consommation* 1965: 4, pp. 59–89.

12 P. de Boisguilbert, *Pierre de Boisguilbert et la naissance de l'économie politique*, 2 vols., Paris, 1966; J.-C. Perrot, *Histoire de la population française*, vol. II, Paris, 1988, pp. 499 ff.

13 C.-E. Labrousse, *Esquisse du mouvement des prix et des revenus en France au XVIIIᵉ siècle*, Paris, 1933, and, especially, *La crise de l'économie française à la fin de l'Ancien Règime et au debut de la Révolution*, Paris, 1944, reprinted 1990 with a preface by J.-C. Perrot.

14 P. Ariès, *L'enfant et la vie familiale*, Paris, 1960.

15 A. Pardailhé-Galabrun, *La naissance de l'intime; 3,000 foyers parisiens, XVIIᵉ–XVIIIᵉ siècle*, Paris, 1988. On the influences of ageing, cf. O. Ekert-Jaffé, 'Vieillissement et consommation. Quelques résultats tirés des enquêtes françaises sur les budgets des ménages', *Population* 1989: 3, pp. 561–71.

16 C. Beutler, 'Un chapitre de la sensibilité collective: la littérature agricole en Europe continentale au XVIᵉ siècle', *Annales, Economie, Société, Civilisations;* 1973: 28, pp. 1282–94.

17 J. M. Barbier, *L'économie du quotidien*, Paris, 1981.

18 J.-L. Flandrin, *Famille et parenté à l'époque moderne*, Paris, 1976; A. Farge, *La vie fragile, violence, pouvoirs et solidarités à Paris au XVIIIᵉ siècle*, Paris, 1986.

19 P. Vidal de la Blanche, *Tableau géographique de la France*, vol. I of *Histoire de la France rurale*, E. Lavisse (ed.), Paris, 1903.

20 G. Bertrand, 'Pour une histoire écologique de la France rurale', in *Histoire de la France rurale*, G. Duby (ed.), vol. I, Paris, 1975.

21 Bertrand, 'Pour une histoire', but particularly vol. II of *Histoire de la France rurale*.

22 R. Dion, *Histoire de la vigne et du vin en France des origines au XIXᵉ siècle*, Paris, 1959; M. Lachiver, *Vins, vignes et vignerons. Histoire du vignoble français*, Paris, 1988; G. Garrier, *Histoire sociale et culturelle du vin*, Paris, 1996.

23 Garrier, *Histoire sociale*, pp. 55–64, 120–39.

24 Roche, *La France des Lumières*, Paris, pp. 39–47.

25 G. Sigaut, 'Histoire rurale et sciences agronomiques. Un cadre général de réflexion', *Histoire et Sociétés rurales*, 'L'histoire rurale en France', 1995: 3,

pp. 203–14.

26 G. Durand, *Vins, vignes et vignerons en Beaujolais, XVIe–XVIIIe siècle*, Lyons, 1979.

27 A. Corvol, *L'homme et l'arbre dans l'Ancien Régime*, Paris, 1984; D. Woronoff and M. Vovelle (eds.), *Révolution et espaces forestiers*, Paris, 1988.

28 G. R. Ikni, 'La question paysanne dans la Révolution française; pour une vision synthétique', *Histoire et Sociétés rurales* 1995: 4, pp. 177–211.

29 J.-M. Moriceau, *Les fermiers de l'Ile de France. L'ascension d'un patronat agricole, XVe–XVIIIe siècle*, Paris, 1994.

30 M. Morineau, 'Simples calculs relatifs à une prétendue révolution agricole survenue en France au XVIIIe siècle', *Revue historique* 1995: 1, pp. 91–108.

31 Perrot, *Histoire*, pp. 505–7, and *Pour une histoire intellectuelle de l'économie*, Paris, 1994.

32 E. Briand, *La mesure de l'Etat. Administrateurs et géomètres au XVIIIe siècle*, Paris, 1994.

33 F. Dagognet, *Des révolutions vertes. Histoire et principes de l'agronomie*, Paris, 1973.

34 Levi, 'Comportements', p. 195.

35 J.-M. Boehler, 'Tradition et innovation dans un pays de petite culture au XVIIIe siècle', *Histoire et Sociétés rurales* 1995: 4, pp. 69–103, and *Une société rurale en milieu rhénan, la paysannerie de la plaine d'Alsace, 1648–1789*, 3 vols., Strasbourg, 1995.

36 T. Leroux, 'Une géographie économique de la France à travers les archives du maximum, les contrastes régionaux de l'espace français à la fin du XVIIIe siècle', master's degree memoir, Paris, 1995, supervised by D. Woronoff and D. Margairaz (typescript).

37 *Ibid.*, pp. 130–3, 162–76, and conclusion, pp. 223–8.

2 TOWNS, TRADE AND INVENTIONS

1 J.-C. Perrot, *Pour une histoire intellectuelle de l'économie*, Paris, 1994, pp. 214–15.

2 D. Roche, *La France des Lumières*, Paris, 1993, pp. 120–31.

3 R. Cantillon, *Essai sur la nature du commerce en général*, 1755, T.Tsuda (ed.), Tokyo, 1979, Chapter 7. I am grateful to D. Margairaz for references on this point.

4 R. Bigo, 'L'octroi de Paris en 1789', *Revue d'Histoire économique et sociale* 1931: 1, pp. 97–113.

5 Paris, 2 vols., 1784, vol. I, p. 87.

6 A. Martin, Paris, 1789, pp. 287–8.

7 Moreau de Beaumont, *Traités des impositions*, Paris, 5 vols., 1784, vol. V, p. 463.

8 Bigo, 'L'octroi', p. 104; Bibliothèque nationale, MS NAF 2644 and LF 11 74.

9 R. Philippe, 'Une opération pilote: l'étude du ravitaillement de Paris au temps de Lavoisier', *Annales, Economie, Société, Civilisation;*, 16: 3, May–June 1961, pp. 560–8.

10 B. Lepetit, *Les villes dans la France moderne (1750–1830)*, Paris, 1988. I have followed its main conclusions and refer the reader to the exhaustive bibliography.

11 J. Dupâquier (ed.), *Histoire de la population française*, 4 vols., Paris, 1984, vol. II, *De la Renaissance à 1789*.

12 A. Lemaitre, *La Métropolitée*, Amsterdam, 1682.

13 D. Roche, *The People of Paris*, Leamington Spa, 1987, pp. 20–4; J.-F. Dubost, S. Juratic, V. Milliot, D. Roche, J.-M. Roy, 'Mobilité et accueil à Paris (1650–1850)', PIR–Villes report, 1996, pp. 52–70 (typescript).

14 F. Raison, *Les Auvergnats de Paris au xixe siècle*, Paris, 1976; A.-M. Moulin, *Les maçons de la Haute-Marche au xviiie siècle*, Clermont-Ferrand, 1986; A. Corbin, *Archaïsme et modernité en Limousin au xixe siècle, 1845–1880*, 2 vols., Paris, 1975.

15 C. E. Labrousse, *Esquisse du mouvement des prix et des revenus en France au xviiie siècle*, Paris, 1993; Grenier, 'Les mécanismes de la croissance', in *Histoire de la population française*, vol. ii, pp. 437–51 – see the chronological evolution, pp. 452–9. I follow Grenier's propositions, which need to be compared with the extensive analysis in his *L'économie d'Ancien Régime*, Paris, 1996.

16 J.-C. Perrot, *Genèse d'une ville moderne: Caen au xviiie siècle*, 2 vols., Paris, 1975, vol. ii, pp. 679–701.

17 J.-F. Solnon, *La Cour de France*, Paris, 1987.

18 A. Guéry, 'Les finances de la monarchie française sous l'Ancien Régime', *Annales, Economie, Société, Civilisations;* 1978: 2, pp. 216–39: see also R. Descimon and C. Jouhaud, *La France du premier xviie siècle*, Paris, 1996, pp. 104–15.

19 M. Fogel, *Modèle d'Etat et modèle social de dépenses: les lois somptuaires en France de 1485 à 1660. Prélèvement et redistribution dans la genèse de l'Etat moderne*, Paris, 1987: G. Levi, *Comportements, resources, procès: la micro-analyse à l'experience*, Paris, 1996, pp. 192–3.

20 F. Hincker, *Les Français devant l'impôt sous l'Ancien Régime*, Paris, 1971; Y. Durand, *Les fermiers généraux au xviiie siècle*, Paris, 1972; D. Dessert, *Argent, pouvoir et société au Grand Siècle*, Paris, 1984.

21 *Théorie de l'impôt*, Paris, 1760; *Les maximes générales d'un bon gouvernement*, Paris, 1701; *La richesse de l'Etat*, 1763; *La Dîme royale*, Paris, 1707; *Le détail de la France*, Paris, 1695.

22 Again I thank D. Margairaz for her collaboration and her help in reading the *Economistes fiscalistes*.

23 'L'Impot indirect. Observation sur les mémoires récompensés par la Société d'Agriculture de Limoges' (1768), in *Les Ecrits économiques*, preface by B. Cazès, Paris, 1970, pp. 189–210.

24 Roche, *La France*, pp. 127–56.

25 D. Woronoff, *Histoire de l'industrie en France, du xvie siècle à nos jours*, Paris, 1994.

26 N. Coquery, 'De l'hôtel aristocratique aux ministères. Habitat, mouvement, espace à Paris au xviiie siècle, doctorate thesis, University of Paris 1, 1995 (typescript).

27 J.-L. Harouel, *L'embellissement des villes. L'urbanisme français au xviiie siècle*, Paris, 1993.

28 D. Roche, *The Culture of Clothing*, Cambridge, 1994, pp. 257–329.

29 *Ibid.*, pp. 326–9; P. Verlet, 'Le commerce des objets d'art et les marchands merciers à Paris au xviiie siècle', *Annales, Economie, Société, Civilisations;* 1958: 12, pp. 10–29.

30 J. Savary des Bruslons, *Dictionnaire universel du commerce, d'histoire naturelle et des arts et métiers*, Copenhagen, 1761, vol. iii, pp. 849–53.

31 Verlet, 'Le commerce', pp. 16–17, 23.

32 Lepetit, *Les villes*, pp. 122–71.

33 B. Lepetit, *Chemins de terre et voies d'eau. Réseaux de transport et organisation de l'espace en France (1740–1840)*, Paris, 1984.

34 J.-M. Goger, 'La politique routière en France de 1716 a 1815', thesis supervised by J.-C. Perrot, 6 vols., E.H.E.S.S., Paris, 1988 (typescript).

35 J.-M. Goger, 'Transport' in *Dictionnaire des Lumières*, M. Delon (ed.), Paris, 1997.

36 D. Margairaz, *Foires et marchés dans la France pré-industrielle*, Paris, 1988 and 'Foires et marchés' in *Dictionnaire des Lumières*.

37 J.-Y. Grenier, *L'économie d'Ancien Régime, un monde de l'échange et de l'incertitude*, Paris, 1997.

38 S. Kaplan, *Les ventres de Paris, pouvoirs et approvissionnement dans la France d'Ancien Régime*, Paris, 1988; J.-A. Miller, *Les marchés céréaliers à la veille de la Révolution: le modèle de l'économie pragmatique, la Révolution française et l'homme moderne*, C. Mazauric (ed.), Rouen and Paris, 1989.

39 *Voyages en France*, del Litto (ed.), Paris 1992 (Collection de la Pléiade), pp. 346–56.

40 Roche, *La France*, pp. 466–94, 603–5.

41 L. Bergeron, *Paris dans l'organisation des échanges intérieurs français à la fin du XVIIIe siècle. Aires et structures du commerce français au XVIIIe siècle*, P. Léon (ed.) Lyons, 1973, pp. 237–63.

42 R. Chartier, M. Compère and D. Julia, *L'éducation en France au XVIIIe siècle*, Paris, 1976; Roche, *La France*, pp. 381–90.

43 H. Chizick, *The Limits of Reform in the Enlightenment, Attitudes toward the Education of the Lower Classes in Eighteenth-Century France*, Princeton, NJ, 1981; M. Albertone, *Fisiocrati, istruzione e cultura*, Turin, 1979.

44 G. Feyel, 'La presse et l'information en France', State doctorate thesis, University of Paris I, 1994, 5 vols. (typescript).

45 J. Raven, 'Imprimé et transactions économiques en Angleterre aux XVIIe et XVIIIe siècles', *Revue d'Histoire Moderne et Contemporaine* April–June 1996: 43–2, pp. 234–65.

46 C. Lienhardt's thesis will show the impact achieved by this work, succesfully published all over Europe, which contained various wise observations on economic matters.

47 L. Hilaire-Pérez, 'Inventions et inventeurs en France et en Angleterre au XVIIIe siècle', doctorate thesis, University of Paris I, 1994, 4 vols. (typescript); J. Schlanger, *L'invention intellectuelle*, Paris, 1983.

48 Schlanger, *L'invention*, pp. 214–22.

49 A. Guillerme, 'L'histoire des techniques, tendances actuelles', *Bulletin de la Société française d'histoire des sciences et des techniques* 1990: 26, pp. 5–12.

50 Paris, 1763, pp. 6–10.

3 ORDINARY CONSUMPTION AND LUXURY CONSUMPTION

1 J.-M. Boehler, 'Tradition et innovation dans un pays de petite culture au XVIIIe siècle', *Histoire et Sociétés rurales* 1994: 4, p. 69.

2 L. Fontaine, *Le colportage ein Europe du XVIe au XIXe siècle*, Paris, 1994, and *Le*

voyageur et la mémoire. Colporteurs de l'Oisans au XIXe *siècle*, Lyons, 1984.

3 G. Levi, 'Comportements, ressources, procès: avant "la révolution de la consommation"', in J. Revel (ed.), *Jeux d'échelles, la micro-analyse à l'expérience*, Paris, 1996, p. 192.

4 P. Perrot, *Le luxe, une richesse entre faste et confort,* XVIIIe–XIXe *siècle*, Paris, 1995.

5 L.-R. Villermé, *Tableau et l'état physique et moral des ouvriers, employés dans les manufactures de coton, de laine et de soie*, 2 vols., Paris, 1840, reprinted 1989.

6 A. Desrosières, *La politique des grands nombres. Histoire de la raison statistique*, Paris, 1993, pp. 289–330.

7 G. Stigler, 'The early history of empirical studies of consumer behaviour', *Journal of Political Economy*, 1954: 62, pp. 95–102; C. Berthomieu, 'La loi et les travaux de Engel', *Consommation* 1965: 4, pp. 61–2.

8 C. Baudelot and R. Establet, *Maurice Halbwachs, Consommation et société*, Paris, 1994; M. Halbwachs, *La classe ouvrière et les niveaux de vie. Recherches sur la hierarchie des besoins dans les sociétés industrielles contemporaines*, Paris, 1913. This contains a sociological theory of needs and ways of life which is of fundamental importance.

9 The content of this chapter is due mainly to the contribution made by the seminar I conducted along with J.-C. Perrot in 1991, certain conclusions of which I have brought together here. It was clarified through discussion between C. Grignon and G. Postel-Vinay in other contexts in 1993–4. The interpretations and, of course any mistakes, are my responsibility, but I wish to give full credit to my intellectual influences.

The history of budgets benefits from the pioneering work of C.-E. Labrousse, *Esquisse du mouvement des prix et des revenus en France au* XVIIIe *siècle*, Paris 1993, vol. II, pp. 450–60, and from the analysis by M. Morineau, 'Budgets populaires en France au XVIIIe siècle', *Revue d'histoire économique et sociale*, 1972: 2–3, pp. 203–37.

10 J.-F. Pelissier, 'L'économie politique des années de crise', 3rd cycle thesis, University of Paris I, 1984: L. Rothkrug, *Opposition to Lóuis XIV. The Political and Social Origins of the French Enlightenment*, Princeton, NJ, 1905

11 J.-C. Perrot, 'Les économistes, les philosophes et la population', in *Histoire de la population française*, vol. II, pp. 499–545.

12 E. Cornaert (ed.), *Projet d'une dîme royale*, Paris, 1933, pp. 74–85.

13 Baudelot and Establet, *Maurice Halbwachs*, pp. 98–100.

14 P. Léon and C. Carrière, 'La montée des structures capitalistes', in F. Braudel and C.-E. Labrousse, *Histoire économique et sociale de la France*, Paris, 1970, vol. II, pp. 161–257.

15 Baudelot and Establet, *Maurice Halbwachs*, pp. 62–5.

16 S. Kaplan, *Le meilleur pain du monde. Les boulangers de Paris au* XVIIIe *siècle*, Paris, 1996, pp. 9–10, 47–50.

17 *Ibid.*, p. 48.

18 S. Linguet, *Annales politiques, civiles et littéraires au* XVIIIe *siècle*, Brussels, 1788, vol. VII, pp. 165–9; Kaplan, *Le meilleur pain*, p. 53.

19 M. Lachiver, *Les années de misère: la famine au temps du Grand Roi, 1680–1720*, Paris, 1991.

20 Kaplan, *Les ventres de Paris, pouvoirs et approvisionnement dans la France d'Ancien Régime*, Paris, 1988.

21 Lepelletier, *Mémoire pour le rétablissement du commerce de la France*, Rouen, 1701; Pottier de la Hestroye, *Réflexion sur le traité de la Dîme royale de M. le Maréchal de Vauban*, n. p., 1716; H. de Boulainvilliers, *Etat de la France*, 2 vols., London, 1727; E. Lescuyer de la Jonchère, *Système d'un nouveau gouvernement en France*, 4 vols., Amsterdam, 1720.

22 M. Morineau, 'Simples calculs relatifs à une prétendue révolution agricole survenue en France au XVIIIe siècle', *Revue historique*, 1995: 1, pp. 210–19, 221–4, 449–51.

23 *Ibid.*, pp. 225–9.

24 D. Roche, *La Culture des apparences, une histoire du vêtement, XVII ^e siècle*, Paris, 1989, pp. 86–108; J.-Y. Grenier, 'Modèle de la demande sous l'Ancien Régime, *Annales, Economie, Société, Civilisations;* 1987: 3, pp. 497–527.

25 Morineau, 'Simples calculs', pp. 229–30, 452–4.

26 O. Hufton, *The Poor of Eighteenth-Century France, 1750–89*, Oxford, 1974; C. Duprat, *Pour l'amour de l'humanité. Le temps des philanthropes, la philanthropie parisienne des Lumières à la monarchie de Juillet*, Paris, 1993.

27 *Oeuvres de Lavoisier publiées par les soins du ministère de l'Instruction publique*, 6 vols., Paris, 1862–93, vol. III, pp. 603–705.

28 N. Pellegrin, *Les bachelleries. Organisation et fêtes de la jeunesse dans le Centre–Ouest, XV ^e–XVIII ^e siècle*, Poitiers, 1982.

29 R. Beck, 'Jour du Seigneur, jour de fête, jour de repos. Les mutations du dimanche en France, 1700–1900', doctorate thesis, University of Paris VII, 1995, 2 vols. pp. 153–83 (typescript).

30 *La Dîme royale*, Paris, 1707, pp. 80–1.

31 J.-P. Gutton, *La société et les pauvres: l'exemple de la généralité de Lyon, 1534–1789*, Paris, 1971; D. Roche, *Le Siècle des Lumières, Province, académies et académiciens, 1660–1789*, 2 vols., Paris, 1978, vol. I, pp. 331–55.

32 J. Faiguet de Villeneuve, *L'économie politique, projet pour enrichir et pour perfectionner l'espèce humaine*, Paris, 1763.

33 D. Roche, *The People of Paris*, Leamington Spa, 1987, pp. 108–10.

34 Berthomieu, 'La loi'.

35 J.-L. Ménétra, *Journal de ma vie*, D. Roche (ed.), Paris, 1984, pp. 333–51. (Eng. trans., J.-L. Ménétra, *Journal of my Life*, New York, 1986, p. 298).

36 J. Godard, *L'ouvrier en soie. Monographie du tisseur lyonnais*, Lyons, 1899; M. Garden, *Lyon et les Lyonnais au XVIII ^e siècle*, Paris, 1970, pp. 298–309, 551–72: 'Doléances des maîtres ouvriers fabriquant en étoffe d'or, d'argent et de soie de la ville du Lyon', Lyons, 1976, introduction by F. Rudle, pp. 5–31.

37 W. Sewell, *Work and Revolution in France. The language of labour from the Old Regime to 1848*, London and Cambridge, 1980 (French trans. 1983).

38 R. Chartier, *L'Académie de Lyon au XVIII ^e siècle. Nouvelles études lyonnaises*, Geneva, 1969, pp. 133–250.

39 Perrot, *Les économistes*, pp. 5–106. I am grateful to D. Margairez for the additional information on this matter that she sent me.

40 R. Philippe, 'Une operation pilote: l'étude du ravitaillement de Paris au temps de Lavoiser', *Annales, Economie, Société, Civilisations;* 1961, pp. 564–7.

41 L. Chevallier, *Classes laborieuses et classes dangereuses*, Paris, 1958.

42 H. Bremond, *Histoire littéraire du sentiment religieux en France, depuis la fin des guerres de religion jusqu'à nos jours*, 11 vols., Paris, 1936.

43 Here I am using data from the 'Consumption–Production' seminar.

44 Kaplan, 'Les ventres', but also his *Bread, Politics and Political Economy in the Reign of Louis XV*, The Hague, 1976 (French trans. 1988): for reference, E. P. Thompson, 'The moral economy of the English crowd', *Past and Present*, 1971: 50, pp. 76–136.

45 J.-P. Dupuy, *Le sacrifice et l'envie*, Paris, 1992, pp. 75–106, 314–16.

46 A. Fillon, 'Louis Simon, étaminier (1741–1820) dans son village du haut Maine au Siècle des Lumières', doctorate thesis, University of Haut-Maine, 2 vols., Le Mans, 1983 (typescript).

47 C. Port (ed.) *Souvenirs d'un nonagénaire*, Paris, 1880.

48 N. Elias, *La Société de Cour*, Paris, 1974, and 1985, with introduction by R. Chartier. (Eng. trans. from German original, *The Court Society*, 1983).

49 C. Walter, 'Les lois somptuaires ou le rêve d'un ordre social. Evolution et enjeux de la politique somptuaire à Genève, XVIe–XVIIIe siècle', *Equinoxe*, 1994: 11, pp. 111–26; J. Sékora, *Luxury, the Concept in Western Thought*, London, 1977.

50 D. Margairaz, 'Luxe', in *Dictionnaire des Lumières*, M. Delon (ed.). For a comparison with the early modern period, see R. Muchembled, *Luxe et dynamisme social à Douai au XVIIe siècle. Nouvelles approches concernant la culture de l'habitat*, R. Baetens and B. Blondé (eds.), Turnhout, 1991, pp. 197–211.

51 A. Hirschman, *Bonheur privé, action publique*, Paris, 1983, pp. 99–102.

52 P. Grateau, 'Nécessité réelle et nécessité factice: doléances et culture matérielle dans la Sénéchaussée de Rennes en 1789', *Annales de Bretagne et des pays de l'Ouest* 1993: 3, pp. 299–310.

4 RURAL AND URBAN HOUSES

1 F. Braudel, *Civilisation and Capitalism Fifteenth to Eighteenth Century*, vol. I, *The Structures of Everyday Life: The Limits of the Possible*, London, 1981.

2 S. Roux, *La maison dans l'histoire*, Paris, 1976.

3 M. Eleb-Vidal and A. Debarre-Blanchard, *Architecture de la vie privée, XVIIIe–XIXe siècle*, Archives d'architecture moderne, Brussels, 1989.

4 M. de Certeau, L. Giard, P. Mayol, *L'invention du quotidien*, 2 vols., Paris, 1980, vol. I, *Art de faire*, vol. II, *Habiter et cuisiner*.

5 P. Deffontaines, *L'homme et sa maison*, Paris, 1972.

6 J. Cuisenier, *La maison rustique, logique sociale et composition architecturale*, Paris, 1991.

7 *Ibid.*, pp. 49–65; C. Estienne, *L'agriculture et maison rustique*, Paris, 1564.

8 Cuisenier, *La maison rustique*, pp. 49–65.

9 G. Bachelard, *La terre et les rêveries du repos*, Paris, 1948, pp. 95–6.

10 A. Pardailhé-Galabrun, *La naissance de l'intime 3,000 foyers parisiens, XVIIe–XVIII siècle*, Paris, 1988.

11 D. Roche, *The People of Paris*, Leamington Spa, 1987, pp. 116–23.

12 M. Segalen, *Maris et femmes dans la société paysanne*, Paris, 1980; *Sociologie de la famille*, Paris, 1981.

13 P. Bonnin, M. Perrot and M. de la Soudière, *L'Ostal en Margeride*, Paris, 1983.

14 Cuisenier, *La maison rustique*, pp. 16–17; A. Soboul, *La maison rurale*, Paris, 1955, reprinted 1996.

15 Cuisenier, *La maison rustique*, pp. 22–3, 27.

16 G.-H. Rivière, 'Le chantier 1425, un tour d'horizon, une gerbe de souvenirs', *Ethnologie française* 1973: 1–2, pp. 9–14.

17 A. Schweitz, *La maison tourangelle au quotidien, façons de bâtir, manières de vivre, 1850–1930*, Paris, 1997, pp. 80–1.

18 Cuisenier, *La maison rustique*, pp. 50–7; J.-M. Moriceau, *Les fermiers de L'Ile de France. L'ascension d'un patronat agricole, XVᵉ–XVIIIᵉ siècles*, Paris, 1994, vol. II, pp. 350–5.

19 Schweitz, *La maison tourangelle*, p. 82.

20 Cuisenier, *La maison rustique*, pp. 67–119.

21 N. Coquery, 'De l'hôtel aristocratique aux ministères: habitat, mouvement, espace á Paris au XVIIIᵉ siècle', 3 vols., thesis, University of Paris I, 1995, vol. I, pp. 290–311.

22 Roche, *The People*, pp. 98–116; J.-C. Perrot, *Genèse d'une ville moderne. Caen au XVIIIᵉ siècle*, Paris, 1994, vol. II, pp. 554–60.

23 D. Rabreau, 'Appollon en Province', University of Paris IV, thesis, 1985, pp. 399–450 (typescript).

24 A. Farge, *La vie fragile, violence, pouvoirs et solidarités à Paris au XVIIIᵉ siècle*, Paris, 1986, pp. 17–30.

25 *L'escalier dans l'architecture de la Renaissance*, transactions of colloquium at Tours, 22–26 May 1975, Paris, 1985, collection of architectures; also M. M. Fontaine, 'Images littéraires de l'escalier' in *ibid.*, pp. 111–16.

26 A. Farge, *Le vol d'aliments*, Paris, 1974, pp. 151–88; Roche, *The People*, pp. 120–7.

27 J. M. Roy, 'La géographie de l'accueil en garnis à Paris dans la seconde moitié du XVIIᵉ siècle', in *Mobilité et accueil à Paris (1650–1850)*, 1996, pp. 119–87.

28 S. Kaplan, *Le meilleur pain du monde. Les boulanges de Paris au XVIIIᵉ siècle*, Paris, 1996, pp. 280–284.

29 J. Jacquart, *L'habitat rural en Ile-de-France au XVIIᵉ siècle. La qualité de la vie au XVIIIᴱ siècle*, 7th colloquium of the C.M.R., Marseilles, 1977, pp. 69–74.

30 L. Gambi, 'Per una storia della abitazione rurale in Italia', *Rivista storica italiana*, 1964, pp. 430–51; E. Luzatti-Gregori, 'Cultura materiale, Storia sociale: note sulle case rurale dell'arca dell'insediamento sparso mezzadriale', *Societi e storia* 1983: 19, pp. 137–64.

31 Cuisenier, *La maison rustique*, pp. 137–8.

32 *Ibid.*, p. 140; M. Rosenfeld, *S. Serlio on Domestic Architecture*, New York and London, 1978, reproduces the original text and plans.

33 M. Rossi, *Il trattato di architettura di Sebastiano Serlio*, vol. II, *Il sesto libro delle habitation e di tutti le gradi degli Uomini*, Milan, 1967, pp. 61–5; Rosenfeld, *S. Serlio*, pp. 30–5.

34 Cuisenier, *La maison rustique*, pp. 166–7.

35 G. Désert, 'Maisons rurales et urbaines dans la France traditionnelle', in P. Chaunu, (ed.), *Le bâtiment. Enquête d'histoire économique, (XIVᵉ–XIXᵉ siècle)*. Paris and The Hague, 1971, pp. 35–119.

36 G. Cabourdin, *Terres et hommes en Lorraine, 1550–1635: Toulois et comté de Vandémont*, Nancy, 1977, pp. 543–60, 679–86.

37 P. Bousselle, *La maison, la vie populaire en France du Moyen Age à nos jours*, Paris, 1965, vol. III, pp. 11–150.

38 A. Croix, *La Bretagne aux XVIe et XVIIe siècles; la vie, la mort, la foi*, Paris, 1981, vol. II, pp. 781–804.

39 P. Goubert, *Beauvais et le Beauvaisis, 1600–1730. Contribution à l'histoire sociale de la France au XVIIe siècle*, Paris, 1960, pp. 151–78; *La vie quotidienne des paysans français au XVIIe siècle*, Paris, 1982, pp. 56–66.

40 G. Durand, *Vins, vignes et vignerons en Beaujolais*, Lyons, 1979, pp. 325–35, 385–7.

41 Moriceau, *Les fermiers*, pp. 249–65.

42 Jacquart, *L'habitat rural*, pp. 71–3.

43 I am grateful to C. Pascal for his comments and references.

44 P. Gouhier, 'La maison presbytérale en Normandie', in Chaunu (ed.), *Le bâtiment*, pp. 123–90.

45 Cuisenier, *La maison rustique*, pp. 338–9.

46 M. Garden, 'Quelques remarques sur l'habitat urbain. L'exemple de Lyon au XVIIIe siècle', *Annales de démographie historique, démographie et environnement*, 1975, pp. 29–35; Hugues Neveux, 'Recherche sur la construction et l'entretien des maisons à Cambrai de la fin du XVe siècle au debut du XVIIIe siècle', in Chaunu (ed.), *Le bâtiment*, pp. 123–275; J.-P. Bardet 'La maison rouennaise aux XVIIe et XVIIIe siècles. Economie et comportement', in *ibid.*, pp. 315–83.

47 R. Deseimon and C. Jouhaud, *La France du premier XVIIe siècle*, Paris, 1996, pp. 10–21.

48 J.-L. Harouel, *L'embellissement des villes. L'urbanisme français au XVIIIe siècle*, Paris, 1993, pp. 128–32, 148–88.

49 Perrot, *Genèse*, vol. II, pp. 639–42, 679–702.

50 M. Philipponeau, *La vie rurale de la banlieue parisienne. Essai de géographie humaine*, Paris, 1956.

51 C. Nières, *La reconstruction d'une ville au XVIIIe siècle. Rennes, 1720–1760*, Rennes, 1972, pp. 92–112, 277–330.

52 A. Picon, *Architectes et ingénieurs au Siècle des Lumières*, Marseilles, 1988.

53 P.-D. Boudriot, 'Une source pour l'étude de l'habitat parisien au début du XVIIe siècle: Pierre le Muet', *Histoire, Economie et Société*, 1985: 1, pp. 29–41.

54 Kaplan, *Le meilleur pain*, pp. 85–7.

55 D. Roche, *The Culture*, pp. 308–29.

56 C. Pascal's thesis has here and now changed our view of Paris in the seventeenth and eighteenth centuries where these points are concerned.

57 A. Guillerme, 'Technique et culture matérielle', E.H.E.S.S., 14 March 1995 (typescript), quotes Abbé Dillon, *Mémoire sur les trottoirs*, Paris, 1804, and *Second mémoire sur les trottoirs*, Paris, 1805.

58 P. Ariès, *L'enfant et la vie familiale sous l'Ancien Régime*, Paris, 1960, pp. 377–459.

59 J.-P. Goubert, *Du luxe au confort*, Paris, 1988, pp. 15–30.

60 P. Pinon, 'A travers révolutions architecturales et politiques', in L. Bergeron (ed.), *Genèse d'un paysage*, Paris, 1989, pp. 147–216.

61 Coquery, 'De l'hôtel', vol. I, pp. 305–9.

62 *Versailles, lecture d'une ville*, research report, CORDA, Versailles, 1978; P.-D. Boudriot, 'La construction locative parisienne sous Louis XV. De l'inerte à l'animé', 3rd cycle thesis, University of Paris IV, n.d. (1985), 2 vols. (typescript).

63 Nières, *La reconstruction*, pp. 92–130.
64 Garden, 'Quelques remarques', pp. 31–2.
65 M. Garden, *Lyon et les Lyonnais au XVIII ͤ siècle*, Paris, 1970, pp. 12–14, 410–15.
66 B. Hénin, 'La maison et la vie domestique à Marseille du XVII ͤ au XVIII ͤ siècle', 3rd cycle thesis, Aix-en-Provence, 1984, 3 vols. (typescript).
67 Roche, *The People*, pp. 104–8.
68 Pardailhé-Galabrun, *Naissance*, pp. 199–205.
69 Schweitz, *La maison tourangelle*, pp. 50–2.

5 LIGHTING AND HEATING

1   A. Schweitz, *La maison tourangelle au quotidien, façons de bâtir, manières de vivre. 1850–1930*, Paris, 1994, pp. 42–3. He stresses the progressive disappearance of this habitat during the nineteenth century, but estimates that it constituted about eight per cent of the dwellings subjected to inventory.
2   M. Boucher and J. Furic, *La maison rurale en Haute-Marche. Contribution à un inventaire régional*. Nonette-Saint-Germain-Lembron, 1984, pp. 8–10, 55–8.
3   *Ibid.*, pp. 35–6, 39–41, 48–9, 56–7.
4   D. Roche, *The People of Paris*, Leamington Spa, 1987, chapter 2.
5   J.-C. Perrot, *Genèse d'une ville moderne. Caen au XVIII ͤ siècle*, Paris, 1975, vol. II, pp. 913–15.
6   J.-L. Ménétra, *Journal of my Life*, D. Roche (ed.), pp. 299–316.
7   J. Vassort, *Une société provinciale face à son devenir: le Vendômois aux XVIII ͤ et XIX ͤ siècles*, Paris, 1996, pp. 330–50.
8   N. Belmont, *Mythes et croyances dans l'Ancienne France*, Paris, 1973, provides the principal bibliography.
9   G. Bachelard, *Psychanalyse du feu*, Paris, 1949; *Poétique de l'espace*, Paris 1957.
10 Bibliothèque nationale, Ms. FFr, 12671 (1698); P. Barbier and F. Vernillat, *Histoire de France par les chansons*, vol. II, *Mazarin et Louis XIV*, Paris, 1956, pp. 124–5.
11 J.-C. Perrot, *Gènese*, vol. II, pp. 663–4.
12 F.-G. Pariset, *Georges de La Tour*, Paris, 1948; J. Thuillier, *Georges de La Tour*, Paris, 1973, emphasises the link between light and the spirituality of childhood, pp. 7–8.
13 F. Braudel, *Civilisation and Capitalism, Fifteenth to Eighteenth Century*, vol. I, *The Structures of Everyday Life: The Limits of the Possible*, London, 1981, pp. 310–11.
14 H. R. d'Allemagne, *Histoire du luminaire depuis l'époque romaine jusqu'au XIX ͤ siècle*, Paris, 1891; E. Rebke, *Lampen, Lanternen, Leuchten*, Stuttgart, 1962; S. S. Wechsler-Kummel, *Chandeliers, appliques et lampes*, Freiburg, 1963; M. and P. Deribère, *Préhistoire et histoire de la lumière*, Paris, 1979.
15 Braudel, *Civilisation*, p. 310.
16 M. Sonenscher, *Work and Wages, Natural Law, Politics and the Eighteenth-Century French Trades*, Cambridge, MA, 1989, pp. 174–210; S. Kaplan, 'Réflexion sur la police du monde du travail, 1700–1815', *Revue historique 1979*, pp. 17–18.

17 V. Milliot, *La ville en bleu. Les représentations de la ville dans la littérature populaire, XVII*ᵉ*–XVIII*ᵉ *siècle*, Paris, 1996.

18 S. Kaplan, *Le meilleur pain*, pp. 247–53.

19 Sonenscher, *Work*, pp. 180–5.

20 The question of wages and that of productivity linked with the form of wages (by the hour, or piece work) and the problem of the way wages were paid (daily, weekly, monthly) conceal the argument about the exact length of the working day, which is, furthermore, inseparable from the length of the working week. It is therefore difficult to answer the question of the necessary technical arrangements on which we need to find evidence: cf. P. Minard, *Typographes des Lumières*, 1989, pp. 62–4. The fine imposed for forgetting to extinguish a candle was five sols, *Anecdotes typographiques de Nicolas Contat dit Le Brun*, G. Barber (ed.), Oxford, 1980, p. 87.

21 Roche, *The People*, pp. 100–18, 242–77; A. Farge, *Vivre dans la rue au XVIII*ᵉ *siècle*, Paris, 1979, pp. 21–37; T. Brennan, *Public Drinking and Popular Culture in Eighteenth-Century Paris*, Princeton, NJ, 1988, pp. 177–227.

22 R. Chartier, 'La ville dominante et soumise', in Histoire de la France urbaine, in G. Duby, (ed.), *La ville classique*, vol. II, Paris, 1981.

23 F. Souchal, *Les Slodtz, sculpteurs et décorateurs du roi*, Paris, 1967, pp. 426–7; S. Rials, 'La lumière à Paris au Siècle des Lumières', master's degree memoir, University of Paris X, 1973, pp. 150–4.

24 A.-C. Gruber, *Les grandes fêtes et leur décor à l'époque de Louis XVI*, Geneva and Paris, 1972, pp. 1–9; D. Roche, *Les Français et l'Ancien Régime*, vol. II, *Culture et Société*, Paris, 1984, pp. 255–68.

25 H. Lagrave, *Le Théatre et le public à Paris de 1715 à 1750*, Paris, 1972, pp. 204–6, 208–56.

26 Rials, 'La lumière', pp. 79–107.

27 *Mercure de France*, 1763, No. 2, pp. 105–12, 'Quel genre de décoration et quelle manière d'illuminer conviennent dans les églises', quoted in Rials, 'La lumière', pp. 106–7.

28 M. Lours, 'L'éclaircissement des églises parisiennes aux XVIIᵉ et XVIIIᵉ siècles', master's degree memoir, University of Paris I, 1995 (typescript).

29 *Ibid.*, pp. 42–4.

30 *Ibid.*, pp. 102–22.

31 *Ibid.*, p. 56: P. Le Vieil, *L'art de la peinture sur verre et la vitrerie*, Paris, 1774, p. 199; Abbé Laugier, *Observation sur l'architecture*, Paris, 1765, p. 129; J.-B. Thiers, *Dissertations ecclésiastiques sur les choeurs des églises*, Paris, 1688.

32 Chateaubriand, *Génie du christianisme*, 1802, Bibliothèque de la Pléiade, Paris, 1978, pp. 893–920.

33 S. Mercier, *Blanchisseurs d'église*, Tableau de Paris, vol. XII, p. 149. The clergy were here accused of having fostered a 'taste for luxury' in the churches.

34 D. Julia, *La Réforme post-tridente en France d'après les procès-verbaux de visites pastorales, ordres et resistances*, La Società religiosa nell'età moderni, Naples, 1973; I. Brian, 'Les génovéfains et la Contre-Reforme à la Révolution', doctoral thesis, University of Paris I, 2 vols., vol. I, pp. 300–1 (typescript), quoting Bibliothèque Sainte-Geneviève, MS. 1885, fo. 227; J. Berenger-Féraud, *Traditions et réminiscences populaires de la Provence*, Paris, 1886, pp. 135–57, 'Les feux de joie'.

35 J. Sgard, 'La métaphore nocturne', in *Eclectisme et cohérence des Lumières*, Festschrift for Jean Erhard, Paris, 1992, pp. 249–55.

36 J. Starobinski, *L'invention de la liberté, 1700–1789*, Paris, 1964, 86–7.

37 Rials, 'La Lumière', p. 122.

38 Perrot, *Genèse*, vol. II, pp. 641–56; Roche, *The People*, pp. 12–35.

39 A. Mérot, *Demeures mondaines*, Paris, 1990.

40 J.-B. Lemaitre, *La police de Paris en 1770*, with introduction and notes by A. Gazier, Paris, 1879, pp. 104–5; A. Williams, *The Police of Paris*, Baton Rouge, LA, 1979, pp. 222–3; P. Piacenza, *Policia e città, strategie d'ordine, conflitti e rivolte a Parigi tra sei e settecento*, Bologna, 1980, pp. 101–87; J. Chagniot, *Nouvelle histoire de Paris, Paris au XVIIIe siècle*, Paris, 1988, pp. 138–9.

41 H. Defrance, *Histoire de l'éclairage des rues de Paris*, Paris, 1904; Cdt Herlaut, 'L'éclairage des rues de Paris à la fin du XVIIe siècle et au XVIIIe siècle,' *Mémoires de la Société de l'Histoire de Paris et de l'Ile-de-France*, vol. XLIII, 1916, pp. 130–240; *L'éclairage de Paris à l'époque révolutionnaire*, Paris, 1932.

42 P. Patte. *De la manière la plus avantageuse d'éclairer les rues d'une ville pendant la nuit*, Amsterdam, 1766; Herlaut, 'L'éclairage des rues', p. 257 – he gives the number of lamp-posts as 3,500.

43 A. Guillerme, 'Technique et culture matérielle', E.H.E.S.S. seminar, Etudes sur les sciences et la technique, 14 March 1995, pp. 8–10 (typescript).

44 Perrot, *Genèse*, vol. II, pp. 662–3. Sources of light doubled between 1740–9 (257) and 1780–9 (500). The periphery of Caen was somewhat less well lit than the centre: 100 lamp-posts for 73 per cent of the town's area (27%), as against 270 for 27 per cent of the area, where 58 per cent of the population lived.

45 Lemaitre, 'La police', pp. 104–5; Herlaut, 'L'éclairage des rues', pp. 133–49, and *L'éclairage de Paris*, pp. 238–63. In 1794 the Sangrain lease counted 8,911 lamp-posts operating for 2,360 hours, and 4,375 operating for 1,375 hours, costing altogether 633,000 *livres* for oil.

46 Paris, 'Floréal, An X', B.N. Li 16 20.

47 M. Baulant, 'L'appréciation du niveau de vie. Un problème, une solution', *Histoire et Mesure* 1989: 4; pp. 267–302; F. Warro-Desjardins, 'La vie quotidienne dans le Vexin au XVIIIe siècle', in *L'Intimité d'une société rurale*, Pontoise, 1992, pp. 147–65; J.-M. Moriceau, *Les Fermiers de l'Ile de France. L'ascension d'un patronat agricole, XVe–XVIIIe siècles*, Paris, 1994, p. 754–70; F. Abollivier, 'La vie quotidienne d'après les inventaires après décès à Roscoff au XVIIIe siècle', master's degree memoir, University of Rennes II, 1993 (typescript); J. Burtin, 'Quatre-vingt-trois ans de vie quotidienne à Auxerre, 1741–1822', master's degree memoir, University of Paris XII, 1985, pp. 55–200 (typescript); S. Dinges, 'Culture matérielle des classes sociales inférieures à Bordeaux', *Bulletin de la Société archéologique de Bordeaux* 1986: 77, pp. 85–95; F. Vignot, 'Espaces domestiques et manières d'être en Brie, 1690–1767, une approche de la culture matérielle à Nangis à travers l'inventaire après décès', master's degree memoir, University of Paris XII, 1989, 2 vols., vol. I, pp. 155–61 (typescript).

48 F.-Y. Besnard. *Souvenirs d'un nonagénaire. Mémoires de F.-Y. Besnard publiés sur le mémoire autographe par Célestin Port*, Paris, 1880, pp. 28ff., describes the house of his great-grandmother about 1750–60, with its customs dating from

the seventeenth century, at La Chapelle-sur-Doué, in Anjou. 'A slender candle of resin (an *oribus*) stuck in one of the corners was almost all the lighting in poor households, and often rendered the same service on some evenings in the houses of people who could be thought comfortably off. Alternatively they might use a very simply made lamp, of copper or tin, fuelled with hempseed oil, the smell of which always seemed to me more unbearable than that of resin. Not only was the use of the wax taper unknown at the time, but candles which cost one *livre* for four or six were a sort of luxury. As a rule, they used one of the kind obtainable at eight or twelve per *livre*, and there was never more than one set on a table of the usual size.'

49 D. Diderot, *Oeuvres*, Bibliothèque de la Pléiade, 1962, *Lettre sur les aveugles à l'usage de ceux qui voient* (1749) pp. 811–72. The debate between sight, hearing and touch, from the sensualistic standpoint, is an important part of the history of sensibility and the senses. Diderot points out the principal difficulty in the problem: 'The aid that our senses give to each other prevents them from perfecting themselves', (p. 86). 'I conclude that we certainly draw considerable benefits from the co-operation of our senses and our sense-organs. It would be quite a different matter if we were to use them separately', (p. 819). The primacy of the visaul could be measured only by comparison.

50 Mercier, *Tableau de Paris*, vol. v, pp. 180–1; J.-F. Blondel, *Cours d'architecture ou traité de décoration. Distribution et construction des bâtiments*, Paris, 1771–7, 9 vols., vol. v, pp. 60–1; Rials, 'La Lumière' pp. 42–3.

51 J. Barrelet, *La verrerie en France, de l'époque gallo-romaine à nos jours*, Paris, 1971; Rials, 'La lumière', pp. 44–5: J.-F. Belhoste, 'La fabrication du verre plat en France xviie–debut xixe siècle)', in *Le verre, matériau de construction*, Ecole nationale du patrimoine, 6–7 May 1996: G.-M. Leproux, *L'apparition de la fenêtre à petit bois à Paris au xviie siècle*; S. Lagabrielle, *La baie à travers l'iconographie (xve–xviiie siècle)*, forthcoming.

52 F.-Y. Besnard, *Souvenirs*, pp. 12–13: 'The few windows in each house were small, either in width or in height, and often consisted of a single pane. The glazing of almost all of them was made of small lozenge-shaped pieces of glass fitted into small strips of lead which were folded over their edges. However, people were beginning to instal bigger windows . . . with astragals separating the panes.'

53 Mérot, *Demeures mondaines*, pp. 59–65; P. Thornton, *L'époque et son style, 1620–1920*, Paris, 1986 (*Authentic Decor: Domestic Interior, 1620–1920*, London, 1994).

54 Roche, *The People*, pp. 152–4: A. Pardailhé-Galabrun, *Naissance de l'intime. 3 000 foyers parisiens, xviie*, pp. 366–401.

55 Pardailhé-Galabrun, *Naissance*, pp. 343–8. For Paris the average was five lighting-sources per inventory. This increased a little after 1760. The figure varied greatly between socal categories, but was not lower for the lower orders than for the other groups: three or four lighting-sources in about 1700, five or six towards 1780. Better relative lighting did not become a privilege of the rich before the technological revolutions of the nineteenth century.

56 I am grateful to Robert Descimon for this information.

57 A. N., Z^1 652, 24 November 1774, fo. 3.

58 Perrot, *Caen*, vol. II, pp. 906–17.

59 D. d'Allemagne, *Les casernes françaises*, Paris, 1990.

60 B. Bensaude, *Lavoisier, Mémoires d'une Révolution*, Paris, 1993; F. Abbri, *Le terre, l'acqua, le arie*, Bologna, 1984.

61 I am most grateful to M. D. Blouin, whose thesis which was supervised by F. Caron, will definitely change our view of the technologies, science and heat-economy of the eighteenth and nineteenth centuries, for the advice he has generously given me.

62 M. Vernus, *La vie comtoise au temps de l'Ancien Régime*, 2 vols, Lons-le-Saunier, 1982, vol. I, pp. 135–59, vol. II, pp. 25–39.

63 Schweitz, *La maison*, pp. 70–9.

64 Boudriot, 'Une source', and 'La maison à loyer. Etude du bâtiment à Paris sous Louis XV', *Histoire, Economie et Société*, 1982: 2, pp. 115–25.

65 Boudriot, 'Une source', p. 38.

66 Mérot, 'Demeures', pp. 35–41, quoting P. Collet, *Pièces d'architectures où sont compris plusieurs cheminées*, Paris, 1653, and J. Le Pautre, *Cheminées à la moderne*, Paris, 1661, *Cheminées a l'italienne*, Paris, 1665; P. Verlet, *La maison du XVIIIe siècle*, Paris, 1966.

67 Mérot, 'Demeures', pp. 68.

68 Boehler, *Une société rurale en milieu rhénan, la paysannene de la plaine d'Alsace, 1648–1789*, 3 vols., Strasbourg, 1995, vol. II, pp. 1574–85.

69 *Espargnebois*, i.e.: 'New and hitherto neither common nor well-known invention of certain and diverse artifical furnaces, by the use of which one can save, every year, a vast amount of wood and other combustibles, and nevertheless maintain from stoves a heat both comfortable and more salubrious: written first in German, for the public good and profit of Germany and made known through pictures showing the said furnaces. Published now in French for the public good and profit of France and of all who use that language.' Oppenheim, H. Galler for J. Théodore de Bry, 1619, quarto, 72 pages, five plates (copy in B. N. V11152).

70 F. Keslar, *Epargne-Bois*, Oppenheim, 1619, p. 57.

71 Mercier, *Tableau de Paris*, vol. X, p. 303.

72 *Mémoires d'outre-tombe*, Bibliothèque de la Pléiade, 2 vols., Paris, vol. I, pp. 79–83.

73 Roche, *The People*, pp. 133–4; Pardailhé-Galabrun, *Naissance*, pp. 289–92, 335–8, 388–94.

74 Perrot, *Caen*, vol. II, pp. 914–16.

75 Mercier, *Tableau de Paris*, vol. I, p. 49, vol. X, pp. 306–7; see also vol. VII, *Bois à bruler*, pp. 85–7, and vol. XII, *Bois flotté*, pp. 204–8.

76 Roche, *The People*, pp. 139–41.

77 D. Roche, 'L'économie et la sociabilité de l'accueil à Paris, XVIIIe–XIXe siècle', in *Mobilité et accueil à Paris, 1650–1850*, pp. 189–269.

78 J. Boissière, 'Populations et économies du bois dans la France moderne. Contribution à l'étude des milieux forestiers entre Paris et le Morvan au dernier siècle de l'Ancien Régime (vers 1685–vers 1790)', 3 vols., state doctorate thesis, University of Paris I, 1993, vol. III, 'Consommations urbaines', pp. 29–108.

79 H. Bourquin, L' Approvisionnement en bois de Paris de la Régence à la Révolution, law degree thesis, Paris, n.d.

80 Boissière, 'Populations', vol. III, pp. 133–7, where he comments learnedly on the material in Mercier's *Tableau de Paris*.

81 *Les Arts des Mines*, 3 vols., 1768–74, reprinted Geneva 1988, vol. II, pp. 643–95 for the trade, vol. III, pp. 1115–299 for industrial and domestic uses. Cf. also *Mémoirs sur les feux de houille ou charbon de terre*, vol. III, pp. 2–14, where the writer refutes the arguments of this opponents and discredits travellers' stereotypes, such as Grosley on English melancholy due to coal fires, or Baron de Polnitz on the bad smell of Liège, p. 28–33.

82 Mercier, *Tableau de Paris*, vol. X, pp. 310–11.

6 WATER AND ITS USE

1 J.-P. Goubert, *La conquête de l'eau du XVIIIe au XXe siècle*, Paris, 1986.

2 A. Guillerme, 'Quelques problèmes de l'eau dans les villes du Bassin parisien au Moyen Age', 3rd cycle thesis, E.H.E.S.S, 1981, 2 vols. , vol. I, pp. 119–35 (typescript); cf. also the revised version *Le Temps de l'eau, la cité, l'eau et les techniques, Nord de la France, fin XVIIe–début XIXe siècle*, Paris, 1983.

3 G. Bertrand, 'Pour une histoire écologique de la France rural', in *Histoire de la France rurale*, G. Duby (ed.) vol. I, pp. 37–111; Schweitz, *La maison tourangelle au quotidien, façons de bâtir, manières de vivre, 1850–1930*, Paris, 1997, pp. 75–6.

4 J. Gélis, *L'Arbre et le fruit. La naissance dans l'Occident moderne (XVIe–XIXe siècle)*, Paris, 1984; Y. Verdier, *Façons de dire, façons de faire*, Paris, 1979.

5 G. Bachelard, *L'eau et les rêves*, Paris, 1942, pp. 5–6, 170–210.

6 P. Saintyves, *Le corpus du folklore des eaux en France et dans les colonies françaises*, Paris, 1934: P. Sébillot, *Les eaux douces*, Paris, 1983; B. Caulier, *Les cultes thérapeutiques autour des fontaines en France du Moyen Age à nos jours*, Paris, 1990.

7 L. Chevalier, *Classes laborieuses et classes dangereuses*, Paris, 1958.

8 Guillerme, 'Quelques problèmes', vol. I, pp. 105–9.

9 A. L. Lavoisier, *Oeuvres*, J.-C. Perrot (ed.), Paris, 1862–93, 6 vols. pp. 142–4.

10 Bertrand, 'Pour une histoire', pp. 68–9, 78–9.

11 Guillerme, 'Quelques problèmes', vol. II. pp. 109–10.

12 J.-P. Babelon, *Demeures parisiennes sous Henri IV et Louis XIII*, Paris, 1967; M. Gallet, *La maison parisienne au XVIIIe siècle*, Paris, 1969.

13 I. Backouche, 'La Seine et Paris, 1750–1850. Pratiques, aménagements, représentations', doctorate thesis, E.H.E.S.S., 1996, 2 vols. (typescript).

14 A. N. Z^te, 307–8; Caroline Cammel, 'La Bièvre du XVIIe au XIXe siècle. Eau et industrie', master's degree memoir, University of Paris I (typescript); H. Burstin, *Le faubourg Saint-Marcel a l'époque révolutionnaire. Structure économique et composition sociale*, Paris, 1983, pp. 24–7.

15 A. Parmentier, *Dissertations sur la nature des eaux de la Seine*, Paris, 1787: C. Audin-Rouvière, *Essai sur la topographie physique et médicale de Paris*, Paris, an II (1794). C. Lachaise, Topographie médicale de Paris, Paris, 1822; D. Menuret de Chambaud, *Essai sur l'histoire médico-topographique de Paris*, Paris, 1786.

16 J. Favier, *Nouvelle histoire de Paris, Paris au XVe siècle, 1380–1500*, Paris, 1974, pp. 28–30: J.-P. Babelon, *Nouvelle histoire de Paris, Paris au XVIe siècle*, Paris, 1987, pp. 284–93; R. Pillorget, *Nouvelle histoire de Paris: Paris sous les premiers Bourbons*, Paris, 1988, pp. 153–5, 166–7; G. Dethan, *Nouvelle histoire de Paris: Paris au temps de Louis XIV, 1660–1715*, Paris, 1990, pp. 78–80, 400–1; J.

Chaignot, *Nouvelle histoire de Paris, Paris au XVIIIe siècle*, Paris, 1988, pp. 110–17, 168–71, 280–94.

17 Backouche, 'La Seine'.

18 B. Fortier, *La Maîtrise de l'eau, XVIIIe siècle*, Paris, 1977, pp. 193–201.

19 Backouche, 'La Seine', pp. 177–229.

20 J.-M. Chaplain, *La Chambre des tisseurs, Louviers, cité drapière, 1680–1840*, Paris, 1984.

21 J. Jacquart, *L'habitat rural en Ile de France au XVIIe siècle*. La qualité de la vie au XVIIIe siècle, 7th colloquium of the C.M.R., Marseilles, 1977, pp. 69–73: J. Jacquart, *Aspects de l'architecture rurale en Ile-de-France*. Exposition, Paris, 1975; O.Tulippe, *L'habitat rural en Seine-et-Oise. Essai de géographie du peuplement*, Paris–Liege, 1934; J. Jacquart, *La crise rurale en Ile-de-France, 1550–1670*, Paris, 1974, chapters 1 and 18.

22 J.-J. Rousseau, *Essai sur l'origine des langues* in *Oeuvres completes*, vol. X, Paris, 1995: introduction by J. Starobinski, clxv–cciv.

23 Starobinski, introduction to Rousseau, *Essai*, pp. clxxxiv–clxxxvi.

24 Rousseau, *Essai*, pp. 405–6.

25 Caulier, 'Les cultes', pp. 60–82.

26 J.-Y. Hugoniot, *L'architecture de l'eau en Berry*, Actes du congrès national des Sociétés savantes, Poitiers, 1986; *Usage et représentation de l'eau*, Paris, 1986, pp. 213–44.

27 Guillerme, 'Quelques problèmes', pp. 60–2; P. Diffré, 'Historique de l'alimentation en eau de Paris, *Bulletin du B.G.R.M.* 1967, pp. 3–22.

28 P.-S. Girard, *Recherches sur les eaux de Paris*, Paris, 1812; P.-S. Girard, *Des puits forés et artésiens*, 1833; E. Belgrand, *Travaux souterrains de Paris*, Paris, 1877–82, 5 vols., vol. III; Diffré, 'Historique', pp. 16–17; Hurtaut and Magny, *Dictionnaire historique de la ville de Paris et de ses environs*, Paris, 1779, 2 vols., vol. II, pp. 678–9: the authors considered 20 *pintes*, per day per inhabitant were needed, or 18.6 litres; for 800,000 inhabitants nearly 15 million litres would be needed – five million from the aqueducts and the pumps and the remaining two-thirds from the water-carriers.

29 S. Kaplan, *Le meilleur pain du monde. Les boulangers de Paris au XVIIIe siècle*, Paris, 1996, pp. 87–8, with references on pp. 630–2.

30 L. Baumont-Maillet, *L'eau à Paris*, photographs by J.-F. Baumard, Paris, 1992.

31 Guillerme, 'Quelques problèmes', p. 64.

32 J. Grinewald, 'L'architecture hydraulique au XVIIIe siècle, un paradigme vitruvien. Contribution à une sociologie historique des techniques', *Itinéraire* 1979, pp. 150–210.

33 Fortier, *La maîtrise*, pp. 199–200.

34 J. Payen, *Capital et machine à vapeur au XVIIIe siècle: les frères Périer et l'introduction en France de la machine à vapeur de Watt*, Paris and The Hague, 1969; J. Bouchary, *Les compagnies financieres à la fin du XVIIe siècle*, Paris, 1939–43.

35 Fortier, *La Maîtrise*, p. 200.

36 A. Mousset, *Les Francine*, Paris, 1930: until Eric Souillard's thesis on the waters of Versailles is ready, see 'Les eaux de Versailles', master's degree memoir, Paris, 1988 (typescript) and 'Recherches sur la technique des eaux a

Versailles aux xviie et xviiie siècles', DEA memoir, University of Paris 1, 1994.
37 D. Roche, *The People of Paris: an Essay in Popular Culture in the Eigheenth Century*, Leamington Spa, 1987 pp. 157–8. The figures in the following table give an idea of the average and modal distribution and of its evolution, calculated on the basis of the capacity of the utensils recorded by the registrar.

Quantity		1695–1715 Wage-earners (61)		Servants (38)		1775–1790 Wage-earners (14)		Servants (88)	
1 pail	15l	10	17%	10	26%	1	7%	12	13%
2 pails	30l	15	25%	9	24%	3	21%	73	82%
3–4 pails	58l	25	39%	10	26%	8	56%	3	5%
More than 4 pails	87l	11	19%	9	24%	2	14%	–	–
Average per family		49 litres		28 litres		43 litres		61 litres	

38 D. Roche, *The Culture of Clothing*, Cambridge, 1994, pp. 364–95.
39 G. Vigarello, *Le Propre et le sale*, Paris, 1985, and *Le Sain et le malsain*, Paris, 1993.
40 J. Guillerme, *Le malsain et l'économie de la nature*, xviiie siècle, Paris, 1979, pp. 61–72.
41 F. Loux and P. Richard, *Sagesse du corps. La santé et la maladie dans les proverbes français*, Paris, 1978, pp. 24–30, 105–8.
42 F. Gaiffe, *L'envers du Grand Siècle*, Paris, 1924.
43 N. Elias, *La civilisation des moeurs* (French trans.), 1973; Eng. trans. *The Civilising Process, vol. I, The History of Manners*, Oxford, 1978.
44 Roche, *Culture*, pp. 118–83.
45 Vigarello, *Le Propre*, pp. 90–5.
46 *Ibid.*, pp. 84–7.
47 R. Chartier, *La civilité entre distinction et divulgation*, Historische Lexicon der Politisch-sozialen Grundbegriffe in Frankreich von Ancien Régime zur Revolution, 1680–1820, Munich, 1986; J. Revel, 'Les usages de la civilité', *Histoire de la vie privée*, ed. P. Ariès and R. Chartier (eds.), vol. III, pp. 169–210.
48 Erasmus, *La civilité puerilé*, trans. A. Bonneau, P. Ariès (ed.), Paris, 1977, p. 71.
49 Chartier, *La Civilité*, pp. 11–12; A. de Courtin, *Nouveau traité de la civilité qui se pratique en France parmi les honnêtes*, Paris, 1671, pp. 28–9; J.-B. de La Salle, *Les règles de la bienséance et de la civilité chrétienne*, Reims, 1703, pp. 101–2.
50 C. Rimbault, 'Le corps à travers les manuels de civilité', master's degree memoir, University of Paris VII, 1977.
51 Vigarello, *Le Propre*, pp. 49–89.
52 L. Pérez, Le vêtement dans les logiques médicales à la fin du xviiie siècle et au debut du xixe siècle, master's degree memoir, University of Paris 1, 1982.
53 F. Loux and P. Richard, *Sagesse du corps. La santé et la maladie dans les proverbes français*, Paris, 1978, pp. 124–6.
54 N. Pellegrin, 'Chemises et chiffons. Le vieux et le neuf en Poitou au xviiie et xixe siècle', *Ethnologie française* 1986: 3, pp. 283–94.
55 Roche, *Culture*, pp. 370–8.
56 S. Mercier, *Tableau de Paris*, Paris and Amsterdam, 1782–9, vol. v, pp. 117–18.

57 *Mémoires de la Société d'agriculture de Paris*, vol. III, n.d., pp. 312–28, on the laundering of linen in the American islands by Count Moreau-Saint-Méry. I am grateful to D. Margairaz for bringing this passage to my notice.

58 *La science de la santé, soit pour le moral, soit pour le physique, ou Hygiène encyclopédique*, Avignon, 1813, pp. 54, 82–3.

59 L.-C.-H. Macquart, *Dictionnaire de la conservation de l'homme*, Paris, year VII, 2 vols., vol. I, pp. 352–5.

60 A. Pardailhé-Galabrun, *La Naissance de l'intime, 3,000 foyers parisians, XVIIe–XVIIIe siècles*, Paris, 1988, pp. 360–5.

61 D. Massounié, 'L'architecture des bains privés, 1650–1810', master's degree memoir (art history), Paris, 1993, pp. 55–75. I am grateful to D. Rabreau and D. Massounié for their help on this point.

62 N. Restif de la Bretonne, 'Les nuits de Paris', in *Paris le jour, Paris la nuit*, D. Baruch (ed.), Paris, 1990, pp. 912–14.

63 J.-C.Perrot, *Genèse d'une ville moderne: Caen au XVIIIe siècle*, 2 vols., Paris, 1975, vol. II, pp. 906–16; Roche, *The People*, pp. 44–52.

64 A. Corbin, *Le miasme et la jonquille. L'odorat et l'imaginaire social*, Paris, 1982; P.-R. Gleichmann, *Des villes propres et sans odeur*, Urbi, 1982, pp. 88–100.

65 Fortier, *La Maîtrise*, p. 194.

7 FURNITURE AND OBJECTS

1 F. Braudel, *Civilisation and Capitalism, Fifteenth to Eighteenth Century*, vol. I, *The Structures of Everyday Life: The Limits of the Possible*, London, 1981, pp. 303–6.

2 F. Dagognet, 'Preface' to B. Deloche, *L'Art du meuble*, Lyons, 1985, pp. 12–13.

3 M. Praz, *The House of Life*, London, 1964, and *An Illustrated History of Interior Decoration*, London, 1964.

4 S. Tardieu, *Le Mobilier rural traditionnel français*, Paris, 1976, pp. 10–11.

5 *Ibid.*, pp. 13–14.

6 D. Roche, *The People of Paris, an Essay in Popular Culture in the Eighteenth Century*, Leamington Spa, 1987, pp. 118–20; A. Schweitz, *La Maison tourangelle au quotidien*, pp. 114–18.

7 B. Deloche, *L'Art du meuble. Introduction à l'esthetique des arts mineurs, suivis de L'Art du meuble a Lyon au XVIIIe siècle et Formaliser l'analyse stylistique*, Lyons, 1985. I should like to pay tribute to this work, which was not widely read and is now out of print and can be consulted only in the Sorbonne library (Sibil 448.096).

8 G. Bachelard, *Poétique de l'espace*, Paris, 1957, pp. 82–3.

9 H. Lafon, *Les décors et les choses dans le roman français du XVIIIe siècle, de Prévost à Sade*, Oxford, 1992.

10 M. Pradines, *Traité de psychologie générale*, vol. II, *Le génie humain*, Paris, 1947, pp. 336–45, quoted in Deloche, *L'Art du meuble*, p. 24; P. Francastel, *Le style Empire*, Paris, 1939, p. 26.

11 B. Deloche, 'Le statut de l'artisan, un test de la modernité de l'Encyclopédie', *Milieux*, 1984–5: 19–20, pp. 79–87.

12 E. E. Viollet-le-Duc, *Dictionnaire raisonné du mobilier français*, Paris, 1871–5;

H. Havard, *L'art à travers les moeurs*, Paris, 1882 and *Dictionnaire de l'ameuble-ment*, Paris, 1887–9; for peasant furniture, J. Cuisenier, *L'art populaire en France*, Freiburg, 1975.

13 Deloche, *L'art*, pp. 24–5, 28.

14 *Ibid.*, pp. 33–5.

15 Tardieu, *Le mobilier*, pp. 48–51; see also *La vie domestique dans le Mâconnais pré-industriel*, Paris, 1964, which uses post–mortem inventories of the eight-eenth and nineteenth centuries.

16 S. Giedion, *La mécanisation au pouvoir*, Paris, 1980, pp. 269–78 (French trans. of *Mechanisation Takes Command*, Oxford and New York, 1948); B. Deloche, *Le mobilier bourgeois à Lyon au XVIIIe siècle*, Lyons, 1983, pp. 14–25, 153–4.

17 Lafon, *Les décors*, pp. 260–2.

18 Pradines, *Traité*, vol. II, p. 341: Deloche, *L'art*, pp. 49–70.

19 Roche, *The People*, p. 148.

20 J. Arnaboldi, *La table dans la vie populaire en France du Moyen Age à nos jours*, Paris, 1965, *Les Français et la table*, preface by J. Cuisenier, Paris, 1986; Z. Gourerier, *Modèles de cour et usages de table: les origines, Versailles et les tables royales en Europe*, Paris, 1993, pp. 15–34: C. Arminjon, *Les objets de table royaux français du XVIe au XVIIe siècle*, Paris, 1993, pp. 33–9; B. Saule, *Tables royales à Versailles, 1682–1789*, Paris, 1994, pp. 41–68.

21 H. Juin, *Le lit dans l'art*, Paris, 1980; P. Dibie, *Ethnologie de la chambre à coucher*, Paris, 1987, pp. 81–180.

22 Tardieu, *Le mobilier*, pp. 94–8; A. Croix, *La Bretagne aux XVIe et XVIIe siècles: la vie, la mort, la foi*, Paris, 1981, vol. II, pp. 803–4.

23 A. Pardailhe-Galabrun, *La naissance de l'intime, 3,000 foyers parisiens, XVIIe–XVIIIe siècles*, Paris, 1988, pp. 255–66, 275–87: Roche, *The People*, pp. 130–2.

24 J.-L. Flandrin, *Familles, parenté, maison, sexualité dans l'ancienne France*, Paris, 1976; F. Lebrun, *La Vie conjugale sous l'Ancien Régime*, Paris, 1975.

25 Pardailhé-Galabrun, *Naissance*, pp. 279–80.

26 J.-C. Bans and P. Gaillard-Bans, 'Maisons et bâtiments agricoles dans l'Ancien Régime en Vannetais', *Revue d'histoire moderne et contemporaine* 1984: vol. 31, pp. 3–26.

27 Pradines, *Traité*, vol. III, pp. 340–5; Deloche, *L'Art*, pp. 56–7.

28 N. Elias, *La Société des Coeurs*, p. 77.

29 Tardieu, *Le mobilier*, pp. 72–85.

30 Deloche, *L'art*, pp. 71–95.

31 P. Verlet, *Société, décoration, mobilier. La maison du XVIIIe siècle en France*, Paris, 1966; above all we have the essential work by C. Sargentson, *Merchants and Luxury Markets. The Marchands Merciers of Eighteenth-Century Paris*, London, 1996; see also L. Auslander, *Taste and Power. Furnishing Modern France*, Berkeley and Los Angeles, CA and London, 1996.

32 A. Thillay, 'Le faubourg Saint-Antoine et la liberté du travail sous l'Ancien Régime', *Histoire, Economie, Société* 1992: 2, pp. 217–36.

33 Tardieu, *Le mobilier*, pp. 13–14.

34 Roche, *The People*, pp. 129–34.

35 J.-M. Boehler, *Une société rurale en milieu rhénan, la paysannerie de la plaine d'Alsace, 1648–1789*, 3 vols., Strasbourg, 1995, vol. II, pp. 1620–51.

36 F. Waro-Desjardins, 'Permanences et mutations de la vie domestique en

France au XVIIIe siècle, un village du Vexin français', *Revue d'histoire moderne et contemporaine* 1993: 40, 1993 and 'La vie quotidienne dans le Vexin au XVIIIe siécle', in *L'intimité d'une société rurale*, Pontoise, 1992, pp. 46–110.

37 Verlet, *Société*, pp. 32–4.

38 N. Coquery, De l'hôtel aristocratique aux ministères. Habitat, mouvement, espace à Paris au XVIIIe siècle, doctorate thesis, University of Paris I, 1995 (typescript). vol. I, pp. 35–220.

39 D. Roche, 'Le Marais au milieu du XVIIIe siècle', master's degree memoir, University of Paris-Sorbonne, 2 vols., 1959, pp. 75–108.

40 Tardieu, *Le mobilier*, pp. 148–76.

41 E. Kant, *Critique of Pure Reason*, Bohn's Philosophical Library, London, 1897, p. 167.

42 P.-D. Boudriot, 'La maison à loyer. Etude du bâtiment à Paris sous Louis XV', *Histoire, Economie et Société* 1982: 2, pp. 33–4.

43 Roche, *The People*, p. 130; Pardailhé-Galabrun, *Naissance*, pp. 275–85.

44 S. Dinges, 'Culture matérielle des classes sociales inférieures à Bordeaux', *Bulletin de la Société archéologique de Bordeaux* 1986: 77, pp. 90–1.

45 A. Fillon, *Comme on fait son lit on se couche. 300 ans d'histoire du lit villageois, populations et cultures*. Festschrift for F. Lebrun, Rennes, 1989, pp. 153–64.

46 Boehler, *Une société*, vol. II, pp. 1639–41.

47 Waro-Desjardins, 'Permanences', pp. 3–29.

48 Schweitz, *La Maison*, pp. 211–16. In the Touraine of the nineteenth and twentieth centuries the bed is always the sanctuary of domestic life, a secret piece of furniture enclosed by curtains, and is the household's big investment. In nearly 300 inventories we find 600 beds, 275 of them in the common room, 175 in the bedroom, 64 in a second bedroom. Bedding was still essential in order to meet the needs for isolation from the ground, damp, cold and noise.

49 Lafon, *Les Décors*, pp. 199–200, 260–70.

50 Roche, *The People*, pp. 146–50; Pardailhé-Galabrun, *Naissance*, pp. 316–24.

51 Boehler, *Une société*, vol. II, pp. 1634–5.

52 Waro-Desjardins, 'La vie quotidienne', pp. 79–103: F. Vignot, '*Espaces domestiques et matières d'être en Brie, 1690–1767, une approche de la culture matérielle à Nangis à travers l'inventaire après décès*', master's memoir, University of Paris III, 1989, pp. 135–44; J. Burtin, 'Quatre-vingt-trois ans de vie quotidienne à Auxerre, 1741–1822', master's degree memoir, University of Paris XII, 1985, pp. 104–7 (typescript); F. Abollivier, 'La vie quotidienne d'aprés les inventaires aprés décès à Roscoff au XVIIIe siècle', master's memoir, University of Rennes II, 1993, pp. 106–10 (typescript); Schweitz, *La Maison*, pp. 203–10.

53 P. Haudrère, 'Esquisse d'une histoire des intérieurs angevins au XVIIIe siècle,' *Annales de Bretagne et des pays de l'Ouest* 1992: 3, pp. 227–42.

54 Schweitz, *La maison*, pp. 207–8.

55 Roche, *The People*, ch. 8: Pardailhé-Galabrun, *Naissance*, pp. 105–88.

56 Waro-Desjardins, 'La vie quotidienne', pp. 74–6.

57 Schweitz, *La maison*, pp. 210–20.

58 Boehler, *Une société*, vol. II, pp. 1538–1639.

59 I am grateful here to C. Pascal and N. Coquery for their observations and their unflagging help.

8 CLOTHING AND APPEARANCES

1 George M. Darwin, 'Development in Dress', *Macmillan's Magazine* September 1872, pp. 410–16.

2 N. Pellegrin, 'Le vêtement comme fait social', in *Histoire sociale, histoire globale*, C. Charle (ed.), Paris, 1993, pp. 81–94.

3 L. Godard de Donville, *Signification de la mode sous Louis XIII*, Aix–en–Provence, 1978.

4 N. Pellegrin, 'Travestissements', in *Dictionnaire de l'Ancien Régime*, L. Bely (ed.), Paris, 1996.

5 N. Pellegrin, *Vêtements de peau(x) et de plumes: la nudité des Indiens et la diversité du monde au XVI⁰ siècle, voyager à la Renaisssance*, Paris 1987, pp. 509–46; O. Blanc, 'Images du monde et portraits d'habits: les recueils de costume à la Renaissance', *Bulletin du Bibliophile* 1995: 2, pp. 221–61; F. Piponnier and P. Mane, *Se vêtir au Moyen Age*, Paris, 1995.

6 O. Blanc, 'Images', pp. 223–4.

7 N. Pellegrin, 'Costumes regionaux', in *Dictionnaire de l'Ancien Régime* (see n. 4).

8 R. Barthes, 'Histoire et sociologie du vêtement,' *Annales, Economie, Société, Civilisations;* 1957: 3, pp. 430–41.

9 N. Pellegrin, 'Costumes, coutumes', in *Dictionnaire de l'Ancien Régime* (see n.4): for an example of highly typed costume, that of sailors, A. Cabantous, *Citoyens au large*, Paris, 1995, pp. 87–90; C. Lévi-Strauss, 'Histoire et ethnologie', *Annales, Economie, Société, Civilisations;* 1983: 38, pp. 1217–31.

10 D. Roche, *The Culture of Clothing*, Cambridge, 1994; F. Piponnier, *Costume et vie sociale. La Cour d'Anjou, XIV⁰–XV⁰ siècle*, Paris and The Hague, 1970; Y. Deslandres, *Le Costume, image de l'homme*, Paris, 1976; P. Perrot, *Les Dessus et les dessous de la bourgeoisie, une histoire du vêtement au XIX⁰ siècle*, Paris, 1981; Piponnier and Mane, *Se vêtir*.

11 D. Diderot, 'Correspondance litteraire', 15 February 1769, *Oeuvres complètes*, R. Levinter (ed.), Paris, 1967, vol. VIII, pp. 7–13.

12 Roche, *The Culture*, pp. 450–2.

13 G. Audisio, *Des paysans, XV⁰–XX⁰ siècle*, Paris, 1993, vol. I; M. Baulant, 'Niveaux de vie paysans autour de Meaux en 1700 et 1750', *Annales, Economie, Société, Civilisation;*, 1975: 2–3, pp. 505–18; J. M. Boehler, *Une société rurale en milieu rhénan, la paysannerie de la plaine d'Alsace, 1648–1789*, 3 vols., Strasbourg, 1995, vol. II, pp. 1663–73: L. Bouquin, 'Les objets de la vie quotidienne dans la première moitié du XVI⁰ siècle à travers cent inventaires après décès parisiens', *Revue d'Histoire Moderne et Contemporaine:* 1989 36, pp. 464–75; A. Croix, *La Bretagne aux XVI⁰ et XVII⁰ siècles: la vie, la mort, la foi*, Paris, 1981: B. Garnot, *Un declin: Chartres au XVIII⁰ siècle*, Paris, 1991: O. Magyar-Thevenin, 'Etude comparative du mode de vie des recteurs et laboureurs, l'exemple du Vannetais au début du XVIII⁰ siècle', *Annales de Bretagne et des pays de l'Ouest*, 1987: 4, pp. 197–211; J.-M. Moriceau, *Les fermiers de l'Ile-de-France. L'ascension d'un patronat agricole, XV⁰–XVIII⁰ siècles*, Paris, 1994, pp. 754–69; R. Muchembled, *L'Invention de l'homme moderne. Sensibilités, moeurs et comportements collectifs sous l'Ancien Régime*, Paris, 1988, pp. 408–50; N. Pellegrin, *Ruralité et modernité du textile en haut Poitou au XVIII⁰ siècle. La leçon des inventaires après décès. Textile: production et mode,*

Proceedings of the 112th congress of the *Sociétés savantes*, Paris, 1987, pp. 377–96; F. Waro-Desjardin 'La vie quotidienne dans le Vexin au XVIIIe siècle', in *L'intimité d'une société rurale*, Pontoise, 1992, pp. 167–222; F. Vignot, 'Espaces domestiques et manières d'être en Brie, 1690–1767: une approche de la culture matérielle à Nangis à travers l'inventaire aprés décès', master's degree memoir, 2 vols., University of Paris III, 1989, vol. I, pp. 205–30; J. Burtin, 'Quatre-vingt-trois ans de vie quotidienne à Auxerre, 1741–1822', master's degree memoir, University of Paris XII 1985, pp. 108–24; F. Abollivier, 'La vie quotidienne d'après les inventaires après décès à Roscoff au XVIIIe siècle', master's degree memoir, University of Rennes II, 1993, pp. 206–30. I am grateful to A. Croix for having sent me the works of his students.

14 N. Pellegrin, *Les vêtements de la liberté, abécédaire des pratiques vestimentaires françaises de 1780–1800*, Aix, 1989.

15 *Ibid.*, pp. 81–4.

16 H. Medick, 'Une culture de la considération, les vêtements et leurs couleurs à Laichingen, 1750–1820', *Annales, Economie, Société, Civilisations;* 1995, pp. 753–73. It is useful to note the great difference of context between eighteenth-century Swabia and France: in Swabia the sumptuary laws were enforced, and rural society kept watch on the relation between appearance and social status in a way which, as I see it, had no equivalent in France before the nineteenth century.

17 Y. Verdier, *Façons de dire, façons de faire*, Paris, 1979; D. Fabre, 'Passeuses au gué du destin', *Critique* 1980, pp. 1075–99.

18 F.-Y. Besnard, *Souvenirs d'un nonagénaire. Mémoires de F.-Y. Besnard publiés sur le mémoire autographe par célestin Port*, Paris, 1880, pp. 26–8.

19 Roche, *The Culture*, pp. 330–95.

20 M. Leriget, *Des lois et impôts somptuaires*, Montpellier, 1919; M. Fogel, *Modèle d'Etat et modèle social de dépenses: les lois somptuaires en France de 1485 a 1660. Prélèvement et redistribution dans la genèse de l'Etat moderne*, Fontevrault and Paris, 1984–7; C. Walker, 'Les lois somptuaires ou le rêve d'un ordre social. Evolution et enjeux de la politique somptuaire à Gèneve, XVIe–XVIIIe siècle,' *Equinoxe* 1994: 2, pp. 111–27.

21 Mme de Sévigné *Correspondance*, R. Duchesne (ed.), 3 vols., Paris, 1974, vol. II, pp. 974–5.

22 *Journal d'un curé de campagne au XVIIe siècle*, H. Platelle (ed.), Paris, 1965, pp. 114–15; J. Jamerey-Duval, *Mémoires. Enfance et éducation d'un paysan au XVIIIe siècle*, J.-M. Goulemot (ed.), Paris, 1981, pp. 168–70.

23 A. Furetière, *Le roman bourgeois, ouvrage comique*, Bibliothèque de la Pléiade, Paris, 1958, pp. 907–8, 924–5, 930–1.

24 Roche, *The Culture*, pp. 81–150.

25 G. Gayot, 'Les innovations de marketing sur le marché européen des draps fins, XVIIe–XVIIIe siècle,' forthcoming article.

26 P. Minard, 'Les inspections des manufactures en France de Colbert à la Revolution', thesis, University of Paris I, 2 vols., 1994.

27 J.-F. Belhoste, 'Naissance de l'industrie du drap fin en France à l'âge classique. La manufacture du Dijonval et la draperie sedanaise (1660–1850)', *Cahiers de l'Inventaire*, 1984: 2, pp. 10–28.

28 *Journal du voyage de deux jeunes Hollandais à Paris en 1656–58*, A.-P. Faugere (ed.), Paris, 1899, pp. 31–2, 56–7.
29 J.-C. Nemeitz, 'Séjour de Paris', in A. Franklin, *La vie de Paris sous la Régence*, Paris, 1887, pp. 29–30.
30 M. Ferrières, *Le peuple et son patrimoine à Avignon, 1610–1790*', qualification thesis, 3 vols., Aix-en-Provence, 1995, vol. I, pp. 14–33.
31 *Ibid.*, vol. II, pp. 129–31, 206–320.
32 *Ibid.*, pp. 224–6, 267–70. The following tables show, from the pledges in the Mont-de-Piété and the registering of clothes on a person's entry into hospital, the primary elements in the dress of women and men.

Women (10 pledges)	Mont–de–Piété	Hospital (10 entries)
Shift	1.5	10
Camisole	0.7	8
Stiff bodice	0.6	0
Petticoat	1	0
Ganachon (tunic)	2.3	6
Gonnelle (long tunic)	1.7	0
Gown	1.7	6
Fondau (corsage)	0.5	5
Head-dress	0	10
Goularet (shawl)	0	10
Stockings	0	8
Shoes	0	10

Men		
Doublet	6	7
Trunk-hose	4	7
Short trousers	0	1
Coat	1	1
Shirt	10	6
Sleeved waistcoat	–	4
Mantle	10	5
Hat	0	7
Stockings	0	9
Shoes	0	10

Note the difference between the clothes worn by the persons received into the poor–house and those of the clients of the Mont-de-Piété, which are items selected for pawning in accordance with means and temporary needs.

33 Ferrières, 'Le peuple', pp. 238–66.
34 Roche, *The Culture*, pp. 108–20, 134–50, 151–83.
35 J.-A. de Ségur, *Les femmes, leur condition et leur influence dans la vie sociale*, 3 vols., Paris, 1803, vol. III, p. 7.
36 M. Faur-Jeandenans, 'Société et culture à Versailles au XVIIIᵉ siècle', doctoral thesis, University of Paris I, 1993, pp. 174–304.
37 B. Garnot, *Un declin: Chartres au XVIIIᵉ siècle*, Paris, 1991, pp. 215–30: H. Dréant, *Le costume dans le canton de la Roche-Bernard, 1789–1939*, Gaillon, 1995; A. Joffre, 'Le vêtement à Limoges et dans ses environs d'après les inventaires

après décès, 1740–1840', master's degree memoir, Limoges, 1980, pp. 149–51 (typescript).

38 L. Hamelin, 'Le vêtement à Besançon dans la seconde moitié du XVIIIe siècle, 1750–1790, d'après les inventaires mobiliers du presidial de Besançon', master's degree memoir, University of Besançon, 1989, pp. 51–3.

39 J. Berthelé, *Inventaire et documents des Archives municipales de Montpellier*, Montpellier, 1920, vol. IV, pp. 1–163: C. Pascal, 'Société et urbanisme à Montpellier aux XVIIe et XVIIIe siècles, 1665–1781', master's degree memoir, University of Paris I, 1988, pp. 112–13.

40 Waro-Desjardin, 'La vie quotidienne', pp. 167–205.

41 M. Baulant, 'Niveau de vie des paysans autour de Meaux en 1700 et 1750', *Annales, Economie, Société, Civilisations;* 1975, pp. 505–18 and 'Du fil à l'armoire', *Ethnologie Française*, 1986: 3, pp. 273–80.

42 M. Vernus, *La vie comtoise au temps de l'Ancien Régime*, 2 vols., Lons-le-Saunier, 1982, vol. I, pp. 217–38.

43 Abollivier, 'La vie quotidienne', pp. 135–41.

44 L. Simon, quoted in A. Fillon, 'Louis Simon, étaminier (1741–1820), dans son village du Haut-Maine au Siècle des Lumières', thesis Le Mans, 1983, pp. 66–7.

45 L. Fontaine, *Histoire du colportage en Europe, XVe–XIXe siècle*, Paris, 1993, pp. 229–52.

46 S. Chassagne, *Le coton et ses patrons, France, 1760–1840*, Paris, 1991.

47 L. Salmann, *Une croissance industrielle sous l'Ancien Régime: le textile en Bas-Languedoc, XVIIe–XVIIIe siècle*, Paris, 1994.

48 Roche, *The Culture*, pp. 259–329, 330–63.

49 H. Vanier, *Le costume, la vie populaire en France*, Paris, 1965, pp. 187–8, 195–6.

50 P. Guignet, 'Les Tribout et leurs ouvrières. Symboles et artisans de la brève époque des dentelles de Valenciennes', *Revue du Nord*, 1995: 6, pp. 35–72.

9 BREAD, WINE, TASTE

1 J. de Garine, 'Les modes alimentaires. Histoire de l'alimentation et des manières de table, Histoire des moeurs', Encyclopédie de la Pléiade, J. Poirier (ed.), Paris, 1990, vol. I, pp. 1447–630; J. Barrau, *Les hommes et leurs aliments. Esquisse d'une histoire écoligique et ethnologique de l'alimentation humaine*, Paris, 1983.

2 F. Lebrun, 'La qualité de la vie des milieux populaires au XVIIe siècle', *Marseille*, 1977, 109, pp. 43–6.

3 E. Leroy Ladurie, *Histoire du climat depuis l'an mil*, Paris, 1967.

4 P. Gillet, *Par mets et par vins, voyages et gastronomie en Europe, XVIe–XVIIIe siècle*, Paris, 1985; D. Roche, *Sociétés et cultures, les Français et l'Ancien Régime*, Paris, 1984, vol. II, pp. 209–10.

5 J. Meuvret, *Le problème des subsistances à l'époque de Louis XIV, Le commerce des grains et la conjoncture*, 2 vols., Paris, 1988.

6 D. Faucher, 'Les jardins familiaux et la technique agricole', *Annales, Economie, Société, Civilisations;* 1959: 2, pp. 297–307.

7 B. Garnier, Preface, *De l'herbe à la table. La viande dans la France méridionale à l'époque moderne*, transactions of 1993 colloquium, Henri Michel, Anne Blanchard and Elie Pelaquier (eds.), Paul-Valéry University, Montpellier,

1994, pp. 3–14. The author assembles the bibliography of the subject and opens the discussion, showing the interest of an extended analysis of a small town or village and the importance of a systematic study of market regulations.

8 J.-L. Flandrin, *Chroniques de Platine*, Paris, 1992; S. Mennell, *All Manner of Food, Eating and Taste in England and France from the Middle Ages to the Present*, Oxford, 1985; C. Marenco, *Manières de table, modèle de moeurs, XVIIe–XXe siècle*, Paris, 1992; A. Rowley, *A table! La fête gastronomique*, Paris, 1994.

9 Z. Gourerier, 'Le banquet medieval, XIV^{e}e–XVIe siècle', in *Les Français à table*, Paris, 1985, pp. 149–61.

10 J.-L. Flandrin, 'La distinction par le goût', in *Histoire de la vie privée*, P. Ariès and R. Chartier (eds.), vol. II, Paris, 1986, pp. 267–309.

11 *Ibid.*, pp. 272–3; *Histoire de l'alimentation*, J.-L. Flandrin and M. Montanari (eds.), Paris, 1996, pp. 657–704.

12 S. Kaplan, *Le meilleur pain du monde. Les boulangers de Paris au XVIIIe siècle*, Paris, 1996, pp. 55–690; on chestnuts, cf. J.-R. Pitte, *Terre de Castanide. Hommes et paysages du châtaignier en France de l'Antiquité à nos jours*, Paris, 1986.

13 V. Milliot, 'Alimentation', in *Dictionnaire des Lumières*, M. Delon (ed.), Paris, 1996; M. Livi-Bacci, *Popolazione e alimentazione. Saggio sulla storia demografica europea*, Bologna, 1987; M. Montanari, *La fame et l'abbondanza. Storia dell' alimentazione in Europa*, Rome and Bari, 1993.

14 *Pour une histoire de l'alimentation*, J.-J. Hémardinquer (ed.), *Cahiers des Annales*, 1970, Paris; also especially; M. Morineau, 'Conclusion', in J.-J. Hémardinquer, *Marines du Nord*, Paris, 1985.

15 C. Pasty, 'Les Problèmes de l'alimentation des troupes dans la deuxième moitié du XVIIIe siècle', master's degree memoir, University of Paris IV, 1992 (typescript).

16 J.-L. Lahitte, 'L'Alimentation des marins aux XVIIe et XVIIIe siècles', master's degree memoir, University of Paris I, 1995 (typescript); F. Issaly, 'La Vie des marins à la fin du XVIIIe siècle', master's degree memoir, University of Paris I, 1995, (typescript).

17 R. Baetens, 'Les rations de vivres des marins. La théorie confrontée à la réalité', *Les Amis du vieux Dunkerque* 1979: 9, pp. 51–79; J.-J. Hémardinquer, 'A propos de l'alimentation des marins', *Annales, Economie, Société, Civilisations;* 1963, pp. 1141–7. C. Koninckx, 'L'alimentation et la pathologie des déficiences alimentaires', *Revue d'histoire moderne et contemporaine* 1983: 1, pp. 109–38.

18 Issaly, 'La vie des marins', pp. 45–7, 77–80. The food ration, calculated from the works of Dr Poissonnier-Desperières aimed at improving the nourishment of crews and curing victims of scurvy, came to about 4,000 calories: 0.71 litre of wine, 611 g of white bread, 367 g of mutton or 244 g of mutton and chicken, 61 g of rice, 122 g of plums, 122 g of butter or grape jam, one egg, but only 9 mg of vitamin C.

19 B. Bonnin, 'L'alimentation dans les milieux populaires en France au XVIIe siècle. Essai de mise au point', *Marseille* 1977: 109, pp. 75–83.

20 *Ibid.*, pp. 74–7: P. Goubert and D. Roche, *Les Français et l'Ancien Régime*, Paris, 2 vols., 1984, vol. I, pp. 57–114, 151–86.

21 J.-J. Hémardinquer, 'Le porc familial sous l'Ancien Régime', *Annales, Economie, Société, Civilisations;* 1970: 6, pp. 1746–52; C. Fabre-Vassas, *La bête singulière, les juifs, les chrétiens et le cochon*, Paris, 1994.

22 J.-N. Biraben, 'Alimentation et démographie historique', *Démographie historique*, 1976, pp. 23–40; J. Claudian, 'L'alimentation, la France et les Français', *Encyclopédie de la Pleiade*, Michel François (ed.), Paris, 1972, pp. 133–89.

23 R. Beaudry, 'Alimentation et population rurale en Périgord au XVIIIe siècle', *Démographie historique* 1976, pp. 41–59.

24 Y. Castan, *Honnêteté et relations sociales en Languedoc, 1715–1780*, Paris, 1974, p. 274.

25 A. Poitrineau, 'L'alimentation populaire en Auvergne au XVIIIe siècle', *Pour une histoire de l'alimentation*, J.-J. Hémardinquer, (ed)., Paris, 1970, pp. 146–53; M. Ferrières, 'A la table d'une famille cévenole', in Garnier, *De l'herbe à la table* (see note 7), pp. 212–26, gives a precise example based on the family record-book of the Fouze family for 1769–80. The amount of food they produced and consumed themselves cannot be calculated from this, but it is clear that the average hillman was better fed than the plainsman in Languedoc, thanks to chestnuts, fruit and vegetables. Altogether, purchases of meat provided about one pound per person per week, mainly mutton but with some beef. The ratio of purchases of corn to purchases of meat was 100 to 43; 312 *livres* as against 135 *livres* per year. For the nineteenth century, A. Schweitz, *La maison tourangelle au quotidien, façons de bâtir, manières de vivre, 1850–1930*, Paris, 1996, pp. 162–71, and 'Les systèmes alimentaires en Touraine et en Sologne', *Revue française de diététique*, 1925, vol. 188: 2, pp. 29–36; *Histoire de l'alimentation* (see note 11), pp. 549–76, 597–628.

26 J.-C. Perrot, *Genèse d'une ville moderne. Caen au XVIIIe siècle*, 2 vols., Paris, 1975, vol. I, pp. 229–30.

27 M. Lachiver, *Vins, vignes et vignerons. Histoire du vignoble français*, Paris, 1988.

28 B. Garnot, *Un déclin: Chartres au XVIIIe siècle*, Paris, 1991.

29 Kaplan, *Le meilleur pain*, pp. 521–94, 608–9.

30 B. Garnier, *Viande et bêtes. Variations saisonnières de l'approvisionnement de Paris aux XVIIIe et XIXe siècles*, Festschrift for P. Chaunu, J.-P. Bardet and M. Foisil (eds.), Paris, 1993, pp. 147–70: and *Consommation et production de viande* (forthcoming).

31 R. Favier, 'Le marché de la viande à Grenoble au XVIIIe siècle', *Histoire, Economie, Société*, 1994: 4, pp. 583–604.

32 R. Philippe, 'L'alimentation de Paris au XVIIIe siècle', *Annales, Economie, Société, Civilisations;* 1974, pp. 560–7.

33 Kaplan, *Le meilleur pain*, pp. 47–50, 616–7.

34 G. Garrier, *Histoire sociale et culturelle du vin*, Paris, 1995, pp. 37–41, 62–3, 67–72, 84–9; M. Onfray, *Le ventre des philosophes, critique de la raison diététique*, Paris, 1989.

35 J.-C. Bonnet, 'Le vin des philosophes. L'imaginaire du vin', *Marseille* 1983, pp. 151–7.

36 J.-C. Bonnet, 'La table dans les civilités', *Marseille* 1977: 109, pp. 99–104.

37 Schweitz, *La Maison*, p. 175.

38 Z. Gourerier, 'Le banquet', pp. 179–86; A. Lebault, *La table et le repas à travers les siècles*, Paris, n.d., pp. 602–3; Flandrin, 'La distinction', p. 267–74.

39 Z. Gourerier, *Les repas quotidiens dans la société rurale pré-industrielle. Les Français et la table*, Paris, 1985, pp. 316–17; M. Segalen, 'Quinze générations de Bas-Bretons. Mariage, parentèle et société dans le pays bigouden', thesis, University of Paris v (typescript), pp. 676–80; Tardieu, *La vie domestique*, pp. 100–35: G.-H. Riviere and S. Tardieu, *Objets domestiques des provinces de France, dans la vie familiale et les arts ménagers*, Paris, 1953, pp. 40–5; Schweitz, *La Maison*, pp. 173–6; Flandrin, *Histoire de l'imentation*, pp. 516–36, 706–13.

40 M. Baulant, 'L'Appréciation du niveau de vie. Un problème, une solution', *Histoire et Mesure* 1989: 4, pp. 186–8; J.-M. Boelher, *Une société rurale en milieu rhénan, la paysannerie de la plaine d'Alsace, 1648–1789*, 3 vols., Strasbourg, 1995, vol. II, pp. 1686–7.

41 D. Roche, *The People of Paris: an Essay in Popoular Culture in the Eighteenth Century*, Leamington Spa, 1987, pp. 140–5: A. Pardailhé-Galabrun, *La naissance de l'intime, 3,000 foyers parisiens, XVIIᵉ–XVIIIᵉ siècles*, Paris, 1988, pp. 287–90.

42 Z. Gourerier, 'La mutation des comportements', in *Les Français et la table*, Paris, 1985, pp. 189–90.

43 Roche, *The People*, pp. 148–9.

44 D. Roche, *La France des Lumières*, Paris, 1993, pp. 572–5.

45 Here I follow Flandrin, 'La distinction', pp. 267–309, completely, and *Histoire de l'alimentation*, pp. 683–704.

46 M. Morineau, 'La pomme de terre au XVIIIᵉ siècle', *Annales, Economie, Société, Civilisations;* 1970: 6, pp. 1767–85. It should be noted that cultivation of the potato favoured an increase in rearing of pigs, e.g. in the Jura and Auvergne, though less, perhaps, in the North of France.

47 *Traité de la culture des pommes de terre*, 1782. I am grateful to M. A. Poirot, director of the municipal library, for having supplied me with this rare publication.

48 A. Maurizio, *Histoire de l'alimentation, depuis la préhistoire jusqu'à nos jours*, Paris, 1932; Barrau, *Les hommes et leurs aliments. Esquisse d'une histoire écologique et ethnologique de l'alimentation humaine*, Paris, 1983, pp. 34–57: R. Tannahill, *Food in History*, New York, 1973.

49 For comparison, see J. C. Drummond and A. Wilbraham, *The Englishman's Food. A History of Five Centuries of English Diet*, London, 1939; revised and completed by D. Hollingsworth, London, 1958.

50 J. Meyer, *Histoire du sucre*, Paris, 1988: S. Mintz, *Sweetness and Power. The Place of Sugar in Modern History*, London, 1986; Flandrin and Montanari, *Histoire de l'alimentation*, pp 629–42.

51 H. Lafon, *Les decors*, pp. 163–77, 329–36.

52 F. Mauro, *Histoire du Café*, Paris, 1992.

53 Roche, *The People*, pp. 247–64.

54 N. Harwich, *Histoire du chocolat*, Paris, 1992; P. Camporesi, *Le goût du chocolat. L'art de vivre au Siècle des Lumières* (French trans.), Paris, 1991; S. D. Coe and M. D. Coe, *The True Story of Chocolate*, London, 1996.

55 Roche, *The People*, pp. 142–145; Pardailhé-Galabrun, *Naissance*, pp. 300–03.

56 L. Dermigny, *Le commerce à Canton, 1719–1830*, 3 vols., Paris, 1964, vol. II, pp. 577–80.

57 A. Girard, 'La cuisinière bourgeoise. Livres culinaires, cuisine et société aux XVIIe et XVIIIe siècles', *Revue d'Histoire Moderne et Contemporaine* 1977, pp. 437–523; J.-L. Flandrin, P. Hyman and M. Hyman. *Le cuisinier français*, Paris, 1983: J.-C. Bonnet, 'Le réseau culinaire de l'Encyclopédie', *Annales, Economie, Société, Civilisations;* 1976: 5, pp. 891–915.

58 J. Lambert, 'Le chirurgien de papier. La naissance de l'hygiène', thesis, University of Paris I, 1991, 3 vols. (typescript), vol. I, pp. 187–90; J.-P. Aron, 'Biologie et alimentation à l'aube du XIXe siècle, in Hémardinquer, *Pour une histoire*, pp. 23–8, J.-R. Pitte, *Gastronomie française. Histoire et géographie d'une passion*, Paris, 1991.

59 M. Onfray, *Le ventre des philosophes, critique de la raison diététique*, Paris. 1989, pp. 36–7, 58–63; M. Foucault, *Histoire de la sexualite*, 3 vols., Paris, 1976–84, vol. II, *L'usage des plaisirs* pp. 111–23.

CONCLUSION

1 D. Poulot, 'Une nouvelle histoire de la culture matérielle', *Revue d'histoire moderne et contemporaine*, Paris, 1997, pp. 3–4; P. Glenne, *Consumption within Historical Studies. Acknowledging Consumption, a Review of New Studies*, D. Miller (ed.), London and New York, 1995, pp. 164–203.

2 L. Weatherill, *Consumer Behavior and Material Culture in Britain, 1660–1760*, London and New York, 1988.

3 S. Kaplan, *Le meilleur pain du monde. Les boulangers de Paris au XVIIIe siècle*, Paris, 1996, pp. 526–7.

4 A. Schweitz, *La maison tourangelle au quotidien, façons de bâtir, manières de vivre, 1850–1930*, Paris, 1996, pp. 152–3.

5 Condillac, *Oeuvres complètes*, Paris, 1821–2, 18 vols., vol. III, 'Essai sur l'origine des connaissances humaines', pp. 49–50.

6 *Ibid.*, vol. IV, 'Le commerce et le gouvernement considérés relativement l'un à l'autre', pp. 6–7.

7 *Ibid.*, pp. 31–50.

8 *Ibid.*, pp. 264–72.

9 *Ibid.*, pp. 350–87.

10 H. Mendras, *La seconde Révolution française*, Paris, 1989, and *La fin des paysans*, Paris, 1984.

Bibliography

Abbri, F., *Le terre, l'acqua, le arie*, Bologna, 1984.

Abbollivier, F., 'La vie quotidienne d'après les inventaires après décès a Roscoff au XVIIIe siècle', master's degree memoir, Rennes, 1993 (typescript).

Albertone, M. *Fisiocrati, istruzione e cultura*, Turin, 1979.

Allemagne, J. R. d', *Histoire du luminaire depuis l'époque romaine jusqu'au XIXe siècle*, Paris, 1891.

Angiolini, F. and Roche, D., *Culture et formation négociante*, Paris, 1995.

Ariès, P., *L'enfant et la vie familiale sous l'Ancien Régime*, Paris, 1960.

Arminjon, C., *Les objets de table royaux français du XVIe au XVIIIe siècle*, Paris, 1993.

Arnaboldi, J., *La table, dans la vie populaire en France du Moyen Age à nos jours*, Paris, 1965.

Les Français et la table, preface by J. Cuisenier, Paris, 1986.

Aron, J.-P. 'Biologie et alimentation à l'aube du XIXe siècle', in J.-J. Hemardinquer (ed.), *Pour une histoire de l'alimentation*, pp. 23–8.

Audin-Rouvière, C., *Essai sur la topographie physique et médicale de Paris*, Paris, an II (1794).

Audisio, G., *Des paysans, XVe–XIXe siècle*, Paris, 1993.

Auslander, L., *Taste and Power: Furnishing Modern France*, Berkeley and Los Angeles, CA, London, 1996.

Babelon, J.-P, *Demeures parisiennes sous Henri IV et Louis XIII*, Paris, 1967.

Nouvelle Histoire de Paris: Paris au XVIe siècle, Paris, 1987.

Bachelard, G., *L'eau et les rêves*, Paris, 1942.

La terre et les rêveries du repos, Paris, 1948.

Poétique de l'espace, Paris, 1957.

Psychanalyse du feu, Paris, 1949.

Backouche, I., 'La Seine et Paris, 1750–1850. Pratiques, aménagements, représentations', doctorate thesis, 2 vols, E.H.E.S.S., 1996 (typescript).

Baetens, R. 'Les rations de vivres des marins. La théorie confrontée à la réalité', *Les Amis du vieux Dunkerque* 1979: 9, pp. 51–79.

Bans, J.-C. and Gaillard-Bans, P., 'Maisons et bâtiments agricoles dans l'Ancien Régime en Vannetais', *Revue d'Histoire Moderne et Contemporaine* 1984: 31, pp. 3–20.

Barber, G. (ed.), *Anecdotes typographiques de Nicolas Contat dit Le Brun*, Oxford, 1980.

Barbier, P. and Vernillat, F., *Histoire de la France par les chansons*, Paris, 1956.

Bardet, J.-P. 'La maison rouennaise aux XVIIe et XVIIIe siècles. Economie et comportement', in P. Chaunu (ed)., *Le Bâtiment. Enquête d'histoire economique (XIVe–XIXe siècles)*, Paris and The Hague, 1971.

Barrau, J., *Les hommes et leurs aliments. Esquisse d'une histoire écologique et ethnologique de l'alimentation humaine*, Paris, 1983.

Barrelet, J., *La verrerie en France, de l'époque gallo-romaine à nos jours*, Paris, 1971.

Barthes, R., 'Histoire et sociologie du vêtement', *Annales, Economie, Société, Civilisations;* 1957: 3, pp. 430–41.

Baudelot, C. and Establet, R., *Maurice Halbwachs, Consommation et société*, Paris, 1994.

Baudrillard, J., *La société de consommation*, Paris, 1970.

Pour une critique de l'économie politique du signe, Paris, 1972.

Baulant, M., 'Niveaux de vie paysans autour de Meaux en 1700 et 1750', *Annales, Economie, Société, Civilisations;* 1975: 2–3, pp. 505–18.

'Du fil à l'armoire', *Ethnologie française* 1986: 3, pp. 273–80.

'L'appréciation du niveau de vie. Un problème, une solution', *Histoire et Mesure* 1989: 4, pp. 267–302.

Baumont-Mallet, L., *L'eau à Paris*, photographs by J.-F. Baumard, Paris, 1992.

Beaudry, R., 'Alimentation et population rurale en Périgord au XVIIIe siècle', *Démographie historique* 1976, pp. 41–59.

Beck, R. 'Jour du Seigneur, jour de fête, jour de repos. Les mutations du dimanche en France, 1700–1900', doctorate thesis, 2 vols., University of Paris VII, 1995 (typescript).

Belgrand, E., *Travaux souterrains de Paris*, 5 vols., Paris, 1877–82.

Belhoste, J.-F. 'La fabrication du verre plat en France (XVIIe–debut XIXe siècle)' in *Le verre, matériau de construction*. Ecole nationale du patrimoine, 6–7 May 1996.

'Naissance de l'industrie du drap fin en France à l'âge classique. La manufacture du Dijonval et la draperie sedanaise (1650–1850)' *Cahier de l'Inventaire* 1984: 2, pp. 10–28.

Belmont, N., *Mythes et croyances dans l'Ancienne France*, Paris, 1973.

Bensaude, B., *Lavoisier, Mémoires d'une Revolution*, Paris, 1993.

Berenger-Féraud, J., *Traditions et réminiscences populaires de la Provence*, Paris, 1886.

Bergeron, L., *Paris dans l'organisation des échanges interieurs à la fin du XVIIIe siècle. Aires et structures du commerce français au XVIIIe siècle*, P. Léon (ed.), Lyons, 1973.

Berthele, J., *Inventaire et documents des Archives municipales de Montpellier*, Montpellier, 1920.

Berthomieu, C., 'La loi et les travaux de Engel', *Consommation* 1965: 4, pp. 59–89.

Bertrand, G., 'Pour une histoire écologique de la France rurale', in *Histoire de la France rurale*, G. Duby (ed.), Paris, 1975.

Beutler, C., 'Un chapitre de la sensibilité collective: la littérature agricole en Europe continentale au XVIe siècle', *Annales, Economie, Société, Civilisations;* 1973: 28, pp. 1282–94.

Bigo, R., 'L'octroi de Paris en 1789', *Revue d'Histoire économique et sociale* 1931: 1, pp. 97–113.

Biraben, J.-N., 'Alimentation et démographie historique', *Démographie historique* 1976, pp. 23–40.

Blanc, O. 'Images du monde et portraits d'habits: les recueils de costumes à la Renaissance', *Bulletin du Bibliophile* 1995: 2, pp. 221–61.

Blondel, J.-F. *Cours d'architecture ou traité de décoration. Distribution et construction des bâtiments*, 9 vols., Paris, 1977, vol. v, pp. 60–1.

Boehler, J.-M., 'Tradition et innovation dans un pays de petite culture au xviiie siècle', *Histoire et Sociétés rurales* 1995: 4, pp. 69–103.

Une société rurale en milieu rhénan, la paysannerie de la plaine d'Alsace, 1648–1789, 3 vols., Strasbourg, 1995.

Boisguilbert, P. de, *Pierre de Boisguilbert et la naissance de l'économie politique*, 2 vols., Paris, 1966.

Le détail de la France, Paris, 1695.

Boissière, J., 'Populations et économies du bois dans la France moderne. Contribution a l'étude des milieux forestiers entre Paris et le Morvan au dernier siècle de l'Ancien Régime (vers 1685–vers 1790)', 3 vols., state doctorate thesis, University of Paris I, 1993.

Bonnet, J.-C., 'La table dans les civilités', *Marseille* 1977: 109, pp. 99–104.

'Le réseau culinaire de l'Encyclopédie', *Annales, Economie, Société, Civilisations;*, 1976: 5, pp. 891–915.

'Le vin des philosophes. L'imaginaire du vin', *Marseille* 1983, pp. 151–7.

Bonnin, B., 'L'alimentation dans les milieux populaires en France au xviie siècle. Essai de mise au point', *Marseille*, 1977: 109, pp. 75–83, pp. 76–7.

Bonnin, P., Perrot, M. and Soudière, M. de la, *L'Ostal en Margeride*, Paris, 1983.

Borghero, C., *La polemica sul Lusso nel settecento francese*, Turin, 1974.

Bouchary, J., *Les compagnies financières à la fin du xviiie siècle*, 3 vols., Paris, 1939–43.

Boucher, M., and Furic, J., *La maison rurale en Haute-Marche. Contribution à un inventaire régional*, Nonette, Saint-Germain and Lembron, 1984.

Boudriot, P.-D., 'La maison à loyer. Etude du bâtiment à Paris sous Louis XV, *Histoire, Economie et Société* 1982: 2, pp. 115–25.

'Une source pour l'étude de l'habitat parisien au début du xvie siècle: Pierre Le Muet', *Histoire, Economie et Société* 1985, pp. 29–41, 38.

'La construction locative parisienne sous Louis XV. De l'inerte à l'anime', 3rd cycle thesis, University of Paris IV, n.d. (1985), 2 vols. (typescript)

Boulainvilliers, H. de, *Etat de la France*, 2 vols., London, 1727.

Bourquin, H., 'L'approvisionnement en bois de Paris de la Regence à la Révolution', law degree thesis, Paris, n.d.

Bourquin, L., 'Les objets de la vie quotidienne dans la première moitié du xvie siècle à travers cent inventaires après décès parisiens', *Revue d'Histoire Moderne et Contemporaine* 1989: 36, pp. 464–75.

Bousselle, P., *La maison, la vie populaire en France du Moyen Age à nos jours*, Paris, 1965.

Braudel, F. *Civilisation matérielle, économie et capitalisme, xve–xviiie siècles*, 3 vols., Paris 1979. (Eng. trans. *Civilisation and Capitalism, Fifteenth to Eighteenth Century*, vol. I: *The Structures of Everyday Life: The Limits of the Possible*, London, 1981.)

Bremond, H., *Histoire littéraire du sentiment religieux en France, depuis la fin des guerres de religion jusqu'à nos jours*, 11 vols., Paris, 1936.

Brennan, T. *Public Drinking and Popular Culture in Eighteenth-Century Paris*, Princeton, NJ, 1988.

Brewer J., and Porter, R., *Consumption and the World of Goods*, London, 1993.

Brewer, J., MacKendrick, N. and Plumb, J. N., *The Birth of a Consumer Society: The Commercialisation of Eighteenth-Century England*, London, 1982.

Brian, L., Les génovéfains de la Contre-Réforme à la Révolution, doctorate thesis, University of Paris I, 2 vols, 1994 (typescript).

Briand, E., *La mesure de l'Etat. Administrateurs et géometres au XVIII* siècle*, Paris, 1994.

Burstin, H., *Le faubourg Saint-Marcel à l'époque révolutionnaire. Structure économique et composition sociale*, Paris, 1983, pp. 24–7.

Burtin, J., 'Quatre-vingt-trois ans de la vie quotidienne à Auxerre, 1741–1822', master's degree memoir, University of Paris XII, 1985 (typescript).

Cabantous, A., *Citoyens du large*, Paris, 1995.

Cabourdin, G., *Terres et hommes en Lorraine, 1550–1635: Toulois et comté de Vandémont*, Nancy, 1977.

Cammel, C., 'La Bièvre du XVIIᵉ au XIXᵉ siècle. Eau et industrie', master's degree memoir, University of Paris I (typescript).

Camporesi, P., *Le goût du chocolat. L'art de vivre au Siècle des Lumières*, French trans., Paris, 1991.

Cantillon, R., *Essai sur la nature du commerce en général*, 1755, T. Tsuda (ed.), Tokyo, 1979 (Eng. trans., London, 1931).

Castan, Y., *Honnêteté et relations sociales en Languedoc, 1715–1780*, Paris, 1974, p. 274.

Caulier, B., *Les cultes thérapeutiques autour des fontaines en France du Moyen Age à nos jours*, Paris, 1990.

Certeau, M. de, Giard, L., Mayol, P., *L'Invention du quotidien*, 2 vols. Paris, 1980.

Chaignot, J., *Nouvelle Histoire de Paris: Paris au XVIII* siècle*, Paris, 1988.

Chaplain, J. M., *La Chambre des tisseurs. Louviers, cité drapière, 1680–1840*, Paris, 1984.

Chartier, R., *L'Académie de Lyon au XVIII* siècle. Nouvelles études lyonnaises*, Geneva, 1969.

'La ville dominante et soumise', in *Histoire de la France urbaine*, G. Duby (ed.), Paris, 1981.

La civilité entre distinction et divulgation. Historische Lexikon der Politischsozialen Grundbegriffe in Frankreich von Ancien Régime zur Revolution, 1680–1820, Munich, 1986.

'Le monde comme représentation', *Annales, Economie, Société, Civilisations;* 1989: 6, pp. 1505–20.

L'ordre des livres, Paris, 1992.

Chartier, R., Compère, M. and Julia, D., *L'éducation en France au XVIII* siècle*, Paris, 1976.

Chassagne, S., *Le coton et ses patrons, France, 1760–1840*, Paris, 1991.

Chateaubriand, *Génie du christianisme* (1802), Bibliothèque de la Pléiade, Paris, 1978, pp. 893–920.

Mémoires d'outre–tombe, Bibliothèque de la Pléiade, 2 vols., Paris, 1951.

Chevalier, L., *Classes laborieuses et classes dangereuses*, Paris, 1958.

Chizick, H., *The limits of Reform in the Enlightenment. Attitudes toward the Education of the Lower Classes in Eighteenth-Century France*, Princeton, NJ, 1981.

Claudian, J., 'L'Alimentation, la France et les Français', in *Encyclopédie de la Pléiade*, Michel François (ed.), Paris, 1972, pp. 133–89.

Coe, S. D. and Coe, M. D., *The True Story of Chocolate*, London, 1996.

Collet, P., *Pièces d'architecture où sont compris plusieurs cheminées*, Paris, 1653.

Condillac, E. B. de, *Oeuvres complétes*, Paris, 1821–2.

Coquery, N., 'De l'hôtel aristocratique aux ministères. Habitat, mouvement, espace à Paris au XVIIIe siècle', doctorate thesis, University of Paris I, 1995 (typescript).

Corbin, A., *Archaïsme et modernité en Limousin au XIXe siècle, 1845–1880*, 2 vols., Paris, 1975.

Le miasme et la jonquille. L'odorat et l'imaginaire social, XVIIIe–XIXe siècles, Paris, 1982. (Eng. trans., *The Foul and the Fragrant*.)

Corvol, A., *L'homme et l'arbre dans l'Ancien Régime*, Paris, 1984.

Courtin, A. de, *Nouveau traité de la civilité qui se pratique en France parmi les honnétes*, Paris, 1671.

Croix, A., *La Bretagne aux XVIe et XVIIe siècles: la vie, la mort, la foi*, Paris, 1981.

Cuisenier, J., *L'art populaire en France*. Freiburg, 1975.

La maison rustique, logique sociale et composition architecturale, Paris, 1991.

Dagognet, F., Preface to B. Deloche, *L'art du meuble*, Lyons, 1985, pp. 12–13.

Eloge de l'objet. Pour une philosophie de la marchandise, Paris, 1989.

Des révolutions vertes. Histoire et principes de l'agronomie, Paris, 1973.

Rematérialiser, matières et matérialismes, Paris, 1985.

D'Allemagne, D., *Les casernes françaises*, Paris, 1990.

Darwin, C., 'L'evolution dans le vêtement', *Revue de l'Université de Bruxelles*, March 1900, pp. 37.

Deffontaines, P., *L'homme et sa maison*, Paris, 1972.

Defrance, H., *Histoire de l'éclairage des rues de Paris*, Paris, 1904.

Deloche, B., 'Le statut de l'artisan, un test de la modernité de l'Encyclopédie', *Milieux* 1984–5: 19–20, pp. 79–87.

L'art du meuble. Introduction à l'esthétique des arts mineurs, followed by *L'art du meuble a Lyon au XVIIIe siècle* and *Formaliser l'analyse stylistique*, Lyons, 1985.

Le mobilier bourgeois à Lyon au XVIIIe siècle, Lyons, 1983.

Deribère, M. and P., *Préhistoire et histoire de la lumière*, Paris, 1979.

Dermigny, L., *Le commerce à Canton, 1719–1830*, 3 vols., Paris, 1964.

Descimon, R., and Jouhaud, C., *La France du premier XVIIe siècle*, Paris, 1996.

Désert, G., 'Maisons rurales et urbaines dans la France traditionnelle', in P. Chaunu, ed., *Le Bâtiment. Enquéte d'histoire économique (XIXe – XIXe siècles)*, Paris and The Hague, 1971.

Deslandres, Y., *Le costume, image de l'homme*, Paris, 1976.

Desrosières, A., *La politique des grands nombres. Histoire de la raison statistique*, Paris, 1993.

Dessert, D., *Argent, pouvoir et société au Grand Siècle*, Paris, 1984.

Dethan, G., *Nouvelle Histoire de Paris: Paris au temps de Louis XIV, 1660–1715*, Paris, 1990.

Dibie, P., *Ethnologie de la chambre à coucher*, Paris, 1987.

Diderot, D., *Oeuvres complètes*, R. Levinter (ed.), Paris, 1967.

Diffré, P., 'Historique de l'alimentation en eau de Paris', *Bulletin du B.G.R.M.* 1967, pp. 3–22.

Dillon, Abbé, *Mémoire sur les trottoirs*, Paris, 1804.

Dinges, S., 'Culture matérielle des classes sociales inférieures à Bordeaux', *Bulletin de la Société archéologique de Bordeaux* 1986: 77, pp. 85–95.

Dion, R., *Histoire de la vigne et du vin en France des origines au XIXᵉ siècle*, Paris, 1959.

Douglas, M., and Isherwood, B., (eds.), *The World of Goods: toward an Anthropology of Consumption*, New York, 1979.

Dréant, H., *Le costume dans le canton de la Roche-Bernard, 1789–1939*, Gaillon, 1995.

Drummond, J. C., and Wilbraham, A., *The Englishman's Food. A History of Five Centuries of English Diet*, London, 1939, edition revised and completed by D. Hollingsworth, London, 1958.

Dubost, J.-F., Juratic S., Milliot, V., Roche, D., and Roy, J.-M., 'Mobilite et accueil a Paris (1650–1850)', PIR–Villes report, 1996 (typescript).

Dupâquier, J. (ed)., *Histoire de la population française*, 4 vols., Paris, 1984.

Duprat, C., *Pour l'amour de l'humanité. Le temps des philanthropes, la philanthropie parisienne des Lumières à la monarchie de Juillet*, Paris, 1993.

Durand, G., *Vins, vignes et vignerons en Beaujolais, XVIᵉ–XVIIIᵉ siècle*, Lyons, 1979.

Durand, Y., *Les fermiers généraux au XVIIIᵉ siècle*, Paris, 1972.

Ekert-Jaffé, O., 'Vieillissement et consommation. Quelques résultats tirés des enquêtes françaises sur les budgets des ménages', *Population* 1989: 3, pp. 561–77.

Eleb-Vidal, M. and Debarre-Blanchard, A., *Architectures de la vie priveé, XVIIᵉXIXᵉ siècle)* Archives d'architecture moderne, Brussels, 1989.

Elias, N., *La civilisation des moeurs* (French trans.) 1973, (Eng. trans. *The Civilising Process vol I, the History of Manners*, Oxford, 1978 from *Uber der Progress der Zivilisation*, Basel, 1939.

Erasmus, *La civilité puérile*, trans. A. Bonneau, P. Aries (ed.), Paris, 1977. [On good Manners for Boys, 1530: *Collected Works of Erasmus*, Toronto, 1979, vol. xxv.]

Escalier dans l'architecture de la Renaissance, L', proceedings of colloquium held at Tours, 22–26 May 1975, collection des architectures, Paris, 1985.

Estienne, C., *L'agriculture et maison rustique*, Paris, 1564.

Fabre, D., 'Passeuses au gué du destin', *Critique* 1980, pp. 1075–99.

Fabre-Vassas, C., *La bête singulière. Les juifs, les chrétiens et le cochon*, Paris, 1994.

Faiguet de Villeneuve, J., *L'économie politique, projet pour enrichir et pour perfectionner l'espèce humaine*, Paris, 1763.

Farge, A., *La vie fragile, violence, pouvoirs et solidarités à Paris au XVIIIᵉ siècle*, Paris, 1986.

Le vol d'aliments, Paris, 1974.

Vivre dans la rue au XVIIIᵉ siècle, Paris, 1979.

Faucher, D., 'Les jardins familiaux et la technique agricole', *Annales, Economie, Société, Civilisations;* 1959: 2, pp. 297–307.

Faur-Jeandenans, M., 'Société et culture à Versailles au XVIIIᵉ siècle', doctoral thesis, University of Paris I, 1993.

Favier, J., *Nouvelle Histoire de Paris.: Paris au XVe siècle, 1380–1500*, Paris, 1974.
Favier, R., 'Le marché de la viande à Grenoble au XVIIIe siècle', *Histoire, Economie, Société*, 1994: 4, pp. 583–604.
Febvre, L., *Pour une histoire à part entière*, Paris, 1962.
Ferrières, M., 'A la table d'une famille cévenole', in Garnier, B., *De l'herbe à la table*.
  'Le peuple et son patrimoine à Avignon, 1610–1790', qualification thesis, 3 vols. Aix-en-Provence, 1995.
Feyel, G., 'La presse et l'information en France', State doctorate thesis, 5 vols., University of Paris I, 1994 (typescript).
Fillon, A., 'Louis Simon, étaminier (1741–1820), dans son village du Haut-Maine au Siècle des Lumières', thesis, 2 vols., Le Mans, 1983 (typescript).
  Comme on fait son lit on se couche. 300 ans d'histoire du lit villageois, populations et cultures. Etudes réunies en l'honneur de F. Lebrun, Rennes, 1989, pp. 153–64.
Flandrin, J.-L., 'La distinction par le goût', *Histoire de la vie privée*, P. Aries and R. Chartier (eds.), Paris, 1986.
  Chroniques de Platine, Paris, 1992.
  Famille et parenté à l'époque moderne, Paris, 1976.
  Familles, parenté, maison, sexualité dans l'ancienne France, Paris, 1976.
Flandrin, J.-L., Hyman, P. and Hyman, M. *Le cuisinier français*, Paris, 1983.
Flandrin, J.-L., and Montanari, M., (eds.), *Histoire de l'alimentation*, Paris, 1996, pp. 657–704.
Fogel, M., *Modèle d'Etat et modèle social de dépenses: les lois somptuaires en France de 1485 à 1660, prélèvement et redistribution dans la genèse de l'Etat moderne*, Fontevrault, 1984 and Paris, 1987.
Fontaine, L., *Le voyageur et la mémoire. Colporteurs de l'Oisans au XIXe siècle*, Lyons, 1984.
  Histoire du colportage en Europe, XVIe–XIXe siècle, Paris, 1993.
  Le colportage en Europe du XVIe au XIXe siècle, Paris, 1994.
Fontaine, M. M., 'Images littéraires de l'escalier', in *L'escalier dans l'architecture de la Renaissance*, Paris, 1985.
Fortier, B., *La maîtrise de l'eau, XVIIIe siècle*, Paris, 1977.
Foucault, M., *L'usage des plaisirs. Histoire de la sexualité*, 3 vols., Paris, 1984.
Francastel, P., *Le style Empire*, Paris, 1939.
Furetière, A., *Le roman bourgeois, ouvrage comique*, Bibliothèque de la Pléiade, Paris, 1958.
Gaiffe, F., *L'envers du Grand Siècle*, Paris, 1924.
Gallet, M., *La maison parisienne au XVIIIe siècle*, Paris, 1969.
Gambi, L., 'Per una storia della abitazione rurale in Italia', *Rivista storia italiana*, 1964: 76, 2.
Garden, M., 'Quelques remarques sur l'habitat urbain. L'exemple de Lyon au XVIIIe siècle', *Annales de démographie historique, démographie et environnement* 1975, pp. 29–35.
  Doléances des maîtres ouvriers fabriquant en étoffe d'or, d'argent et de soie de la ville de Lyon, introduction by F. Rudle, Lyons, 1976.
  Lyon et les Lyonnais au XVIIIe siècle, Paris, 1970.

Garine, J. de. 'Les modes alimentaires. Histoire de l'alimentation et des manières de table. Histoire des moeurs', *Encyclopédie de la Pléiade*, J. Poirier (ed.), Paris, 1990, pp. 1447–630.

Garnier, B., 'Preface', *De l'herbe à la table. La viande dans la France méridionale à l'époque moderne*. Proceedings of 1993 colloquium, compiled by Henri Michel, Anne Blanchard and Elie Pelaquier, Paul-Valéry University, Montpellier, 1994, pp. 3–14.

Consommation et production de viande (forthcoming).

Viande et bêtes. Variations saisonnières de l'approvisionnement de Paris aux XVIIIe et XIXe siècles. Miscellany for P. Chaunu, J.-P. Bardet and M. Foisil (eds.), Paris, 1993.

Garnot, B., *Un déclin, Chartres au XVIIIe siècle*, Paris, 1991.

Garrier, G., *Histoire sociale et culturelle du vin*, Paris, 1996.

Gayot, G., 'Les innovations de marketing sur le marché européen des draps fins, XVIIe–XVIIIe siècle' (forthcoming).

Gélis, J. *L'arbre et le fruit. La naissance dans l'Occident moderne, XVIe–XIXe siècle*, Paris, 1984.

Giedon, S., *La mécanisation au pouvoir* (French trans.), Paris 1980 (*Mechanization Takes Command*. Oxford and New York, 1948).

Gillet, P., *Par mets et par vins, voyages et gastronomie en Europe, XVIe–XVIIIe siècle*, Paris, 1985.

Girard, A., 'La cuisinière bourgeoise; Livres culinaires, cuisine et société au XVIIe et XVIIIe siècles', *Revue d'Histoire Moderne et Contemporaine*, 1977: 24, pp. 437–523.

Girard, P.-S., *Des puits forés et artésiens*, Paris, 1833.

Recherches sur les eaux de Paris, Paris, 1812.

Gleichmann, P.-R. *Des villes propres et sans odeur*, Paris, 1982.

Glenne, P., *Consumption within Historical Studies. Acknowledging Consumption, a Review of New Studies*, D. Miller (ed.), London and New York, 1995.

Godard de Donville, L., *Signification de la mode sous Louis XIII*, Aix-en-Provence, 1978.

Godard J., *L'ouvrier en soie. Monographie du tisseur lyonnais*, Lyons, 1899.

Goger, J.-M., 'Transport', in *Dictionnaire des Lumières*, M. Delon (ed.), Paris, 1997.

'La politique routière en France de 1716 à 1815', thesis, E.H.E.S.S. J.-C. Perrot (ed.), 6 vols, Paris, 1988 (typescript).

Goubert, J.-P., *Du luxe au confort*, Paris, 1988, pp. 15–30.

Goubert, P., *Beauvais et le Beauvaisis, 1600–1730. Contribution à l'histoire sociale de la France au XVIIe siècle*, Paris, 1960.

La vie quotidienne des paysans français au XVIIe siècle, Paris, 1982.

Goubert, P., and Roche, D., *Les Français et l'Ancien Régime*, 2 vols., Paris, 1984.

Gouhier, P., 'La maison presbytérale en Normandie', in P. Chaunu, (ed)., *Le Bâtiment. Enquete d'histoire economique (XIVe–XIXe siècle)*, Paris and The Hague, 1971.

Gourerier, Z., *Le banquet médiéval, XIVe–XVIe siècles. Les Français à table*, Paris, 1985.

Les repas quotidiens dans la société rurale pré-industrielle. Les Français et la table, Paris, 1985.

Modèles de cour et usages de table: les origines, Versailles et les tables royales en Europe, Paris, 1993.

Grateau, P., 'Nécessité réelle et nécessité factice: doléances et culture matérielle dans la Sénéchaussee de Rennes en 1789', *Annales de Bretagne et des pays de l'Ouest* 1993: 3, pp. 299–310.

Grenier, J.-Y., 'Consommation et marché au XVIIIe siècle', *Histoire et Mesure* 1995: 10, 3–4, pp. 371–380.

'Les mécanismes de la croissance', *Histoire de la population française,* J. Dupaquier (ed.), 4. vols, Paris, 1984.

'Modèle de la demande sous l'Ancien Régime', *Annales, Economie, Société, Civilisations;* 1987: 3, pp. 497–527.

L'économie d'Ancien Régime, un monde de l'échange et de l'incertitude, Paris, 1997.

Grinewald, J., 'L'architecture hydraulique au XVIIIe siècle, un paradigme vitruvien. Contribution à une sociologie historique des techniques', *Itineraire* 1979, pp. 150–210.

Gruber, A.-C., *Les grandes fêtes et leur décor à l'époque de Louis XVI,* Geneva and Paris, 1972.

Guéry, A., 'Les finances de la monarchie française sous l'Ancien Régime,' *Annales, Economie, Société, Civilisations;* 1978: 2, pp. 216–39.

Guignet, P., 'Les Tribout et leurs ouvrières. Symboles et artisans de la brève époque des dentelles de Valenciennes', *Revue du Nord* 1995: 6, pp. 35–72.

Guillerme, A., 'Quelques problèmes de l'eau dans les villes du Bassin parisien au Moyen Age', 3rd cycle thesis, 2 vols. E.H.E.S.S. Paris, 1981 (typescript).

Le temps de l'eau, la cité, l'eau et les techniques, Nord de la France, fin XIIIe–début XIXe siècle, Paris, 1983.

'L'histoire des techniques, tendances actuelles', *Bulletin de la Société française d'histoire des sciences et des techniques* 1990: 26, pp. 5–12.

'Technique et culture materielle', E.H.E.S.S. (Paris) seminar on studies in the sciences and technology, 14 March 1995 (typescript).

Guillerme, J., *Le malsain et l'économie de la nature, XVIIIe siècle,* Paris, 1979.

Gutton, J.-P. *La société et les pauvres: l'example de la généralité de Lyon, 1534–1789,* Paris, 1971.

Halbwachs, M., *La classe ouvrière et les niveaux de vie. Recherches sur la hiérarchie des besoins dans les sociétés industrielles contemporaines,* Paris, 1913.

Hamelin, L., 'Le vêtement à Besancon dans la seconde moitie du XVIIIe siècle, 1750–90, d'après les inventaires mobiliers du présidial de Besancon', master's degree memoir, University of Besançon, 1989.

Harouel, J.-L., *L'embellissement des villes. L'urbanisme français au XVIIIe siècle,* Paris, 1993.

Harwich, N., *Histoire du chocolat,* Paris, 1992.

Haudrère, P. 'Esquisse d'une histoire des intérieurs angevins au XVIIIe siècle', *Annales de Bretagne et des pays de l'Ouest* 1992, 3, pp. 227–42.

Havard, H., *Dictionnaire de l'ameublement,* Paris, 1887–9.

L'art à travers les moeurs, Paris, 1882.

Heller, A., *La theorie des besoins chez Karl Marx* (French trans.) Paris, 1978. (Eng. trans. *The Theory of Need in Marx,* London, 1976.)

Hemardinquer, J.-J., 'A propos de l'alimentation des marins', *Annales, Economie, Société, Civilisations;* 1963: 6, pp. 1141–9.

'Le porc familial sous l'Ancien Régime', *Annales, Economie, Société, Civilisations;* 1970: 6, pp. 1746–52.

Hemardinquer, J.-J. (ed.), *Pour une histoire de l'alimentation, Cahier des Annales,* 1970, Paris.

Hénin, B., 'La maison et la vie domestique à Marseille du xviie au xviiie siècle', 3rd cycle thesis, 3 vols., Aix-en-Provence, 1984 (typescript).

Herlaut, Commandant, 'L'éclairage des rues de Paris à la fin du xviie siècle et au xviiie siècle', *Mémoire de la Société de l'Histoire de Paris et de l'Ile-de-France,* vol. XLIII, Paris, 1916.

L'éclairage de Paris à l'époque révolutionnaire, Paris, 1932.

Hilaire-Pérez, L., 'Inventions et inventeurs en France et en Angleterre au xviiie siècle', doctorate thesis, 4 vols., University of Paris I, 1994 (typescript).

Hincker, F., *Les Français devant l'impôt sous l'Ancien Régime,* Paris, 1971.

Hirschman, A., *Les passions et les intérêts,* French trans., Paris, 1980 (*The Passions and the Interests,* Princeton, NJ, 1977.)

Bonheur privé, action publique, French trans., Paris, 1983 (*Shifting Involvements: Private Interest and Public Action,* Princeton, NJ, 1982.)

Hufton, O., *The Poor of Eighteenth-Century France, 1780–9,* Oxford, 1974.

Hugoniot, J.-Y., *L'architecture de l'eau en Berry,* National Congress of the *Sociétés savantes,* Poitiers, 1986; 'Usage et représentation de l'eau', Paris, 1984.

Hurtaut and Magny, *Dictionnaire historique de la ville de Paris et de ses environs,* 4 vols., Paris, 1779.

Ikni, G. R., 'La question paysanne dans la Révolution française; pour une vision synthétique', *Histoire et Sociétés rurales* 1995: 4, pp. 177–211.

Issaly, F., 'La vie des marins à la fin du xviiie siècle', master's degree memoir, University of Paris I, 1995 (typescript).

Jacquart, J., *Aspects de l'architecture rurale en Ile-de-France,* exhibition, Paris, 1975.

L'habitat rural en Ile-de-France au xviiie siècle. La qualité de la vie au xviiie siècle, 7th C.M.R. colloquium, Marseilles, 1977.

La crise rurale en Ile-de-France, 1550–1670, Paris, 1974.

Jamerey-Duval, J., *Mémoires. Enfance et éducation d'un paysan au xviiie siècle,* J.-M.Goulemot (ed.), Paris, 1981.

Joffre, A., 'Le vêtement à Limoges et dans ses environs d'après les inventaires après décès, 1740–1840, master's degree memoir, Limoges, 1980 (typescript).

Journal de ma vie. Critical edition of the diary of Jacques-Louis Ménétra, a journeyman glazier in the 18th century, Paris (Montalba), 1982.(Eng. trans. *Journal of My Life,* New York, Columbia University Press, 1986; Italian trans., Milan, Garzanti, 1992.)

Journal de voyage de deux jeunes Hollandais à Paris en 1656–8, published by A.-P. Faugère, Paris, 1899, pp. 31–2, 56–7.

Juin, H., *Le lit dans l'art,* Paris, 1980.

Julia, D., *La réforme post-tridentine en France d'après les procès-verbaux de visites pastorales, ordres et résistances,* La Societá religiosa nell'eta moderna, Naples, 1973.

Kaplan, S., 'Refléxion sur la police du monde du travail, 1780–1815', *Revue historique*, 1979: 1, pp. 17–18.

Le meilleur pain du monde. Les boulangers de Paris au XVIIIe siècle, Paris, 1996.

Le pain, le peuple, le roi, Paris, 1988. (Bread, Politics and Political Economy in the Reign of Louis XV, The Hague, 1976.)

Les ventres de Paris, pouvoirs et approvisionnement dans la France d'Ancien Régime, Paris, 1988.

Koninckx, C. 'L'alimentation et la pathologie des déficiences alimentaires', *Revue d'Histoire Moderne et Contemporaine* 1983: 1, pp. 109–38.

Labrousse, C.-E., *Esquisse du mouvement des prix et des revenus en France au XVIIIe siècle*, Paris, 1933.

La crise de l'économie française à la fin de l'Ancien Régime et au début de la Révolution, preface by J.-C.Perrot, Paris, 1944 (re-issued 1990).

Lachaise, C., 'Topographie médicale de Paris', Paris, 1822.

Lachiver, M., *Les années de misère: la famine au temps du Grand Roi, 1680–1720*, Paris, 1991.

Vins, vignes et vignerons. Histoire du vignoble français, Paris, 1988.

Lafon, H., *Les décors et les choses dans le romain français du XVIIIe siècle, de Prévost à Sade*, Oxford, 1992.

Lagabrielle, S., *La baie à travers l'iconographie (XVe–XVIIIe siècle)*, (forthcoming).

Lagrave, H., *Le théâtre et le public à Paris de 1715 à 1750*, Paris, 1972.

Lahitte, J.-L. 'L'alimentation des marins aux XVIIe et XVIIIe siècles', master's degree memoir, University of Paris I, 1995 (typescript).

Lambert, J. 'Le chirurgien de papier, la naissance de l'hygiène', thesis, 3 vols., University of Paris I, 1991 (typescript)

La Salle, J.-B. de, *Les règles de la bienséance et de la civilité chrétiennes*, Reims, 1703.

Laugier, Abbé, *Observation sur l'architecture*, Paris, 1765.

Lavoisier, A. L., *Oeuvres*, 6 vols., Ministry of Education, Paris, 1862–1893.

Lebault, A., *La table et le repas à travers les siècles*, Paris, n.d.

Lebrun, F., 'La qualité de la vie des milieux populaires au XVIIe siècle', *Marseille*, 1977: 109, p. 43–6.

La Vie conjugale sous l'Ancien Régime, Paris, 1975.

Lefebvre, H. *Critique de la vie quotidienne*, II *Fondements d'une sociologie de la quotidienneté*, Paris, 1961

Le Goff, J., Chartier, R. and Revel, J.(eds.), *Nouvelle Histoire*, Paris, 1978.

Lemaitre, J.-B., *La police de Paris en 1770*, introduction and notes by A. Gazier, 1879.

La Metropolitée, Amsterdam, 1682.

Léon, P. and Carrière, C. 'La montée des structures capitalistes', in *Histoire économique et sociale de la France*, ed. F. Braudel and C.-E. Labrousse (eds.), Paris, 1970.

Le Pautre, J., *Cheminées à la moderne*, Paris, 1661.

Cheminées à l'italienne, Paris, 1665.

Lepelletier, *Mémoire pour le rétablissement du commerce de la France*, Rouen, 1701.

Lepetit, B., *Chemins de terre et voies d'eau. Réseaux de transport et organisation de l'espace en France (1740–1840)*, Paris, 1984.

Les villes dans la France moderne (1750–1830), Paris, 1988.

Leproux, G.-M. *L'apparition de la fenêtre à petit bois à Paris au XVIIe siècle* (forth-coming).

Leriget, M., *Des lois et impôts somptuaises*, Montpellier, 1919.

Leroux, T., 'Une géographie économique de la France à travers les archives du maximum, les contrastes régionaux de l'espace français à la fin du XVIIIe siècle', master's degree memoire, Denis Woronoff and Dominique Margairaz (eds.), Paris, 1995 (typescript).

Le Roy Ladurie, E., *Histoire du climat depuis l'an mil*, Paris, 1967.

Lescuyer de la Jonchère, E., *Systemè d'un nouveau gouvernement en France*, 4 vols., Amsterdam, 1720.

Levi, G., 'Comportements, ressources, procès: avant la "revolution de la consommation"', in J. Revel (ed.), *Jeux d'echelles: la micro-analyse à l'expérience*, Paris, 1996.

Lévi-Strauss, C., 'Histoire et ethnologie', *Annales, Economie, Société, Civilisations;* 1983: 38, pp. 1217–31.

Le Vieil, P., *L'art de la peinture sur verre et de la vitrerie*, Paris, 1774, pp. 199.

Linguet, S., *Annales politiques, civiles et littéraires au XVIIIe siècle*, Brussels, 1788.

Livi-Bacci, M., *Popolazione e alimentazione. Saggio sulla storia demografica europea*, Bologna, 1987.

Lours, M., 'L'éclaircissement des églises parisiennes aux XVIIe et XVIIIe siècles, master's degree memoir, University of Paris I, 1995 (typescript).

Loux, F. and Richard, P. *Sagesse du corps. La santé et la maladie dans les proverbes français*, Paris, 1978.

Luzatti-Gregori, E., 'Cultura materiale, Storia sociale: note sulle case rurale dell'arca dell'insediamento sparso mezzadriale', *Societi e storia* 1983: 19, pp. 137–64.

Macquart, L.-C.-H., *Dictionnaire de la conservation de l'homme*, 2 vols., Paris, an VII (1799).

Magyar-Thevenin, O., 'Etude comparative du mode de vie des recteurs et la-boureurs, l'exemple du Vannetais au début du XVIIIe siècle', *Annales de Bretagne et des pays de l'Ouest* 1987: 4, pp. 197–211.

Mandrou, R., *Introduction à la France moderne*, Paris, 1961.

Mane, P. and Piponnier, F., *Se vêtir au Moyen Age*, Paris, 1995.

Marenco, C., *Manières de table, modèle de moeurs, XVIIe–XXe siècle*, Paris, 1992.

Margairaz, D., 'Luxe', in *Dictionnaire des Lumières*, M. Delon (ed.), Paris 1997.
Foires et marchés dans la France pré-industrielle, Paris, 1988.

Marx, K., *Contribution à la critique de l'économie politique* (French trans.). Paris, 1977 (Eng. trans., Marx and Engels, *Collected Works*, vol. XXVIII, 1986).
Le Capital (French trans.), Paris, 1950 (Eng. trans., Marx and Engels, *Collected Works*, vol. XXXV, 1996).

Massounié, D., 'L'architecture des bains privés, 1650–1810', master's degree memoir (history of art), University of Paris I, 1993.

Maurizio, A., *Histoire de l'alimenatation, depuis la préhistoire jusqu'à nos jours*, Paris, 1932.

Mauro, F., *Histoire du café*, Paris, 1992.

Mauss, M., *Cours d'anthropologie*, Paris, 1947.

McKenzie, D. F., *La bibliographie et la sociologie des textes*, French trans., preface by R. Chartier, Paris 1991. (*Bibliography and the Sociology of Texts*, London, 1986.)

Medick, H. 'Une culture de la considération; les vêtements et leurs couleurs à Laichingen, 1750–1820', *Annales, Economie, Société, Civilisations;* 1995: 4, pp. 753–73.

Mémoires de la Société d'agriculture de Paris, n.d.

Mémoires sur les feux de houille ou charbon de terre, n.d.

Mendras, H., *La fin des paysans*, Paris, 1984. n.d.

   La seconde Révolution française, Paris, 1989.

Mennell, S., *Français et Anglais à table du Moyen Age à nos jours* (French trans.), Paris, 1987. (*All Manner of Food: Eating and Taste in England and France from the Middle Ages to the Present*, Oxford, 1985.)

Menuret de Chambaud, D., *Essai sur l'histoire médico-topographique de Paris*, Paris, 1786.

Mercier, S., *Tableau de Paris*, 2 vols., Paris and Amsterdam, 1782–9, J.-C. Bonnet (ed.), Paris, 1994.

Mercure de France, 1763, 2nd instalment, pp. 105–112, 'Quel genre de décoration et quelle manière d'illuminer conviennent dans les eglises', quoted by S. Rials, pp. 106–7.

Mérot, A., *Demeures mondaines*, Paris 1990.

Meuvret J. *Le problème des subsistances à l'époque de Louis XIV.* vol. I, *Le commerce des grains et sa conjoncture*, 2 vols., Paris, 1988.

Meyer, J., *Histoire du sucre*, Paris, 1988.

Miller, D., *Acknowledging Consumption, A Review of New Studies*, D. Miller (ed.), London and New York, 1995.

Material Culture and Mass Consumption, Oxford, 1987.

Miller, J.-A., *Les marchés céréaliers à la veille de la Révolution: le modèle de l'économie pragmatique, la Révolution française et l'homme moderne*, C. Mazauric (ed.), Rouen and Paris, 1989.

Milliot, V., 'Alimentation', in *Dictionnaire des Lumières*, M. Delon (ed.), Paris, 1996.

   La ville en bleu. Les répresentations de la ville dans la littérature populaire, XVIIe–XVIIIe siècles, Paris, 1996.

Minard, P., *Typographes des Lumières*, Paris, 1989.

'Les inspections des manufactures en France de Colbert à la Révolution', thesis, 2 vols, University of Paris I, 1994.

Mintz, S., *Sucre blanc, misère noire. Le goût et le pouvoir* (French trans.), Paris, 1991 (*Sweetness and Power: The Place of Sugar in Modern History*, London, 1986).

Montanari, M., *La fame e l'abbondanza. Storia dell'alimentazione in Europa*, Rome and Bari, 1993.

Morand, J.-F., *Les Arts des Mines*, 3 vols., 1768–74, reprinted Geneva, 1988.

Moreau de Beaumont, *Traites des impositions*, 5 vols., Paris, 1784.

Moriceau, J.-M., 'La pomme de terre au XVIII siècle, *Annales, Economie, Société, Civilisations;* 1970: 6, pp. 1767–85.

   Les fermiers de l'Ile-de-France. L'ascension d'un patronat agricole, XVe–XVIIIe siècles, Paris, 1994.

Morineau, M., 'Budgets populaires en France au XVIII ᴱ SIÈCLE', *Revue d'histoire economique et sociale* 1972: 2–3, pp. 203–37, 449–81.

'Conclusion' in Hemardinquer, *Marines du Nord*, Paris, 1985.

'Simples calculs relatifs à une prétendue révolution agricole survenue en France au XVIIIᵉ siècle', *Revue historique* 1995: 1, pp. 91–108.

Morize, A., *L'apologie du luxe et le mondain de Voltaire*, Paris, 1919.

Moulin, A.-M., *Les maçons de la Haute-Marche au XVIII ᵉ siècle*, Clermont-Ferrand, 1986.

Mousset, A., *Les Francine*, Paris, 1930.

Muchembled, R., *L'Invention de l'homme moderne. Sensibilités, moeurs et comportements collectifs sous l'Ancien Régime*, Paris, 1988.

'Luxe et dynamisme social à Douai au XVIIᵉ siècle', in *Nouvelles approches concernant la culture de l'habitat*, R. Baetens and R. Blondé (eds.), Turnhout, 1991.

Necker, J., *Traité de l'administration des finances*, A. Martin, Paris, 1789.

Nemeitz, J.-C., 'Séjour de Paris', in A. Franklin, *La vie de Paris sous la Régence*, Paris, 1987.

Neveux, H. 'Recherche sur la construction et l'entretien des maisons à Cambrai de la fin du XIVᵉ siècle au debut du XVIIIᵉ siècle', in R.Chaunu (ed.), *Le Bâtiment. Enquête d'histoire economique, XIV ᵉ–XIX ᵉ siècle*, Paris and The Hague, 1971.

Nières, C. *La reconstruction d'une ville au XVIII ᵉ siècle, Rennes, 1720–60*, Rennes, 1972.

Onfray, M., *Le ventre des philosophes, critique de la raison diététique*, Paris, 1989, pp. 36–7, 58–63.

Pardailhé-Galabrun, A., *La naissance de l'intime, 3000 foyers parisiens XVII ᵉ–XVIII ᵉ siècles*, Paris, 1988.

Pariset, F.-G., *Georges de La Tour*, Paris, 1948.

Parmentier, A., *Dissertations sur la nature des eaux de la Seine*, Paris, 1787.

Pascal, C., 'Société et urbanisme à Montpellier aux XVIIᵉ et XVIIIᵉ siècles, 1665–1781', master's degree memoir, University of Paris I, 1988.

Pasty, C., 'Les problèmes de l'alimentation des troupes dans la deuxième moitié du XVIIIᵉ siècle', master's degree memoir, University of Paris IV, 1992 (typescript).

Patte, P., *De la manière la plus avantageuse d'éclairer les rues d'une ville pendant la nuit*, Amsterdam, 1766.

Payen, J., *Capital et machine à vapeur au XVIII ᵉ siècle: les frères Périer et l'introduction en France de la machine à vapeur de Watt*, Paris and The Hague, 1969.

Pelissier, J.-F. 'L'économie politique des années de crise', 3rd cycle thesis, University of Paris I, 1984.

Pellegrin, N., 'Chemises et chiffons. Le vieux et le neuf en Poitou au XVIIIᵉ et XIXᵉ siècle', *Ethnologie française*, 1986: 3, pp. 283–94.

Les bachelleries. *Organisation et fêtes de la jeunesse dans le Centre-Ouest, XV ᵉ–XVIII ᵉ siècles*, Poitiers, 1982.

Ruralité et modernité du textile en haut Poitou au XVIII ᵉ siècle. La leçon des inventaires après décès. Textile: production et mode. Proceedings of the 112th congress of *Société savantes*, Paris, 1987.

Vêtements de peau(x) et de plumes: la nudité des Indiens et la diversité du monde au XVIIIe siècle: voyage à la Renaissance, Paris, 1987.

'Le vêtement comme fait social', in *Histoire sociale, histoire globale*, C. Charle (ed.), Paris, 1993, pp. 81–94.

'Travestissements', *Dictionnaire de l'Ancien Régime*, L. Bely (ed.), Paris, 1996.

'Costumes, coutumes', *Dictionnaire de l'Ancien Régime*, L. Bely (ed.), Paris, 1997.

Pérez, L., 'Le vêtement dans les logiques médicales à la fin du XVIIIe siècle et au début du XIXe siècle', master's degree memoir, University of Paris I, 1982.

Perrot, J.-C., *Genèse d'une ville moderne. Caen au XVIIIe siècle*, 2 vols, Paris, 1975

'Les économistes, les philosophes et la population', *Histoire de la population française*, J. Dupâquier (ed.), 4 vols., Paris, 1984.

Pour une histoire intellectuelle de l'économie, Paris, 1994.

Perrot, P., *Les dessus et les dessous de la bourgeoisie, une histoire du vêtement au XIXe siècle*, Paris, 1981.

'Notes pour l'élargissement d'une notion et d'une histoire: la consommation', *Bulletin du Departement d'Histoire Economique*. University of Geneva, 1987, pp. 14–19.

Le luxe, une richesse entre faste et confort, XVIIIe–XIXe siècle, Paris, 1995.

Philippe, R., 'Une opération pilote: l'étude du ravitaillement de Paris au temps de Lavoisier', *Annales, Economie, Société, Civilisations;* 1961, pp. 564–8.

'L'alimentation de Paris au XVIIIe siècle', *Annales, Economie, Société, Civilisations;* 1974, pp. 560–8 and five tables annexed.

Philipponeau, M., *La vie rurale de la banlieue parisienne. Essai de géographie humaine*, Paris, 1956.

Piacenza, P., *Policia e città, strategie d'ordine, conflitti e rivolte a Parigi tra sei e settecento*, Bologna, 1980.

Picon, A., *Architectes et ingénieurs au Siècle des Lumières*, Marseilles, 1988.

Pillorget, R., *Nouvelle Histoire de Paris: Paris sous les premiers Bourbons*, Paris, 1988.

Pinon, P., 'A travers révolutions architecturales et politiques', in L. Bergeron, (ed.), *Genèse d'un paysage*, Paris, 1989, pp. 147–216.

Piponnier, F., *Costume et vie sociale. La Cour d'Anjou, XIVe–XVe siècles*, Paris and The Hague, 1970.

Piponnier, F. and Mane, P., *Se vêtir au Moyen Age*, Paris, 1995.

Pitte, J.-R., *Terre de Castanide. Hommes et paysages de châtaignier en France, de l'Antiquité à nos jours*, Paris, 1986.

Gastronomie française. Histoire et géographie d'une passion, Paris, 1991.

Planhol, X. de, *L'eau de neige, le tiède et le frais*, Paris, 1995, especially pp. 204–307.

Platelle, H. (ed.), *Journal d'un curé de campagne au XVIIe siecle*, Paris, 1965.

Poitrineau, A. 'L'Alimentation populaire en Auvergne au XVIIIe siècle', *Pour une histoire de l'alimentation*, pp. 146–53.

Port, C. (ed.), *Souvenirs d'un nonagénaire*, Paris, 1880.

Pottier de la Hestroye, *Réflexion sur le traîté de la Dîme royale de M. le Maréchal de Vauban*, n.p., 1716.

Poulot, D., 'Une nouvelle histoire de la culture matérielle', *Revue d'Histoire Moderne et Contemporaine*, Paris 1997: 44, pp. 344–57.

Pounds, N. J. G., *The Culture of the English People: Iron Age to Industrial Revolution*, Cambridge, 1994.

Pradines, M., *Traîté de psychologie générale*, Paris, 1947.

Praz, M., *La maison de la vie*, 1972 (French trans.), Paris 1993 (*La casa della vita*, Milan, 1979: Eng. trans., *The House of Life*, London, 1964).

Histoire de la décoration intérieure, Paris and London, 1990. (*La filosofia dell'arredamento*: Eng. trans., *An Illustrated History of Interior Decoration*, London, 1964.)

Rabreau, D., 'Apollon en province', thesis, University of Paris IV, 1985 (typescript).

Raison, F., *Les Auverngats de Paris au XIXe siècle*, Paris, 1976.

Raven, J., 'Imprimé et transactions économiques en Angleterre aux XVIIe et XVIIIe siècles', *Revue d'Histoire Moderne et Contemporaine* 1996: 43–2, pp. 234–65.

Rebke, E., *Lampen, Lanternen, Leuchten*, Stuttgart, 1962.

Restif de la Bretonne, N., 'Les nuits de Paris', in *Paris le jour, Paris la nuit*, D. Baruch (ed.), Paris, 1990.

Revel, J., 'Les usages de la civilité', in *Histoire de la vie privée*, P. Ariés and R. Chartier (eds.), Paris, 1986, vol. III pp. 169–210.

Rials, S., 'La lumière à Paris au Siècle des Lumières', master's degree memoir, University of Paris X, 1973.

Rimbault, C., 'Le corps à travers les manuels de civilité', master's degree memoir, Univerity of Paris VII, 1977.

Rivière, G.-H. 'Le chantier 1425, un tour d'horizon, une gerbe de souvenirs', *Ethnologie française* 1973: 1–2, pp. 9–14.

Rivière, G.-H., and Tardieu, S., *Objets domestiques des provinces de France dans la vie familiale et les arts ménagers*, Paris, 1953.

Roche, D.,'Le Marais au milieu du XVIIIe siècle', master's degree memoir, 2 vols., University of Paris-Sorbonne, 1959, pp. 75–108.

Le Siècle des Lumières en province. Académies et académiciens provinciaux, 1689–1789, 2 vols., Paris, 1978.

Le Peuple de Paris. Essai sur la culture populaire au XVIIIe siècle, Paris, 1981. (Engl. trans., *The People of Paris: an Essay in Popular Culture in the Eighteenth Century*, Leamington Spa, 1987.)

Les Français et l'Ancien Régime. I: *La Société et l'Etat*, II *Culture et Société* (in collaboration with P. Goubert), Paris, 1984, pp. 209–10.

La Culture des apparences. Une histoire du vêtement, XVIIe–XVIIIe siècle, Paris, 1989. (Eng. trans., *The Culture of Clothing*, Cambridge, 1994.)

'La culture des apparences entre economie et morale, XVIIe–XVIIIe siècles', *Bulletin de la Société d'histoire moderne* 1990: 17–2, pp. 14–17.

La France des Lumières, Paris, 1993.

'L'économie et la sociabilité de l'accueil à Paris, XVIIIe–XIXe siècles', in *Mobilité et accueil à Paris, 1650–1850*, Paris, 1996.

Rosenfeld, M., *S. Serlio on Domestic Architecture*, New York and London, 1978.

Rossi, M., *Il trattato di architettura de Sebastiano Serlio*, II, *Il sesto libro delle habitationi e di tutti i gradi degli Uomini*, Milan, 1967.

Rothkrug, L., *Opposition to Louis XIV, The Political and Social Origins of the French Enlightenment*, Princeton, NJ, 1905.

Rousseau, J.-J., *Essai sur l'origine des langues in Oeuvres complètes*, introduction by J. Starobinski, Paris, 1995.

Roussel de La Tour, *La Richesse de l'Etat*, 1763.

Roux, S., *La maison dans l'histoire*, Paris, 1976.

Rowley, A., *A table! La fête gastronomique*, Paris, 1994.

Roy, J.-M. 'La géographie de l'accueil en garnis à Paris dans la seconde moitié du XVIIᵉ siècle', in *Mobilités et accueil à Paris, 1650–1850*, 1996.

Saintyves, P., *Le corpus du folklore des eaux en France et dans les colonies françaises*, Paris, 1934.

Salmann, L., *Une croissance industrielle sous l'Ancien Régime: le textile en Bas-Languedoc, XVIIᵉ–XVIIIᵉ siècles*, Paris, 1994.

Sargentson, C., *Merchants and Luxury Markets. The Marchands Merciers of Eightteenth-Century Paris*, London 1996.

Saule, B., *Tables royales à Versailles, 1682–1789*, Paris, 1994.

Savary des Bruslons, J., *Dictionnaire universel du commerce, d'histoire naturelle et des arts et métiers*, Copenhagen, 1761.

Schelle, G., *L'art de se promener* (1802), French trans., Paris, 1996. (From *Die Spatzergange oder die Kunst spatzien zu gehen.*)

Schlanger, J., *L'invention intellectuelle*, Paris, 1983.

Schweitz, A. 'Les systèmes alimentaires en Touraine et en Sologne', *Revue française de diététique*, 1925: 188–2, pp. 29–36.

  La maison tourangelle au quotidien, façons de bâtir, manières de vivre, 1850–1930, Paris, 1996.

  Science de la santé, soit pour le moral, soit pour le physique, ou Hygiène encyclopedique, Avignon, 1813.

Sébillot, P., *Les eaux douces*, Paris, 1983.

Segalen, M., *Maris et femmes dans la société paysanne*, Paris, 1980.

  'Quinze générations de Bas-Bretons. Mariage, parentèle et société dans le pays bigouden', thesis University of Paris V (typescript).

  Sociologie de la famille, Paris, 1981.

Sévigné, Madame de, *Correspondance*, 3 vols., R. Duchesne (ed.), Paris, 1974.

Ségur, J.-A. de, *Les femmes, leurs conditions et leur influence dans la vie sociale*, 3 vols., Paris, 1803.

Sékora, *Luxury: the Concept in Western Thought*, London, 1977.

Séris, J.-P., *La technique*, Paris, 1994.

Sewell, W., *Work and Revolution in France. The language of labour from the Old Régime to 1848*, Cambridge, 1980 (French trans. 1983).

Sgard, J., 'La métaphore nocturne', in *Eclectisme et cohérence des Lumières*, Festschrift for Jean Erhard, Paris, 1992.

Sigaut, G., 'Histoire rurale et science agronomiques. Un cadre général de réflexion', *Histoire et Sociétés rurales* 1995: 3, 'L'Histoire rurale en France', pp. 203–14.

Simmel, G., *Philosophie de l'argent* (French trans.), Paris, 1987 (Eng. trans., *The Philosophy of Money*, London, 1978.)

Soboul, A., *La maison rurale*, Paris, 1955, reissued 1996.

Solnon, J.-F., *La Cour de France*, Paris, 1987.

Sombart, W., *Luxus und Kapitalismus*, Munich, 1913. (Eng. trans., *Luxury and*

Capitalism, Ann Arbor, MI, 1967.)

Sonenscher, M., *Work and Wages, Natural Law, Politics and the Eighteenth-Century French Trades*, Cambridge MA, 1989.

Souchal, F., *Les Slodtz, sculpteurs et décorateurs du Roi*, Paris, 1967.

Souillard, E., 'Les eaux de Versailles', master's degree memoir, University of Paris I, 1988 (typescript).

'Recherches sur la technique des eaux à Versailles aux XVIIe et XVIIIe siècles, D.E.A. memoir, University of Paris I 1994.

Starobinksi, J., *L'invention de la liberté, 1700–1789*, Paris, 1964.

Stendhal, *Voyages en France*, del Litto (ed.), Collection de la Pléiade, Paris, 1992.

Stigler, G., 'The early history of empirical studies of consumer behaviour', *Journal of Political Economy* 1954: 42.

Tannahill, R., *Food in History*, New York, 1973.

Tardieu, S., *La Vie domestique dans le Mâconnais pré-industriel*, Paris, 1964.

Le mobilier rural traditionnel français, Paris, 1688.

Théorie de l'impot, Paris, 1760.

Thiers, J.-B. *Dissertations e'cclesiastiques sur les choeurs des églises*, 1688.

Thillay, A., 'Le faubourg Saint-Antoine et la liberté du travail sous l'Ancien Régime', *Histoire, Economie, Société* 1992: 2, 217–36.

Thompson, E. P., 'The moral economy of the English crowd', *Past and Present* 1971: 50.

Thornton, Peter, *L'époque et sons style, 1620–1920* (French trans.), Paris, 1986. (Authentic Decor: Domestic Interior, 1620–1920, London, 1994.)

Thuillier, G., *Pour une histoire du quotidien au XIXe siècle, Paris, 1977*.

Thuillier, J., *Georges de La Tour*, Paris, 1973.

Trité de la culture des pommes de terre, Paris, 1782.

Tulippe, O., *L'habitat rural en Seine-et-Oise. Essai de géographie du peuplement*, Paris and Liège, 1934.

Turgot, A.-R.-J., 'L'impot indirect. Observation sur les mémoires récompensés par la Sociéte d'Agriculture de Limoges' (1768), in *Les Ecrits Economiques*, preface by B. Cazes, Paris, 1970, pp. 189–210.

Vanier, H., *Le costume: la vie populaire en France*, Paris, 1965.

Vassort, J., *Une société provinciale face à son devenir: le Vendômois aux XVIIIe et XIXe siècles*, Paris, 1996.

Vauban, S. Le P., *La Dîme royale*, Paris, 1707.

Les maximes générales d'un bon gouvernment, Paris, 1701.

Verdier, Y., *Façons de dire, façons de faire*, Paris, 1979.

Vérin, H., *Entrepreneur, enterprise, histoire d'une idée*, Paris, 1982.

Verlet, P., 'Le commerce des objets d'art et les marchands merciers à Paris au XVIIIe siècle, *Annales, Economie, Société, Civilisations;* 1958: 12, pp. 10–29.

Le maison du XVIIIe siècle, Paris, 1966.

Société, décoration, mobilier, la maison du XVIIIe siècle en France, Paris, 1966.

Vernus, M., *La vie comtoise au temps de l'Ancien Régime*, 2 vols., Lons-le-Saunier, 1982.

Versailles, lecture d'une ville, research report, CORDA, Versailles, 1978.

Vidal de la Blache, P., *Tableau géographique de la France*, vol. 1 of *Histoire de France*, E. Lavisse (ed.), Paris, 1903.

Vigarello, G., *Le sain et le malsain*, Paris, 1993.

Le propre et le sale, Paris, 1985. (Engl. trans., *Concepts of Cleanliness*, Cambridge, 1988.)

Vignot, F., Espaces domestiques et manières d'être en Brie, 1690–1767: une approche de la culture matérielle à Nangis à travers l'inventaire aprés décès, master's degree memoir, 2 vols., University of Paris III, Paris, 1989 (type-script).

Villermé, L.-R., *Tableau de l'etat physique et moral des ouvriers, employés dans les manufactures de coton, de laine et de soi*, 2 vols., Paris, 1840, reissued 1989.

Viollet-le-Duc, E. E., *Dictionnaire raisonné du mobilier français*, Paris, 1871–5.

Walker, C., 'Les lois somptuaires ou le rêve d'un ordre social. Evolution et enjeux de la politique somptuaire à Genève, xvie–xviiie siècles', *Equinoxe* 1994: 2, pp. 111–27.

Waro-Desjardins, F., 'Permanences et mutations de la vie domestique en France au xviiie siècle, un village du Vexin français', *Revue d'histoire moderne et contemporaine*, Jan.–March 1993: 40–1, pp. 3–29.

'La vie quotidienne dans le Vexin au xviiie siècle', in *L'intimité d'une societé rurale*, Pontoise, 1992, pp. 147–65.

Weatherill, L., *Consumer Behaviour and Material Culture in Britain, 1660–1760*, London and New York, 1988.

Wechsler-Kummel, S., *Chandeliers, appliques et lampes*, Frieburg, 1968.

Williams, A., *The Police of Paris*, Baton Rouge, LA, 1979.

Woronoff, D., and Vovelle, M. (eds.), *Révolution et espaces forestiers*, Paris, 1988.

Histoire de l'industrie en France, du xvie siècle à nos jours, Paris, 1994.

Index